PLATO'S "LAWS"

PLATO'S "LAWS"

THE DISCOVERY OF BEING

Seth Benardete

THE UNIVERSITY OF CHICAGO PRESS
CHICAGO AND LONDON

SETH BENARDETE is professor of classics at New York University. His many books include *The Argument of the Action,* published by the University of Chicago Press.

The University of Chicago Press, Chicago 60637
The University of Chicago Press, Ltd., London
© 2000 by The University of Chicago
All rights reserved. Published 2000
Printed in the United States of America

09 08 07 06 05 04 03 02 01 00   1 2 3 4 5
ISBN: 0-226-04271-5

Library of Congress Cataloging-in-Publication Data

Benardete, Seth.
    Plato's "Laws" : the discovery of being / Seth Benardete.
        p. cm.
    Includes bibliographical references and index.
    ISBN 0-226-04271-5 (alk. paper)
    1. Plato. Laws. 2. Plato—Contributions in ontology. 3. Ontology—History.
    I. Title.
    B398.O5 B46 2000
    321'.07—dc21

                                                    00-009052

RICHARD KENNINGTON
1921–1999

οὗτος μὲν πανάριστος ὃς αὐτὸς πάντα νοήσῃ

'Twas a good Fancy of an old Platonic: the Gods which are above Men, had something whereof Man did partake, an Intellect, Knowledge, and the Gods kept on their course quietly. The Beasts, which are below Man, had something whereof Man did partake, Sense and Growth, and the Beasts lived quietly in their way. But Man had something in him, whereof neither God nor Beast did partake, which gave him all the Trouble, and made all Confusion in the World; and that is Opinion.

JOHN SELDEN

CONTENTS

PREFACE

Every Platonic dialogue represents the relation being has to soul. The disparity between what something is and how an opinion or opinions about it show up in someone of a particular character is always the engine of any Platonic argument. Glaucon's request to Socrates, that he show what justice and injustice severally are and what power each has in the soul, can be said to be paradigmatic for every dialogue, even if the issue is not stated with such clarity everywhere. Glaucon's question ultimately takes the form of the relation between being and the good, but it is of the greatest importance that Glaucon did not know that that question lurked behind the difference between his table of goods and his account of justice and injustice (cf. *Republic* 504e7–505a4). The question what is being and nonbeing, to which the Eleatic Stranger comes after Theaetetus has not discerned the difference between Socrates, the sophist noble by descent, and the sophist he is to discover in his separateness from the philosopher, turns out to be inseparable from the question of soul and mind, even though it seems that the Stranger intends to lead Theaetetus to the problem of being without inducing in him the experiences of deception and enlightenment (*Sophist* 234d2–e6). The question what is the holy, which Socrates discusses with Euthyphro, cannot be separated from piety, and hence from the power the holy has on the soul, even though the word "soul" never appears in the *Euthyphro*: the self-righteous, funny, and mystical Euthyphro makes up for its absence. Timaeus's cosmology has psychology at its core no less than the *Republic*'s psychology has ontology. At first glance, the *Laws* seems to be an exception to this general rule. In the *Minos* Socrates says at the beginning, "Law wants to be the discovery of what is," and at the end he is ashamed to confess he cannot answer this question: "What in the world are those things that make the soul better when the good legislator and shepherd [distributor] distributes them to it?" (*Minos* 315a2–3; 321d1–3). The *Laws* seems to be the answer to Socrates' question, but without subscribing to or explicating Socrates' definition of law. The *Laws* certainly proposes a psychology for the interpretation of law, but ontology is conspicuously absent.

The self-motion of soul, which is at the core of the Stranger's theology, is independent of the being of the beings, and nothing is said to be superior to the priority of the becoming of soul. The primary purpose of this book on the *Laws* is to try to uncover its concealed ontological dimension and explain why it is concealed and how it comes to light. The first sign of its presence is that Clinias implies through his experience of the laws of Minos that war is the king and the father of all things.

The *Republic*, however, as it seems to make the *Laws* superfluous, blocks the way to any ontologic import of law. Once the philosopher-king is in place, law could only be an obstacle to his rule, for it would set its own willfulness, which is deaf to reason, in opposition to the free exercise of wisdom (*Statesman* 294a10–c6). Even though Socrates proposes that the philosopher could frame laws in light of the beings that he alone knows, he never suggests what a single law would look like if it were to be deduced from knowledge of the beings (*Republic* 500e5–501c2), for surreptitiously Socrates has replaced the philosopher who knows his own ignorance with the simply wise man whose comprehensive knowledge of the beings and their relations with one another would presumably supply him with a way to translate that knowledge into lawful opinion. Insofar as there is law in the best city in speech, it is no more than a safety net, designed to make up for the possible failure of the education of the guardians. Just as the institution of the communism of property, women, and children guarantees a transparency to the actions of the guardians regardless of whether their souls are properly ordered or not, so law would transform through habit the virtue of soul into "so-called virtues of soul" that are properly to be ascribed to the body (*Republic* 518d9–e2). The opacity of meaning that invariably accompanies such a transformation gives law its strength and makes it indifferent. Nothing shines through the law. It is just the way of a people from which they cannot be dislodged without ceasing to be what they were. The sacrifices to which Cephalus feels obliged to attend represent all that must be set aside of the law if nothing is to hamper the discussion of justice. Socrates prepared for Cephalus's departure by omitting obligatory sacrifices to a god as part of Cephalus's understanding of justice (*Republic* 331b2–c3); and when the sacred does return in the argument about holy matrimony it is strictly identified with the most useful (*Republic* 458e3–4).

Plato's gentle way of setting the condition for political philosophy has its counterpart in the violence that prepares the way for the discussion of regimes in Herodotus. The coup against the false Smerdis, which required for its success that the Persian law to tell the truth be abandoned (Herodotus 3.72.4–5; cf. 118.2), incited the Persians to kill all the priests they could find. Only after that did the conspirators deliberate about all matters (περὶ τῶν πάντων πρηγμάτων), and "speeches were spoken, unbelievable to some of the Greeks, but all the same they were spoken" (3.79.2–80.1; cf. 6.43.3). Whereas Plato dismisses Cephalus and all he stands for at the beginning of the *Republic*—truth-telling is dropped as soon as his son Polemarchus takes over—, Herodotus does not get around to his small equivalent to the *Republic* until the middle of the third book. He arranged for this Persian achievement not by sidestepping the issue of law but by first confronting it head on. It is therefore worthwhile to examine both how he came to that issue and how he got around it. His experiential procedure will offer us a way to understand why Plato had to return to law in the *Laws* despite his easy way out in the *Republic*: Cephalus left with a laugh.

Herodotus begins with a Persian rationalization of Greek myths. The heroes of old were just traders or pirates and the heroines willing victims of rape (1.1–4). In leaving us in doubt whether he accepts this Persian version, Herodotus introduces the principle that governs the nondigressive portion of his *Inquiries*: human happiness has its necessary condition in the injustice of imperial expansion, in which the freedom and greatness of one city entails the enslavement of another (1.5.3–6.3; cf. 9.122). This principle shows up in the two portions of the first book: the fall of Lydia after its expansion in the time of Croesus (1.6–94), and the rise of Persia with the accession of Cyrus (1.95–216). The law plays a minor role in Herodotus's adoption of a hyper-rational version of the Persian viewpoint. Just as the story he chooses to tell of Cyrus's birth is the Oedipus myth stripped of the fateful and the holy, so the account he gives of Persian laws is explicitly stated to be a digression (1.140.3). What puts a stop to a straightforward continuation of his own principle is Egypt.

Egypt forces Herodotus against the drift of his own logos to swerve aside into divine things (2.3.2).[1] These things, about which he holds that everyone knows equally about them, cast doubt on the very assumption behind the necessary connection between happiness and injustice, for the Egyptians replace the just with the holy and question what constitutes

---

1. The structure of Thucydides' first book is comparable. He ends the "Archaeology" with the assertion that the ἀληθεστάτη πρόφασις for the war was the fear the Spartans had of the growing power of the Athenians (1.23.6); but as this was least spoken about, he proceeds to give the charges (αἰτίαι) each side brought against the other. Corcyra and Potidaea were the two primary points of contention; but the last Spartan embassy to Athens ordered them to expel the curse incurred at the time of Cylon's seizure of the acropolis (1.126). This sequence—Athenian imperialism, justice, and the holy—matches Herodotus's way.

the human. The holy replaces the just in the Egyptian story of Helen. Whereas the attendants of Paris speak of his injustice, both the Egyptian governor and the king speak of his unholy deeds (2.113.3; 114.2–3; 115.3–4). The Egyptians' identification of the unjust with the unholy—Herodotus says they are excessively pious (2.37.1)—implies that everywhere else the holy, though being but part of the just, has shaded it and checked the apparently self-evident equation of the unjust with empire (cf. *Euthyphro* 12c10–d3). The human, on the other hand, ceases equally to be self-evident when the presumably inhuman or the bestial is elevated beyond the human and coincides, for some of its range at least, with the divine. Once Egypt makes the human itself problematic, it can only return in the form of an image: Stesichorus says that Helen herself stayed in Egypt throughout the ten years of the war and only her phantom was at Troy, and even Homer has the Trojan elders admit that Helen merely looked in all her terribleness like the deathless goddesses (*Iliad* 3.158; cf. Herodotus 7.56.2).

The elevation of the bestial at the expense of the human and its partial coincidence with the divine point to suicide as the truth of the human good: Herodotus first breaks his vow not to speak of divine things when he turns to the beasts the Egyptians worship and reports the suicide of cats (2.65.2, 66.3; cf. 7.46.3–4). Suicide had first become an issue in the story of Adrastus, which Herodotus put immediately after Solon's visit with Croesus as an illustration of "*nemesis* from god," for, "to the extent that one can make an image of it" (ὡς εἰκάσαι) Croesus had thought himself the happiest of all men (1.34.1). Adrastus had been the innocent agent of two deaths, his brother's and of Atys, one of Croesus's two sons. Croesus had purified him of the first deed by established law (1.35.2), and forgave him for the second death, but Adrastus still slew himself over the tomb of Atys because "he acknowledged (συγγινωσκόμενος) himself to be the most doomladen of all the human beings he knew (ᾔδεε)" (1.45.3). The story of Adrastus seems to confirm the moral of the story of Cleobis and Biton. Solon had told that story to Croesus as illustrative of whom he regarded as the second in happiness, but he had given first place to Tellus the Athenian (1.30–33). Croesus had asked Solon, who had gone abroad "for the sake of sight-seeing" (θεωρίη), and in order not to be forced to alter the laws he had laid down for Athens, whom of those he had seen (εἶδες) was the happiest (ὀλβιώτατος). Athens was prospering at the time that Tellus had beautiful and good children, all of whom had children who were still alive, and Tellus himself was, for an Athenian, well off, and the end of his life was most brilliant, for he routed the enemy in a battle, died most beautifully, and was buried at public expense on the spot where he fell. Croesus then asked him whom had he seen (ἴδοι) second in happiness; and Solon said it was Cleobis and Biton: they were Argives, with an adequate livelihood, both prizewinners in contests of strength, and it is reported (λέγεται) of them as well that when their mother had to be present at a festival to Hera—she must have been the priestess[2]—and the oxen were not available, her sons yoked themselves to her cart and brought her forty-five stades to the sanctuary, "and the god showed in their case that it was better for a human being to be dead than alive" (1.31.3). The Argive men blessed the strength of the boys, the Argive women their mother, who, standing before the statue of Hera, asked that the goddess grant her sons "what is best for a human being to obtain." The sons fell asleep in the temple and did not rise up again; and the Argives made two statues and dedicated them at Delphi, "on the grounds that they had proved to be the best men." As Solon separates an eyewitness account from hearsay, so he separates the beautiful from the good; he assigns one to the city, the other to the gods, and he warns Croesus not to confuse them and expect that a god would grant a request for the good in the form of the beautiful.

Solon's first answer agrees perfectly with Herodotus's own principle, for it is wholly within a political perspective and lacks only the indispensable ingredient of injustice that had made Herodotus indifferent to the difference between large and small cities. Solon's second answer, however, had not affected Herodotus's own narrative; it seemed to peter out in the heavily poeticized story of Adrastus and be disconnected from Croesus's sudden realization of the truth of Solon's words. Croesus recalled them only when he had lost his empire; they had not registered either at the time of Solon's visit, when he had already discounted his deaf and dumb son, or later when he had lost Atys for whom he mourned for two years (1.86.3).

The divine perspective enters Herodotus's narrative only when it gets embodied in Egypt and forces him to question his right to impose on events a principle not manifest in the understanding of the people themselves (cf. 2.15.2). Cambyses' conquest of Egypt would presumably allow Herodotus to use Cambyses as his own agent in re-rationalizing Egypt and turning it right side up (3.3.3; cf. 2.35.2): Herodotus refers to oracles and divines far less often in the third book than in any other, and Cambyses, to whose epilepsy "some give the name 'sacred disease'" (3.33),

2. Cf. Sextus Empiricus *Pyrrhoniae hypotyposes* 3.231.

kills a god and the priests are forced to bury him in secret (3.27.3–29). Herodotus, however, stands back from Cambyses' action and cites his mockery of sacred things as a proof of his madness. He thus shifts from the moderation of indifference, with which he started, to moderation as sanity. No one, he says, should he be given a choice among all laws would prefer any but his own as the most beautiful (3.38.1). When it comes to law, no one is like Candaules and demands a Gyges to confirm him in his erotic belief, for the law is a covering of man's nakedness that no one ever discards.[3] Most, Herodotus implies, would draw the line at incest— Cambyses married his own sisters—and all would balk at exchanging their funeral customs for others', least of all for money. Money, which equalizes the unequal, cannot find a measure for the sacred. The sacred is a lawful currency (νόμισμα) that is not fungible. Cambyses, then, almost represents the necessary consequence of Herodotus's own principle of narration, but even Cambyses cannot permit cannibalism (3.25.7). Cambyses discovers through the guileless Ethiopians, who outdo the Persians themselves in truthfulness, and whose ways pretend to be of a complete transparency (3.20.2; 24.3), that there are limits beyond which the human, if it is to remain human, cannot go. Herodotus thus returns to the political in a modified way. Herodotus had prepared the ground for the conspirators against the false Smerdis to discuss regimes freely by virtually ceasing to use the word "priest" after 3.37.3: when the word recurs twice more in the sixth book it concerns the beating a king of Sparta had inflicted on the priest of Hera (6.81). Herodotus marks the return to the political by citing Pindar's "law is the king of all" with approval and then plunging into the story of the tyrants Polycrates and Periander (39–60).[4] He juxtaposes all that Antigone represents with all that Creon believes

---

3. "Proclos, son of Philosophos asked Rabban Gamaliel in Acre while he was bathing in the bath of Aphrodite" a question about the law, and "he answered, 'One may not make answer in the bath.'" *The Mishnah*, tr. by Herbert Danby (Oxford 1933), 440. Danby's note 11 runs: "It is forbiden to speak words of the Law while naked."

4. Herodotus's citation from Pindar seems at first to be unrelated to what we know followed it: Callicles quotes the passage in the *Gorgias* and interprets it in light of Pindar's evidence, Heracles' theft of the cattle of Geryon without either asking or paying for them but rather "justifying the most violent" (*Gorgias* 484b4–9). Herodotus, however, does seem to allude to what he does not quote, for his citation follows on Darius's question to Indians and Greeks, for how much money they would adopt the funeral customs of the other. That Herodotus immediately shifts to a discussion of tyranny seems to be equally an allusion to the poem, for Pindar comprehended under the "all" of "Law is the king of all" "mortals" no less than "immortals." "Of mortals" points to tyranny, "of immortals" to divine law. One has to recall as well that the god Cambyses killed was a calf.

he does and leaves us to compose the single plot to which they both belong. It is in a speech of a Persian, in response to Xerxes' joy and subsequent tears, that he himself finally unites these two strands and reveals that suicide is the necessary consequence of imperial expansion as well (7.45–6). The return to the political is not after all an escape from the divine law. Just as "iron," which occurs most frequently in the first book, symbolizes the triumph of the political, so the reemergence of the heroic age at the very end of the *Inquiries*, despite the fact that at the beginning the Persians had rationalized it away and the iron age had literally buried it (1.68), indicates the ineradicable presence of the holy in right (9.116–120).

That the Athenian Stranger has to appeal twice to the Egyptian practice of consecration suffices to show that Plato follows in the footsteps of Herodotus (*Laws* 656d1–657b8; 799a1–b8). He is as aware that priests no longer have the same hold on Athens as they do on Egypt as that Socrates had to answer to the charge of impiety and injustice before the King Archon, who, Aristotle says, "manages virtually all the ancestral sacrifices," and "even now" the wife of the King Archon meets and marries Dionysus (*Ath. Pol.* 3.5; 57.1).[5] The *Laws*, one might say, explicates an enigmatic remark of Aristotle, who, in listing the parts of a city without which it would not be a city, says, "First and fifth is the care of the divine, which they call the priesthood" (*Politics* 1328b11–13). How the Athenian Stranger finds his way through the sameness of and the difference between "the care of the divine," which is the first thing, and "what they call the priesthood," which is the fifth, constitutes the action of the *Laws*. What brings the Stranger face to face with what Herodotus arrived at through his confrontation with Egypt is the experience he undergoes in the seventh book (803b3–804c1). Midway to that experience was the Stranger's imaginary address in the fourth book to the future inhabitants of Magnesia, when he translated his original understanding of the divine (τὸ θεῖον) into a twofold understanding of god (θεός) (715e7–718b6). He had then first mentioned sacrifice (716d6); but in the seventh book, in adding sacrifice there to song and dance so as for the three of them together to comprehend the rightness of play, the Stranger suddenly discovers the difference between the holy and the divine. He is brought to that discovery through his abandoning at a stroke an ambiguity that he had systematically exploited up to that point (799e10–800a4). The word for law (νόμος) also means a musical tune, and all of the Stranger's efforts had been to supplement laws with preludes, or threats with persuasion, and lull

---

5. Cf. *Statesman* 290d5–e8; *Sophist* 235b8–c2.

us into the illusion that "holiday" was the original and "holy day" the derivative, and *Songs* no less than *Laws* could just as rightly translate Plato's *Nomoi* (cf. *Minos* 318b1–c3). Here again he follows Herodotus, who has Arion escape from his lawless crew by singing a νόμος in the middle of the sea and being rescued on the back of a dolphin (1.24). Philosophy is the Stranger's song, the *Laws* his dolphin.

ACKNOWLEDGMENTS

I am grateful to the Carl Friedrich von Siemens Stiftung of Munich, and to its director Dr. Heinrich Meier, for granting me the occasion to fill out the fellowship they gave me in 1994 in fall 1998, so that I could complete the study of Plato's *Laws*. I am also grateful to the Philosophy Department of New School University, and its chairman Richard Bernstein, for allowing me to offer a three-term course on the *Laws*. My friends Robert Berman, Ronna Burger, Michael Davis, Heinrich Meier, Drew Keller, and Martin Sitte have helped me in various ways, and I thank them for their kindness.

I

❧

THE EIDETIC AND THE GENETIC

I   WAR AND PEACE

At the summer solstice (683c4–5), a day of stifling heat (625b3), a Cretan by the name of Clinias, the Spartan Megillus, and an Athenian whose name is never disclosed are taking a walk to a cave where Minos conversed with Zeus more than once and, in conformity with the authoritative utterances (*phēmai*) of his father, laid down laws for all of Crete. The three old men plan to rest frequently under the shade of lofty trees. If we assume that they started out no earlier than five in the morning, and their pace, adjusted for their rest stops, was uniform, we can infer that their talk, but not their walk, lasted almost 24 hours: if 18 pages of Greek text were covered every hour up to high noon (722c8), their conversation would have ended some 16 or 17 hours later. The longest dialogue Plato ever wrote fills up the time of the longest day and shortest night of the year (683c3–4). It comprehends in time the length of the *Symposium*, which went from evening up to dawn, and the *Phaedo*, which went from dawn to dusk. A discussion about law covers the same interval, but with a different ratio between day and night, that two Socratic discussions occupy. It differs from those discussions insofar as it seems to partake more of real time than they do: neither the *Phaedo* nor the *Symposium* is as long in speech as either is said to be in time.[1] In the *Phaedo* Socrates defines philosophy as the practice of dying and being dead, in the *Symposium* philosophy is defined as *erōs*. This double characterization of philosophy seems to be a mythical representation of the life of philosophy, whose unity is left as a riddle. Law too covers a lifetime and sets its stamp on birth and death. Through its incest prohibitions and ceremonies of marriage, law indicates its understanding of *erōs* no less than it does through burial its understanding of the relation between body and soul.

---

1. The *Republic* begins sometime during the day and goes on past dinnertime; but there are no markers of time after the beginning: its ascent is not measured against the clock.

I

Indeed, Socrates' definition of law (*Minos* 315a2–3)—"Law wants to be the discovery of what is"—could equally apply to philosophy. It seems conceivable that if law at its two poles distills what it is throughout its range, law could embody what philosophy is and thus make it plausible for a philosopher to deal with it despite its evident difference from philosophy. Philosophy surely knows that it cannot achieve what it wants, but law apparently cannot know it, and though it is as much a failure as philosophy, it would take its failure as its success and turn what it gets into what it wants and pass off its own inventions for the discovery of what is. Socrates' comrade in the *Minos* took Socrates as saying that law was the discovery of being (315a4).

A discussion about law and what it is can be as philosophical as any discussion about anything, but a discussion about legislation seems to drop below the horizon of philosophy. The *Republic*, however, does not just ask what the city is but answers at the same time what the good city is. So if the *Minos* were part of the *Laws* and its introduction to it, then the *Laws* would be exactly parallel to the *Republic* and answer together the question of the being of law and the question of good legislation; but the *Minos* and the *Laws* are two separate dialogues, one of which has Socrates ask the Socratic question, while a nameless Athenian answers the second apparently un-Socratic question, what is good legislation.[2] Socrates' answer in the *Republic* to the question what would make a city good—the philosopher—, seems to preclude him from ever dealing with the *Laws*' question, since the philosopher essentially rules without laws. Once the philosopher ceases to rule, law in some form has to take over, but whatever form it assumes, law is too circumstantial to allow the philosopher, who has now withdrawn from politics, to recommend reforms, even if they might save his life (*Apology of Socrates* 37a8–b1). Despite, then, the suggestive resemblance of the time frame of the *Laws* and that of the *Phaedo* and *Symposium* together, the philosophic bearing of the *Laws* is obscure. If the *Laws* consisted of the first two books alone, we would not be as puzzled. The Stranger's discussion of the symposium as a counterbalance to the Doric *sussition* leads directly back to the setting of the definition of philosophy as *erōs*, just as the Stranger's discussion

2. If the *Clitophon* is the introduction to the *Republic*, and corresponds to the *Minos* as the introduction to the *Laws*, then Clitophon's criticism of Socrates, that he berates superbly, just as if he were a god from the tragic μηχανή, and praises virtue, but does not offer any guidance for its acquisition, matches fairly well the Socrates of the *Minos*, who knows what law is but will not discuss legislation, for he does not know what those things are by which the good legislator, in distributing them to the soul, makes the soul better (321d1–3).

of the drink of fear cannot but recall Socrates' drinking of hemlock after he has defined philosophy as the practice of dying and being dead. To the extent, then, that philosophy can be thought to be lurking under the discussion of music, the *Laws* could be vindicated for philosophy, but the price would be high. The *Laws* too is a riddle. It quickly frees itself from something like philosophy and stoops to practice without ever becoming practicable. The three old men are on the way to legislation; they do not become legislators. They are, according to the Stranger, like children who are playing at being legislators (712b1–2). The way of the *Laws* thus turns the *Laws* into a dialogue "on the way to," and in this sense gives it a philosophic cast against its evident purpose. The *Laws* ends up with the recommendation of a nocturnal council, which is to discuss the unity of virtue. If the *Laws* ends with a proposal to introduce philosophy into the city of laws, it is on the way to philosophy. "On the way to philosophy" is a formula that holds for every Platonic dialogue: no dialogue answers the question "What is philosophy?" in a completely adequate manner. The *Laws* would be peculiar in starting further back than any other dialogue if it only comes to this question, common to all of the dialogues, at the very end. In coming to this question at the end, it would seem to have been diverted from the question by the issue of legislation. We have to ask why we are forced to descend so far down into the law so as to examine even criminal law, whose premise is that the education in the law of the *Laws* has not been entirely successful (853b4–c3), before we can get back to the question "What is?" The setting of the *Phaedo* is the judicial execution of Socrates. Could it be that only through the criminal law can we get to the question of what is? Φιλοσοφεῖν occurs first in the book on criminal law (857d2).

The answer to the question with which the *Laws* begins, whether a god or human being is to be held responsible for the disposition of Cretan and Spartan laws, seems to find little resonance in the course of the argument. In a sense, Zeus and Apollo were not the legislators of Crete and Sparta respectively; Minos and Lycurgus seem to deserve the designation (632d2–4), and the gods only rarely are said to have legislated (634e2; 662c7; cf. 835c1–3). To lay down laws (*nomothetein*) and to be a legislator (*nomothetēs*) are what men do. Whatever were the authoritative utterances of Zeus, in conformity with which Minos laid down the laws, they were not in themselves in legal form and had to be translated in order to become statutes. Insofar as the laws of the *Laws* are at best paradigmatic and have to be adapted by Clinias and his fellow commissioners in order to become usable, the *Laws* duplicates in its action the original association of Minos with Zeus rather than the subsequent reformulation of

Minos on his own. The Athenian Stranger replaces Zeus and lays out the schematics that Clinias may or may not find useful for the founding of Magnesia. The *Laws*, then, as a whole, is a prelude to laws. It is meant to stand in front of all the laws of the Cretan city. It thus can be understood to be the prelude to any other actual legislation, regardless of whether that legislation has been formulated independently of the *Laws* or not. We are being let into the reconstruction of the conversation between Zeus and Minos, in which Minos had to have been educated in becoming a legislator before he was free to legislate.

If the *Laws* as a whole is a prelude to laws, the first three books are in turn the prelude to the laws of Magnesia (cf. 722d1–2), and the Stranger's proposal, how Clinias ought to have answered his question, stands as a prelude to the prelude that is the *Laws*. The laws of the *Laws* have their own prelude, and each set of laws likewise has its prelude. The five preludes that constitute the *Laws* are so many templates of law. The smaller the template the less easy it is to deduce the details of any law from it; but the smaller template has the advantage of offering a synoptic view of the law that any expansion of the template is liable to obscure. It would be reasonable to suppose that the *Laws* ends at that point where synopsis is no longer possible. It should end at that point where either a deduction from the principles of law cannot be drawn or the laws are wholly indifferent to the principles of law (cf. 835b5–7; 843e3–844a3; 846b6–c3). The *Laws* should end where laws no longer let the principles of law shine through and "law and order" becomes simply "order." This does not appear to be the case. Although the Stranger insists that he is offering just an outline and everything small has been omitted (768c3–d7; 769d1–e2), the outline looks more like a finished picture and the details over-refined. The Stranger has set the principles of law very high. The laws are to be laid down in conformity with the ranking of the eightfold good. The laws are not just to preserve the ranking of the eightfold good but induce in the law-abiding an awareness of that ranking (cf. 705e1–706a4; 743e3–744a3). No good induced by and through the law is to lodge in the soul of a citizen with any other number and size than that which it had in the table of goods at which the legislator looked when he translated the table into law. It is much easier to figure out all the obstacles to such a translation than to imagine the devices that the Stranger must propose to get around those obstacles.

Clinias answers the Stranger's first question on behalf of both himself and Megillus; but he qualifies his answer—"God"—in such a way—"insofar as I limit my answer to what the strictest justice requires" (ὥς γε τὸ δικαιότατον εἰπεῖν)—that it forces us to reconsider the Stranger's question.

We would have been inclined to take it neutrally; but it seems that Clinias detected in the phrase, εἴληφε τὴν αἰτίαν ([Who] has taken the responsibility?), the prelude to a formal charge the Stranger wants to draw up against Dorian laws. He turns out to be not entirely mistaken. Clinias diverts the possible blame to Zeus; indeed, he is so anxious to get Minos off that he reminds the Stranger, gratuitously, of Minos's brother Rhadamanthys, who was most just and was rightly praised by the Cretans for his handling of lawsuits (δίκαι), or more literally "issues of right." Clinias's τὸν ἔπαινον εἰληφέναι picks up the Stranger's εἴληφε τὴν αἰτίαν and exposes to view the touchiness he harbors toward foreigners when it comes to his native laws. Clinias has heard no doubt about the bad reputation the tragic poets of Athens have spread about Minos and the high regard in which Rhadamanthys was held outside of Crete (Minos 318d9–11). The Minos who demanded human sacrifices from the Athenians is not the Minos Clinias wishes to defend (cf. 706a7–b1). Minos was ἄνομος (lawless), and Athenian tragedy denied that "lawless" could mean "superior to the law" no less than "above the law." In conceding to the Stranger the possible criminality of Minos, Clinias inadvertently raises the question whether the originary legislator, who has never yet conformed with the laws he lays down, must always look criminal to anyone brought up within the law, and only someone of more than human stature could stand outside the law and still be just. Clinias's "God, Stranger, God" encapsulates a most just solution to the problem of the origin of law.

The Stranger's second question to Clinias is a minefield of surprises. He asks him whether he agrees with Homer's account, that Minos went every eight years to Zeus for the purpose of association (συνουσία) and laid down laws for Cretan cities in accordance with the pronouncements (φῆμαι) from Zeus. Now we later learn that not much of Homer has come to Crete—"We Cretans do not employ to any great extent the poems of strangers" (ξενικὰ ποιήματα, 680c2–5; cf. 629b3–4)—, and yet this Ionian poet has preserved perfectly a Cretan tradition. Homer, however, preserved the tradition only in a sense; it is the Stranger's interpretation of an obscure line in a lying speech of Odysseus that recovers perfectly the Cretan tradition. This miraculous recovery, moreover, is not just the Stranger's; Socrates had offered it in the Minos, in contradistinction to the ordinary or Ionic interpretation of the line. We may take the coincidence as a sign of either the spuriousness of the Minos or the casual Aristotelian identification of the Athenian Stranger with Socrates (Politics 1264b29, 37). Be that as it may, the line reads

ἐννέωρος βασίλευε Διὸς μεγάλου ὀαριστής (Odyssey 19.179).

Beside the obscurity of ἐννέωρος, which should mean when Minos was nine years of age, ὀαριστής, which seems to contain the word ὄαρ (wife), is said to mean an associate in speeches (συνουσιαστὴς ἐν λόγοις) and not fellow-drinker and playmate (συμπότης καὶ συμπαιστής).[3] Socrates says that ὄαροι means λόγοι, but the Homeric usage makes it plain that the "badinage of lovers" comes closer to its meaning. Homer of course does not say a word about laws, or that Minos had his understanding tested on each visit. The Ionian interpretation of Cretan tradition makes the symposium the setting for the transmission of a god's pronouncements; but that original setting is strictly forbidden by Dorian law, and insofar as it survives at all it is as the συσσίτιον —the common mess or eating together—rather than as a drinking together. Since the Stranger proposes the symposium as the proper model for the understanding of law, the Stranger goes back behind a Cretan tradition and restores both in theory and practice an Ionian way of life. In restoring the symposium, with Minos as Zeus's drinking companion, the Stranger also restores Minos as his playmate. On a level beyond the laws, play (παιδιά) takes precedence over seriousness or σπουδή. Once, however, we have moved so far beyond the law, the Stranger's συνουσία in light of the Homeric meaning of ὀαριστής takes on an erotic coloring, and the pederasty the Stranger later accuses the Cretan of defending by the invention of the Ganymede story is suggested to have been at the start of Minos's legislative activities. If we take Homer literally, Minos was just a boy when he went to Zeus.

If we read the Stranger's second question in light of what lies ahead in the Laws and what Socrates in the Minos denies to be the true meaning of the Homeric line, we are confronted with the possibility that the Laws as a wineless symposium imitates Plato's Symposium in a very austere mode, though we must remember that the Symposium too, since drinking was not then an obligation on the part of the guests, was for most of its length not an ordinary drinking party either and did not become so until Alcibiades burst in upon them and changed its regulations: the word συμπόσιον does not occur in the Symposium. If an Athenian symposium was sober enough to allow for erotic speeches, a Cretan offshoot would be unconstrained enough to allow for speeches about law that do not have to conform with the law. The excellence of Cretan law lets the Stranger divine that it has a provision that permits old men, outside the presence of the young, to discuss the laws. At the same time that the Stranger hints at what he is up to, he suggests a general formula for the difference

---

3. Pierre Chantraine, *Dictionnaire étymologique de la langue grecque* (Paris 1974), gives an account of the problems under ὄαρ.

between an utterance of Zeus and a law of Minos. The emblem for that difference is the difference between συμπόσιον and συσσίτιον. Although the terms are not exclusive elsewhere, they are in Sparta and Crete, and Clinias rests his entire interpretation of Cretan laws on what he infers from the institution of συσσιτεῖν.[4] If what Zeus and Minos did together is to what the Cretans do together as a dialogic communion is to the common mess of warriors, and that proportion represents the problem of translation for the law, then the *Laws* as prelude to laws would be the intelligible envelope of the laws (νόμοι) as lawful practices (τὰ νομιζόμενα). It would be, to borrow a phrase from the *Philebus,* "like an incorporeal order designed to rule an ensouled body" (64b6–7). In the language of the *Laws,* νόμοι as songs would precede νόμοι as laws, and the entire aim of the *Laws* would thus be to investigate how far the laws can be turned upside down and redirected to embody παιδιά as the truth of σπουδή. If the original setting for the establishment of Cretan law was συμπαίζειν, and the defective tradition came out as συσσιτεῖν, then the Stranger's συμπίνειν can be considered to be the proper mean between them.

Clinias and Megillus would not find, the Stranger expects, a discussion about regime and law unpleasant, since they have been brought up in lawful ways that it is not inappropriate to call divine. Insofar as the first two books are about lawful ways as they affect the individuals of a community, and the third about regime, or the ordering principles for rulers and ruled, the Stranger begins by proposing no more than a fourth of the entire bulk of the *Laws.* It would not be unpleasant, he implies, for Clinias and Megillus to look for the traces of the divine in their own lawful habits and ways (ἐν τοιούτοις ἤθεσι νομικοῖς). Their experience of the laws should have yielded an insight into meaning and intent. After Clinias's first exposition, the Stranger praises him for his having been beautifully trained for the discernment of Cretan customs (γεγυμνάσθαι πρὸς τὸ διειδέναι τὰ Κρητῶν νόμιμα, 626b5). The gymnastic of custom has brought about an understanding of custom. Clinias has been led through the body to a logos (cf. 632d4–7). There lurks in the Stranger's remark the tragic formula πάθει μάθος as well as his own suggestion that education begins with the speechless and irrational pleasures and pains of children and shapes them in such a way that they prove to be consonant with the speech and reason of complete human beings (653b1–6). In the case of Clinias, however, his experience of the law leads him to total dissonance

---

4. On the "false" opposition between *sussition* and symposium, see Oswyn Murray, "War and Symposium," in William J. Slater, *Dining in a Classical Context* (Michigan 1991), 90.

with the law. His gymnastic ends in a music that is wholly out of tune. The *Laws* begins with a puzzle: a law-abiding man, whom his fellow citizens have chosen as a founder and legislator of a new colony, harbors in his soul, through the very laws he has fully imbibed, sentiments contrary to the intent of any set of laws whatsoever.[5] This unexpected result is not due to any artful probing on the part of the Stranger; Clinias spills it straight out without any awareness that he has expressed anything shocking or against the law. If divine laws have such an effect, what could one expect of purely human legislation?

The Stranger wishes to know about three Cretan customs: the common mess, the exercises, and the weapons. Clinias answers in the order of exercises, weapons, common mess. For the first he appeals to the nature of the country, which requires training in running; and he believes it follows of necessity that the arms must be light, though one could just as well argue that training in heavy armor would make one all the fleeter when it came to fighting with bow and arrow. Up to this point, law follows the dictates of nature, or so Clinias believes; the Stranger **sees** for himself what the nature of the country demands; neither Minos nor Zeus has to be invoked to justify Cretan ways. Clinias then adds that not only have their exercises and weapons been geared to war, but the legislator arranged everything in light of it. His only example is the common mess. The common mess goes beyond the special conditions to be found in Crete and applies everywhere and always. The legislator, he says,

> in **seeing** that all, whenever they are on campaign, are compelled by the matter itself (ὑπ᾽ αὐτοῦ τοῦ πράγματος) for the sake of their own protection to mess together during that time, seems to me to recognize and condemn the folly (ἄνοια) of the many, since they do not understand that there is always an unending war of everyone throughout their lives against all cities (πᾶσιν διὰ βίου πρὸς ἁπάσας τὰς πόλεις): If when there is war any rulers and ruled must for the sake of protection mess together and be guardians in an ordered way, then one also has to do this in peace. What most human beings call peace, that he realized was only a name, but in deed there is always by nature an undeclared war of all cities against all cities (πάσαις πρὸς πάσας τὰς πόλεις).

An undeclared war (ἀκήρυκτος πόλεμος) is also a war that no truce can call off: if the Cretans ever make a treaty one can expect a first strike at any time. Clinias infers from the necessity of a common mess in wartime, on

5. Cf. Aristotle *Politics* 1324b22–28, 32–36.

the one hand, and from the Cretan practice of a common mess at all times, on the other, that there is always war. He does not conclude that the common mess in peacetime makes it easier to live together on campaign, or that the fellowship of communal dining increases the friendliness among the citizen body, but that peace does not exist. In his first formulation, war is a permanent condition of every man against all cities. It lasts throughout one's life and entails that one be constantly on guard.[6] One's own city as well as every other city is the enemy (cf. 941c4). Clinias tones down this radical implication when he gives his second formulation, where he says what one would have expected the first time, that all cities are on a permanent war-footing. Clinias clearly assigns the second formulation to the Cretan legislator, but it is not as clear whether the first is merely his own inference and does not go back to Minos or Zeus. The Cretan law, in any case, induced in him an understanding of things that the many in their folly do not comprehend. The many therefore should be in a state of war against all cities if cities embrace, either in law or not, the insight embodied in Cretan law, for it stands opposed necessarily to the illusion of most men. They have not grasped the nature of what is; but Cretan law has done so and more than confirms Socrates' definition of law: Cretan law not only wants to be the discovery of what it is, it is the discovery of what is.

The discovery of what is emerges through an observation about a temporal event—"whenever men are on campaign"—combined with a lawful practice that is always in effect. The meaning of the practice comes to light from its timely necessity, but once that meaning has been gained it is detemporalized again through the practice itself and assigned the status of a natural fact. That one should always be alert for the possible or even probable outbreak of war does not satisfy Clinias's interpretation of the common mess. Only if the motto "Stay alert" has its objective counterpart in an unending state of emergency can the real import of the Cretan law be grasped. Once a prudential motto gets incorporated into a practice, its prudential component seems to vanish and get replaced by what is always (cf. 780b2–c2). Clinias's slide from the temporal to the eternal allows one to wonder whether institutions of themselves, provided they offer the slightest purchase for a significance to be grafted onto them, are necessarily taken to point to what is always. If insights such as Clinias's are unavoidable growths on practices of almost any kind, then the legislator, if he is to follow the Stranger's prescriptions and look to

6. The addition of the phrase διὰ βίου shows that πᾶσιν must be taken of individuals.

what is for his laws, has to build safeguards into his laws so that they do
not produce on their own through the experience of them variants on
what is that deviate from his own intention. These safeguards turn out
to be the theme of book 2. Clinias claims that he has recovered the original insight of the Cretan legislator. That insight seems to have diverged
so far from the ordinary understanding of men and so much against the
grain that a god or someone close to a god must plausibly be held responsible. When Clinias finally sees the strange consequences of his experience of the law, whose harshness fully confirms the tragic view of Minos
that he was at such pains at first to cover up, he expresses some surprise
and wonders whether his experience of the law could have possibly failed
to hit upon what the law intended (628e2–5).[7]

After Clinias has recovered the meaning of Cretan institutions, he
gets around to answering the Stranger's question. The Stranger had asked,
"According to what (κατὰ τί) has the law arranged?" for three practices;
and Clinias now says that the legislator fixed his glance on war in arranging all public and private customs, and he transmitted the laws to be
maintained "according to this" (κατὰ ταῦτα), "that there is no use for anything else, either possession or practice, if one does not get the upper
hand in war, and the goods of the conquered become the property of the
conquerors."[8] The answer to the Stranger's question, κατὰ τί, is given in
terms of the good; the insight into the being of things is war. Nothing
Clinias has said about the practices suggests how one gets from "being"
to "good," for the good depends on winning and if there is always war
no one can ever prevail. Clinias does not argue, as Megillus does later
(638a1–2), that Cretan institutions guarantee victory even in wars as they
are ordinarily understood. Clinias seems to have forgotten that Crete is

---

7. Cf. C. Ritter, *Platos Gesetze, Kommentar zum griechischen Text* (Leipzig
1896), 2: Clinias's wonder "kann auf das eine oder andere Glied des vorangehenden
Gegensatzes sich beziehen. Also entweder: ich wundere mich, nach dieser einleuch-
tenden Darlegung, wenn nicht auch unser Gesetzgeber in der That, obgleich ich das
bisher nicht bemerkt habe, die Begründung sicheren Friedens im Auge gehabt habe;
oder: obgleich ich jetz einsehe, dass jenes das Ziel jeder Gesetzgebung sein muss, sollte es mich wundern, wenn man auch von unsern Gesetzen, die ich bisher für vortref-
flich gehalten, nachweisen könte, dass sie jenes richtige Ziel und nicht vielmehr ein
anderes, nämlich den Krieg, im Auge gehabt haben."

8. Cf. Aristotle *Politics* 1324b5–12: "Accordingly, though most laws among most
people have been laid down virtually without system and irregularly, still, if laws do
look at any one thing anywhere, all aim at gaining the upper hand (κρατεῖν), just as in
Sparta and Crete, where their education and the majority of their laws have been ordered for warfare; and further among all the [barbarian] nations that are able to be ac-
quisitive (πλεονεκτεῖν), power of this kind has been held in honor, for example, among
Scyths, Persians, Thracians, and Celts" (cf. *Laws* 637d7–8; Herodotus 2.167).

an island (cf. 662b3–4), and its wars are likely to be fought against cities with institutions identical in kind with those of Cnossos, and Cretan archers lose all the advantage of native terrain if they fight overseas under other conditions. He can hardly believe that the goods of the Celts or Scythians are theirs for the taking. Clinias implies that no one has the right to anything if it is not gained in war, but even then it is a hazardous right. As soon as victory in war becomes the standard, peace and its goods return despite the unreality of peace. If Clinias were to offer the goods of a spurious peace to the many as a bribe for enduring institutions whose inner meaning is eternal hostility, and to claim that rulers like himself are alone aware of the truth and act upon it, then a certain degree of coherence could be imposed on Clinias's account. The insightful rulers would have enlisted in an eternal campaign that had no other end for themselves than its perpetuation, but they were never deluded into believing that any inalienable good belonged to the reality itself. In order to smuggle such a good into the being of things, it will be necessary to enlist Megillus into the discussion and summon a "native" Athenian poet.

In light of what follows, one can say that Clinias's experience of Cretan law led him to the view that there is an eternal war of the superior against the inferior, or of the good against the bad, but this quasi-Manichaeanism in Clinias needs the Stranger's maieutics to bring it out into the open, and at the point where Clinias breaks off, the superior and the inferior are not permanent characteristics of things but merely retrospective determinations that constantly change with the outcome of battles. What holds for cities against cities holds for village against village, village household against village household, man against man, and finally each man is to be thought of as an enemy to himself (626d1–2). Clinias can hardly contain himself at this conclusion. He calls the Stranger "Athenian Stranger" and goes out of his way to justify the designation: "Athenian" does not mean "of Athens"; Ἀττικός, according to Clinias, would have sufficed for that, but "Athenian" refers directly to "Athena," after whom the Stranger deserves to be called. Clinias alludes, perhaps unwittingly, to the fact that Athenian women were always called Ἀττικαί precisely because Ἀθηναία, addressed to an Athenian woman, was indistinguishable from the old Attic form of Athena's own name.[9] Clin-

---

9. Cf. Harmut Erbse, *Untersuchungen zu den attizistischen Lexika* (Berlin 1950), s.v. Aelius Dionysius. One wonders whether this fact does not lie behind Pisistratus's dressing up a woman to look like Athena and spreading the rumor, "Athena is bringing Pisistratus back from exile" (Herodotus 1.60.5). In some sense he would not have been lying.

ias, then, in calling the Stranger Athena-like calls him divine in a somewhat stronger sense than Megillus could have meant when he addressed Clinias a little while before, by Spartan custom, ὦ θεῖε (626c4). The Stranger deserves the epithet for his bringing the argument to its principle (ἀρχή). What Clinias barely got a handle on through his experience of the law the Stranger has traced back to its source. The principle can be applied repeatedly to the series from household to city and reveal that the true meaning of war is not of one city against all others but of each city against itself. The goddess of wisdom who is also the goddess of war has disclosed to an Athenian the inner unity of her double aspect (cf. *Critias* 109c6–d2).

Clinias does not find the notion of a victory of the self over the self or a defeat of the self by the self to be disturbing in its incoherence. He latches onto a common Greek expression that denies what it affirms. If, however, one ignores its incoherence, it does illuminate Clinias's original insight, for this is truly a war that can never be won, goes on undeclared, and does not admit of a truce. One way out of the incoherence would be to assign the victory of the self over the self to the citizen's dedication of himself to the city, and his giving up his own life for its survival; and what Clinias meant by the war of everyone against all cities was the individual's struggle against the patriotic death that carries with it no apparent good for himself. Indeed, one could go further along the same lines, and assert that Clinias implied that the city was the locus of self-alienation and split man permanently against himself. Clinias allows for all men to be the enemies of all in public and everyone severally to be privately an enemy to himself without specifying in what the victory consists; but in the case of the city, if the better win over the many and worse, the city can be strictly said to be better than itself. There would be, then, a better self and a worse self, and the worse self would be analogous to the demos and the better comparable to the rule of the wise (cf. 689a9–b2). The victory of the worse self would seem to mean the defeat of reason by pleasure, and rather than such a victory pointing to cowardice it would imply that the loss of moderation or of self-control is the worst and most disgraceful of defeats. On the level of the self, σωφροσύνη is at issue, on the level of the city the willingness to be killed: Clinias later admits that to succumb to pleasures is worse than to succumb to pains (637e1–6). Man's alienation from the city does not have the same ground as man's enmity to himself. To resist giving up one's own life for the sake of the city is not the same as to be a slave to pleasure. The difference can be likened to that between Socrates' daimonion, which kept him from politics and saved his life, and Socrates' obedience to the oracle from

Apollo, which made him disregard all risks and see himself as another Achilles.

Clinias comes to see the strangeness of his own insight and its extension after he hears the Stranger's version, in which he seems to alter nothing in reversing Clinias's example and speaking of the city that can be strictly said to be inferior to itself; but the Stranger adds not only the fact that they are fellow-citizens (πολῖται) and kin (συγγενεῖς), but he tells a story. The story introduces the elements of time and becoming. Many unjust citizens form a conspiracy and use violence against the just who are fewer in number. Clinias did not tell a story: the better or the worse either win or lose in each city.[10] Once time and change are at the basis of the victory or defeat of any entity, the paradox of the self against the self disappears. "You have surpassed yourself" means "You have never done better," and "I am not myself today" holds out hope for the future. The Stranger's first move against Clinias thus consists in checking his haste in discarding time and getting the law to be the truth of being. This sobering of Clinias, so that what becomes takes precedence over what is, seems to culminate in book 10, where the Stranger argues for the temporal priority of soul to body in becoming, and no appeal is made to that which may be always. Whether such a cosmological psychology is altogether satisfactory can be left aside for the moment, but that it is consistent with the drift of the first three books of the *Laws* will emerge in the course of the discussion. Clinias's first account of Cretan law used εἶναι seven times and γίγνεσθαι once, and he formulated the notion of self-victory and self-defeat in a nominal sentence (626e2–4).[11] The Stranger

10. Cf. David Daube, *Forms of Roman Legislation* (Oxford 1956), 6: "First, then, in early Roman legislation, the form 'If a man murders another man, he shall be put to death' predominates, whereas later the form 'Whoever murders a man shall be put to death' is no less usual. The change reflects an evolution from what we might call folk-lore to a legal system. 'If a man does this or that' tells a story—though of something yet to come. It puts a situation which may arise, and informs you how to meet it. 'Whoever does this or that' refers not to a situation, but to a category, a person defined by his action. It does not inform you how to meet a contingency, but declares the proper treatment of a murderer. It is more general, abstract, detached"; see further his *Ancient Jewish Law* (Leiden 1981), 72–74. Clinias introduces his assertion with a generalizing relative (ἐν ὁπόσαις) in the indicative; the Stranger phrases his in a future more vivid (N.B. ὥς ποτε), and continues with two temporal clauses (ὅταν and ὅπου ἄν). In the laws proper of the *Laws*, there are not more than twenty that begin with "Whoever" (ὃς ἄν or ὃς δ' ἄν); cf. 843b1, c6, 844d8, e5; and contrast 715c2 with 822e8.

11. That the *Laws* is dominated by the issue of becoming shows up in the following way. The ratio of εἶναι to γίγνεσθαι in the *Laws* is 505:198, in the *Republic* it is 544:50; the *Laws* has the present and aorist participle of γίγνεσθαι 291 times, the *Republic* 136; ἦν occurs 137 times in the *Laws*, 127 in the *Republic*; the third-person singular and plural present optative of γίγνεσθαι occurs 83 times in the *Laws*, 44 in

accordingly turns his attention to the family, where kinship (συγγένεια) no longer has a derivative meaning.

The Stranger imagines a case of many brothers, all from the same mother and father, the majority of whom become (γίγνεσθαι) unjust and fewer just; but rather than continuing with his example, he goes out of his way to block any quibbling about the expression of self-mastery on the part of a household, for he says that the issue is the natural rightness and failure (ἁμαρτία) of laws. The propriety and impropriety of expressions are opposed to the nature of successful and unsuccessful laws. In alluding to the philosophical opposition between nature (φύσις) and law, the Stranger seems to be raising the question whether Clinias's mistaken interpretation of law, which subverted all law, did not naturally issue from the self-contradiction of conventional speech. Clinias ultimately based his insight into the naturalness of unending war on the strict interpretation of a Greek idiom. There was a coincidence between his experience of law and the language he speaks, as if his experience had no other end than to restore to his words their literal meaning. To enter experientially into the meaning of the most ancient Greek laws is to recover a beginning (ἀρχή) that is right at one's feet. The Stranger opposes this quasi-tragic experience of Clinias to an inquiry into the natural rightness of laws, the starting point of which is the family and not the city. What such a beginning implies can be seen in the Stranger's later demand, when he discusses the seven competing claims to rule (690a1–c8), that the citizens are to love what is right and hate what is not, and only one of the seven—the rule of father and mother—can be thought to have any natural affection built into it. A reflection on the natural rightness of laws starts from the dissolution of natural fraternity and its restoration through laws. The family of the tragic poets (cf. 663e8–9), who employ catachrestically αὐτός (self) in compounds—αὐτόχειρ, αὐτοκτόνος, αὐτοφόνος [-φόντης], and αὐθέντης—to designate family who are killed by family,[12] initiates the problem of law.

The Stranger imagines three possible outcomes for his family of good and bad brothers, in which the unjust outnumber the just (cf. 838a5). He does not consider the case, which would seem to match the conditions

---

the *Republic;* γεγενῆσθαι occurs 45 times in the *Laws,* eight times in the *Republic;* and γεγονώς occurs 36 times in the *Laws,* 15 in the *Republic.* Perhaps it is in line with this difference that in the *Republic* νῦν occurs 158 times but 411 in the *Laws.*

12. Cf. Ferdinand Sommer, *Zur Geschichte der griechischen Nominalkomposita* (Munich 1948), 83–86, 153–159, for the original function of αὐτο-.

of an ordinary city, where the just outnumber the unjust. A judge with executive power could either (1) kill the bad and order the better to rule themselves,[13] (2) make the good rule but let the worse live and arrange for them to be ruled willingly, or (3) kill no one, reconcile them all, lay down laws for them for the rest of time, and be capable of seeing to it that they remain friends. The first of these possibilities corresponds to what the Eleatic Stranger recommends in the *Statesman* (293a9–e2), the second matches "the city in speech" of the *Republic*, and the third is the premise of the *Laws*. Clinias, in choosing the last, puts friendship above justice and forces us to keep in mind that laws and the prevalence of evil came to light together. Contrary to the impression the Stranger gives when he apologizes for the need to discuss criminal law, law in itself assumes imperfect conditions. The shift from being to becoming brings along with it a rather advanced state of decay. It is certainly better than Clinias's terrifying picture of unremitting war, but the Stranger does lower one's expectation of law if the establishment of friendly feeling is not to be built on the community of the righteous. Right, one might say, belongs to the order of rule; it does not survive in the hearts of the citizens themselves. The "natural" meaning of the Stranger's words to describe the judge whom Clinias chooses—τρίτον δικαστὴν πρὸς ἀρετήν—is that he is third in point of virtue (627e3–4);[14] but one immediately has to add that only in this third case does the Stranger not speak of a conflict between the good and the bad but leaves it at saying that the family is at odds with itself (συγγένειαν διαφερομένην).

If Clinias chooses the third judge not only because he introduces law but because he reconciles those who without being separable into the good and the bad disagree, then Megillus, Clinias, and the Stranger form such a group. They differ at first about many things, yet they are all Greeks and engaged in a common task. The laws of Athens, however, have little in common with either Spartan or Cretan law, and the political arrangements to be found in Sparta do not match those in Crete. It is reasonable to suppose that a consensus of some kind is reached by the

---

13. Note that the expression ἄρχειν αὐτοὺς αὐτῶν (627e1) has nothing paradoxical about it if one adds "in turn" or one takes it to mean that they have no masters (αὐτοκράτορες or αὐτόνομοι).

14. This "third" seems to point directly to the third-best regime that the Stranger later implies would be Clinias's version of the second-best regime of the *Laws* (739b3). England's view, that it means third in an ascending scale, seems forced, for he assumes that Clinias's choice is the same as the Stranger's; cf. 654c3–d4, where Clinias chooses a not evidently superior possibility; cf. *Euthydemus* 306c5.

end of the dialogue. This consensus is brought about by the Athenian Stranger; he brings them together and makes them concurrent (συμφερό-μενοι, 629c3) without abolishing altogether their differences. Their differences are always threatening to break out, at least throughout the first three books, into harsh and disagreeable contention (629a1–3; cf. 685a1). We could then say of the group that it is becoming better than itself or than it was; but we could equally say that the group becomes less than itself if the Stranger condescends in any way to the capacities and habits of Megillus and Clinias. We have had already a sign of his condescension; he implies that to determine whether the worse is ever stronger than the better belongs to a logos longer than even the *Laws* turns out to be (627b1–2; cf. 726a4–5). The Stranger's refusal to address this question amounts to his declining to discuss the nature of the good that is in itself beyond being.[15] The establishment of the priority of soul to body in the element of becoming is as far as he is willing to go in facing this ultimate question. The double movement of the *Laws*, in any case, in which the ascent of the Dorians accompanies the descent of the Athenian (cf. 804b5–c1), seems to be designed to embody the choice of Clinias. We are invited to look at the *Laws* in order to understand the function of law in establishing friendly feeling. It takes some time before Clinias calls the Stranger "friend" (641c8).

It seems at first that the "dysfunctional" family is only a means to get Clinias to give up on the primacy of war, and once the legislator is assigned the task of preventing civil war, the aim of law is put higher than the induction of internal peace and friendly feeling; but though the happiness of a city is mentioned once, it is unclear whether the statesman aims necessarily at the happiness of individuals (628d5), and the model is the healthy body, which never needed treatment, and not the beautiful and strong body, which would have to submit to rigorous training and exercise to achieve such a state. Although the Stranger speaks of "the things of peace," which could well include the highest things, when he argues against legislating them for the sake of "the things of war," he merely says that the legislator in the strict sense must legislate the things of war for the sake of peace (628d7–e1). It is only in the course of an imaginary confrontation between Tyrtaeus and Theognis that the legislator aims higher than peace. Tyrtaeus praises courage, the virtue needed to face bloody slaughter, but he does not praise it as something exclusively Spartan; in none of the fragments we have does he ever mention Sparta;

---

15. Cf. Herwig Görgemanns, *Beiträge zur Interpretation von Platons Nomoi, Zetemata* 25 (München 1960), 204–206.

and in the poem from which the Stranger cites several lines, and which may well be complete, Tyrtaeus speaks of the young warrior fighting and dying on behalf of his country and children (fr. 12.33–34 West), but there is nothing to indicate how his virtue would be bound up with the laws of his country, so that they could be understood to have bred him in such a way as to give to a universal virtue a loyalty to his homeland. The mercenary's virtue also consists in the willingness to die in Tyrtaeus's kind of war (630b3–7). One wonders, then, whether laws framed to promote even complete virtue do not necessarily go beyond the local nature of laws. In one passage the Stranger speaks of a complete man (ἀνήρ), in another of a complete citizen, and in a third of a complete human being (ἄνθρωπος) as possibly being the ultimate aim of education in and through the law (643d1–2, 644e5, 653a9). The Stranger, however, does seem to deny to complete virtue a higher goal than loyalty. Loyalty is the excellence Theognis praises in harsh civil war, and the Stranger argues that it could never arise without the coincidence of justice, moderation, and prudence with courage (630a5–b2). In the context of stasis, loyalty should mean loyalty to a faction, and the Stranger is presupposing that one side has a monopoly on the good;[16] but if that were the case, the possibility of compromise and reconciliation would be out of the question, to say nothing of the fact that civil war would not engender greater enmity than external war if one side were not as fanatically loyal as the other.[17] The trustworthiness to which the Stranger alludes must belong to a man whom both sides trust; he must be the judge whom he had earlier proposed as the conciliator of the family at odds with itself. If the loyal man has not taken sides, if he resists the temptation to treat a fellow-citizen as an enemy, if he refuses to kill for a "principle," he must count something higher than any difference that can show up in stasis. The good that is dependent on the unity of the city is higher than any good that could

16. Cf. England on 630a: "Both Plato and Theognis may be held to have assumed that in a στάσις the right was all on one side." A biographer of John Selden said of him: "There can scarcely be a less disputable mark of integrity and worthiness in an individual than his succeeding in securing the 'golden opinions' of parties opposed to each other in contending for the same object, and concerning which object that individual is known by them to differ from them both. Now of all contentions, history affords uniform testimony that none are so jealous and implacable as those in which are involved the religious opinions and the temporal pre-eminence of the disputants. Mingling in such contentions, Selden passed his life a prominent actor in them all, and yet so moderate, consistent, and talented was his course, that although occasionally supporting and opposing each, the extremes of the conflicting parties looked up to him and sought the aid of his abilities." *The Table-Talk of John Selden*, ed. S. W. Singer (London 1860), 85.

17. Cf. Thucydides 3.82.3–6.

possibly be embodied in a faction. Loyalty involves a suspicion about "absolute" right as it appears politically. This loyalty becomes manifest in Megillus, whose goodwill toward Athens, regardless of her injustice toward Sparta, used to make him when he was a boy defend Athens against her detractors (642b2–d1). Megillus's esteem for what he calls his second fatherland is ultimately based on the unforced and unfeigned spontaneous goodness of some Athenians. That goodness, which he knew of as a saying but came to acknowledge on his own, was the unknown ground of his early affection for Athens. His boyish feelings proved to be consonant with reason. It would seem to be the purpose of the law to bring about deliberately the accidental double loyalty of Megillus (cf. *Republic* 592a5–b1). The citizen must also be "pro-foreign" (πρόξενος).

If it is right to connect the legislator-judge of the discordant family with the loyal and sound man who stands above the fray in stasis, then the model at which he looks in framing the laws is himself. Complete virtue becomes the aim of the legislator in order to eliminate the possibility of stasis (cf. 636b1–4). The political result seems to be pitched too low for so lofty a goal; but that at which the legislator looks and that which his laws establish prove to be of very different orders. In stating what he believes Clinias should have said on behalf of Cretan laws, the Stranger takes a sideswipe at contemporary legislators, who handle changes in the law piecemeal, as the need arises, and set before themselves species (εἴδη) that do not match the species in accordance with which Minos sought the laws for his people (630d9–e4). The Stranger connects in an apparently arbitrary manner Clinias's failure to see that Minos must have looked at the whole of virtue and not a part, and the fourth part at that, and the contemporary failure of legislators to look beyond species like inheritance and outrage. The species of right, with which they now deal, differ in kind from the species on which Minos tried to model his laws. The Stranger implies that the model Minos used for his laws was not simply the whole of virtue and its four parts. In the speech that the Stranger wishes Clinias himself to have made he draws a distinction between what we may call the eidetic structure of good and the genetic structure of law.[18] It is this difference in species to which the Stranger refers (cf.

---

18. "Eidetic" is short for what results from an analysis of something into its kinds, "genetic" stands for the result of examining the coming into being of a genus or one genus from another. The equivalent in the *Republic* to the difference between the eidetic and genetic is to be found in the twofold requirement that the class structure of the city be rigid yet allow for movement between the classes if any member of

632e3–6).[19] In order to understand this difference it is necessary to set side by side the order of good and the order of law (631b3–d1):

"Stranger," you should have said, "it is not in vain that the laws of Cretans are exceptionally esteemed among all the Greeks. The laws are right, accomplishing and completing the happiness of those who use them.

"The laws supply all the goods. Goods are (ἐστιν) twofold, some human, some divine. The others depend on the divine [goods]; and if a city receives the greater, it acquires the lesser as well;[20] if not, it is deprived of both.

The lesser are (ἔστι) those in which health leads, second beauty, the third strength in running and all other motions of the body, wealth is fourth, not blind but with keen sight, if it comes along with good sense (φρόνησις).	He must take care of marriages, through which a mutual sharing occurs, in honoring and dishonoring them in the right manner, and after this, in the generation and upbringing of children, all who are male and all who are female, both when they are young and when they are growing older up to old age, and in all their associations he must have investigated and kept a careful watch on their pains, their pleasures, their desires, and the zealous intensities of their loves (ἔρωτες), blaming and praising them in the right manner through the laws themselves;
It is that which leads (ἡγεμοῦν ἐστιν) the divine goods, good sense, second, if it is with mind (νοῦς), a moderate (σώφρων) condition of soul, and justice would be (ἂν εἴη) third	and, in turn, in fits of anger and on occasions of terror, all the disturbances that occur (γίγνονται) for souls on account of bad fortune, and all the flights from occasions of that kind [that occur] on ac-

---

a class at birth or later deserves to be shifted from his original place (cf. *Timaeus* 19a1–5).

19. Cf. Stallbaum ad loc.: *posteaquam de universa virtute explicaverimus, etiam haec quae modo commemoravimus (inde a p. 631d περί τε γάμους usque ad 632c extr.), illuc (ad virtutem) spectare docebimus;* see also England at 632e6; H. Görgemanns, *Beiträge zur Interpretation von Platons Nomoi,* 116 note 1.

20. This follows Eusebius in omitting τις (631b8); otherwise Badham's correction παρίσταται for πόλις κτᾶται has to be accepted.

from a mixture of these [the first two] along with manliness.

count of good fortune, and all the events (παθήματα) that befall human beings as they occur (γιγνόμενα) in illness, wars, poverty, or their contraries, in the case of all things of this kind he must teach and define what in their several dispositions [is] the beautiful and [what] not.

And after this [it is] a necessity that the legislator see to the possessions and expenditures of the citizens, in what manner they are to occur (γίγνηται), and he must survey the partnerships and dissolutions that all have with one another, both voluntary and involuntary, in what way they do each of them, and the just and the not [just], in what things they are (ἔστιν) and in what they are missing;

and he must assign honors to those who obey the laws, and impose set penalties on the disobedient;

until having come to the end (τέλος) of the entire regime, he sees in what manner to each of the dead the burials are to be (γίγνεσθαι) and what honors are to be assigned to each;

All of the latter have been arranged and ordered by nature before the former, and it is in just this way that the legislator too must order and arrange them. After these things, he must proclaim, in an exhortation to the citizens, that all his other ordinances (προστάξεις)

and he who laid down the laws, once he observes who will be the guardians, will set them over all of the laws, some who proceed through good sense (φρόνησις), some through true opinion, in order that mind, with a binding together of all of these things, may show that they go along with are looking to them, and of them the human look to the divine, and all the divine look to their leader, mind. [These ordinances are:] moderation and justice, not with wealth, let alone ambition.

The natural order of the eightfold good, which the legislator is to order in the same way, makes for the happiness, not this time of the city, but of the citizens. These goods, however, must undergo a translation in order to become law. The first translation consists in spreading out the four virtues over a lifetime: the verb to become (γίγνεσθαι) occurs only in the outline of the law. The temporal schema of the law goes in some sense from birth to death but in another from marriage to burial. The lawful equivalents take precedence over natural becoming. The virtue of moderation, as it is commonly understood, stands behind the pleasures, pains, and desires that the Stranger assigns to his summary of the early years of children. Courage likewise is suggested in the handling of good and bad fortune: terror and anger are mentioned by name, hope and compassion are not. The just and the unjust are plainly stated to be the categories in light of which the third class is to be understood; but, astonishingly, the wisdom to which this movement in time seems to be pointing is replaced by burial as the end (τέλος) of the regime; and the guardians of the laws are only partly chosen for their good sense.

Apart from the riddle of what the Stranger could possibly mean in locating the culmination of the regime in burial, as if he were stooping to a bad pun on end (τελευτή) and completion (τέλος),[21] he ends up by speaking of only two virtues as being manifest in the statutes, moderation and justice; and in confining himself to these two, he also drops the good in favor of the beautiful and the just.[22] The perspective of the law transforms the good and bad into noble and base, on the one hand, and, on the other, into just and unjust.[23] Pleasure and pain, either as constant

21. Cf. Aristotle *Physics* 194a28–33.

22. That the same shift occurs at the beginning of Aristotle's *Nicomachean Ethics* is well known: the hierarchy of good finds its highest exemplification in politics, but politics handles the beautiful and the just (1094b14–15). Aristotle makes this shift immediately after he has remarked that one must not seek precision in all speeches alike.

23. The articulation of the law is indicated in various ways. The first section of the first half is set off by τε from the second's τε αὖ (631d6, 632a3); the second half is divided from the first by μετὰ δὲ ταῦτα (632b1), its second section is weakly separated by καί (632b7). Μέχρι γήρως (631e2) occurs at the beginning, μέχριπερ (632c1) at the end. Although honor and dishonor run through the entire proposal, praise and blame are mentioned only in the first section of the first half (632a2), and punishments

features of life, or when men experience extreme versions of them, terror
and joy, dominate the genetic structure of law; but in the eidetic structure
of good, whose aim is happiness, there is no mention of pleasure and
pain. No experiences go along with the goods; and there are no such experiences because there is no being to which the eightfold good is assigned.
If θεῖα and ἀνθρώπινα are taken strictly, the higher goods belong exclusively to gods, and only heroes could be the patients of both their goods
and those of human beings (cf. 732d8–e3). If θεῖα and ἀνθρώπινα are not
taken so strictly, the divine goods belong to soul, the human to body, but
there is no ensouled body in which they are said to inhere. This split in
the goods seems to be reflected in the Stranger's ascription of burial to
the end of the regime. The separation of body and soul has its lawful
equivalent in "Hades" (cf. 828c6–d5).[24]

This program of law fits fairly well books 4–9: the very first law the
Stranger offers as an example of prelude and law are the marriage laws
(721a9–d6). The program, however, seems not to comprehend the sequence of criminal law in book 9, theology in 10, and civil law in 11; it
certainly stops short of the nocturnal council of book 12. Gods are not
mentioned except adjectively, and "mind" does not show up in the eightfold good except as an accompaniment of a moderate condition of soul,
and again as the leader to which all the divine goods look, and finally as
that which binds together all the laws and proves them to be consequences of the two middle virtues, moderation and justice. The temporal
order of law and human life takes moderation out of its middle rank and
makes it first; but in becoming first, perhaps in even more than a temporal way, it seems to lose what made it second of the virtues and bound
it with mind. If Clinias's experience of Cretan law led him to an understanding of war as the nature of what is, and a poet revealed that the
highest good was courage, would the experience induced by the Stranger's
laws lead to an understanding that the highest good was mind or even
good sense? Once the question is put, one notices that the Stranger has
no equivalent to Clinias's insight into that which is. The good as happi-

---

(δίκαι) in the second section of the second half (632b8): the legislator is under necessity only in the second half (632b2). He is to see (632c2, 632c4).

24. Nothing better illustrates the ambiguous status of θεῖος than the Stranger's at-
tribution of it to the regime's reviewers (εὔθυνοι) (945c2), only to allow that they too,
though they are all priests, may be subject to review, if they prove to be bad and show
their human nature (947e7), and that Rhadamanthys could in his time, when many
were born from gods, decide cases quickly only because he entrusted the issue to the
gods by whom the litigants swore (948b3–c2). Elaborate funeral rites distinguish these
reviewers from all other citizens (947b3–4).

ness, on the one hand, and the good as moderation and justice, on the other, seem to be as high as the eidetic structure of good and the genetic structure of law can go respectively. How they are related to one another is left obscure. The eight goods are presented as if the lower depended on the higher and the higher were somehow involved in the production of the lower; but in the case of justice, courage must be mixed in with it. Such an inverse dependence deepens the mystery of how the "tumbling" effect of the virtues works out in becoming. Could courage preserve experientially its lower status than justice if it must become together with what is higher than justice? Beauty and strength, moreover, are higher than health though dependent on it; but moderation and justice are not as evidently higher than good sense or soundness of mind, though the parallelism of health and φρόνησις makes one suspect that the latter is not more than an indispensable condition. If the eidetic structure of good should have in this way a double arrangement built into it, so that in one sense the higher the item the less complete it is—so justice looks like the complete virtue (cf. 630a8–b1, c6; 957e2–3)—, but in another the lower the item it has exactly the rank it deserves—an arrangement that is clearly meant to hold for courage and wealth—then the implausibility that a city, any.more than an individual, could acquire in any sense the four virtues of soul while it was sick, ugly, weak, and poor would be somewhat mitigated. It would also help to explain why mind is finally taken out of the order entirely and given a place of its own. If the order of goods, however, is read straight, as it seems we should read it, the Stranger sets up a hierarchy outside of time. It thus seems to suffer from the same defect as Clinias's account did, in which he moved so easily from the temporality of circumstance to the eternal being of war. Clinias had coupled being and good in a very loose way, for he could not show that preparedness for war, let alone the knowledge of the truth of war, led to victory in war and the acquisition of the goods; and the Stranger now has the comparable problem of showing how the experience of his laws would instruct the law-abiding in the true rank of the goods, let alone that the goods follow one another in real time.

From Clinias's take on the law, the Stranger's biggest alteration has been to divide human life into its ordinary course, over which moderation is to have control from birth to old age, and life's upheavals, to which war belongs, along with the sudden reversals of fortune of any kind. If courage belongs anywhere as a virtue separable from moderation it is here; but insofar as moderation and justice are said to comprehend the intent of the law, one could equally well say that wisdom and courage have been pulled away from the law entirely and reassigned exclusively to the legislator-judge. Such a reassignment recalls Callicles' attempt in the *Gorgias* to celebrate those two virtues apart from any grounding in moderation and justice. Could the curious way in which Clinias's experience of the law led to a radical understanding of things make him fit to be a legislator and unfit to be a citizen? The Stranger himself proposes a young tyrant as the best possible ally of the legislator (709e6–710b2), and someone on the order of Callicles and Clinias combined might suit him.

2   COURAGE AND MODERATION

The *Laws* is the only Platonic dialogue in which talking and walking are coupled throughout; everywhere else walking is done in silence, or, if there was talking, its content goes unrecorded.[25] The only exception is the *Phaedrus*, which begins with Phaedrus leading Socrates from the city to the country (230a6–7), where they rest and discuss, among other things, the relation between writing and law.[26] In the *Laws*, the reality of space goes along with the reality of time. Walking is the primary activity; the talking is designed to distract the old men from the effort of the journey. The Stranger speaks of their talk as παραμύθια (632e5; cf. 625b6); and when he does so he speaks of their talk as the telling of stories (διαμυθολο-γοῦντες). The verbs δι[εξ]έρχεσθαι and διεξιέναι, which occur so frequently in the *Laws*,[27] are constant reminders of the distance traversed in their going through the argument.[28] It is not at once obvious why these playful allusions in speech to motion should obtrude on the *Laws*; but one may suggest that the painful effort of their journey should remind them of the constraints of the law, and that the liberation from the law that a discussion of the law can induce is not to be taken as being outside the law (cf. 685a6–b1). The law is to sanction their departure from the law within the law. Clinias's experiential transgression of the law has to be reined in corporeally if reflection on the law is not to pass beyond the boundaries of the law.

    25. Cf. *Symposium* 174d4; *Gorgias* 447c6–9; *Lysis* 206d7–e9; *Protagoras* 314c3; *Theaetetus* 143b2.
    26. Cf. Seth Benardete, *The Rhetoric of Morality and Philosophy* (Chicago 1991), 189–190.
    27. 632e2; 635e4; 638e1; 699e1; 702b5; 743e6; 793a9; 811c8; 857e4; cf. especially 768c8–d7; 779d2–6.
    28. One may compare the odd way in which in the *Statesman* shorter and longer ways of division are suddenly put in real time and imagined to involve a difference in real effort (265a1–b5); cf. Seth Benardete, "The Plan of the *Statesman*," *Metis* 7, nos. 1–2 (1992): 35–37.

Clinias had inferred from the law the truth about things; through the citation of a poet the Stranger had shifted from "being" to "good" and indicted Minos, or Clinias's misinterpretation of Minos, for having failed to focus on the whole of virtue. Whereas Clinias had spoken of the legislator as looking to war but legislating in light of the good (626a7), the Stranger spoke of the legislator as looking to the eightfold good and did not separate that perspective from the pattern in light of which he was to lay down the laws.[29] For the second round, the Stranger proposes that they examine first the practices of courage, and with that as a paradigm show that the appropriate part in the genetic structure of law looks to that virtue (632d9–e7). Clinias had started with practices, jumped over the virtue or virtues they fostered, and came directly to what is. The Stranger proposes, more cautiously, that they proceed from the practices of a virtue to their lawful equivalents: what do the laws praise and blame, and are the practices as experienced in agreement with the laws? This summary of the Stranger's proposal, however, accounts for only one of its strands. The sequence of tasks, as he presents it, requires that every species of virtue be examined first; but once courage has been made paradigmatic, they are to tell stories of all the rest, and only then, subsequent to a survey of virtue in its entirety, are they to prove the consonance between its practices and the laws. The Stranger never does get past the Cretan and Spartan practices of courage and their inadequacies; the examination of moderation, which is initiated, is not carried through,[30] even though the entire first two books of the *Laws* are concerned with nothing else than moderation. As for justice and good sense, they are dealt with even more obliquely; but the kind of systematic treatment that the Stranger outlines seems to be broken off rather early and never resumed. To ascribe this change of plans to the Stranger's revelation that the nocturnal council is to handle the unity of virtue is, as far as the entire argument goes, true enough; but at the moment it is drunkenness that sends them off course.

29. Clinias's πρὸς τοῦτο βλέπων (625e1) and εἰς τὸν πόλεμον . . . ἀποβλέπων (626a6–7) are both common expressions in Plato—there are some 200 instances—for the standard at which one aims or that in light of which one understands (i.e., either the good or being), but nowhere else, as far as I know, is such an expression associated with anything like Clinias's κατὰ ταῦτα (626e7) that separates being from good; cf. *Republic* 484c6–d3; 501b1–7.

30. As soon as Megillus goes back in the argument and defends Spartan ways as they are, σωφροσύνη itself drops out of the first book, and σώφρων and σωφρονέω occur only once each (647d3, 648e6); on the unsystematic character of the argument, see Gerhard MXller, *Studien zu den platonischen Nomoi, Zetemata* (München 1968), 19 note 1.

The more sober Megillus now takes over the discussion. He seems to be rather eager to have Clinias, "this here praiser of Zeus," put in his place again (633a1–2); but the Stranger says that each of them is to be subject to scrutiny. The examination of practices cannot be done apart from an examination of those who have experienced them. The law is tested through the patient of the law. Megillus adds several practices to the common mess and exercises: hunting, various kinds of endurance of pain, the secret-service. He is slightly embarrassed by the well-known Spartan practice of theft (ἐν ἁρπαγαῖς τισιν, 633b8), but apparently not at all by the secret execution of rebellious Helots that the secret-service carried out (cf. Thucydides 4.80.2–4). Megillus implies that the practices of courage are inconsistent with the practices of justice; but the Stranger does not point to the difficulty of harmonizing the various purposes of the virtues; instead, he turns to the exposed side within Megillus's understanding of courage. The issue is whether courage can be understood as equally applicable to the struggle against desires and pleasures, which turn the spirit of even the high and mighty into wax.[31] The Stranger asks Clinias whether Minos and Lycurgus legislated courage so as for it to be capable of standing its ground on the left but made it lame on the right.[32] The immediate cause for their departure from an eidetic handling of the virtues is the intrusion of pain and pleasure. Pain and pleasure, in becom-

31. In the seventh book of the *Iliad*, the Achaeans and Trojans call a truce in order to bury the dead; both sides weep, but only Priam forbids the Trojans to weep (VII.423–432); Lessing pointed out that the implied capacity of the Achaeans to weep and to fight without losing their edge distinguishes the civilized from the barbarian. Such an example would have sufficed to show how courage can be of the same order when it comes to pleasure and pain; but the example requires an understanding of poetry that Megillus and Clinias each in his own way lack.

32. The Stranger's sentence is remarkable: Ὁ Διὸς καὶ ὁ Πυθικὸς νομοθέτης οὐ δήπου χωλὴν τὴν ἀνδρείαν νενομοθετήκατον. Immediately after "the Pythian legislator" come the particles οὐ δήπου in an unusual position for Plato (cf. *Gorgias* 496d7), followed by the word "lame" (χωλήν). Between an allusion to Apollo and "lame" comes the interrogative οὐ δήπου, "surely not?" This Sophoclean pun on Oedipus's name (cf. *OT* 1042; *Antigone* 381) does seem intrusive. If, however, one recalls that the sequence at the beginning of the *Laws*, from city to family to individual, is the same as that of *Oedipus Tyrannus*, where the question, "Who killed the king?" ends up with "Who am I?" through the ordained crimes of patricide and incest, one might suspect that Oedipus's intelligence and Oedipus's lack of self-knowledge does resemble Clinias's stumbling onto a deep understanding of the city, however mistaken, and his bewilderment at its unlawful character. Insofar as the Stranger will later assert that the one-sidedness of Dorian law led to pederasty and the looseness of Spartan women, and Oedipus's father, whose name means "left" (λαιός), was known as the first pederast, and Oedipus's ultimate crime is incest, one is forced to wonder whether the issue of tragedy does not lurk behind that of the law from the very beginning of the *Laws*.

ing thematic for the understanding of law, no longer allow the species of virtue to be discerned. Pleasure and pain abolish the separation between body and soul, which was central for the eidetic structure of good, and presuppose the unity of a single being through feeling. In accordance with the genetic structure of law, pleasure and pain put the human being in time and blur whatever distinguishes one species of virtue from another: at the very moment the Stranger admits that an enumeration of practices might be the only way to comprehend a virtue, he drops the word εἴδη for the virtues and calls them parts, "or whatever else they should be called" (633a7–9). The breakup of wholes into fragmentary ways weakens the link between the end of a virtue and its means. Megillus admits that the toughening of Spartan youth is done through many beatings (633b8), and hence that fearlessness, which belongs to courage as a virtue, partly has its source in fear. The authorities can never be sure that the citizens have not been hardened even against the law.

Spartan law induces resistance to pain through pain. The Stranger asks, on the basis of this practice, whether the resistance to pleasure should likewise be induced through pleasure. The Dionysia are taken to be the model for the indulgence in pleasure but not for the resistance to pleasure. The Stranger works his way from an actual practice to a practice in speech, in which one can imagine that it would have an effect comparable to Spartan training in endurance. A matchup is made between a species of virtue and its counterpart in lawful practice through the construction of an imaginary symposium. The *Laws* had begun with Clinias expressing his experience of the law; now Megillus, while undergoing something comparable to Clinias's experience, is going to see that Spartan practices are defective; but the Stranger readily admits that in his own case, though he has seen many symposia and thoroughly questioned virtually all of them, he does not know of any nondefective symposium (639d5–e3). We are made to ask, "What possibly could be inferred from a model, to which by definition no experience can be attached, about the probable experiences of it, which would neither yield an insight against the intent of the practice nor be in its consequences inimical to other demands of the law?" We have heard from Clinias himself how his experience of the law contravened law, and the Stranger will explain how the common mess led on its own to immoderation within and without (of its members within and of the women without), but it seems impossible to foresee the effects of a proposal that only exists in speech. We are thus led to apply the symposium in speech to those who hear of it and ask whether the exhilaration of the topic does not affect them in the way the

Stranger proposed and induce in them a kind of moderation that counter-
balances the harshness that has become second nature to them. The symposium in speech, which the Stranger makes up, has its reality in the
argument of the *Laws*.[33]

The drift of the argument, through which the Stranger gets to the
symposium in speech, is confusing and obscure. Only through provoking
Megillus, so that he defends Spartan practices and lashes out at Dionysia,
does the Stranger manage to get to it. The Stranger has to turn from courage to moderation before Megillus goes back in the argument and denounces Athenian ways. Megillus and Clinias are perfectly willing to extend courage to cover pleasures no less than pains and admit that they
cannot put forward any laws that on a large scale minister to the resistance to pleasure (634b7–c4); but Megillus at least cannot see that the
Stranger's extension of courage is apparently nothing but the ordinary
understanding of moderation, for when the Stranger asks for exceptional
Cretan and Spartan practices that deal with moderation, Megillus believes the exercises and common mess have been beautifully found for
both virtues (636a2–3). On the one hand, then, courage is admitted to
have a left and right side, and Dorian law to be unequally prepared to defend both sides, and, on the other, courage and moderation are admitted
to be two different virtues, in accordance with both the eidetic structure
of the good and the genetic structure of law, and the same Dorian laws
are adequate to induce both. If courage is indeed capable of being equally
armed against pleasure and pain, courage would cease to be fourth of the
virtues and rise to second place, and the paradox of justice's reliance on
what is below it would disappear. Courage would then be just below good
sense, and if it is mated with mind as moderation had been in the eidetic
structure of the good, it would seem to usurp all of virtue (710a3–6). If,
on the other hand, Megillus is right, and the common mess and exercises
induce moderation no less than courage, the unity of the virtues is embedded in a single set of practices and their differences are more a matter
of speech than experience. If one puts the matter as sharply as possible:
courage as a symmetrical one does not show up in the law, courage and
moderation as a separable two show up in one and the same set of practices. The first formulation lets the Stranger pose a problem—why did
Minos, in a unique opposition to all other legislators, Greek and barbarian, enjoin the abstention from the greatest pleasures and pastimes
(παιδιαί) and urge the confrontation with toils, fears, and pains (635b2–

---

33. Compare the Stranger's τὸ περὶ τῆς ἐν τοῖς οἴνοις διατριβῆς . . . οὐκ ἀπάξιον
(645c3–6) with Clinias's reply, τῆς γε νῦν διατριβῆς ἄξιον (645c7–8).

c3)? It is this question that Megillus answers after the Stranger has turned to the second species of virtue, moderation (636e4–637b6). Megillus unites moderation with courage by denying that they are induced symmetrically: moderation follows not from a practice but from prohibition. The law as commandment suffices when it comes to pleasure; pain can only be overcome through training. The law simply removes from view what it does not allow and obedience automatically follows: any Spartan would punish on the spot with the greatest penalty anyone caught in drunken revelry. Megillus goes back to the figure of the hoplite, with his shield on the left arm and his spear in the right, which the Stranger had introduced, and says the shielded defense against pains is matched in Spartan law by the spear-expulsion of pleasures. It drives out what it cannot withstand: the Spartans are notorious for their practice of ξενηλασία.[34] Megillus means, then, that the asymmetry of Spartan custom is due to the difference between the punitive and the educative aspects of the law; but the education in pain was, as Megillus presented it, primarily punitive too, and the difference between the threat of punishment and the customary infliction of beatings seems slight.

Once Megillus and Clinias admit their bafflement before the Stranger's question—what Dorian practices allow one to taste pleasure?[35]—the Stranger postpones criticizing them by reminding them of what must be a most beautiful provision of their own laws, if in fact they have been arranged in a measured way. That provision forbids any of the young to investigate which laws are beautiful or not, but with a single voice from a single mouth they all are to say in consonance, "With the gods as legislators everything has been laid down beautifully,"[36] and if anyone speaks otherwise, they are altogether not to put up with listening to them; but if some old man reflects on something of the laws, he is to be allowed to speak before a magistrate or a contemporary, provided no young are in his presence (634d7–e6). Clinias says that the Stranger, as if he were a diviner, has guessed at the thought of the legislator, even though he was absent from it. Unlike Clinias, who had to experience the law in order to under-

34. Thucydides has the Athenians at Sparta remind the Spartans how they throw off not only Spartan laws, which are immiscible, as soon as they go abroad, but the ways of all the rest of Greece as well (1.77.6); they are referring primarily to Pausanias (1.130.1).

35. Both Megillus and Clinias misunderstand the Stranger's question; it is not what other institutions train one to resist pleasure, but what promotes equally a resistance to pleasure and pain (634b2–6).

36. The phrase θέντων θεῶν recalls Herodotus's etymology of θεοί: ὅτι κόσμῳ θέντες τὰ πάντα πρήγματα καὶ πάσας νομὰς εἶχον (2.52.1).

stand the law, the Stranger bypassed experience and deduced from the general excellence of the laws both the blanket prohibition against criticism of the law and the loophole in the law. The Stranger figures out that Dorian law must have built into it a license that belies its strictness. The law is an all-encompassing law, which enjoins uniform praise of the laws and inserts an exemption for the old. The law seems to exemplify an institutional arrangement of moderation; but Megillus at least does not see it. He does not see that both the compliance with the law, which the law instills through the command for the young to praise the law, and the departure from the law, which the law grants to the old, are equally forms of moderation. If he had wanted to keep the difference between courage and moderation, he could have appealed to this divination of the Stranger and argued that moderation, which is contrary to two vices at once, madness and insolence (637a3), is distinct from courage, and in its indulgence of the old allows for a measured degree of pleasure in the element of thoughtfulness. In order to get Megillus and Clinias to make use of the license the law already has given them, the Stranger has to call them names—"You are hypocritical pederasts and your women are sluts"—before Megillus responds in kind to the first charge—"You are nothing but drunks!"—and they settle down enough to listen to his symposium in speech. The raillery that is part and parcel of Dionysia (637b2–3)—ἐν ἁμάξαις is proverbial for hubristic mockery—goes out of bounds and spills over into the abuse they hurl at one another. They participate in a wineless Dionysia in speech. We may call it a Dorian comedy,[37] through which a way is opened up for the establishing of institutions of moderation that will match the prescription of moderation that the Stranger divined Dorian law already has.

The systematic review of lawful institutions in light of the eidetic structure of the good gets no further than moderation. It gets no further because, on the one hand, the Stranger has already undermined the difference between courage and moderation, and, on the other, the turn to moderation incites Megillus to defend the lopsidedness of Spartan law once the Stranger points out that any training of a part tends to damage another part (636a7–b1). The Stranger suggests not only that defectiveness is built into any piecemeal practice but that the partiality of a part infects every other part adversely. The fit between speech and deed, so that what the law commands is indisputably on a par with what results from the

---

37. Cf. England on the phrase καὶ εἴτε παίζοντα εἴτε σπουδάζοντα ἐννοεῖν δεῖ τὰ τοιαῦτα (636c1–2): "the effect of this parenthesis is somewhat as follows: 'the comic poet, if you will let him, will tell you as readily as the philosopher.'"

law, is hard to establish. Only a comprehensive set of institutions could check the tendency of any practice to extend its domain beyond the intent of the practice and lead to consequences that lodge in custom without being either authorized by or in conformity with law. Clinias had drawn an utterly lawless consequence from the single practice of the common mess, and now the Stranger points to the civil strife it occasioned in Miletus, Boeotia, and Thurii, and its corruption of a law that is thought to be both ancient and natural.[38] Clinias had disregarded both the virtue the common mess presumably promotes and the unforeseen consequences it has on marriage, which the Stranger had put at the head of his genetic structure of law. The Stranger is not criticizing pederasty in itself but for its being an unreflective offshoot of another practice that in isolating the women from the men left the women uncontrolled, and in gathering the men together led to an act of high daring, the discovery of what is: sexual pleasure and the law, which marriage seems to unite indissolubly, are utterly separable. The incontinence of pederasty (δι᾽ ἀκράτειαν ἡδονῆς) showed that the failure of Dorian law to promote equally a resistance to pleasure and pain did not entail the suppression but rather the induction of pleasure without any lawful constraints. Pederasty necessarily prevented Dorian law from establishing a consonance between the law and the experiences of pleasure and pain. The hatred of what was painful was bound to follow from the lawful inculcation of pain, and the love of what was pleasurable was bound to follow from what the law did nothing to guide.

The Stranger brings in another indictment against the Cretans: "We all accuse them of inventing (λογοποιησάντων) the story (μῦθος) of Ganymede, since their settled belief that their laws had come from Zeus made them attach this story against Zeus, in order that in following the god—if you can believe it (δή)—they may reap this pleasure too" (636c7–d4).[39] The Stranger implies that, though pederasty came along with the common mess, the Cretans were guiltily aware that it was not an explicit element of the law, and in order to square a practice with the divine origin of their laws, they bypassed the law as commandment and went directly to the author of the law so that they could claim to be imitating him. Emulation of Zeus emerges from behind and through the obedience to

38. The text is difficult, and παλαιόν <τε> νόμον (636b4) would be one way to make it clearer that it is the object of διεφθαρκέναι.

39. The Stranger's criticism of the Cretan Ganymede is all the more telling if one recalls that in the "Ionian" version Zeus snatched Ganymede in order for him to be his wine pourer (*Iliad* 20.232–5).

Zeus. An end run is made around the law as if it were an advance to a higher level, but instead the indulgence in pleasure is dressed up to look like something else. Clinias had discerned in a custom a principle. That principle, if one were telling stories, would be called "Ares." The Stranger, in looking at the same custom, has now observed in it as a byproduct another principle, which, if it were likewise to be given a mythical name, would be "Aphrodite." Ares and Aphrodite emerge together as the embodiments of the antinomian implications of the law itself. If the law has not been so elaborated that any leakage around the edges of the law, in the form of unauthorized meanings and customs, has been sealed off, theology-laden stories threaten to undermine it. Either the stories suggest of themselves that the law is fundamentally defective and something better and contrary to it lies just behind it, or the stories in glossing over defects in the law make it impossible to correct them. The glamour of divinity hides the rot in the law. The rehearsal of the original conference between Minos and Zeus, which the Stranger is now working up, is certainly designed to hinder the contravention of the law even if one goes behind it, but it is not as clear whether the Stranger has a way to block excrescences on the law itself. The Stranger replaces the unauthorized license of pederasty with the fully lawful license of dialogic συνουσία. It is a new kind of mythmaking within the confines of the law.

At this point, in dismissing myth and turning back to law, the Stranger asserts that the thorough scrutiny of laws is almost entirely a scrutiny of pleasures and pains. If we reflect on the course of the argument, from war and civil strife to peace and friendly feeling, with war linked with pain and peace with pleasure, and courage either as the comprehensive virtue, regulating all pleasures and pains, or as half of a whole, and moderation as either the second highest good or a complement of courage, the Stranger has already made his case. Megillus, however, cannot quite square the argument with his feelings of disgust when he recalls the Dionysia he once saw in Attica and Tarentum. The Dionysia, he implies, are in their extreme form of self-indulgence the counterpart to the Spartan training in endurance, and like the Ganymede story carry in their name a divine excuse. A practice, arising perhaps alongside an Ionian way of life (cf. 680d1), likewise needed a god to defend it. Megillus thereby ignores the difference between a festive letting-go, which law fences around, and an irregular practice that only a story excuses (cf. 775b4–6; Aristotle *Politics* 1336b14–16). Still, Megillus has a point: an entire city drunk leaves itself wide open to a surprise attack (cf. Thucydides 7.73.2), and to become addicted to wine cannot be conducive to sobriety. The Stranger does not defend Dionysia; he does not even defend a correctly conducted symposium. He argues merely that nothing can be inferred from something badly done as to whether it would be beneficial if it were rightly done. The Stranger had offered this line of defense to Clinias and Megillus. The deficiencies in Dorian law when it came to courage did not mean that they could not have devised a no less ideal form of *sussition* that would have been equally adept at facing pleasures and pains. Clinias declined the challenge after the Stranger had invented the speech the legislator should have addressed to himself (635c3–d6). Clinias was given the opportunity to improve on the city as an armed camp and suggest the communism of women (cf. *Republic* 458c6–d3), which would have solved at a stroke the two defects the Stranger mentions as inherent in the Dorian *sussition*. It is not surprising if neither Clinias nor Megillus sees this way out; but even Socrates' solution had the defect that he did not prove that communism was in accordance with human nature, whereas it is the first purpose of the Stranger's symposium in speech to reveal human natures (650b6–8). The symposium in speech is a thought-experiment on man himself.

3   DRUNKENNESS

If one looks back to Clinias's radical interpretation of a law, and Megillus's presentation of the extreme severity of Spartan training, one might conclude that laws have a tendency to lose sight of the Aristotelian mean, which depends on an on-the-spot determination of when, where, and how much (cf. 636e1; 638c7–8). Despite the fact that a habit as such is already "measured" through its constancy, it seems to be incapable of holding itself in check, but like a precept it fixes everything except its own timely use. Regardless, moreover, of the "key" at which a habit pitches the soul's state, the habit looks as though it partakes of the mean even if it may really be immoderate in itself. We call even an addiction a "habit." Departures from custom, which look at the time of their intrusion excessive, pass themselves off as moderate if they succeed in getting incorporated into the law. Almost any dance one can think of was thought at first to violate decorum, but in time it came to seem orderly and proper when compared to the indecency of the next novelty (cf. 797e2–798a8 with 802c4–d3).[40] Moderation, then, seems to be the same as the familiar, and

40. Cf. Rémi Hess, *La valse: Révolution du couple en Europe* (Paris 1989), 49 (criticism of the "volta" in the sixteenth century), 115 (only married women danced the waltz in the early nineteenth), 153 (Alfred de Musset in 1836 on the waltz).

anything out of the ordinary exaggerated and immodest. Forms of custom are always orderly, the content of custom rarely if ever in order. It might seem a vain project, then, even to try to translate the eidetic structure of the good into the genetic structure of law, or in reverse to trace in the genetic structure of law the true ranking of the eightfold good. The evident incompleteness in the examination of moderation might be taken as an admission that the Stranger's project was bound to fail. The Stranger's response to Megillus's attack on Dionysia looks at first as if he were willing to admit that from the outside every custom, in looking strange, violates propriety, and from the inside, every custom has a universal defense: "It is just our way, stranger; you perhaps have another" (637c6–8). It seems, then, that there is no perspective from which a custom can be criticized or praised, and only a madman, as Herodotus says, would go about ridiculing alien ways (3.38).[41]

The Stranger frees them from the impasse they have reached by reminding them that their discussion concerns the virtue and vice of legislators and not all the rest of mankind (637d1–3). If the Stranger really means that they are no longer to look at the virtues and vices of men, who take their imprint from the laws under which they live, he would be talking nonsense. Megillus claims, absurd though the exaggeration is, that the superiority of the Spartan abstention from drink shows up in the defeat on the battlefield of all the tribes, most of whom the Spartans have never faced, who indulge in wine more or less excessively (637d5–e7). The Stranger denies that victory or defeat is a safe criterion, but says rather that prior to their asking whether something is useful or not in its effect they have to determine what is its correct use in itself. The right way of conducting a symposium has first to be figured out, then the good it aims at has to be evaluated, and finally that good has to be considered in light of whether the symposium will impart to that good its proper rank. The Stranger proposes the discussion of drunkenness itself (μέθης αὐτῆς πέρι) as the model they should have followed from the start. They had not started with the "common mess itself," but rather had accepted Clinias's and Megillus's impression that the common mess did not have a correct form: συσσιτεῖν was just what it was, for as a necessity of wartime it did not admit of varieties in its mode (cf. *Symposium* 180e4–

41. The connection of thought at 637b7–c2 is obscure. πάντα τὰ τοιαῦτα seems to refer to Dionysia, but if so, the self-defense of an Athenian, by pointing to the looseness of Spartan women, does not follow (ταχὺ γάρ . . . ἄν). "All things of the sort" refers, I believe, to Megillus's outrage at Dionysia, to which the Athenian responds in kind. It is rather stupid (βλακικώτερα) of Megillus, in borrowing so freely from Dionysiac license, to be so intemperate in criticizing it.

181a4). They then proceeded to attribute to it a virtue, without ever asking how a virtue could show up in the mere fact of eating together. The Stranger had countered with two criticisms; it led to pederasty and the looseness of women, but the co-presence of those vices with συσσιτεῖν did not establish any causal relation, for no proof was given that συσσίτια as such engender those vices, any more than that excessive drinking on occasion makes a people poor fighters. Now, however, the Stranger, in shifting to a theoretical perspective, in which the form of an action will be analyzed in itself, has the opportunity to show what necessarily belongs to it and how it can be controlled. This pure model can then guide what the Stranger suggests are its institutional equivalents in the genetic structure of law. Education is the reality of the ideal symposium.

The peculiar and special relation the discussion about "intoxication itself" has to legislation is first suggested by an idiom of the "later" Plato. After saying that their talk is about the vice and virtue of legislators, the Stranger says: ἔτι γὰρ οὖν εἴπωμεν πλείω περὶ ἁπάσης μέθης (637d3–4). We could translate this as, "Let us speak at still greater length about drunkenness as a whole," were it not for the particles γὰρ οὖν. "In a few passages in Plato's later works," J. D. Denniston says, "γὰρ οὖν and γὰρ οὖν δή are used where the context would appear rather to demand a forward-pointing connective, οὖν or δή. That is to say, the sequel is regarded as implicitly contained in, rather than following from, the preceding thought: explanatory γάρ being pushed almost beyond its proper limits."[42] In what sense is drunkenness "contained" in the excellence or defectiveness of legislators? To be drunk is to be out of control, in mind as well as in body; the drunk, like the old, are twice children (646a4–5). To be a child, especially to be less than a year old, is to move and shout in a completely disordered and random way. It is to be in a condition that is prior to the orderliness and regularity that habit and law impose. Drink thus reproduces the prelaw state of human beings both collectively and individually. It brings before the eyes of the legislator precisely that condition which the laws he lays down are to handle. Drunkenness alone shows him what he has to contend with, the prerational beginning of any rational order (cf. 672c1–5). The recovery of this starting-point is the corrective

---

42. *The Greek Particles* (Oxford 1954), 447. Édouard des Places, *Études sur quelques particules de liaison chez Platon* (Paris 1929), 123–124, fills in what is missing as follows: "*En effet*, entrons dans quelque détail au sujet des différents excès de l'ivresse (et nous jugerons mieux les législateurs); car ce point n'est pas de mince importance, et ce n'est pas à un législateur médiocre qu'il appartient de le régler." This makes the issue a practical one, albeit paradigmatic, rather than recognizing that the legislator deals with nothing else than that which drunkenness represents.

of Clinias's experiential insight into law. Not war, which may well be the political condition of men, but disorder, which antedates any political arrangement, is the truth of whatever becomes. This prepolitical condition fills in some of the gap between the genetic structure of law and the eidetic structure of the good. It shows what the sobering of man involves: if it were possible for man to be neutrally disposed toward pain and pleasure, so that he could face both from a standpoint beyond either, the ranking of the eightfold good could possibly be experienced through the law. If, however, man is always on the brink of disorder, as his susceptibility to intoxication of any kind reveals, then the prepolitical state of man is his permanent condition, which the law manages to conceal rather than alter. The antinomian experience of Clinias proves to be but the surface truth about the law.

The Stranger seems to imply that had he been present at what Plato titled a symposium he would have found fault with it. Phaedrus, who was in charge, had a poor head for wine, and Alcibiades would probably not have been allowed to enter and change the rules, and certainly the late revelers would have been barred altogether. These defects, as well as the disturbance in the order Aristophanes' hiccups caused, are perhaps enough to qualify it as somewhat too disorderly for the Stranger's taste, though he could not argue that a greater cheerfulness and friendliness were not promoted through the playfulness of Aristophanes, the Gorgianic jingles of Agathon, and the ardor of Alcibiades. Socrates was not the ruler of the symposium, though he was the only one present who would pass the Stranger's test of sobriety. Under less than ideal conditions, then, the *Symposium* still manages to let everyone show himself as just what he is as a lover. Their erotic natures were revealed on their own and Socrates was there to guide one in understanding how they severally had hit upon the truth and fallen short of it. It is unclear, then, what a tighter control of the circumstances would have achieved, unless we take into account the missing conversation Socrates had with Aristophanes and Agathon, which, had Aristodemus stayed awake and passed on their argument to Apollodorus, would have filled in the time till dawn. That conversation concerned the Socratic thesis that a tragic poet by art was also a comic poet, and the knowledge of how to make a comedy and a tragedy belongs to the same man (*Symposium* 223d2–6). When Socrates finally did get to be in charge, and a symposium in the strict sense was under way, Aristodemus nodded off and did not have the wit to ask Socrates what the argument was, in which Socratic wisdom was pitted against the chief votaries of Dionysus (cf. 175e9, 177e1). Surely, a symposium that ended in this way would come near to being the perfect party. The closest approximation to it Plato ever wrote was the *Laws*. The *Laws* supplies not only Socrates' argument, in a setting that partakes of the hilarity of communal wine drinking, but it also puts itself to the test, once it is acknowledged to be a rightly organized symposium, whether it is to be praised or not. It passes this test if and only if it can show that the way to the laws lies through songs, and the way through music leads to the god who sponsors Dionysia and presides over tragedy and comedy (643a6–7). A sign that the *Laws* is meant to make up for Aristodemus's negligence is the Stranger's astonishing statement that they do not need the tragic poets: "We are ourselves the makers of the most beautiful and best possible tragedy" (817b2–3). If the Stranger made by art what he calls "really" (ὄντως) the truest tragedy, he was also capable of making a comedy.

The Stranger's reason for turning away from real symposia to a symposium in speech is twofold. One cannot rely on the evidence of partisan witnesses, for if they did, the Spartan and the Cretan would be overwhelmed by the number of tribes who maintain different customs. It is to the advantage of Clinias and Megillus not to enter a contest in which their two cities could not possibly win. The sheer variety of ways seems to make the symposium a matter of indifference. Secondly, a strict division must be made between the correct and the good. That distinction is of decisive importance in the Stranger's analysis of imitation, but at the moment it seems to point in general to the difference between art or science and its use. Despite the fact that the origin of an art may always be traced to a need or desire, and hence its usefulness precedes ordinarily its invention, an art by itself can neither determine when it is to be applied nor argue on the basis of what it knows and knows how to do that the need or desire the art satisfies ought to be satisfied. The Stranger, therefore, in order to neutralize the symposium, has to assimilate it to any partnership in which there is a common action so that he can introduce the knowledgeable ruler. There had not been a word so far about knowledge in connection with either war or courage. The Stranger now couples knowledge and virtue. Though he begins his examples with a flock of goats, which have wandered into cultivated fields, where the goatherd has only to be skilled and not immune to the smell of goats, he mentions that the sea captain must not suffer from nausea and the general of an army not be a coward. The Stranger denied that he was concerned with the permission or the prohibition of wine drinking, but only with drunkenness in its entirety (637d5–6). He seems to be alluding to the extension of "drunkenness" to cover any ecstatic state: he himself speaks of the cowardly general as one who is seasick by the drunkenness of fear—ὑπὸ μέθης τοῦ φόβου ναυτιᾷ—and he does not say he is speaking metaphorically (639b7).

From the difference in degree between the brave man and the coward—terrors disturb him less—the Stranger concludes that they should appoint a general who is totally without fear (640b2–3). A fearless general might well be oblivious of the fears of others and lead his troops to face dangers that will necessarily break them. The general's knowledge is meant to prevent this; while terror should never impair his judgment, he should know what his men can stand. In the parallel case of the symposium, the sober leader is to have the knowledge of how to maintain and increase friendly feeling among friends. The parallel looks odd for two reasons. Neither the captain nor the general induces the state from which he himself is free; but the symposiarch presides over a gathering in which he is responsible for inducing the disorder he is supposed to regulate. The external forces of disorder, whether winds and waves or the enemy, confront the captain or general with a state that he would prefer not to face; but the symposiarch must upset and put in disarray what he is to regulate. He is deliberately to run the risk of drawing out the hidden enmity among friends in order to arrange for their greater friendship: the Stranger called Clinias and Megillus friends for the first time after Megillus's indignation at un-Spartan ways, which the Stranger had deliberately provoked, threatened to break up the discussion (637d1). The second lack of parallelism follows from this. The general and the captain are at risk along with their men, and if they manage to save them they save themselves; but just as the sober symposiarch runs no risks at all, either because he does not drink or drink does not affect him, so he does not become more friendly toward his drinking companions. As a means whereby the legislator comes to know the natures of those he rules, the symposium itself is effective, even if he never conducts one, for it reminds him what men are before they become law-abiding; but the need that would drive him to set up a symposium in deed must be the occurrence of the starting point of the Stranger's argument: the friends whom he gathers in a symposium consist of the just and the unjust, and he must reconcile people who are on the verge of cutting each other's throats. The existence or the threat of stasis would then stand for the storm at sea or the approach of the enemy, and the symposiarch would counter that disorder with one of his own. The legislator is an expert in homeopathic medicine.

Clinias had asserted that peace was just a word and war the permanent condition of man. The Stranger has now revised the antinomian implications of Clinias's assertion. The antinomian meaning of the law as Clinias experienced it has yielded to the essential lawlessness of man in his becoming in time. Disorder is the condition into which everyone is born, and disorder precedes whatever political order is established. The theme of book 3 is thus already prepared. The legislator promotes friend-liness not by getting rid of the bad or arranging for their voluntary sub-mission to the good, but by giving to them all a "buzz" or making them "high," so that the rule of reason can take over in the form of laws. Laws must be intoxicating if a consonance is to be achieved among those who if they were cold sober would never agree. The citizens must be disarmed: the mind of some must lose their edge and the hearts of others be exalted. The symposium in speech thus stands for both the prelaw condition of man, when they are in complete disorder, and the condition of men once their disorder gets to be in order. To blame a symposium for its disorderli-ness cannot be sound unless one knows whether or not a symposium is in order if it is in disorder. A flock of goats is in order if they do not stray beyond the confines of the pasture (νομός) the goatherd has assigned them. They do not have to be lined up in rows to be an orderly flock. This standard of order is very low if one compares it with what either a ship in a storm or an army under attack requires, but politically its analogue is nonimperialism: the law is to confine the city to the region the ruler manages (νέμει). The laws are designed to check expansion without and dissension within. Friendly feeling—φιλοφροσύνη—also seems to be a not very grand ambition for a city; but perhaps it too has to be taken as liter-ally as νόμος has been, and in the form of *φιλο-φρονεῖν[43] point not only to the reason and good sense (φρόνησις) with which the feelings are to coincide through the laws, but also to φιλο-σοφεῖν as that to which the city must become friendly.

The Stranger had reminded Clinias of the paired expressions "to be superior to oneself" and "to be inferior to oneself." He now seems to be proposing the examination of the state of being "beside oneself" without pairing it with "being oneself," ἐκτὸς ἑαυτοῦ by itself without ἐν ἑαυτοῦ. The regulated derangement he suggests is designed at first to be a theoret-ical spectacle of human natures (cf. 639c5); but Clinias, though he ac-cepts the difference between the right and the good (641a4–5), is impa-tient and wants to know what great good would result to either individuals or the city if a symposium were rightly managed. He agrees that a drunk and unwise ruler, unless he were very lucky, would produce a great evil (640d5–7); but he seems to deny that the production of greater

43. Liddell-Scott-Jones lists under φιλοφρονέομαι III the doubtful cases of it as an active.

friendliness would deserve to be called a great good. That he is about to call the Stranger "friend" (641c8) for the first time does not count in favor of their kind of symposium. The differences among them, which the Stranger ascribes to well-known national traits, seem to guarantee that they cannot come together in any harmony. Athenians love to talk and at great length, the Spartans do not, and the Cretans' thinking is wide-ranging and pithy. If the ultimate result of laws shows up in these kinds of differences, however little they may apply to an individual member of a city, the issue of law concerns not only how laws are to enfold the eightfold good but also whether laws, even if they achieve a transparency for the reception of the eidetic structure of the good, are not necessarily shot through with "slubs" that work their way into the fabric of laws and are at least as important as the genetic structure of law. If the Stranger's character is a growth, however spontaneous, out of the loquacious soil of Attica, and it is inconceivable without such a condition, then either the legislator has no way of either favoring or hindering its nurture, or else, if laws can affect anything in this regard, the legislator must let up on the compulsion of the laws, which, Megillus acknowledges, prevails in Sparta and makes the exceptional and unfeigned natural goodness some Athenians have impossible (642c8–d2). As the tumultuousness of Dionysia, in which everyone lets go under official auspices, would symbolize the conditions under which the Stranger flourished, so the symposium in speech exemplifies the model for the dissonance of natures despite the uniformity of law. The symposium thus looks two ways, to the disorderliness of man prior and subsequent to law, and to the law's accommodation to deviations from the genetic structure of law that in no sense can be called either lawless or spontaneous.

The most obvious deviation from the genetic structure of law is to be found in language itself, and at the very moment Megillus expresses his fondness for the Attic dialect, Plato has him use an expression in quoting the Spartan companions of his youth—ἡ πόλις ὑμῶν ἡμᾶς οὐ καλῶς ἢ καλῶς ἔρρεξε—that deviates from Attic usage and seems to be exclusively Laconic (642c2).[44] The logos of the law always comes to light in a language or dialect of a language (cf. 704b1).[45] Except for Megillus's ὦ θεῖε, Plato

44. Cf. England ad loc.: "Acc. to Boeckh κακῶς ῥέζειν τινά is a Laconism. It is certainly not ordinary Attic." The most notable other Dorism is the postponement of ἄν in relative clauses; this begins at 777c6; cf. J. Wackernagel, cited by England at 890a5.

45. The problematic relation between language and divine law is first adumbrated by Herodotus (2.2–3), who follows up his story of Psammetichus's experiment to discover the first language with an avowal of human ignorance about τὰ θεῖα τῶν

had up to now made the language of the speakers uniformly Attic, so that, one might suppose, if his readers are presumed to have Attic as their native tongue, neither the Spartan nor the Cretan would appear ridiculous; but here our attention is called to the fact that he has done so, when the Stranger is about to embark on a long discourse of a custom that neither Clinias nor Megillus could tell even if they saw it whether it was being rightly done or not (639e4–640a2). We know then that Clinias, if he ever applies the Stranger's proposals to Magnesia, must literally translate the *Laws* into the dialect of Crete. This translation would involve at least as much of a departure from the *Laws* as Megillus's quotation would undergo if its Attic equivalent were given. Such alterations would certainly affect the experience of the law and alter the behavior of its adherents. They seem to be incalculable and render once more the Stranger's project vain. One might guess that even the most exact transcription of the *Laws* into another dialect or language would make it unrecognizable, if not at once, at least over time. These unavoidable imperfections in the actual law, so that within its language a network of connections is formed independent of the intent of the law, would seem to be behind the Stranger's insistence on the ecstatic as the proper starting point for the understanding of law. The symposium in speech is designed to be a solvent of everything that stands in the way of taking in the logos of the law.

Clinias supplies the opening to education through his catachresis of the verb παιδαγωγεῖν (641b1). He wants to know what great thing would happen should a symposium be rightly conducted (συμποσίου ὀρθῶς παιδαγωγηθέντος). He seems to use the verb sarcastically. Just as children must be brought to and from school by slave παιδαγωγοί, to keep others from diverting them and themselves from straying, so a symposium needs a monitor if its members are not to get falling down drunk or to act outrageously. We call such παιδαγωγοί "designated drivers." The Stranger picks up on παιδαγωγεῖν in the forms of παῖς and παιδεύειν and argues that education never yields a Cadmeian victory, in which the winner loses. Fratricidal warfare, he implies, is never the outcome of education. In thus alluding back to their earlier discussion about stasis, the Stranger links education with friendliness, and, as he had done before, makes victory in war depend on it. At this point, Clinias makes an imaginative leap that we would not have suspected he was capable of doing:

ἀπηγημάτων, where he leaves it unclear whether our ignorance is no less of the gods than of their names; Socrates spells out the ambiguity in the *Cratylus* 400d6–9. If the text is sound, and, according to the fourth hand of the Vatican MS, θεοῖς was obelized in some copies, Clinias expresses inadvertently the same thought at 891e1–3.

"We think, friend, that you are speaking of the common pastime in wine drinking, if it rightly becomes, as pertaining to a large share of education" (641c8–d2). Clinias calls the Stranger "friend" at exactly that moment when he has to have seen that φιλοφροσύνη was the middle term between the aim of the symposium and the aim of civil peace. The Stranger had not said anything explicitly about the connection between education and symposium. It seemed as if he had disregarded Clinias's disparaging allusion to the menial task of παιδαγωγοί and pounced on the verb in itself, which more easily lent itself to "education" than to "symposium."[46] That there is something inspired about Clinias's guess comes out in the Stranger's own way of linking the symposium to education. The natural rightness of intoxication would never gain adequate clarity without the rightness of music, and music in turn, never without the entirety of education (642a3–5). Clinias divined the connection between symposium and education without having the least notion that the connection lay through music. The Stranger had even hinted at music when he added the proper guidance of a single chorus as a possible alternative to that of a single child (641b3); but Clinias did not take him up on it and zeroed in on education by himself. Clinias thus confirms in himself the reputation of the Cretans for πολύνοια and the divinatory powers of Epimenides, with whom he claims a family connection (642d6).

4   THE PUPPET MASTERS

The Stranger does not follow exactly the sequence of themes he proposes. He does not go from education to music to intoxication, for though he starts with education he soon brings in intoxication, and only when he has established what the advantage of symposia might be for the legislator does he turn back to music and education. He discusses wine drinking before he gets to the god Dionysus, who is not mentioned by name before the very end of book 1 (650a1). One could say that wine neat comes before the god who is to be put in charge of his own chorus. Intoxication in theory is Dionysus in law. Dionysus is the refined and elevated dilution of intoxication itself. There is, then, a double form of education that the Stranger is separating and putting together in the course of his argument. The education of the legislator himself is coupled with and uncoupled from the education of citizens. The symposium gives him access to the

---

46. The verbal element in παιδαγωγέω is picked by the Stranger in ἡ τοῦ λογισμοῦ ἀγωγή (645a1; cf. a5–6).

souls of its guests—"truth and wine," as the proverb says—without risk, for he joins with them in the spectacle of Dionysus (συγγενόμενον μετὰ τῆς Διονύσου θεωρίας). Ἡ Διονύσου θεωρία means both the festivals dedicated to Dionysus and the theoretical speculation of Dionysus, where "of Dionysus" is both an objective genitive—the theoretical gazing on the indulgence in wine—and subjective—the legislator adopts and joins in the vantage point of the god.

The Stranger does not explain why intoxication has to be brought together with education and music. In the *Republic*, after all, Socrates discussed education and music without any recourse to Dionysus. One could say that Dionysus stands for the quasi-identification the Stranger is going to make between education (παιδεία) and play (παιδιά). To be engaged in play is παίζειν or προσπαίζειν, and προσπαίζειν means not only to play and make fun of but to celebrate gods in song (804b1; *Epinomis* 980b4). What is not serious is more serious than what is serious, and, as the argument develops, what we are to delight in before we become serious imitates the eidetic structure of the good before we have experienced it in the genetic structure of law. Education, then, in representing the completion of becoming in images, looks away in its representing from what is becoming. Its images as images make sport of what they image. The funniness of man is inseparable from the business of becoming human. Education is "funny business." The tragedy and comedy of life, which is commonly held to be the truth of life, is also nothing but an image of life.

The Stranger offers a double definition of education. The first is based on a general reflection of how one becomes good at anything. The examples are the builder and the farmer, the carpenter and the knight. Either toy instruments are involved or playful actions. The future horseman rides a hobbyhorse, the future carpenter builds with blocks and weighs and measures with scale models of ruler and balance. The educator tries to divert the pleasures and desires of children toward that point where on their arrival they themselves are complete (τέλος ἔχειν). Τέλος ἔχειν could well be a euphemism for death (717e2, 740c2, 772c1). Correct upbringing will to the highest degree draw the soul of the player to a love (ἔρως) of that in which when he becomes a man (ἀνήρ) he will have to be perfect (εἶναι τέλεον) in regard to the virtue of the matter (643d1–3). There is not a word about pain. The pleasure in playing with the unreal is to be joined with a desire for the real. The unreal is to be known as unreal. The second definition of education is intended to reserve the name for education toward virtue, making the child a desirer and a lover of becoming a perfect citizen (ἐπιθυμητήν τε καὶ ἐραστὴν τοῦ πολίτην γενέσθαι τέλεον), with the knowledge of how to rule and be ruled with justice (643e2–6). The second definition says nothing about the achievement of perfection: since perfection consists solely in knowledge, the law would become superfluous if the lover ever obtained his goal. It is perhaps for this reason that the definition is phrased in terms of "becoming" rather than of "being." The Stranger stresses that it should be possible, if any deviations from education occur, to make corrections throughout one's life (644b2–4). There is, moreover, not a word in the definition about either pleasure or games, and it is equally silent about the soul. If one thinks of children's games that imitate ruling and being ruled, one recalls how in Giant Steps, for example, the rules of the game involve strict obedience to the arbitrary orders of the ruler, strict compliance with which guarantees that one will tag the ruler and force everyone else to run back to the starting line without getting caught; the one caught becomes the ruler. The aim is to stay in power as long as possible by fooling one's subjects, and the subjects take pleasure in disobeying the ruler without getting caught. The fun of disobedience is matched by the fun of ruling, but the knowledge imparted is not wholly desirable. The role of umpire would fit more closely what the Stranger might have in mind. Here partisanship, however, which would incline those playing the game to dispute the umpire's decisions and tempt the umpire himself not to be fair, would act powerfully enough to make the role of umpire extremely unpleasant and not anything children would want to assume. The players too would only take pleasure in their own indignation and not in the necessity to abide by the decisions of the umpire. After all, even professional players never take turns at being the umpire.[47] One could argue, on the other hand, that the expression "to play by the rules" does indicate what education is to achieve, and "sportsmanship" the fusion of umpire and player into one. "Sportsmanship," however, seems to be the goal of gymnastic, and it is hard to discern in it any direct education of the soul. The law-abiding habits of Clinias were a gymnastic that led to his insight about war and conquest.

At this point, the Stranger introduces an image. Prior to the introduction of images in music education, an image is introduced to lead up to music education. The education of the legislator is also through images. He looks at man as an hypothesis and an image. The hypothesis consists of three elements: each of us is one; each possesses two senseless and opposed advisers, pleasure and pain; and in addition to them each possesses

---

47. Pollux (9.110) mentions a game called βασιλίνδα, which in form is the same as the one Cyrus played as a boy (Herodotus 1.114), and Xenophon tells of the lesson Cyrus learned when he was appointed a judge as a boy (*Cyropaedeia* I.3.16–17).

opinions of the future, whose common name is expectation, but fear is the expectation prior to pain, and confidence for its contrary. The Stranger adds not too mysteriously, if one recalls the genetic structure of law, that a calculation ranges over all of these possessions as to which of them is better or worse, and if that calculation becomes the common opinion or resolve of the city (δόγμα πόλεως κοινόν), it has the name law (644c4–d3). The definition of law is not an hypothesis, but a name for an opinion which arises from a calculation, regardless of whether it is right or not, about what is better or worse. Λογισμός is alone nonhypothetical.[48] It figures out the good or bad in whatever one hopes or fears. Pleasure and pain, in this hypothesis, are not simple experiences but experiences with arrows; they tell us what to pursue and what to avoid and are closer to desires than anything limited to the present. Everything is prospective, either experientially or dogmatically, but there is in the one each of us is no awareness. Our singularity depends on the absence of any inside to us. We are either pushed or pulled. Man is by hypothesis future-oriented.[49] He does not have a past. Both Megillus and Clinias admit that they cannot follow the Stranger perfectly. Their experience of perplexity in the present is precisely what the Stranger's hypothesis does not allow; but they have such confidence in the Stranger that Clinias urges him to go on speaking as if he were following. He jumps into the unknown future with the hope that the Stranger will supply an opinion he can share. That opinion is an image. The image is of each of us as a puppet (θαῦμα). A puppet is an object of wonder; it is not a being which wonders. The Stranger says this puppet is divine (θεῖον). As the two ways which the Stranger gives of interpreting it show, "divine" is ambiguous: εἴτε ὡς παίγνιον ἐκείνων εἴτε ὡς σπουδῇ συνεστηκός. If θεῖον is the equivalent of a substantive in the genitive, the puppet belongs to the gods and is their plaything; if, on the other hand, θεῖον is strictly adjectival, it could mean that we partake of the divine, and we have been put together for some serious purpose.[50] The Stranger professes not to know what his own image

48. This is shown by the dropping of the construction introduced by τιθῶμεν (644c4) that continues up to 644d1.

49. For the connection between law and future good, see *Theaetetus* 178a5–10.

50. The essential ambiguity of θεῖον first occurred in the label attached to the goods of the soul. That ambiguity recalls the beginning of the *Sophist*, where Socrates suggests that Theodorus has inadvertently introduced him to a god in the disguise of a stranger; Socrates, as the Athenian Stranger does at the beginning of the *Laws*, cites a passage from the *Odyssey*, and he does so because Theodorus had introduced the Eleatic Stranger as a kind of stranger (τινὰ ξένον) and failed to give him a name; Theodorus denied that the Stranger was a god, and certainly not a refutative god, but he is θεῖος, πάντας γὰρ ἐγὼ τοὺς φιλοσόφους τοιούτους προσαγορεύω (216c1). The Athenian

means: he too cannot follow what he is saying. We might suppose that
we are divine if we are capable of the divine goods, and we are playthings
if we are only capable of the human goods: the puppet, as an image, implies that we are purely corporeal. In our relation to the gods, however,
we might be exactly in the same position as playthings are to children.
The educational toys of children were imitations of the real thing; the
real thing now turns out to be possibly a toy. Are the gods, then, on the
way to becoming perfect, and are we the means to their becoming serious
at last? Do we reflect something higher than the gods, and are we thus
objects of wonder to them? This is admittedly a strange reading of the
Stranger's image but unavoidable in light of its place in the argument.

Hope and fear are about the future. If the law is to be a common
opinion about them, the future would need to be noncontingent and non-
circumstantial. The law transforms pleasures and pains into protases
with necessary apodoses: "If this, then that shall be." Every "this" is a
pleasure or a pain, to every "that" good or bad is attached. If we follow
the genetic structure of law, these conditionals of the law attach either
"just"/"unjust" or "beautiful"/"ugly" to what the Stranger here calls
"good" and "bad." According to the genetic structure of law, the future is
between birth and death; but now that the gods may possibly be the puppet masters, the future could also be our ultimate future. The ultimate
future involves the gods insofar as they would be the permanent objects
of our fears and our hopes in a fourfold way. The gods as just would in
one sense be the ultimate objects of our fears, and the gods as beautiful
the ultimate objects of our hopes; but in another sense the gods would
also be the ground of hope insofar as we are victims of injustice, and they
would be the ground of despair insofar as we are defective. The law would
thus become divine law if the temporal horizon of the genetic structure
of law were to be in this way expanded. The divine puppet already looks
forward to the theology of book 10. However this may be, the harshness
of the law, if the conditionals of the law are punitive as well as beneficent,
does not fit the Stranger's own account of his image. The Stranger separates what he knows from what he does not know about it. He does not
know who pulls the strings or for what purpose, but he does know the

---

Stranger, once he hears that gods are responsible for Cretan and Spartan law, suggests
the suitability of a discussion on regime and laws, ἐπειδὴ ἐν τοιούτοις ἤθεσι τέθραφθε
νομικοῖς (625a1), where his τοιούτοις, in alluding to the gods, signals the same problem
as Theodorus's τοιούτους. The Eleatic Stranger when abroad commits patricide, the
Athenian Stranger exposes the roots of the ancestral.

experiences in us are like the strings attached to each joint of a puppet. These strings in their mutual opposition pull us toward contrary actions. Among these iron strings there is just one of soft gold. This golden thread of λογισμός is beautiful and gentle; it therefore needs helpers if the golden genus (γένος) in us is to win out over all the other genera. The Stranger assigns to the golden thread only the beautiful and denies to it the just. Fear and despair, then, might be thought to be the harsh strings that are to be summoned to contribute to the leading string of beauty; but it is not easy to see how such helpers would not contaminate the draw of reason. If its helpers are to be only pleasure and confidence, as the characterization of education would suggest, the lure of pleasure might mimic too easily the gold of reason.

The Stranger says that his image clarifies the incoherence of "better than oneself" and "worse than oneself." The strings of the puppet match our experiences because everything in our experiences is outside the unitary self in the form of the future. The projections of time in the form of either hope or fear allow one to say in the present that one is better than oneself if the prospect is good and worse than oneself if the prospect is bad. The image implies that the pull of a string of pleasure or pain points to some immediate or distant future; around that future an opinion forms about future pleasure and pain; and as that future pleasure or pain is good or bad, the puppet is now better or worse than it is. Since the puppet's present state is the result of the past projections into the future, its present state is either good or bad insofar as it conforms with the good or bad of its past prospect. If its projection and realization are always consistent, then it is either good or bad; but if either alters, then either the good of its future labels its present bad better or the bad of its future labels its present good worse. The consequence of this image is the essential jerkiness of experience; there is no experiential continuity unless the manifold of projections over time are always the same and hence the strings never twitch, for one would then be without either hope or fear. In order to restore experiential continuity, the Stranger would have to introduce pleasant or painful pictures in the present that accompany the opinions about future pains and pleasures.[51] This he does not do, any more than he considers present pleasures and pains in their presentness; he treats them solely as impulses toward the future. Consequently, when the

---

51. Cf. *Philebus* 38e12–40b2, where Socrates understands expectations as speeches but adds pictures to the speeches in order to account for present experiences of future hopes and fears.

Stranger proposes plying the puppet with drink, he is doing nothing more than emphasizing the lack of smoothness in its motions.[52] The puppet represents us as being put under a microscope, in whose field the stop-and-go character of our actions would become evident. The puppet strips us of the envelope of habit and shows us drunk within.

The puppet represents the Stranger's first attempt to connect the eidetic structure of the good with the genetic structure of law. Calculation stands for the determination in time of the eightfold good; pleasures and pains are then linked with the better and the worse through opinions about future pleasures and pains, on which calculation pronounces whether they are in conformity with virtue or vice. So far the account is applicable to an individual. The Stranger at first, however, identifies the golden thread with what is called a city's law (645a2,5); but then, as he proceeds to separate the myth of virtue from its logos, he says that to take "the true logos" about these drawings (ἕλξεις) and to follow it in one's life is only possible for an individual, whereas a city inherits a logos from a god or one who came to understand these things, and this is positive law (654b4–8). This difference between the individual and the city emerges in the Stranger's complication of his image, so that the entire advantage the puppet as an image has might be thought to have been lost. He says that the golden thread needs helpers, "in order that the golden genus (γένος) in us may win out over all the rest" (645a7–8).[53] The puppet is suddenly a composite, with an inside that can be made to respond to the golden thread outside. The Stranger seems to imply that there is no gold in the city, or that the city cannot have any purely golden thread. The impurity of its thread would then show up, if we follow the genetic structure of the law, in the reconnection of the just with the beautiful.

However dexterous the puppet masters are, the puppets themselves are always in disorder, and the possibly perfect order of motion is outside them. If this picture is applied to ourselves, it suggests that, no less than our movements, our speeches, in which everything looks rational and in order, consist of ill-fitting constituents whose grammatical correctness conceals their difference. Clinias had spoken of the Stranger's divination in guessing that the Dorians had a certain kind of law, and he said he thought the Stranger was speaking the truth exactly (σφόδρα ἀληθῆ λέγειν,

---

52. The intimate connection between the puppet and intoxication seems to be hinted at by the double τοῦτο at 645d4, in which a communion occurs between them (τοῦτο κοινωνῆσαν τούτῳ).

53. If Eusebius's addition of ἐν at 645a7 is rejected, the Stranger's remark would fit the noble lie of the *Republic* and have a purely political implication.

635a2).[54] Clinias attaches σφόδρα to truth-telling in order to express his feeling about a true speech that it is consonant with a true speech. We do not notice such linkages, which are part of everyday speech, until we become incoherent in our speech, when our pleasures, pains, rages, and desires become more intense (σφοδροτέρας) and our perceptions, memories, opinions, and thoughts loosen their hold on us (615d6–e3). In this sense we never grow up and the sounds of ourselves as babies get clothed in conventional "words" and vanish from view. Only the laugh and the wail, as explosive noises, retain a version of our original state. In this way, the temporal dimension of human life collapses into a single state of intoxication that the law takes as its hypothesis. Clinias finds this state undesirable, for he does not see how necessary it is for the law to adopt it as an hypothesis. He does not see that if it is not the hypothesis of the law it becomes the experience of the law, as he himself has shown in its effect on himself. The Stranger gets Clinias to see an advantage of the law's hypothesis by drawing a parallel between those who go voluntarily to the doctor or trainer and those who go voluntarily to the symposium. The sick or weak know beforehand that they will be in greater pain than they now are in before they get well or strong. They set before themselves an immediate fear and a more distant hope. No measure is assigned to either the pain or the pleasure. It is enough for them to efface the imminent and enhance the prospective. The Stranger does not say how this fits the symposium. If the symposiast approaches with a confidence about his imminent pleasure, does he also have a more distant picture that terrifies him? Does the hangover correspond to the result of the cure? If the result is shame, he does not have to go to the party with a double vision, but he will be susceptible to the induction of shame regardless of whether he anticipates it or not. The Stranger's own parallel between the treatment of body and treatment of soul shows that the more distant prospect belongs exclusively to the symposiarch as legislator. He has the confidence that he can bring about a kind of terror through pleasure.

The Stranger had criticized the one-sidedness of Dorian courage; he had argued that it could become complete only if it were capable of facing pleasures and desires no less than pains and fears. He did not suggest how it could be made complete. Now he splits fear into two species, one of a future evil about which we have an opinion, the other of a future opinion about ourselves as evil. This second fear is universally called shame

---

54. Σφόδρα μὲν οὖν occurs at 640b5, four times in the *Philebus*, and nowhere else in Plato; πάνυ μὲν οὖν σφόδρα occurs at *Apology of Socrates* 26d7; *Cratylus* 425c8; cf. Seth Benardete, *The Tragedy and Comedy of Life* (Chicago 1993), 142–147.

(αἰσχύνη).[55] It faces and stands opposed to pains and fears, and it faces and stands opposed to the greatest and most overwhelming pleasures. The Stranger does not say that it faces off against the greatest hopes. Shame thus turns out to be a two-legged version of double-sided courage; it differs from that kind of courage because it no longer operates, or better perhaps because it cannot be induced, except among others. At the same time that it is not courage, for it stands up to fear only through fear, shame is not moderation either, for it likewise stands up to pleasure only through fear. Shame, unlike moderation, is not bound up with mind. Shame thus looks like the first translation of two elements in the eidetic structure of the good into the genetic structure of law. Shame is an image of courage and moderation. Its imagistic nature shows up in the shift that fear has undergone in the Stranger's analysis. Fear was defined originally as an expectation before pain; now fear is of evils (τὰ κακά). If one sticks to the first definition, shame faces pain of two kinds. If we face one kind, a pain in all probability comes; if we face the other, we avoid a pain. The pain we avoid is, in its mildest version, the pain of a blush, a showing to others that we believe we are defective. Shame is the concealment of our presumed defectiveness; it is not an excellence. The genetic structure of law, it seems, can translate the eidetic structure of the good only by turning virtue into the hiding of vice (cf. 841a8–b5).

Moderation and courage had been respectively the second and fourth of the virtues; courage had been allowed to take over at least in part the functions of moderation; moderation had then been presented separately as a virtue contrary to the sexual license the common mess inadvertently bred. One-sided courage was not just defective but hostile to moderation and incompatible with it. A revision of courage was thus required that would be fostered with moderation. Shame is the result of that revision. It puts before its patient the patient himself as the evil he must overcome, so that he can literally be better than himself. Shame masks one's defectiveness so that socially one is better than one is (cf. *Symposium* 178e1–179a8). The politicization of virtue occurs through one's own opinion becoming the common opinion of which one would always falls short if one were left to oneself. Shame is the first helper the Stranger enlists to support the gentle thread of reason. Experientially, it does not rank the vir-

---

55. In light of the fact that Herodotus uses αἰδώς only once, in a speech by a non-Greek (1.8.3), and Thucydides also has it only once in the mouth of a Spartan (1.84.3), who immediately shifts to αἰσχύνη, it is striking that the Stranger, though he says that everyone calls this fear αἰσχύνη, has the lawgiver immediately afterwards call it αἰδώς (647a10). Likewise, in both the Herodotean and Thucydidean passages αἰδώς is intimately connected with law.

tues but sets them as a single species above oneself. Virtue becomes one through its image. No sooner, however, does the Stranger propose the lawful inculcation of fear as the means to establish fearlessness as well than he turns around and resplits shame into moderation and courage (647c3–d7). This resplitting is necessary because shame as fear reraises the issue of the induction of fear. If shame is terror before an opinion of future pain, then one has to have a means to induce an absolute despair that is one's own opinion about oneself and not one's opinion about the opinion others have about oneself. In his second formulation, in which the struggle against shamelessness is to lead to being perfectly (τελέως) moderate, the Stranger speaks of logos, art, and experience as the helpers.

The drink of fear is as imaginary as the symposium in speech. It is conceived as a means to break the connection entirely between our experiences and what is. It sets before each of us opinions about our various states that are "all in our heads" and make us believe (νομίζειν) that we are unfortunate (δυστυχεῖς) until we come into total terror (εἰς πᾶν δέος).[56] If this terror is on the same line as shame, it involves the belief that what one is is what one most despises. Total terror arises from the conviction that one cannot face whatever one is. Before such terror one must experience complete hopelessness and helplessness. Oedipus must blind himself once he knows that what he is in his pride he cannot will to be in his knowledge. Adrastus, whom Croesus first purified of involuntary manslaughter, and then forgave for the accidental killing of his son, killed himself over the grave of Atys in the inner knowledge (συγγινωσκόμενος) that he was the most unfortunate of all the human beings he knew (Herodotus 1.45.3). The Stranger imagines a drink that acts as powerfully as Adrastus's imagination; it is almost but not wholly harmless, for its final draft is irresistible and cannot be drunk by anyone. Why does the Stranger conceive of a drink that no one can take without fear? Some imaginary picture would make one afraid regardless of how well one trained oneself in previous drinking bouts. The drink of fear ultimately produces a terror that one cannot have anticipated or steeled oneself against. The Stranger seems to have in mind the hemlock Socrates drank, which at the end made him cover his face more than once in the presence of his friends (*Phaedo* 118a6, 12). He foresaw something that he was ashamed for his friends to see on his face. The Stranger recommends the drink of fear on the grounds that it offers a wonderfully easy training regardless of whether

---

56. This is the first time that the present of νομίζειν has occurred in the *Laws* (647e3); it occurs next at 679c7. The stative perfect was first at 637e5; it concerned the Scythian and Thracian lawful beliefs about their practice of wine drinking.

one practices it alone, with a few, or with any number (648c7–e5); but only if one were in a symposium of fellow-drinkers would the drink of fear correspond to the drink of hope. The alternative to the solitary drinker is he who, in trusting himself and believing he has been beautifully prepared by nature and practice, does not hesitate to put himself on display, exercising with several symposiasts, "overrunning and mastering the drink's unavoidable capacity to bring about an alteration [of self-alienation]." Socrates says that death as the practice of dying and being dead is philosophy. As he practices it, it is in the company of others as well as by himself. If we identify philosophy as the antidote to the drink of fear, it must consist in overcoming the imaginary opinion the drink of fear produces. Philosophy, then, would represent the triumph of the real over opinion: there is nothing to fear. Such a victory would be of the soul over the ensouled body and equivalent to the separation of soul and body; but the separation of soul and body is nothing other than the basis of the eidetic structure of the good, which had assigned half the goods to the gods and half to men. Although Socrates' experience would imply that it is not possible to prevail finally over the imagination or opinion, the drink of fear would also suggest that to the degree that opinion is overcome it is overcome only through the facing of opinion. The facing of opinion is what Socrates calls his second sailing. It is entirely in speech and through speech that one seeks what is.

On the basis of the more or less incorrect symposia the Stranger knew about, either directly or by hearsay, he proposed the construction of a symposium in speech. The symposium was in speech but the drink was real. Now, as a parallel to the symposium in speech that exhilarates and enhances our own virtues and expectations, he proposes another symposium in speech that would plunge us into utter misery. Only a drink in speech can minister to this symposium in speech. This drink in speech is tragic speech. Its antidote is philosophic speech that has the capacity to recognize tragic speech as opinion. Philosophic speech makes one immune to the power of what is not. This power has no counterpart in the education of the perfect citizen. The law does not have the means to overcome terror. This ceiling on the law does not hold, apparently, for its power to dispel the fantastic hopes of men. Moderation or something that can pass for moderation, and not double-sided courage, seems to be within the capacity of the law; but insofar as education concerns the directing of pleasures and desires toward a certain goal, the desires and pleasures that urge us to shamelessness and injustice must be different from the former. They must arise after the education has over time lost its hold. We no longer desire what it urged us to desire. Moderation, then, would always be a secondary development within the law; it would be the experiential virtue. The third chorus of Dionysus supplements the choruses of the Muses and Apollo. It follows on their failure. We have witnessed such a corrective of lawful education in the first book of the *Laws*. Clinias's experience of the law signified not only the entire breakdown of the law but also the desire for universal empire, in which the goods of everyone else would belong to the Cretans, who alone knew the truth about war and peace. Megillus too betrayed an equally extravagant belief: the Spartans defeat every other martial people even if they have never faced them in battle. The Stranger has been somewhat successful in tamping down these beliefs. He has induced a true form of moderation on representatives of so-called moderate regimes.

EDUCATION AND IMITATION

I THE BEAUTIFUL

At the end of book 1, the Stranger had left the impression that the symposium, if it were rightly conducted, would not only allow for the safe observation of men's natures and characters, but also, in strict parallelism
with the imaginary drink of fear, would promote self-control on the part
of its guests, so that they would lose by constant practice vainglorious
self-confidence and become over time modest and abashed. It turns out,
however, that the large-scale benefits to be expected from the symposium
do not involve the symposium as such. The symposium in speech is a
species that has to be translated in order to become useful in a nontheo-
retical way. Its translation assumes the form of a corrective of the genetic
structure of law. The very temporality the Stranger imposed on the primary translation of the eidetic structure of the good into the genetic
structure of law carried with it an experiential deviation from the genetic
structure of law itself. The symposium in speech, when suitably translated, is designed to restore what is lost over time. Clinias, when he first
hears about the symposium as a restorative of education, implies that the
Stranger is boasting, μέγα λέγεις (653a4). If it is a boast, it is stated cautiously. The Stranger is only making a guess (τοπάζω) that the symposium
will act as a restorative, and he urges all of them to pay close attention,
"lest at some point or other we are tripped up by the logos." The obstacle
the logos has put in their way is time. Time opens up fissures in the
apparently smooth progression from birth to death that the genetic structure of law cannot handle. The temporal character of the genetic structure of law was only in speech and did not come to grips with what happens in real time. That the genetic structure of law might be defective
was already suggested in the beautiful and the just being its lawful translation of the good. How the just comes to be experienced might eventu-
ally overwhelm if not obliterate the innocence of the beautiful.

As the Stranger first presented his argument, "the god" was to come
at its end, after he had gone through education (643a4–7); but the good of

"theory," which the symposium offered, forced the Stranger to get ahead of his argument. In returning, however, to education, the Stranger picks up something from his understanding of the law that had not been part of either his general or political characterization of education (643b4–644a5). Pain had not entered into the shaping of the perfect artisan or citizen. There were models of what children were to desire to become, but there were no models of what they were to loathe.[1] One wonders whether the right hatreds, which now define education no less than the right affections, do not increase the need for the symposium as a corrective of experience. Could the experiences the symposium has to overcome be the very experiences in the initial education? Does the symposium in some sense represent the constant correction that has to be made to whatever course has been set? The gods, the Stranger says, in pity for the race of human beings in its natural laboriousness, gave them festivals in order that they might gain a respite from toils and troubles (653c7–d5). These toils and troubles bring about a corruption and loosening of the initially correct education of pains and pleasures; but there has never yet been the right education, and still there are festivals. The gods arranged festivals, apparently, in order to correct the deviations that arise in every kind of mistaken education, and they foresaw that the first correct education, which the Stranger is about to propose, would not be any more successful at obviating the need for correction. The disorderly order of the symposium seems to be the only form education could possibly take in which there would never be any need for correction; but such a symposium is only in speech.

The consonance (συμφωνία) between feelings of pleasure or pain and logos is virtue in its entirety. It is a consonance and not an agreement or ὁμολογία because the feelings in themselves are never rational. They are ἄλογα. Their initial form is in sounds (φωναί), which are not yet articulate speech, and when the sounds are articulated into speech, the logos is still inseparable from the sounds of pleasure and pain. Παιδεία in the literal sense is that stage of education when love and hate are rightly induced as habits in those who do not yet understand rationally (λόγῳ λαμβάνειν), and to understand rationally (λαβεῖν τὸν λόγον) means either to speak or to reason. The Stranger leaves it terribly unclear how much is to be ex-

---

1. The word "desire" (ἐπιθυμία, ἐπιθυμεῖν) virtually disappears from book 2: at 652b3 it refers to the Stranger's desire to recall the definition of right education; later in the book it refers to the desire to be a tyrant and do whatever one wants (661b2, 662a1); in book 3 it has the same sense at 687b1, and then at 688b3 reverts to the sense it had in book 1 (643c7).

pected of education. Virtue and vice depend, he says, on pleasure and pain, but anyone is lucky who gets even in old age good sense and the stability of true opinions, and though a human being is perfect or complete if he possesses good sense and true opinions as well as all the goods dependent on them, it seems not to be anything the city can do much about (cf. 951b4–7). The Stranger had spoken of law as the city's inheritance of a logos (λόγον παραλαβοῦσαν) from whoever had taken the true logos in himself (τὸν ἀληθῆ λόγον λαβόντα ἐν ἑαυτῷ, 645b6–7; cf. 783a5–7); but now he seems to allow for even more slippage between the truth and education as the virtue of children. Consonance seems to be the Stranger's word for the imprecise matchup between the eidetic structure of the good and the genetic structure of the law. Consonance, one might say, is the affective equivalent of the rational structure of musical scales. And just as there is never a perfect match between the acoustical and the mathematical systems, since the musical scales themselves always involve a remainder (*leimma*), so the childish experiences of virtue cannot be expected to answer exactly to the species of virtue.

The difficulty one has in following the Stranger's argument emerges clearly if one sets out in order his various pronouncements at the beginning of the second book. He first states as a guess that the symposium is a means of restoring (σωτηρία) the right education (653a1–3); he next asserts that it is due to the loosening and corruption of the right upbringing of pleasures and pains in the course of a lifetime that the gods gave us the Muses, Apollo, and Dionysus to be the correctors (ἵν᾽ ἐπανορθῶνται, 653d4). He then puts the question whether the logos that is now being dinned into their ears—he speaks as if it were a song in celebration of the gods (ὑμνεῖται)—is true according to nature (ἀληθὴς κατὰ φύσιν). The logos no longer just holds for the human race; it is true of virtually every young animal that it is incapable of keeping still in either body or voice, and some jump and skip, as if they were dancing with pleasure and joining in sport (προσπαίζοντα), and others utter all kinds of sounds. The logos no longer speaks of pains. In going back to the beginning, the pains and toils, which belonged both to human education and the divine alleviation of human experiences, have disappeared. Even when the Stranger now returns to human beings, pain does not come back. He says that the gods who have been given to us as fellow-choristers also granted us a pleasurable awareness of rhythm and harmony, and they string us together (συνείροντας) by means of songs and dances, whose joint name "χορός " they derived from χαρά (joy). The Stranger concludes by asking whether they are to assume that the first education is through the Muses and Apollo.

If we say that Dionysus is lurking behind the first guess of the

Stranger—the symposium is the restorer of the right education—, then
it is plausible to assume that the Stranger alludes to some versions of
tragedy and comedy as the symposia he has in mind; and the triad of
Muses, Apollo, and Dionysus seems no less to designate them as the
sponsors of comic and tragic festivals, which are meant to relax and correct us. That Dionysus now disappears as a sponsor of elementary education is consistent with this if pain and suffering are not attendant on
human life from the beginning. The answer, then, to the Stranger's question, whether or not the logos is true according to nature, must be "No."
Such an answer necessarily entails that Dionysus be restored as a sponsor
of elementary education, and along with his restoration pain must follow
as copresent with pleasure from the beginning. The Stranger's logos, by
ascribing something like dancing and play to nonhuman animals dis-
guises the fact that before we sing and dance together we must learn to
speak and walk, and that we do this before we join in any common play.
There is a rhythm and harmony in walking and talking that we learn far
earlier than their musical equivalents. By skipping over what was really
at the beginning for us, the Stranger implies that his logos begins in falsehood. The falsehood comes to light in a sentence of bad grammar and
poorer sense: τὰ μὲν οὖν ἄλλα ζῷα οὐκ ἔχειν αἴσθησιν τῶν ἐν ταῖς κινήσεσιν
τάξεων οὐδὲ ἀταξιῶν, οἷς δὴ ῥυθμὸς ὄνομα καὶ ἁρμονία (653e3–5). The sentence starts out clearly enough: "Now all other animals," [the logos as-
serts], "do not have an awareness of orders in their motions, any more
than they have an awareness of disorders." It would be hard to prove that
birds are aware when they are singing out of tune, or that dolphins sense
that something is amiss if one of their group does not bob up and down
in some regular fashion; and we can let the Stranger dismiss Arion's dolphin and the nightingale—the "singer" in Greek (ἀηδών)—as fairy tales;
but what are we to make of his relative clause? "The name," he continues, "for these orders and disorders in motions is rhythm and harmony."
The name for orderly and disorderly motion is rhythm and harmony! If
we take him at his word, the Stranger has skewed a standard definition
of rhythm and harmony (664e8–665a3) so that it could support a deviant
sense that precisely fits nothing else than his own symposium in speech,
whose very nature was to combine order and disorder. His symposium in
speech would thus be the true model for even elementary education.

Elementary education is the same as musical education, and musical
education is choral education. Choral education makes education an ordering of a group. Χορεία has built into it the prefix in συμπόσιον. Whether
it orders pleasure only or pain as well, it is a collective order. The gods,
then, gave us an awareness not only of order in motion but of collective

order. Each one is in step and in tune with everyone else. No one sings or dances by himself. The pleasure to be taken in such performances would thus primarily belong to the spectators, for no performer would have a synoptic view of his own chorus. The audience experience a respite from toils. The Stranger later admits as much: the old set up contests for children in order to remind themselves of their youth (657d1–6). That the Stranger silently denies the experience of pain to the young arises from his adoption of the perspective of the old. The chorus of the young gives them nothing but joy. One can say, then, that the triad Muses, Apollo, Dionysus stands to the dyad Muses and Apollo as restoration stands to education. Dionysus sets the purpose the Muses and Apollo carry out. The connection therefore between the pleasures and pains proper to elementary education and the pleasures of the spectators is obscure. The participants in a symposium take pleasure in the symposium, but does the chorus take any pleasure in what they are doing beyond the pleasure they have in delighting the audience and earning their praise? At the end of book 1, the symposium was to display the natures and ways of its guests to the symposiarch. Its translation into the chorus will display orderly motions of body and sounds to an audience whose pleasure will be mixed with the regret of longing. Their restoration could be complete only if they were to forget entirely their own experiences and were to see and hear before them a representation of what they were once supposed to be. If, however, the chorus were to represent what they then were supposed to loathe, would the pleasure they took in the representation override the pain of the hateful? Whatever they liked or disliked could be indifferently the noble or the base and be solely dependent on the technical competence of the chorus. The symposium in speech had no such drawbacks: the unconstrained display of the ugly and base was for the symposiarch only food for thought. The Stranger raises this question as soon as he has won Clinias's agreement to the identification of the adequately educated (πεπαιδευμένον ἱκανῶς) with the competent choral member (ἱκανῶς κεχορευκότα, 654b1).

The Stranger first gets Clinias to concede that to be beautifully educated means to be able to sing and dance beautifully. He then adds that what one sings and dances is to be beautiful (654b6–c2). The Stranger then proposes a third condition: "What about this point? Is he to believe that the beautiful things are beautiful and the ugly things ugly, and does he handle them in just the way he believes?" (654c3–4). If this condition were not met, the competent performer could well be indifferent to whatever he performs and have no beliefs about the beautiful and the ugly. He would be the perfect sophist (cf. *Sophist* 267e10–268a4). The Stranger does not allow Clinias to answer this question; instead, he refines the question in a surprising way (654c4–d3):

> Will someone of this kind have been better educated in choral music, if, though on each occasion he is able to serve competently with his body and voice whatever he thought through to be beautiful (τὸ διανο-ηθὲν εἶναι καλόν), still he takes no pleasure in the beautiful things and does not hate the not beautiful things, or will it be that one, whoever is scarcely able to get it right with his voice and body in the way he intends (ἢ διανοεῖται),[2] but does get it right in pleasure and pain, cherishing everything beautiful and loathing (δυσχεραίνων) all that is not beautiful?[3]

Clinias says the difference in education is vast, and he clearly prefers the second to the first; but whether the Stranger agrees with him is not as clear. This second-best education can describe only the old, who no longer can sing and dance but still retain the feelings their elementary education was to instill. The alternative education, which produces perfect competence and understanding but indifferent feelings, also does not suit the young, for their education precedes any understanding and at best is to be consonant with reason. This alternative education can only be a version of what a translation of the eidetic structure of the good would strictly entail if the beautiful replaced the good—if virtue were to be understood as beautiful and not good—so that whoever embodied the translation would take on a semblance of what the genetic structure of law required. If, moreover, one considers the human capacity for dissimulation, to which the Stranger later calls attention (656a1–5), the subjective criterion of pleasure and disgust has no effective importance unless the Stranger is thinking of the symposium as the means whereby the statesman gets to know the true sentiments of his subjects; but the statesman-symposiarch, to whom human natures and ways are exposed, can only be the same as the one whose education Clinias now rejects. The indifference to the beautiful and the not beautiful would follow from not only the primacy of the good, but it would be due as well to the

---

2. This is Badham's reading for the manuscript's ἢ διανοεῖσθαι, which, if kept, would make for three possibilities: the competent but indifferent, the incompetent to execute, and the incompetent to understand.

3. The difference between the two men recalls Adimantus's distinction between the one who, in knowing that justice is best, can prove that what he and Glaucon have said is false, but does not get angry at the unjust, and the one who by a divine nature loathes (δυσχεραίνων) being unjust and the doing of injustice (Republic 366c3–d1).

understanding of the beautiful as not necessarily good and the not beautiful as not necessarily bad. This latter implication emerges plainly from
the Stranger's answer to the next puzzle: what are they to understand by
the beautiful?

Despite Clinias's choice of the man of proper feeling as far superior
to the man of understanding, the Stranger demands that all three of them
know and be able to recognize (γιγνώσκομεν) the beautiful in song and
dance, for were they to be unacquainted with this, they would not know
who was rightly educated and who not, and they would be unable to decide whether there was a protection (φυλακή) of education and where it
might be found (654d5–e1). There are, then, two dimensions of the beautiful: it can be either understood or felt. Insofar as it provokes delight, it
acts as the link between the good and pleasure and suggests to what extent pleasure can be taken as either equivalent to the good or the sign of
the presence of the good. Much of the Stranger's subsequent argument
concerns no less the degree to which he believes they are equivalent than
the degree to which the law, in its limitations, must accept their equivalence. For all the fanfare, however, with which the Stranger introduces
the question of the beautiful—he starts off with a not entirely suitable
image (654e3)—and declares the vanity of their discussion unless they
track down the beautiful gesture and song, a partial answer is soon found
and extended without argument to all the rest of virtue.

> Stranger: Come, when a manly soul is caught in the grip of toils
>   (πόνοι), and a cowardly soul is in the grip of the same and equal
>   toils, does it turn out that their gestures and sounds are alike?
> Clinias: Just how could that be, when not even their complexions
>   (χρώματα) are?
> Stranger: Beautifully put, comrade. But as a matter of fact, though
>   there are gestures and songs in music, since music is about
>   rhythm and harmony, so that there is the rhythmic (εὔρυθμον)
>   and the harmonic (εὐάρμοστον), it is not possible by making a
>   likeness (ἀπεικάσαντα), as the choral producers make a likeness
>   (ἀπεικάζουσιν), to speak rightly of either a song or gesture as
>   εὔχρων (with a healthy complexion), but there is gesture and
>   song of the coward and the manly, and it is right to address the
>   traits of the manly as beautiful, and the traits of the cowards
>   as ugly (shameful). And in order that we not have an over-
>   whelmingly long speech about all these things, let it be this
>   simple and without qualification: all the gestures and songs
>   connected or dependent on virtue of soul or body, regardless of

whether they are of the virtue itself or some image (εἰκών), are
to be beautiful, and those connected or dependent on vice, they
are to be entirely the contrary (654e10–655b6).

This passage is difficult not only because of the Stranger's apparently
gratuitous swipe at a technical term—it is as if one were now to object
to the "colors" and "flavors" of elementary particles—but because the
Stranger, by putting the image of virtue on a par with virtue itself, characterizes the beautiful as indifferent to its own reality (cf. *Republic* 472d4–
8). The translation of the eidetic structure of the good into the genetic
structure of law involves the abandonment of being: "becoming," one recalls, appeared only in the genetic structure of law. It is no wonder, then,
that the man of understanding takes no pleasure in the beautiful. The
indifference, however, of the beautiful to being is not complete; otherwise the Stranger could not criticize the image implicit in εὔχρως. Clinias
implied that the paleness of the coward differed from the ruddiness of the
brave; but the Stranger, in denying that complexion can be translated into
either song or gesture, admits that the images of the brave and the coward
cannot be complete representations of the reality. And what holds for the
paleness of the coward also holds for the blush of the modest. The blush,
which surely belongs to the youthful traits at least of moderation, cannot
be shown in song and dance. If, moreover, the slink and whimper of the
coward do show up mimetically, are there characteristic sounds and gestures of the moderate that are as easily identifiable as the coward's? When
it comes to justice, one is simply baffled how there can be images of it.
Folly perhaps would not be as difficult to represent, but correct images of
good sense (φρόνησις) cannot easily be imagined. Insensitivity (ἀναισθησία)
would try to pass itself off as the truth of every genuine virtue. The
Stranger's choice of courage and cowardice seems to be due to either their
intrinsic corporeality or the ease with which the vice and the virtue appear on the body: φόβος (fear) originally meant flight.

Clinias's response to the Stranger's question was not entirely appropriate. The Stranger did not ask about the gestures and sounds of the
brave and coward caught in the grip of terrors and alarms, but about those
in the grip of toils and troubles. Among those who are in the grip of
such toils are Clinias, Megillus, and the Stranger: they have to make an
extraordinary effort to discover the beautiful song and dance. The effort
they need prompted the Stranger to liken themselves to bitches (καθάπερ
κυσὶν ἰχνευούσαις). The gender of hunting dogs in Greek, just as of horses
and swine, is usually but not consistently feminine; the gender, one
might say, is grammatical and not sexual; but in the context, in which

courage is of the manly soul (ἀνδρικὴ ψυχή), one wonders whether the Stranger is not just criticizing Clinias for his restricted understanding of courage, so that it applies only to the battlefield, but he is also forcing us to contrast his image with the incorrect image in εὔχρως. His image is perhaps not shameful, though Clinias and Megillus may believe it to be, but it is funny, or, as Aristotle says, ugly but harmless. It raises the question whether the smile the image elicits, when one looks away from it and back to three old men walking at their ease, and whether the Stranger's program of education demands its censorship, since it holds up to mild ridicule the age which everywhere nowadays is thought to be the best (658e3–4). If the image should inspire Megillus and Clinias to engage even now in a more thoughtful manliness than what they are used to, still the pleasure one takes in its absurdity links the beautiful and the not beautiful in a way which the Stranger apparently wants to avoid. The manner of the image is not beautiful, but the objective correlative of the image—the quest for the beautiful—is perhaps not unbeautiful. Clinias had accepted as satisfactory an education which made one delight in the beautiful and loathe the not beautiful but was incompetent to represent the beautiful beautifully. In dropping the manner and keeping the beautiful, Clinias would have to acknowledge that the Stranger's image has kept the beautiful and sacrificed "beautifully." Just as he would be very reluctant, one suspects, to admit that the funny too can be beautiful, so he would be slow to see that the Stranger's "Beautifully put, comrade" is as much in admiration for his noting the complexion of the coward as that of the brave.

In admitting that not everything that belongs to courage can be matched up in its image, the Stranger opens up a gap between being and image that might be fatal to the maintenance of any virtue over time. The image of a virtue, though it will be defective in light of the virtue itself, will not appear to be defective. It will complete and connect on its own whatever it can represent in a way that will have no counterparts in the virtue. An illusion will be fostered through the image that will prove experientially to be false. The most obvious instance of the difficulty lies in courage, for if one recalls Megillus's description of Spartan training, and grants that however less severe the right discipline would be, still everything painful that belongs to courage itself would have to be subtracted from its image, in order that children may find it wholly attractive, and in turn everything painful would have to be assigned to the image of cowardice, so that children may find it utterly loathsome (cf. 659e3–660a8). Even if there is something of a natural base for this distribution, it cannot be wholly true—Clinias had admitted that terrors perturbed the brave less than the coward (64a11–b1)—and the weaning away of the children from the image to its reality would be a delicate matter. Otherwise, if there were no further instruction about the nonbeing of the image, the reaction to one's experience would be fundamentally of two kinds: either shame and ultimately despair before one's failure to realize what the image proposes or rejection of the virtue itself as no more than a dream: Brutus, it is said, exclaimed at Philippi, ὦ τλῆμον ἀρετή, λόγος ἄρ' ἦσθα.[4] If, then, experience necessarily corrupts and relaxes the hold of elementary education, the need to find a restorative that is also a corrective is all the more pressing. The intrusion of Dionysus into the band of the Muses and Apollo is not just unavoidable but to be welcomed. Pain, according to the Stranger, is to enter education at the age of three (793e3–5).

2 KINDS OF PLEASURE

What directs the Stranger's argument throughout book 2 is not the education of the young but the inevitable corruption of that education in the course of time. Were it not that the Stranger has left unresolved the issue of the ugly image of the beautiful and the beautiful image of the ugly, it would seem to follow, if the images of the virtues were as beautiful as the virtues themselves, that all songs and dances of virtue should delight everyone alike. Clinias is emphatic in denying that any such uniformity exists (655c2). The Stranger offers several explanations for this lack of uniformity without exploring all of them equally; but the drift of his argument seems to force him to condemn the shame he had recommended in book 1 as the lawful equivalent of the twin virtues of moderation and courage. What the law wants and succeeds in effecting stands in the way of the law being effective. The law contains within itself the cause of its own overthrow. The experiential deviation from whatever the law lays down leads necessarily to a split between what one praises and what one feels, and whatever one comes to delight in effects of necessity an assimilation to it. It is not pleasure in itself, but pleasure as the experiences of life shape it, that seems to defeat the Stranger's wish to enlist pleasure on the side of the law. The Chorus of Dionysus has its work cut out for it.

The first possibility the Stranger raises, which would explain why not everyone enjoys alike all songs and dances, seems to be dropped as soon as he raises it (655c3–5). Could it be, he asks, that the beautiful things

4. Dio Cassius 47.49.2.

are not the same for all of us, or, though they are the same, they are
thought not to be the same? This question amounts to asking after the
necessary conventionality of the beautiful (cf. Aristotle *EN* 1094b14–16),
for appearance, which clings to the beautiful, brings along with it the
perspectival, and the perspectival in turn, however much it may depend
on one's own state, is inseparable from the light that lets the beautiful be
observed, and if the beautiful is not the same as the good, it is hard to
conceive of that light as being wholly neutral. The Stranger denounces
the most common view that pleasure determines what is right in music,
for if that were the case the disparity in men's pleasure when it comes to
songs and dances would occasion no surprise and obviate the need for the
Stranger to pose his question. The Stranger's question can only be raised
as a question if pleasure necessarily accompanies something from which
it cannot be separated. The hedonistic abstraction from what elicits the
pleasure is contrary to the nature of the supplement that always attends
the pleasure and of which the pleasure is a pleasure. It thus turns out
that the relation of pleasure to what we take pleasure in runs exactly
parallel to the relation of image to that of which it is an image, and to
determine correctly what belongs in the pleasure to that in which one
takes pleasure is of the same order of problem as to assign in an image
what belongs to its reality. The distaste we suspected Clinias would have
felt had he reflected on himself as a bitch hot on the trail applies equally
to his rejection of a less "manly" but more thoughtful courage.

The Stranger imagines two possible cases that could explain the non-
uniformity of response to songs and dances. In the first case, one's nature,
habits, or both coincide with what one is representing; in the second case,
if one's nature is good but lawful ways bad, or one's nature is not good
and the lawful ways are good, one does not outwardly declare that what
delights one is beautiful, but one keeps one's pleasure to oneself. The
main difference between the two cases consists in the fact that in the
first the Stranger is speaking of a performer but in the second of a spectator who has not been called upon to represent ways either inferior or
superior to his nature. In the first case, the Stranger distinguishes between two aspects of choral imitation (655d5–7). One involves the imitation of ways (τρόποι) as they show up in actions and circumstances (τύχαι);
the other involves the explication by each performer of those actions and
circumstances by means of his character and imitative capacities (καὶ
ἤθεσι καὶ μιμήσεσι), or, by way of hendiadys, by the imitative capacities of
his character. If we think of a play, one can say that the Stranger distinguishes between plot and character, in which the plot does not have to

coincide with any event in the performer's own life, and the performer's own character modifies in his performance what his imitative capacities can do. If, then, the speeches, songs, or dances match the performer's own way (πρὸς τρόπου), it is necessary that he rejoice in them, praise them, and address them as beautiful. This matchup does not involve the understanding: "the beautiful is now entirely dependent on pleasure." The matchup takes its bearings from the Stranger's own example of the brave and the coward caught in the grip of the same toils: the brave man will delight in and praise how he imagines he himself would behave in the same circumstances that the story presents, but is it as clear that the coward will likewise delight in and praise the actions and speeches of the coward he represents? Not every coward is a Falstaff. So if it is to be assumed that the brave man, if he is called upon to do so, will loathe the coward he represents and label his behavior ugly and disgraceful, will the coward take no pleasure in his representation of the brave and label his behavior shameful? The indifference as to the cause of the consonance with or dissonance from what the performer is representing—the Stranger says it could be due to nature, habit, or both—suggests that the Stranger is not thinking of these complications. His performer is someone relatively young, and no clash between nature and nurture has yet had time to show itself; but in the second case, where the spectator is ashamed to sing and dance what pleases himself before others whose good sense he respects, nature has already begun to put up a resistance to the law and its constraints. This resistance of nature certainly sets limits to what law can effect, for the Stranger goes on to argue that assimilation to whatever pleases one must occur despite one's public disapproval of it, for the blame will be by way of a joke and not in earnest.

The answer to the Stranger's question, What causes men to feel differently about what the lawful representations of virtue show? seems to be twofold. The first, which was not spelled out, was that the translation of the good into the beautiful necessarily leads to a manifold of lawful opinions: Megillus's disgust at Dionysia has no ground in the nature of drunkenness itself. The second answer had two parts to it. The first was that one's makeup, however it was formed, restricted the range of one's pleasure and praise. The second part to the second answer was that pleasure had a natural basis, and this over time, if given a chance to develop, took over from whatever the law declared to be beautiful. It would seem to follow from this answer that a strict regulation of what the poets themselves arbitrarily delight in and then represent to others would deprive any nature that was out of tune with the law of the support it would need for its expansion and expression, and hence, on the surface at least, any deviation from the law that had its source in nature could never spill out into a full-grown departure from it. Egypt, according to the Stranger, discovered this solution ten thousand years ago. The consecration of every kind of representation, whether it was painting, sculpture, or poetry, was powerful enough to suppress the restless search for innovation on the part of pleasure and pain; but the Stranger does not approve of everything Egyptian and condemns other things as paltry and mean (ἕτερα φαῦλα).[5] The Egyptian solution requires that νόμος in its double meaning as law and song have the same author, and this author either be a god or a divine man (657a8–9). This entails in effect that the Greek split between Zeus and Apollo as the authors or sponsors of the law and the poets, whose authority goes no higher than the Muses, who tell lies like the truth whenever they wish, be dissolved (cf. 776e7),[6] and divine revelation cover both the law as code and the law as story (or song).[7] Egypt, then, stands in the Stranger's account for what we know as the traditional understanding of the Bible. He implies by his disapproval of other Egyptian things that, though the consecration of everything in Egypt carries with it an acknowledgment of the separation of the divine goods from the human— it is a separation he himself had left as problematic—such a radical disjunction necessarily leads to human self-contempt (cf. 716a4–b3)—nothing is as vile and unworthy as man—and man's all-too-human reaction to his own self-denigration is the unchecked and imperceptible development of criminal cleverness (πανουργία), whose chief good is the illiberal love of money (747b6–d1).[8]

It might be argued that the Stranger, by enlisting Apollo as well as the Muses into being the cosponsors of elementary education, had negotiated

5. Herodotus represents the unchangeableness of Egyptian laws by never using either συμφορή or τύχη and its compounds throughout the second book. Neither word is absent from any of the other eight books.

6. Note the way the Stranger, at the start of book 2, distinguished and blurred the difference between the gods who, in pity for the human race, assigned them not only the round of festivals to the gods (τοῖς θεοῖς) but also the refreshment (τροφαί) the gods were to support (μετὰ θεῶν), and the gods the gods gave as fellow-celebrants, who were to correct the festivals (653c9–d5). Τοῖς θεοῖς is as difficult to specify as μετὰ θεῶν. At the end of the book, the Stranger seems at first to say that Apollo, the Muses, and Dionysus have been the causes of gods (672d2), and it takes a moment to treat "of gods" in θεῶν αἰτίους as a partitive genitive (cf. *Ion* 534c7–d4); Cornarius's τούτων is highly implausible.

7. Horace has the partisan of antiquity go so far as to claim that the Muses spoke the laws of the twelve tables (*Epistulae* II.1.23–7).

8. The Stranger mentions in this passage that one possible cause of this vice is that the legislator was base and mean (φαῦλος).

between Apollo the author of Spartan laws and Apollo the author of songs and dances, but this is not a Spartan reconciliation of law and song and involves in any case only a nominal identity. It is true that Clinias will later claim that Sparta and Crete are almost Egyptian in their maintenance of the same music over time (660b1–c1), but Clinias does not assert that either Zeus or Apollo (or either Minos or Lycurgus) supplied the music to their laws. It turns out, moreover, in the next phase of the Stranger's extraordinarily complex argument, that the Egyptian solution, though it affords no purchase in poetic representations to whatever the law forbids to show itself, takes no account of experientially induced deviations from the law, so that the surface uniformity of representations in Egypt does not and cannot check the breakdown in the effectiveness of the law over time. All the Egyptian law does do is conceal from the guardians of the legislation that such a breakdown has occurred, for every outlet for its expression has been blocked. The Stranger, then, has been working out simultaneously the role that pleasure and pain have no less in the genetic structure of law than in poetry; and now that he has temporarily cut off the threat that poetry poses to law through its usurpation of the domain of pleasure and pain for itself, he raises the question of the relation between pleasure and the good. The Stranger, in other words, goes from the apparent coextensiveness of the beautiful and poetic imitation to the equatability of pleasure and the good. The shift is not as great as it appears, for just as the Stranger himself had allowed the image and the reality of virtue to be labelled beautiful, so he now asks, "Do we enjoy whenever we believe we are faring well, and whenever we enjoy, do we believe we are faring well?" (657c5–6). The good, then, in terms of our welfare (εὖ πράττειν), is our belief about it, and as the Eleatic Stranger had maintained in the *Sophist*, the problem the nonbeing of the image poses has a structure identical to the problem of false opinion (*Sophist* 240c7–241b4). The apparently necessary subjectivity of welfare puts the poet back in the running, and even if one banishes him for his transgressions of the lawfully beautiful, he still has the power of convincing everyone that they are happy, while the law is simply not up to the task of pleasing everyone.

Clinias is not disinclined to have the poets supply our pleasures, particularly since the Stranger has reminded him of the pleasure old men such as themselves take in watching the choral performances of the young (657d1–7); but the Stranger, in urging greater caution, imagines a contest of every kind, whose prizewinner will be determined solely by the degree to which he delights the spectators (658a4–b8). The Stranger mentions, in apparent haphazardness, the exhibitor of epic rhapsody, lyre playing, tragedy, comedy, and puppetry; and he had earlier flung open the contest to gymnastics and horse racing as well. He then asks who would win, and Clinias, quite sensibly, replies that no one could say before he had heard them for himself. The Stranger, however, offers an answer based on what in general delights each age: the puppeteer wins the vote of the very small children, older boys will choose the exhibitor of comedy, educated women, young men, and the majority of the audience will judge tragedy most pleasing, and men as old as themselves will declare the winner to be the rhapsode who beautifully recites the *Iliad, Odyssey,* or one of the works of Hesiod.[9] Apart from the striking omission of the exhibitor of tragedy, so that the preference of most is for tragedy itself apart from whoever performs it (cf. *Symposium* 215d3–6), the list of winners is graded in terms of time, from earliest youth to old age. The arts of imitation, strictly on the basis of pleasure, have discovered forms that match the range from birth to death that the genetic structure of law was supposed to handle. Imitation has got there first. At first glance, it seems inconceivable that the law could succeed in inducing small children, who might have just begun to talk, to give up the puppeteer for the rhapsode, if, as the Stranger says, the choice of the old should determine the good of the pleasure; but one realizes, as soon as one recalls what he had said in the first book, that only the very small children take pleasure in what is proleptically consonant with reason. The pleasure of the children, who see on the stage an exaggerated version of their own prior awkwardness, anticipates by way of feeling what reason will disclose to them to be the truth about man: he is a divine puppet, either a plaything of the gods or put together for some serious purpose. The surprise (θαῦμα) of the contest is what is not surprising (οὐ θαυμαστόν) in the contest (658b9–c1). The problem, then, is not how to ram the choice of the old down the throats of the young, but how to induce the old to accept with understanding the pleasure of the young. This turnaround is as wonderful as anything in Plato, and though the Stranger has prepared us for it, ever since he introduced the symposium in speech and the notion of order in disorder, one is not quite prepared for it when it comes. The old have to be loosened up so that they can experience, in the inadequacy of their performance, the puppet-wonder (θαῦμα) man is.

Once one sees that the Stranger is perfectly willing to give up all of poetry if he can only find a means to make the highest understanding stretch itself enough to link up with the hidden truth in puppets, one realizes that if this could be done smoothly, then the genetic structure of

9. Aristophanes has Aeschylus say that teachers instruct little children (τοῖς παιδαρίοις), but the poets instruct those in their prime (τοῖς ἡβῶσι) (*Ranae* 1055).

law would induce over time the recognition of the ranking of the eightfold
good set out in the eidetic structure of the good. Two obstacles stand in
the way of there ever being such a smooth transition from pleasure to
reason. The first is comedy, the second tragedy. Comedy represents everything that young men experience that is contrary to what moderation has
striven to control. Comedy catches perfectly the first experience in time
of the corruption and loosening of the law. It is the first experiential deviation from the genetic structure of law. The second is tragedy, and as the
Stranger hints by having the majority choose tragedy as if it were life and
not an imitation, tragedy stands for everything that induces, on the level
of feeling, the greatest departure from the lawful images of virtue. In
short, just as comedy makes an assault on moderation, so tragedy lays
siege to justice and tramples it underfoot. That the latter is the case, and
holds regardless of whether one has ever seen a tragedy, comes to light in
Clinias, who proves to have the same tastes as Polus and Callicles combined, though in a more exaggerated form. This should be no surprise, for
the unlawful insight Clinias originally gathered from his experience of
the law could only lead to this result.

The only remaining puzzle in the Stranger's list of prizewinners is the
epic rhapsode. He does not let Clinias, who has little knowledge of foreign poetry, voice his assent, but he decides on his own, and asks him
another question, Who would rightly win? His answer assumes the truth
of the universal opinion nowadays in all cities that the aged's way (ἔθος)
is best; but this answer precedes the total exposure of Clinias as being as
corrupt as one could possibly imagine. If, then, we set aside the Stranger's
answer, both in light of what has preceded about the puppeteer and what
will follow in the turning of Clinias inside-out, then Homer seems to be
a placeholder for the use to which the Stranger will put him, once he
turns from music to gymnastic and the history of the Dorians. In the
Stranger's hands, Homer becomes the historical equivalent to the truth
contained in the puppet show of children. The same mixture of order and
disorder will link the epic poet with the puppeteer. Homer will supply
the story in which the puppet will act.

3 THE JUST

In order that children never get accustomed either to like anything contrary to whatever the law has laid down, or in turn to dislike anything in
conformity with the law, the Stranger proposes that whatever the speech
of the law has declared to be right be confirmed by the concordant opin-

ion, experientially confirmed, of the old, whom the law has persuaded (659c9–d6). The young are to conform to the law through emulation of the old, who are to represent the indissoluble link between justice and pleasure, so that what the young absorb as enchantments of their souls, without any experience of earnestness or distress, coincides exactly with what the old maintain and represent, even though they know that not all base things are unpleasant and not all good things pleasant. The Stranger leads up to this proposal through a reflection on how the theatrical audience nowadays instructs and intimidates the judge, whereas the true judge ought to combine good sense and courage. He needs good sense and courage to resist the imperious pleasures of the uneducated audience. This elaborate image, which makes the young the audience and the old the judges, entails in its political counterpart that however much right reason may support the consonance of young and old, it is a community of pleasure that now is to bind the city together. Such a bond turns out to be no stronger than myth, for the Stranger admits that his argument for the greater unpleasantness of the unjust life over against the just life may not be cogent, and a Sidonian tale may be a necessary supplement to the law (663d6–e2). The possible need for myth is the Stranger's way of acknowledging that the perfect solution he had hinted at, the puppet and its double meaning, cannot be politically effective: tragedy stands in its way.

Clinias's failure to follow the Stranger's image, so that he believes not only that the Stranger claims that all cities now do what the Stranger recommends, but that Crete and Sparta alone among Greek cities have their poets sugarcoat the good and embitter the bad, foreshadows what proves to be the greatest disagreement between Clinias and the Stranger as it provokes the Stranger into his strongest denunciation of the Spartan and Cretan way of life. Clinias believes that unchanging musical forms, whose changes the law alone dictates, involve a coincidence between what the music declares and the law demands. It is not just that Clinias did not notice the Stranger's partial disapproval of Egyptian ways, but he did not grasp the significance behind pleasure's adoption of forms that catch perfectly the experiential deviation of law. He did not grasp it because he himself embodies unwittingly this experiential deviation. Indeed, were it not unwitting, the problem it poses for the law would not be as refractory to a solution as it is. At this point, the Stranger equates the principles of the genetic structure of law—moderation and justice—with the happiness that initially belonged to the eidetic structure of the good. He asks Clinias whether Sparta and Crete compel their poets to say that the moderate and just man is happy and blessed (660d11–661d4). In expounding on the fundamental premise of the law, the Stranger asserts that all the so-called goods, including life itself, are bad for the unjust and good for the just, and he opposes this view to that of the many, who rank health the highest, beauty second, and wealth third, and in adding to them the perfect functioning of the senses, top it all off with one's becoming deathless as soon as possible so as to do tyrannically whatever one desires. If one looks back at the eidetic structure of the good, one sees that this notion of blessedness entails the mapping of the divine goods, with suitable modifications, onto the human goods, which now guide the divine. Such a mapping is nothing but the ordinary understanding of the Olympian gods insofar as they are beautiful and not just. The Stranger's caution, in presenting the manifold of the eightfold good, without allowing it to inhere in a unitary entity, now has its reason. The Egyptian and Greek inventions of a being to which the goods could be attached look as if they offer the only possible solutions to the Stranger's neutral disjunction of the divine and the human. Either one goes the way of the Egyptians, cancels the human goods, and spirits everything away into the gods, or one takes the way that Homer and Hesiod suggested and collapses the divine and the human into a deathless human being, who in transgressing the law is indistinguishable from the tyrant, which a deathless perfection has now glamorized.

The Stranger puts the tragic formula—it is best not to be born, and its corollary, it is second-best to live as short a time as possible—in a new setting. The new setting is laid down by the eidetic structure of the good. The tragic formula never had such a setting; it was meant to apply to human life as such regardless of the structure of the good. Once, however, the abstraction from the good implicit in the tragic formula is canceled, the formula is declared to be true if and only if one is unjust. The tragedy of life thus consists in the experience of life as wholly divorced from justice, and this almost universal experience brings along with it the conviction, in which Clinias fully shares, that the life of pleasure without justice is good and possible. Tragedy is the drink of fear: it says that life is unlivable because the best life is the criminal life (cf. *Republic* 619b7–d1). The Stranger's teaching is his first explication of the eidetic structure of the good, and what he meant by having the human goods dependent on the divine. The human goods are good only for the good, but the vices of soul transform them into evils; and the vices of soul, in turn, if they are allied with human evils—sickness, ugliness, weakness, and poverty— turn them into goods, so that only if the virtues of soul are present are human evils really evil. The Stranger, however, wants the poets to declare that the moderate and just man, that is, the man of the genetic structure of law but without either good sense or courage, is happy regardless of whether he is tall and strong or short and weak, and has wealth or not; but he does not speak of beauty and health. The pictures the young are to receive must not associate the painful, whether it be the ugly or the sick, with the attractiveness of the virtues: Socrates, it seems, would have to be made young and beautiful before he could be their model. Though Socrates without a cosmetic overhaul might be the serious intent of the Stranger's teaching, he would be as such insupportable.

The startling addition of deathlessness as the completion (τέλος) of total blessedness makes one realize once more the deliberate ambiguity in the Stranger's designation of the goods of soul as divine. Since "divine" lends itself so easily to be understood as equivalent to "of the gods," as the Stranger had pointed out when he confessed to his own uncertainty how "divine puppet" was to be taken, the shift from "divine" to "deathless" points to the central difficulty in the translation of the eidetic structure of the good into the genetic structure of law. The genetic structure of law had been as silent about the gods as the eidetic structure of the good: the end (τέλος) of the regime was burial. The Stranger thereby had stopped short of the theology of book 10 in his law-scheme; and it now turns out that its exclusion was meant to raise the question whether any theology was compatible with education. The divine, once it is translated into a being, is a standing threat to the eidetic structure of the good, for as a being it gathers all of perfection into itself without the good and becomes, as the arbitrariness of the will replaces knowledge and mind, indistinguishable from eternal tyranny. The Stranger even goes so far as to imagine, after he has sworn by Zeus and Apollo, that those gods too might say that the most just and the most pleasant life are two, and it would be no more than odd (ἄτοπον) but not inconsistent with their own lives were they to say that those who live the most pleasant life are happier. The Cretan myth of Ganymede agrees perfectly with this answer. The Stranger does not link the life of pleasure with the life of injustice when he has himself quizzing the gods, for even if the gods are just they cannot possibly be understood as living most justly. To whom would they be obedient, and with whose laws would they conform? Through this difficulty the Stranger finally reveals what was implicit in the translation by the genetic structure of law of the eidetic structure of the good into the just and the beautiful: the opacity of that translation, once the gods are part of the law, has the experiential consequence that in the immoderate and the unjust lies the good.

On the decisive issue, whether the union of health, wealth, complete tyranny, strength, and courage along with deathlessness makes for misery if injustice and insolence accompany it, Clinias parts company with the Stranger, but, like Polus, he grants that whoever lives such a life lives shamefully (αἰσχρῶς), though not that he lives badly, unpleasantly, or to his own disadvantage (661d5–662a8). The Stranger ascribes Clinias's view to virtually everyone except himself; it somehow matches the equally universal view, which the Stranger had wished to combat, that pleasure is the sole criterion for musical correctness. Music and life are judged in exactly the same way, and the apparent reality of the one and the unreality of the other qua image seem hardly to matter. This is the deeper significance of the Stranger's substitution of tragedy for the expected exhibitor of tragedy when it came to the question whom would most men prefer in a wide-open contest of showmanship, for if reality and its image are blurred experientially, with scarcely anyone noticing their coalescence, then the task of the legislator is to reseparate them and persuade that a perspectival distortion has occurred, and where one stands makes all the difference in the judgment of appearances:

> Whatever is seen at a distance supplies to virtually everyone and in particular to children the experience of dizziness and whirling around in darkness (σκοτοδινᾶν),[10] unless a legislator, by the removal of the darkness, will set up an impression or opinion (δόξα) contrary to it, and will persuade in some way or other by means of habits, praises, and speeches that the just and unjust things are shadow-paintings (ἐσκιαγραφημένα), the unjust things appearing (φαινόμενα) in a way contrary to that which characterizes the just, being observed as pleasant from the perspective of the unjust and bad, while the just things appear most unpleasant, whereas from the perspective of the just everything to everyone is observed contrarily in regard to both. (663b6–c5)

If one borrows the language of the *Sophist*, the Stranger is saying that the images of the just and the unjust look to everyone as if they were the products of eikastics, where the proportions of the original do not alter regardless of any changes in size, but in fact their images are the products of phantastics, in which one has taken into account that the images of the real, if they are not adjusted to the stance of the viewer, do not preserve their true proportions (*Sophist* 235c8–236c7). If this distinction is applied to the manifold of the eightfold good, then the human goods are

---

10. The anagram of "all" in "children" in the Stranger's phrase—πᾶσίν τε ὡς ἔπος εἰπεῖν καὶ δὴ καὶ παισί—seems to imply that hardly anyone grows up, and the old do not become twice children: *non bis pueri sumus, sed semper.*

already on a level with the human line of sight, and we cannot help but
believe we see them as they are; but the divine goods, in standing higher
and further away from us, look smaller than they are, completely out of
reach, and infinitely laborious to attain. If the human perspective is to be
corrected for, then the divine goods in their images must be lengthened
and the human goods shrunk if they are to regain anything like their
true proportions; indeed, the phantom images must give more than their
seemingly true proportions if pleasure is to suffuse the shadow-painting
of the just, and pain is to splatter the shadow-painting of the unjust. The
difficulty of the task consists in affording to the worse soul access to
the perspective of the better soul, for otherwise the perspectives of the
two are simply different and mutually unintelligible. The Stranger thus
swings back to his starting point, where Clinias's choice of the legislator
for the family in which the unjust outnumbered the just brothers required the establishment of friendly feeling against the grain. Clinias's
choice has never been far from the Stranger' thoughts, for Clinias himself, as he has just now revealed, represents the obstacle to Clinias's own
choice (662b1–2).

The possible unpersuasiveness of the Stranger's argument for the in-
separability of the just, the pleasant, the beautiful, and the good consists
in the difference, if not incommensurability, between the pleasure in justice the just take and the pleasure in doing whatever one pleases (cf. Philebus 12c8–e2). That the unjust life is more unpleasant convinces only
those whom honor and glory move (663a2–7), and even they might calcu-
late that only the unsuccessful tyrant meets with obloquy but the successful overwhelms the spitefulness of the envious. If the city splits between those like Achilles and those like Thersites, a myth of some kind
would be necessary if inferior natures were to be elevated into a semblance of the higher. The Stranger assumes throughout the early books
of the Laws that Odysseus's ruthless suppression of Thersites is a last
resort and incompatible with the persuasive rule of law (663e1–2). The
Stranger does not say what kind of lie would accomplish this, but he is
more convinced than Clinias is that stories prove to be easily persuasive,
however unpersuasive they are. He cites the story of armed men who
sprang up from the sowing of teeth. He seems to disregard its significance—that the city comes to be from fratricidal warfare, once the land
of the city has been staked out as exclusively the possession of its autoch-
thonous inhabitants—and assume that the Thebans believed the story;
but what he means is that Clinias, with his insight into the war of all
against all, is the true believer. The story recalls the Stranger's own suggestion, that one possible solution for a family at odds with itself was for

the arbitrator to kill the unjust.[11] The story also recalls Socrates' "noble lie," which put together the land as the common mother of all the citizens with the three classes as composed of different metals. These stories seem to have one thing in common, that the law as the bond of the city must override differences in kind without canceling them, and that to reconcile the city's horizontal equality with its vertical hierarchy necessarily involves the art of phantastics. The Stranger is recommending that that art be diverted away from both philosophy and poetry, which have previously made use of it, to serve the law (cf. 811c6–812a11). Such a diversion finds its expression in the *Laws*, as the prelude of preludes of law, and in the preludes of the *Laws* (cf. 66b3–7).

4 THE CHORUS OF DIONYSUS

If the chief burden of the choruses is to declare that the gods say the same life to be the best and the most pleasant (664b7–8)—the formula for denying any difference between the eidetic structure of the good and the genetic structure of law—it is surprising to learn that everyone in the city, whether they be men or boys, free or slaves, males or females, must enchant the whole city with this message, which is to remain the same while constantly changing in the complexity of its presentation, so that the singers are never sated with the pleasure of their hymns (665c2–7). Nothing could show up better Clinias's complete misunderstanding of the Stranger's reflections on Egyptian art than the Stranger's present acceptance of musical novelty; but one still ought to be puzzled how he proposes to maintain the message if its forms undergo constant change. That, moreover, no dissonance between the experience of slaves and their songs and dances would arise seems most unlikely, particularly if the appropriate form for slaves are animal stories, through which they can say what they think without their masters noticing.[12] We learn later, in any case, that only slaves and hired strangers are to perform in comedies (816d9–e6). The Stranger seems to be demanding the self-enchantment of the entire city, and not just of the children, so that the pleasure in the songs and dances will spill over into the attractiveness of the doctrine,

11. That the Stranger speaks of the city as a συνοικία at this point (664a5) shows how much this story still affects the Stranger's argument.

12. Cf. C. Ritter, *Kommentar*, 50; Phaedrus *Fabulae* III. Prologus 33–37. A similar difficulty shows up in the *Statesman*, where the statesman's cloak is to enfold everyone in the city both slaves and free, despite the statesman's unwillingness to include anyone who is bad (308c1–d3, 311c3–4).

and the pleasure in the play will be the pleasure in life as play. The chorus of children would thus be alone in leading the best life, and everyone else in the city be continuously coming closer to despair as they departed more and more from what time by itself would put out of reach.

The Stranger's account of the choruses is confusing from the start. There are four groups but only three choruses (664c4–d4). The Muses sponsor the first, which consists of the children; Apollo sponsors the second, and he is to be invoked to bear witness to the truth of what is said and implored to show his complaisant graciousness to the young; the third do not at first have a sponsor, but they are over thirty and less than sixty; the fourth, whom the Stranger mysteriously designates as "those after these things" (τοὺς μετὰ ταῦτα), cannot carry a tune, but they have to be storytellers (μυθολόγοι), left over to recount through a divine report (διὰ θείας φήμης) the same ways (ἤθη) as those of which three choruses sing. The Stranger, in explaining to Clinias where the third chorus fits in, summarizes the beginning of book 2; but now, in abbreviating his original story, he ascribes to human nature by itself an awareness of rhythm and harmony, without any pleasure in such awareness, and restricts the gods' role to the sponsorship of choral dances (664e3–665a6). The pleasure, it seems, in rhythm and harmony is a gift of the gods. Clinias finds it odd that Dionysus is to lead a chorus of elders, but he does not make it clear whether the thirty-year range in the membership of the chorus surprises him more, or that Dionysus should join the Muses and Apollo. The Stranger remarks that the third chorus has been the purpose of pretty nearly the largest part of their speeches. That purpose has been, we suspected, a radical reform of comedy and tragedy, so that what now confirms the experiential departure from the law will restore the law against experience. Within this larger purpose was the reformation of Clinias, whom the Stranger had to persuade to abandon his longing for eternal tyranny and turn away from seeing the law through his experience of it as the teacher of lawlessness.

No sooner has the Stranger proposed the chorus of Dionysus than he begins to dismantle it, so that one hardly knows what survives his deconstruction. On the one hand, they are not to let the presumably wisest part of the city go; on the other, the older and more moderate they are, the more they would be reluctant to sing, and they would take little pleasure in doing it: should they be compelled, they would be even more ashamed, and this shame would increase if they had to stand up in front of an audience of all sorts of men; finally, had they to train in order to compete, they would in their embarrassment sing wholly without pleasure and eagerness. Wine is supposed to overcome some of these difficulties, but not for those between thirty and forty, who are not allowed to get drunk. As for the rest, wine softens them up and makes them forget their gloominess (δυσθυμία), but only to the point that they might be willing to sing before a small audience of their own kind. The Stranger cancels the universal incantation of the whole city by the whole city and imagines a case that hardly seems capable of conferring the greatest goods on the city. It is clear that the third chorus do not dance, so that the unity of music and gymnastic in choral dancing has now broken apart, and the Stranger is now concerned solely with words set to music. There is only one way in which a chorus which is not a chorus can withdraw from the public and still be public, and that is if what they say is written and published. Written speeches, recorded when the tongues of the speakers have been loosened, are alone capable of maintaining the proper mean between the symposium, in which utter license lets the ruler discern the natures and ways of his subjects, and the private party, where only a chance set of circumstances could lead to the disclosure of its speeches. If writing is what the Stranger now has in mind, his subsequent recommendation that the *Laws,* once the guardian of the laws and educator have arranged for its transcription, become the most suitable textbook for the young (811d2–e5), would confirm it.[13] This of course is a funny remark, for the educator-guardian is Plato himself, and he has not allowed the Athenian Stranger to wait around until Clinias or anyone else translates his recommendation into reality.[14]

The restorative that is the *Laws* works independently of the law. The Stranger, moreover, in bringing the *Laws* into line with the revised third chorus, calls our attention to the two extremes of imitation, whose possible join has been the underlying thread of the first two books. If the puppet show made the truth about man manifest to all, but only the very small children awarded it first prize for the pleasure it gave, its peculiarity consisted in the fact that it could not be written and had to be performed in order to please or show; but the third chorus have nothing to show the city and can only be written. These two extremes, in which gesture and speech are wholly apart, would presumably bring about, if they could be joined, a consonance between feeling and reason that virtue entire is meant to be. Such a consonance, however, between puppet show and

---

13. C. Ritter, *Kommentar,* 45–46, in discussing the question the Stranger raises at 666d3, beautifully remarks, "Demnach scheint es als ob geradezu die Kritik der Kunst der Inhalt ihrer 'Gesänge' (ᾠδαί) sein sollte, also ob sie die καλλίστη μοῦσα wäre."

14. Cf. H. Görgemanns, *Beiträge zur Interpretation von Platons Nomoi,* note 3, 59–61.

writing seems to be rather a myth than an argument, a juxtaposition of disjoint elements rather than any genuine whole. It would seem that only if the written element could contain within itself an action on its own would the difference concealed in "show and tell" be overcome. This was, I think, the suggestion of Leo Strauss when he called his book *The Argument and the Action of Plato's Laws.* One wonders, in any case, whether the split between the eidetic structure of the good and the genetic structure of law does not reflect and is not meant to reflect the teaching of the *Phaedrus*—that a perfect writing, whose parts form a whole, is still read in time, and the temporal order has to be enfolded into the atemporal structure in order for the animal, which a perfect writing is, to become alive.

Clinias's answer to the Stranger's question, What song will "divine men" sing? provokes the Stranger into an apparently spontaneous assault on Crete and Sparta; it perplexes Clinias so much that he can only say rather helplessly, "I do not know how it has come about, Stranger, but in some way or other once more you utterly degrade our legislators" (667a6–7). Clinias's answer was that neither Cretans nor Spartans could sing any other song than that of choruses with which they had become familiar; and the Stranger says that is likely (εἰκότως), since they have really and truly (ὄντως) not gained an acquaintance with the most beautiful song. Dorian education comes close to training in savagery, for the regime is that of an army camp and never allows for individual and private grooming away from the herd. Clinias must be astonished to hear this disparagement of choral unison, and that a more beautiful song than that of choruses is what their chorus, which is not a chorus, out of shame before the common theatrical sort of chorus, seeks (667a11–b3). The Stranger claims that he was following the logos and had no intention, if in fact he did so, of degrading Minos and Lycurgus (or Zeus and Apollo). He seems to mean that Crete and Sparta got exactly what they deserved, and one would have to go much farther to vilify their uncivilized state. Once he had turned to the way things are (ὄντως), he could no longer permit the illusions of image (εἰκότως) to dictate what he said. This is a curious preface to the Stranger's discussion of the charm (χάρις) of the image, and the importance of not mistaking that of which an image really and truly is (ὅτου ποτ᾽ ἐστὶν εἰκὼν ὄντως, 668c7).[15] One could say that the Stranger

---

15. The choice of the word χάρις for pleasure seems meant to recall Pindar *Olympian* I.30–32, where χάρις is used to characterize myths that in their complex falsehoods surpass τὸν ἀλαθῆ λόγον: χάρις δ᾽ ἅπερ ἅπαντα τεύχει τὰ μείλιχα θνατοῖς, ἐπιφέροισα τιμὰν καὶ ἄπιστον ἐμήσατο πιστὸν ἔμμεναι τὸ πόλλακις.

preserves a kind of continuity by starting off book 2 with the derivation of "chorus" from "joy" and by now looking at "charm," but the difference is obvious: χορός came from χαρά by way of a story of divine naming, χαρά and χάρις are self-evidently cognate. It is now clear, in any case, that the Stranger's search for the beautiful song did not end at the beauty of the virtues and their images.

The Stranger allows some of the third chorus to get drunk, so that the bitter dryness of old age will be diminished, and the iron of their soul, plunged into the fire of drink, become more malleable. They are to undergo a pseudo-experience, for they do not recover their youth but its semblance. Dionysus is to initiate them into a playfulness that is not theirs. The issue of image necessarily follows from the induction of the unreal into the old. They become the image of the very young; indeed, were they to act out before them what their shame must hide, they would look to them as if the puppets which delight them have become alive. The song they severally are to sing must be a song against their acquired disposition. It must be a song they believe to be untrue and repellent to everything they have really experienced. Clinias and Megillus each in his own way are in such a state. They have been constantly charmed and cajoled from the start to sing in tune with the Stranger and out of tune with themselves. Their condition recalls that of Teiresias and Cadmus in Euripides' *Bacchae,* whom not only Pentheus would believe to be hardly sober and lost to all shame when they are prepared to dance in honor of the new god Dionysus (*Bacchae* 204–209, 321–324). They must lean upon each other for mutual support, "for it is a disgrace for a couple of old men to fall down" (364–5). They are the only men in Thebes who welcome Dionysus, and Cadmus advises Pentheus to join them, "for even if the god is not, as you assert, let him be said to be; lie beautifully, in order that Semele be thought to have given birth to a god and honor accrue to us and the entire family" (333–336). Teiresias offers equally sophistical reasons why Pentheus is mistaken to resist, none of which establish the godness of the god, and all of them together do not evidently inhere in a single being who came to be. Their speech and behavior seem to be the model, however remote, for what the Stranger wants Clinias and Megillus to experience soberly.[16] They are to keep their heads while letting go.

---

16. In the *Bacchae,* Tiresias defends Bacchic rites against the charge of promoting unchastity by asserting that σωφρονεῖν is by nature, and that at least the chaste woman (ἥ γε σώφρων) will not be corrupted even in Bacchic rites (314–318). The Stranger seems to pick up on this and propose a training in moderation through temptation: Dionysus is now the god who compels σωφροσύνη harmlessly.

They are put in the strange position of neither being symposiarchs nor symposiasts. They stumble along with the Stranger's argument, they are not in step with it. The perspective of the young, which the drunk adopt willy-nilly, images the headiness they undergo without an elevation of their reason. They have become more lighthearted but not more rational. We are meant to keep our eye on them as the Stranger discusses of what an image really is.

The Stranger begins by introducing a new term for pleasure, "charm" or "grace" (χάρις). Charm seems to designate a pleasure that cannot be isolated from whatever it accompanies (667d9–e3). Charm is pleasure that blurs the difference between χάρις as graciousness and χάρις as gratitude. It stands between, as "lovely" does, the subjective and the objective. In its weakest sense, χάρις expresses the grammatical relation of χαίρειν to its supplementary participle, where the participle fixes the pleasure to the actions it designates, whether it be "I enjoy walking" or "I enjoy thinking," and suggests a preference for what one does regardless of the pleasure. The Stranger says that in all cases in which charm accompanies something, either it is the most serious element, or either "rightness" or "benefit" is (667b5–c7). The two examples he gives do not distinguish between rightness and benefit. Every kind of food and drink with which pleasure goes along has in its healthiness what is beneficial and right; and truth, in the delight of learning, accomplishes both its rightness and benefit; and they, in turn, seem to be equivalent respectively to the beautiful (τὸ καλῶς) and the good (τὸ εὖ). Is the Stranger now denying, after he has argued for the goodness of falsehood, that truth could be right and not good? For the eikastic arts, right and good are distinct, and for this reason truth presumably could not be that which brings them about. Truth, however, determines what he calls equality, and equality produces rightness. Truth, then, is capable of splitting its effects, and right and good do not always follow in its train. The Stranger, moreover, seems to have forgotten shadow-paintings, where the reproduction of the equal would appear unequal unless the image of the equal were unequal. The Stranger is silent now about appearances, even though the song the third chorus would be willing to sing depends on their altered state in which they are not seeing straight.

At the same time that the Stranger restores truth as the judge of imitation, he downgrades play (παιδιά) to harmless pleasure (667e5–8). What was pretty nearly the equivalent of children's education is now unworthy of any serious account. The puppets are not to be judged in light of truth. What, then, is to take their place, which keeps the size and quality of the imitated (668b6–7)? In order to recognize what poems are, one must know their being (οὐσία), what each wants or intends (βούλεται), and of what an image really is (668c6–7), for an error about this will lead to a failure to discern the rightness or mistakenness of the intention (ἡ ὀρθότης τῆς βουλήσεως ἢ καὶ ἁμαρτία αὐτοῦ). No sooner, then, does truth come back than "being" belongs to the image, and we are concerned with the intention of the image in its being. It is not the case, then, that the Stranger has forgotten the art of phantastics, but he has switched his attention from the perspective of the viewer to the perspective of the poem: what was it looking at when it gave us an image? This means, if we revert to the issue of the puppets, that if we look at the puppet-master, there is nothing more in his show than their charm for small children; but if we look past the puppet-master to the image the Stranger devised, which preceded the contest for pleasure, then its intention is at issue, and whether in its being it is right. This new formulation likewise entails that neither comedy nor tragedy can be judged by the pleasure each affords to those whose experiences find an echo in them (cf. 670b8–c2), but rather the intention of the imitation must be figured out if one is to know of what it is really an image. When Achilles says of Agamemnon that he has the eyes of a dog and the heart of a deer (*Iliad* I.225), it is not enough to stop at the nonbeing of the being he invokes, but it is necessary to discover its twofold intention: Agamemnon fawns and trembles, but Achilles has the heart of a dog and the eyes of a deer, and hence combines the highest bravery with the greatest beauty, for Achilles would not have delivered the perfect insult unless he had concealed in it the perfect praise. When the watchman says in Sophocles' *Antigone* that Antigone keened over her brother Polynices as a mother bird does over an empty nest (*Antigone* 423–427), one has to supply what he does not say to know what his image intends: the dust she poured and the guards brushed off was the life of the corpse. What the watchman says does not fit Antigone through equality but through inequality, which by inversion proves to be right.

The Stranger's argument brings back, once Socrates' definition of law is factored in, the problem posed by the relation between the eidetic structure of the good and the genetic structure of law. That the good shows up in the law as the beautiful and the just now seems to raise a similar question to that which the being of imitation raised. Are the beautiful and the just, as the standards in light of which every law is to be judged, no more than images, whose intention is to be traced to the good? Whether a law hits or falls short of the mark of the beautiful or the just would be a secondary consideration; the true problem would be whether it has aimed past either and come close or not to the good. The immediate consequence of this new perspective would be that the injustice and the ugliness in the law would not necessarily be an objection to it, however much coloring the storytellers would have to apply to them. Just as the easy recognition of the right order and parts of the human body in a painting would not suffice for knowledge of its beauty (668e7–669a7), so the right number and arrangement of the kinds of law in the genetic structure of law would be very misleading if they were taken by themselves and the rightness of their intention were unknown. The very fact that the manifold of the eightfold good keeps soul and body apart means that the experiential bond, which is assumed between them in the genetic structure of law, already distorts it, regardless of how many of the goods and their true rank show up in the translation.

This difficulty can be measured by the analogous problem that music notoriously has. "If," Horace says in a poem as apparently monstrous as its initial image, "a painter were to wish to join the neck of a horse to a human head, and feather over limbs put together from all quarters, so that a beautiful woman above would end disgracefully in a black fish, would you, friends, if admitted to look, hold back a laugh?" (*Ars Poetica* 1–5). The answer, of course, would obviously be "No" if one did not know what the painter wanted, and even if one did know one might laugh anyway, if his real intention were as playful as it looked. Plato's *Statesman* does not suddenly gain a noble simplicity and quiet grandeur once one understands the necessity for its disarrangements and disproportions. The Stranger now speaks of poets who, in composing the words of real men, assign them the colors and songs of women (669c3–5); but he himself had done just that when he urged Clinias and Megillus to search for the beauty of song as if they were bitches tracking their quarry. The near impossibility of figuring out what the intention of monstrous images is and what they resemble should lead to the conclusion, if one recalls Socrates' perplexity when it came to the effect of rhythm and harmony on the soul (*Republic* 400a2–c6), that the third chorus should stick to plain speeches, for once they raise their voices in song they will be as baffled as we are to figure out the connection between modes and moods (cf. 815c2–c7). The deepest link between νόμος as law and νόμος as song seems to be this: the equal difficulty of discerning in either what follows from their becoming part of a way of life.[17] Compared to the puzzle that the

---

17. The Stranger lists eight things poets and musicians do which the Muses would not: (1) speeches of men with the complexion and song of women (e.g., Sophocles' Ajax or Heracles); (2) songs and gestures of free men with the rhythm of slaves; (3) a free song to accompany rhythms and gestures of slaves (e.g., the Stranger's own

intention of images poses for laws no less than for music, it was a feat of easy brilliancy for the Stranger to notice how the Dorian laws of courage destroyed even the basis for moderation.

The Stranger does not make it clear what the connection is between the chorus of Dionysus, insofar as they have been individually educated to know what songs they are to sing, and the same chorus, insofar as they become in a symposium more and more obstreperous, full of free speech, and disobedient (670c8–672a4). If they know what songs suit them, they must know they would only sing them when they are not themselves and "in some sense" compelled to sing voluntarily (670c9). When, then, did they learn what the songs were? It could not be when they were sober, for no song would then appear to them to be suitable; and it cannot be when they are drunk, for one of the first things that would go would be their understanding (645e1–4).[18] If, moreover, they know what song suits every age (670d7–671a1), they must be the lawgivers; but they are not the lawgivers: when they are getting drunk they are ruled by those over sixty, who do not drink and cannot sing. They are ruled by the "sympotic laws" formulated by the same lawgiver who molded the souls of the young: the Stranger casually admits that Dionysus is in charge of elementary education. If, moreover, we take the Stranger at his word, the lawgiver is to educate the already completely educated. The purpose of their drinking under the rule of the symposiarch is to make them greater friends than they were before, and whether they sing, get up to dance, or just talk more freely than they would otherwise seems to be irrelevant. The harmless pleasures their singing is to afford them make those pleasures, according to the Stranger's own assertion, unserious. What is serious is the most beautiful terror, united with justice (μετὰ δίκης), which the sympotic laws are supposed to be capable of inserting into the symposium in

---

recommendation at 665c2–3); (4) a speech contrary to the rhythms; (5) sounds of beasts, men, instruments, all sounds, "as if they were imitating some one thing" (e.g., the soul Socrates describes at the end of *Republic* IX, 558b10–e1); (6) separation of rhythm and gesture from song; (7) speeches stripped of song in meter (e.g., the rhythmic clausulae of Plato's *Laws*); (8) instrumental music without words (e.g., the shouts and disordered movements of infants). The eighth also includes the flute nomes of Marsyas and Olympus, which, according to both Socrates and Alcibiades, reveal those who are in need of gods (*Minos* 318b4–c1; *Symposium* 215c2–6); they are known to Clinias (677d4).

18. Cf. C. Ritter, *Kommentar*, 53–54, 57–60. England, 331, notes two difficulties that bear on the question: first, ἡμῖν (670d9) could imply, if it is taken with ᾄδειν and not as a "genitival dative," "that it was not *real* singing that was expected of them"; second, England thinks Plato could not mean "what he appears to say, that the power of right selection will follow as the result of the power to take an intelligent part in a chorus."

order to combat the nonbeautiful confidence the symposiarch-lawgiver-reshaper deliberately induced. These paradoxes only make sense if they are components of an image the rightness of whose intention consists in the dialogic action of the *Laws*. Clinias and Megillus are partners and not partners of the Athenian symposiarch. They have been educated as they have been intoxicated by the bare speeches of the Stranger, who could not have educated them if he had not made them drunk.

Drunkenness generates an illusory form of unjust desire; it renders harmless what otherwise festers in the souls of the old, whose impotence turns them sour as they reflect on what their experiential departure from the law now declares to be good. The Stranger had elicited from Clinias, without having to get him really drunk, the same sentiments. He had saved him from the embarrassment of becoming the repellent object of ridicule on the part of the young by keeping the chorus of Dionysus, in which Clinias must have believed he was to participate, behind closed doors. The split between the beautiful and the just, which was built into the genetic structure of law and experienced in the desire for eternal tyranny, is now resolved in the Stranger's identification of the most beautiful terror of reverence and shame with what he calls "divine fear." This resolution seems to involve a theology in which the gods are most beautiful and most just. It is the theology of the tenth book. This theology is as novel as that of the *Republic*, in which the gods are most beautiful and the causes of all goods, but they are not just. It is meant to correct a widespread report that Dionysus gave men wine to punish them for the madness Hera had inflicted on him (672b3–7). That story seems to imply that were it not for the gods man would never be crazy; but what the Stranger knows is that "every living being, for any of which it is fitting to have mind (νοῦς) on maturity and completion (τελεωθέντι), is never born with it to the extent it is to have it, and in that time in which it does not yet possess its own good sense (οἰκεία φρόνησις), it is entirely mad and shouts in disorder, and, in turn, as soon as it stands upright, it jumps around in disorder" (672b8–c5). Athena, in short, is a fiction; she is the divine version of the eidetic definition of man as rational animal. Man cannot believe he is in his becoming defective. He apparently needs the gods to acknowledge it and therefore experience it as shame. The genetic structure of law, despite its silence about the gods, seems to need the gods to complete it; but in their completing it, the insolence of man becomes more prominent than his madness. Σωφροσύνη, therefore, which combines in itself both sanity and moderation, and accordingly ranked just below, on a par with, or even higher than good sense in the eidetic structure of the good, lost its higher element in the genetic structure of law. The Stranger's imitation of the symposium in speech, in which disordered order was the goal, brought back together mind and shame. Their reconjunction cannot but remind us of the biblical story, in which the "eidetic" being of man is neither male nor female, but as soon as Adam and Eve gain knowledge of good and evil they become ashamed as they look at one another and see they are defective in light of their eidetic creation. In becoming at that moment a generational being in time they are made to give up the possibility of being forever.

If one looks back to the first book and the Stranger's demotion there of courage to fourth place in the goods of soul, one realizes with a start that the Stranger has now gone through in some kind of order moderation, justice, and good sense. Good sense suddenly emerged from the Stranger's hint that one hesitates to speak before the many of the greatest gift Dionysus bestows, since the common story about Dionysus's madness and revenge stands in the way. Dionysus reveals the permanent truth about man in his becoming, without the understanding of which the statesman and the lawgiver do not have a chance to solve the political problem. The Eleatic Stranger had made it just as plain in the *Statesman* how little importance man's presumed rationality has politically; but he had not equally stressed the problem of the becoming of mind in time. At the very moment the Athenian Stranger brings back mind as of decisive importance, he splits choral song into its two parts, whose origins are to be traced back to the difference between the disordered sounds of the infant and the disordered movements of the young who are already standing up, and whose control belongs to two separate arts, music and gymnastic (672c5–6). The movement, then, in book 2 has been to divide at its end what the Stranger had put together at its beginning; and this division represents the result of a movement, in the context of the genetic structure of law, back to the eidetic structure of the good, which had kept apart the divine goods of the soul from the human goods.[19] Despite, however, all his talk about gesture, which the Stranger now says is the peculiar name for the rhythmic motion of body (672e8–9), he has only managed to discuss music, and he asks Clinias and Megillus whether they are to take up gymnastic (673b1–4). Clinias answers as if the answer were obvious, since the question was put to a Cretan and a Spartan; and the

---

19. England's plausible excision of ῥήμασί τε καὶ μέλεσι καὶ τοῖς ῥυθμοῖς (669b2–3), on the grounds that it contradicts the generality of καὶ ἐν γραφικῇ καὶ ἐν μουσικῇ καὶ πάντῃ (669a8), could be resisted if the Stranger is hinting at this movement, especially if γραφική could possibly mean the art of writing, as it does in Hippocrates (*De prisca medicina* 20.8). At *Phaedrus* 275d4–5 γραφή is said to be truly like ζωγραφία; cf. *Laws* 769a7–e2, where τὰ ζῷα of painters are called τὰ γεγραμμένα; also 934c1–2.

Stranger looks as if he is prepared to satisfy them easily, for their experience in gymnastic is greater than in music: the Stranger alludes to what appeared to him to be Clinias's gymnastic insight into the laws of Crete (φαίνη μοι γεγυμνάσθαι πρὸς τὸ διειδέναι τὰ Κρητῶν νόμιμα, 626b5–6). Now it is not difficult to suspect that the third book is the Stranger's version of gymnastic. It deals with the necessarily imperfect beginnings of cities and their regimes, and thus corresponds in its "historical" presentation to the imperfect beginnings of man's rationality. The conditions under which political life comes to be and develops are primarily "material" and thus correspond to what would happen if the eidetic structure of the human goods were examined under its transformation by the genetic structure of law.[20] That this is in fact the case remains to be shown; but what one can now say, by way of anticipation, is that if the second book proves to be to the third as music is to gymnastic, then the Stranger would have accomplished dialogically the split that was already within the eidetic structure of the good, and he would have done so in time.[21] That, in any case, the dialogic purpose outweighs any legislative end becomes clear in the Stranger's summary of the use of drunkenness. If and only if a city will employ this practice as a serious business (ὡς οὔσης σπουδῆς), with the support of laws and order, on the grounds that its use is for the sake of moderation, and will indulge in all other pleasures likewise solely for the sake of their mastery, does the Stranger sanction it;

20. The splitting of music from gymnastic recalls Socrates' procedure in the *Republic*, where music education is first presented as if it were designed to civilize the thumoeidetic, but ends up as concerned solely with the love of the beautiful, and gymnastic becomes the art that is to control the thumoeidetic.

21. The difference between the eidetic and the genetic understanding of things comes out clearly in the apparent repetitions the Stranger indulges in when he summarizes what they have done. Clinias acknowledges that their story about wine declares that it has not been given for the punishment of human beings but for the sake of the acquisition of virtue of soul, and health and strength of body (672d11), but he does not understand the half of χορεία they have finished off, and the half that they still have to decide how to handle (672e4). The Stranger then speaks of their starting point (cf. 654b3–4), that ὅλη χορεία was education, and one part was the rhythm and harmony of sound, and the other of corporeal motion. Music is then defined, "for want of a better term" [England's translation of οὐκ οἶδα ὅντινα τρόπον], as concerned with the soul's education for virtue, and gymnastic, in the form of dancing, pertains to the virtue of body (673a3–11). This cutting of χορεία in two is then opposed to their rejoining, which occurs in the human animal when, with its natural habit of jumping, once it becomes aware of rhythm, it generates and gives birth to dancing (ἐγέννησέν τε ὄρχησιν καὶ ἔτεκεν), and when song recalls and awakens rhythm, the pair form a partnership with one another and give birth (ἐτεκέτην) to χορεία καὶ παιδιά (673c9–d5). In the splitting of χορεία body and soul are simply apart; in their recombination (N.B. the dual) there is the human animal and the coming to be of χορεία.

otherwise, he proposes to be more severe than Cretan and Spartan law and not allow wine drinking under most circumstances. What began as an indispensable correction of Dorian harshness is now put virtually out of reach: the Stranger is silent about the lawgiver-symposiarch. Clinias and Megillus are thus granted permission to revert to the primacy of courage and war.

III

HISTORY

I HOMER

The immediate connection between the end of book 2 and the beginning of book 3 consists in the parallelism between the Stranger's denial that thoughtfulness can be at the beginning for any animal, and his thesis that the arts in their full development are not found at the beginning of political society. The Cyclopean way of life precedes the presence of mind no less than does the disorderly motion and cries of infants. The parallelism goes even deeper. In order for children to become rational in the proper way, the Stranger recommended the regularization of motions and sounds in the form of rhythm and harmony on the way to their consonance with the law. He did not make it entirely clear whether the law was completely rational or an indispensable link between feelings and logos. In the political parallel, law in the strict sense is not prior to writing and hence relatively late in the development of the arts. But again the Stranger does not make it entirely clear whether mind can come into its own only with or after written law. The Stranger, moreover, had argued for the need of disorderly order if there was to be the highest kind of thinking; and such a condition, if the becoming of the city and man were to run exactly parallel, would imply that departure from the law must occur prior to the coming-to-be of mind. Neither virtue nor vice were at the beginning of political society, and when they did come to be they came to be simultaneously (676a5–6). Progress (ἐπίδοσις) toward virtue was progress toward vice.

In a sense, the Stranger begins the third book with the same question with which the *Laws* opened. The question was whether a god or man was to be held responsible for Cretan and Spartan laws. The answer put Zeus and Apollo at the beginning of Cretan and Spartan legislation. This beginning was both in and outside of time. It was outside of time insofar as those gods stood for the ultimate principle of the law regardless of whether the transmission of that principle necessarily had to occur in time. If Zeus and Apollo simply stand in for what the Stranger calls the

divine goods, only one of which showed up in Cretan and Spartan practices, then the *Laws* started from the notion of ἀρχή as principle of law,
and after two books it turns to ἀρχή as the beginning of political life (πολι-
τεία). Such a schema is far too simple for the argument of the *Laws*. The
Stranger had almost at once posed the issue in terms of becoming from
birth to death in the genetic structure of law, and had gone on to look at
man not only at the beginning but also in his experiences in time. Law
was at the heart of this examination, but not law in a political setting.
The political dimension of the law had been minimized through the
Stranger's displacement of Clinias's insight into the centrality of war for
the city by his own more general proposal about disorder. The Stranger
now returns to war, but war is no longer at the beginning of political life.
There is political life before there is the polis and war. In returning to
political life, the Stranger does not begin by asking what is its principle,
either in the sense of its natural ground or in the sense of its organizing
principle. Neither the natural sociality of man nor justice as the common
good is at the start of his analysis. Though justice was in a way complete
virtue, justice as the characterization of the order of the city does not
start off the Stranger's analysis of political life. The Stranger leads up to
an articulation of political right, but political right proves to be seven
competing claims to rule, to all of which accommodation must be made.
This splitting of right seems to be due primarily to the Stranger beginning
with the beginning of political life. The necessarily imperfect beginnings
of political life necessarily obscure the principle of political life.

The Stranger asks for a vantage point from which one would observe
the beginning of political life most easily and beautifully, and that at the
same time would allow one to see the simultaneous progression of cities
toward virtue and vice (676a1–6). The first question by itself would allow
one to suggest the family, with its successive expansions into village and
city, but the second question implies that the beginning cannot be neutral
if good and bad are built into any departure from it. The beginning has
to be defective if one is not to insert arbitrarily vices and virtues as it
changes in time. The Stranger had begun with a family of many brothers,
most of whom were unjust, in order to get Clinias to agree that the task
of the judge-legislator was to establish friendly feeling among them. The
justice and injustice of the brothers were simply assigned to them, and
Clinias thought it was not implausible for this to be the case. Now, however, the beginning has to have such conditions attached to it that it is
on a bias from the start, and this bias, in turn, in working itself out in
time, affects the structure of whatever comes after it. Man is now in a
setting that is not the result of his will. The imperfect beginnings of polit-

ical life have their counterpart, in the Stranger's earlier analysis, in the experiential departure from the law that the poetry of comedy and tragedy know how to represent to those who had undergone it. Now another kind of poetry, the poetry old men were supposed to favor, is going to represent the defective setting of political life. The Stranger now supplies the plot in which man enacts his life.

The Stranger says the vantage point from which his two questions can be answered—the beginning of political life and its changes toward virtue and vice—is an incomprehensible length of time. This interval, which starts with a flood, though the Stranger implies he could have begun with a different disaster, turns out to be the Hellenic past. So what looked as if it were going to be a speculative reconstruction of man's political beginnings becomes a speculative reconstruction of the antecedents to Peloponnesian history. Myth, Homeric poetry, and Spartan tradition are stitched together in order to give an account of Dorian failure.[1] This failure proves to be connected with the Stranger's criticism of Dorian law. He thus goes back to where he departed in the first book in turning aside into a discussion of music and drunkenness (682e8–11). A digression of some sixty-six pages of Greek text brings him almost back to the beginning (cf. 683b5). They return to the beginning through beginning with the beginning of political life. This dialogic return is effected by making up a story about the beginning that proceeds by sleight of hand into the beginning of Sparta. The digression departed from the beginning by putting music before gymnastic or soul before body. It took the primacy of soul as a dialogic priority without asking whether it had such a priority in real time. In restoring priority to the conditions for the possibility of either virtue or vice, the Stranger cannot put those conditions in real time. It would seem that the gap that opens up between the priority of soul in becoming, which is the teaching of the tenth book, and its posteriority in "historical" time can be filled only by way of mythology and poetry. A lie like the truth has to negotiate between what is first in becoming and what is first in time.

Clinias cannot conceive of the length of time in which there have

---

1. It is worth noting that exactly these three elements constitute the evidence Thucydides uses in his Archaeology. Minos corresponds to the flood (1.4.1), though Thucydides does mention Deucalion, the survivor of the flood (1.3.2), Homer is the key to the whole account, and Spartan tradition is reported at some length (1.9.2; cf. *Laws* 682e4–6). At 682c10 ἀφόβως ἤδη πάντων χρωμένων τῇ θαλάττῃ, applied to the time of the Trojan War, recalls directly Thucydides' ἀλλὰ καὶ τὴν στρατείαν θαλάσσῃ ἤδη πλείω χρώμενοι ξυνεξῆλθον (1.3.4), again of the Trojan War. Thucydides 1.12.1–2 agrees more or less with *Laws* 682d5–e4 about the aftermath of the war.

been cities and men living politically (676b3–6). The Stranger allows us to infer that there have not always been cities; whether there have always been men is left open (cf. 781e6–782a3), since conditions could have thwarted the rise of cities. In this incomprehensible length of time, thousands upon thousands of cities, the Stranger says, have come to be and perished, and in each region cities have often changed their regimes in every way, become greater from smaller and smaller from greater, and worse from better and better from worse. The Stranger wants to grasp "the cause of this change," for the cause might show them the first genesis and transformation of regimes. The cause of the instability and impermanence of any city or regime, regardless of its size or excellence, is at the root of the first coming into being of regimes. Old stories supply the cause that is otherwise not known to the Stranger; and from these old stories of human destruction, he chooses the story of a flood. By choosing the flood, the Stranger chooses the survivors, whose way of life establishes the beginning of political life. In light of his choice, the cause of political change is identified with the cause of the vanishing of the city. The city thus comes to be from the noncity. This was not the impression his quasi-Herodotean characterization of cities conveyed (1.5.3–4), in which the Stranger seemed to be speaking of impermanence within a permanent order of political life. Taken by itself, that characterization would have led one to suppose that he was going to attribute the cause of impermanence to a purely human lack of thoughtfulness, and not to something outside of human control. Now, however, what causes political life to be unstable causes political life to disappear. The imperfect beginnings of political life make political life forever imperfect.

At the end of book 3, Clinias proposes, in order to resolve the two questions the Stranger then poses, that they put together a city in speech, "as if we were founding it from the beginning." If Clinias means that a fully rational city is to be imagined that from the start would not bear traces of an imperfect beginning, his proposal would duplicate Socrates' city in speech of the *Republic*. Socrates' "true city" put together the needs of the body with the arts that satisfy them; Clinias's city has conditions attached to it that do not allow the Stranger to start from scratch. Yet it does seem that those conditions are still much less liable to make the city defective than the imperfect beginnings with which the third book began. In the guise of the arts, reason comes relatively late to the city, and political wisdom comes far later than the arts. If the Athenian Stranger himself represents the intrusion of such wisdom into Crete, then a completion of a certain kind is being imagined in the progress toward virtue. This wisdom is intrusive because it does not come naturally in the course of the development of Dorian institutions. It is as lucky an accident as the occurrence of good sense and the stability of true opinions in old age (630a7–9). The most one could say is that Crete is ripe for the intrusion, but only after the Stranger has altered Clinias's perspective in the previous two books.[2] Courage has been abandoned as the sole virtue, and the life of injustice is no longer the best life. A sobering of Clinias has occurred that is inseparable from his elevation. The Stranger has corrected a radically defective understanding of virtue so that it becomes possible for Clinias to make his proposal; but one could still suspect that the foundation is not solid enough to make the edifice more than a jerry-built affair. Clinias the future legislator has been enlightened, but the enlightenment has not put down roots deep enough to overcome his originally defective understanding. The shift from a historical mythology, with which the book begins, to a rational construction seems to be illusory. After the Stranger's myth we are still entangled in myth.

The first consequence the Stranger draws from the flood is that the survivors must have been shepherds living on mountaintops. By speaking of them as small sparks of the human race (677b2), the Stranger seems to imply that the flood was worldwide; but, as he goes on in his account, an area that was self-contained and through geographic features effectively cut off from the rest of the earth would suffice. Indeed, after he has described all the losses an isolated group of shepherds would have sustained, the Stranger admits that there is still in many places among Greeks and throughout the barbarians the way of life he has been at such pains to put at the temporal beginning of political life (680b1–3). It would have been possible, then, for him to look at the beginning without putting it in time; but such a beginning would not have been a beginning that altered through the slow recovery of what had been lost. There would not have been the gradual diminution in terror that the Stranger can now postulate on the basis of the flood. The flood gives him a ribbon of time on which he can place stages of political development that look as if they follow of necessity from the point of origin. The city thus comes to be apart from the terror that old stories ascribe to the founding of cities. The forgetting of an initial terror rather than its memory brings the city to be. Man is made more innocent than he ever was. The Stranger does not mention that the Cyclops ate six of Odysseus's men.

---

2. The parallel to the Stranger's intrusion into Crete is the importation of philosophic books into Athens (primarily Parmenides' and Anaxagoras's) that seemed to have brought about the conditions there for the possibility of Socrates.

The mountainmen who survived the flood were herdsmen (νομῆς). They grazed (νέμουσιν) cattle and goats. They lived at a time when the verb and agent-noun from the root *νεμ were literally true, and if νομος were ever used its accent was oxytone and meant "pasturage" (cf. νομή, 679a1). Νόμος was latent in their way of life, but there was not yet law. Nothing forbids us from thinking that these shepherds had pipes, and νόμος already designated a tune.[3] The Stranger denies them laws (νόμοι) because he denies them legislators. Laws are associated with writing because a written code presupposes the promulgation of a new set of laws; it represents a departure from whatever prevailed before its establishment (cf. 793a9–c5).[4] Laws, then, belong to a time of radical change. They are an acknowledgment that the tradition of the fathers has been consciously abandoned; but the old ways live on despite the laws because the laws cannot possibly cover everything that has become customary over time.[5] A split, then, occurs in the law between those parts that are subject to conscious change, in which the criterion is the better, and those areas that if they change alter without either deliberation or any awareness, except perhaps on the part of the elders, that anything has changed (cf. 797c4–6; 798a8–b4). This difference played no role in the first two books of the *Laws*. If, however, the aim of elementary education is to bring about a consonance between feelings and law, then the feelings are more likely to form around the ways of the fathers than in response to the laws

3. Dietmar Korzeniewksi, *Griechische Metrik* (Darmstadt 1968), 183, discusses the double sense of νόμος to be found elsewhere as well as at the end of Timotheus's *Persae*. One may add that Socrates, in likening his own state to that of Corybants, because he is now deaf to anyone else except the laws of Athens, who he has imagined were speaking and arguing with him, presupposes the pun on νόμος (*Crito* 54d3–6).

4. Cf. F. W. Maitland, "A Prologue to a History of English Law," *Select Essays in Anglo-American Legal History* (Boston 1907), vol. 1, 19: "In many instances the desire to have written laws appears as soon as a barbarous race is brought into contact with Rome. The acceptance of the new religion must have revolutionary consequences in the world of law, for it is likely that heretofore the traditional customs, even if they have not been conceived as instituted by gods who are now becoming devils, have been conceived as essentially unalterable. Law has been the old; new law has been a contradiction in terms. And now about certain matters there must be new law." Compare with this 948d1–3. In Justinian's *Institutes*, 1.2.10, Sparta is said to be the source of unwritten and Athens of written law; cf. Plutarch *Lycurgus* 13.1–4; R. Hirzel, *Agraphos Nomos* (Leipzig 1900), 73–74 note 1.

5. Cf. David Daube, "The Self-Understood in Legal History," in *Collected Studies in Roman Law* (Frankfurt 1991), vol. 2, 1281–1282: "The earliest list of punishments, in Leviticus 20, starts by prescribing the death penalty for intercourse with the step-mother. It is totally silent on the mother, as also on the daughter"; and again, 1283: "The more fundamental an institution—fundamental in the sense of embedded in the fabric of society—the more apt it is to be accepted without ado and to remain unformulated."

proper. Choral song was in a sense the Stranger's formula for keeping the two kinds of law together; but the result of the Stranger's own argument was to split choral song into two different arts, music and gymnastic, as if that argument were reproducing the gradual development of the arts. In going back to a time when that split had not yet occurred, the Stranger is rehearsing his original argument in real time.

The Stranger makes his shepherds as ignorant of the arts in general as of the devices men severally employ in cities to profit at each others' expense. Their isolation into families would suffice, it seems, to account for their innocence, regardless of whether more of the arts survived on the mountains than the two the Stranger allows them (679a6). The connection the Stranger makes between the arts and immorality recalls Rousseau, but the Stranger does not offer any argument. He deepens the puzzle by linking the disappearance of wisdom (σοφία), whether political or of another kind, with the disappearance of tools. Their joint disappearance must be assumed in order to account for the novelty of invention at the present time. If the Stranger alludes to the discovery of Socratic political philosophy no less than to the invention of the latest machine, then the three cities in the *Republic* are not so much sequential as contemporaneous. The true city, with the highest development of the productive arts and the simplicity of manners and morals of the survivors of the flood, is pure fiction; and the city of fevered heat, in which the arts of consumption are as highly developed as the arts of production, becomes the condition for the possibility of philosophy and the rule of the philosopher-king. Corruption, then, is the indispensable condition for either laws or wisdom. Neither could want to wipe out the conditions for its own coming-to-be. Neither can recover innocence without condemning itself to a gradual or sudden extinction. The symposium in speech, whose principle was disorder in order, now seems to be the paradigm of a historical becoming over which no symposiarch presides. How any surgery could proceed to cut out the unnecessary and unsound elements of corruption and keep the sound seems to lie beyond even the imagination. The conditions for becoming perfect in virtue are equally the conditions for becoming perfect in vice (678b1–3). The Stranger will soon say that no human being ever legislates anything (709a1–2).

Clinias agrees that any serious discovery in the arts and wisdom was virtually yesterday, but he gives a strange list of examples as proof: Daedalus, Orpheus, Palamedes, Marsyas and Olympus, and Amphion. With the exception of Palamedes, all the others were innovators in the imitative arts, and four of these five were involved in music. Of the musicians, three met violent ends, Orpheus, Marsyas, and Amphion. The Greeks at

Troy condemned Palamedes unjustly to death, and Daedalus threw his
nephew Talos down from the walls of the Athenian acropolis. The criminal grows alongside the inventive: Amphion punished Dirce by arranging
for a bull to drag her alive over rocks until she was torn to pieces. What
became manifest (φανερά) to these inventors was for thousands and thousands of years utterly invisible (διελάνθανεν) to the survivors of the flood
and their descendants. Clinias acknowledges the difference between the
thousand years or two of Greek memory and the time when the Stranger
must suppose the flood to have occurred, but he seems to miss the Stranger's suggestion of the constant innovation that political life fostered. He
is silent about Zethos, who argued with his brother Amphion for the
superiority of the "music of politics" (Gorgias 486c5). It would seem that
the Stranger has been almost too successful in turning Clinias away from
war and the city. The Stranger, at any rate, calls our attention to Clinias's
failure to grasp the city as the locus of innovation, and to the far greater
concern in his account with the anonymous rediscoverers of metallurgy
than with the darlings of the Muses. He praises Clinias's modesty for
failing to cite Epimenides, who was literally yesterday and perfected, according to the Cretans, the art of medicine that Hesiod had merely divined. The Stranger brings Clinias up to date and obliquely chides him
for believing that a Cretan had finished off pharmacology a century ago.

The virtually complete loss of memory of city, regime, and legislation
that followed the flood ensures that its survivors did not come to restore
them on the basis of any half-remembered models (678a3–5). Whatever
happened subsequently—cities and regimes, arts and laws—developed on
its own. If in the prepolitical era there were the good and the bad, they
still were not perfectly good or bad. They were inexperienced in the many
beautiful and ugly things that are prevalent in cities. Man's inhumanity
to man is strictly a political phenomenon. By his deliberate silence about
the cannibalism of Polyphemus and the incest entailed by the Cyclopean
way of life, to which he appeals in order to illustrate what everyone calls
"dynasty" (680b1–2), the Stranger would seem to imply that bestiality in
any form is a concomitant of political life and does not belong to a more
primitive stage. Since, however, the laws or customs prohibiting incest
and cannibalism are more likely to precede written laws than be first
enacted in a code, the Stranger leaves it unclear to what point of his
scheme these laws belong. Are they remnants of the preflood era that the
mountainmen preserve intact? If we say that these two prohibitions belong to a larger class of lawful prohibitions, all of which reflect an awareness on the part of all men that man is not man unless he does not do
everything of which he is capable, then the Stranger has chosen to replace

the possibly slow humanization of man, which is only negatively determined, by an original terror that made man gentle and friendly at the start of each postcataclysmic event. The Stranger would thus have separated the humanization of man from his politicization or civilization to the extent that the former might be ascribed to the law, and instead put together the politicization of man with the cultivation of mind. Those who lived the Cyclopean way of life were more moderate, more just, and braver than those who lived either before or after (679e2–3), but they were not wiser. It was therefore impossible for the ancestral laws to have translated correctly the eidetic structure of the good, in which good sense heads the virtues of soul and mind guides the eightfold structure of good. Law, then, in the strict sense is bound more closely to mind than it otherwise would have been had the Stranger acknowledged the way in which ancestral law divines the nature of man and anticipates the primacy of mind.

Terror kept the herdsmen from descending into the plains, and the mountains isolated them from each other. Their fewness made them glad to see one another, and the abundance of pasturage guaranteed that no stranger posed a threat. They were not vegetarians; they killed the cattle they raised, and hunting supplemented their diet. The Stranger goes out of his way, before he cites Homer on the Cyclopes, to assure us that he is not describing the Cyclopes. Polyphemus neither hunted nor killed his own sheep and lambs, and he was hardly glad to see the stray visitor. By depriving his people of any means of transport, either by land or sea, the Stranger calls our attention, in terms of his temporal account, to Homer's juxtaposition of one past with another, as if it were possible for a Polyphemus, who knows all about ships and piracy, to be as innocent as he must be for the story. Odysseus lies to his face and presumably gets away with it, though one must immediately add that Polyphemus's silent response to Odysseus's lie is to eat two of his companions. The further failure of the Cyclopes to see through Odysseus's adopted name, "No one," involves the confrontation of an earlier way of life with mind. Through the unsuspected pun on "No one" and mind (οὔ τις and μῆτις [μή τις]), Odysseus can lie concealed in the cave from the Cyclopes and ultimately escape from Polyphemus, whose name means "Of many voices." By stripping Homer's story of everything but the account of the Cyclopes, the Stranger seems to imply that Homer's fiction primarily consists in letting the triumph of mind appear contemporaneously with a simple way of life that had to have vanished before mind could have won so overwhelming a victory. Mind, the Stranger says, looks back to the time of the isolated family and mistakes it for the savagery of cannibalism. It refuses to see in its own lying and stealing anything reprehensible and charges innocence with bestiality. The anonymity of mind, which is rootless and without a past, cannot comprehend its own origin in time.

The Stranger's reinterpretation of Homer continues and expands the problem that the difference between the eidetic structure of the good and the genetic structure of law first raised. At the head of the eidetic structure of the good was precisely mind in its anonymity, for there was no being in which the eightfold structure of good inhered. The story of the Cyclops, in the Stranger's allusion to it, represents the difficulty in the translation of the eidetic structure of the good into the genetic structure of law not as a problem of attaching an atemporal nonbeing to the temporal becoming of man but as a problem of connecting the temporal becoming of mind with the becoming of the virtues apart from mind. The virtues of justice and moderation were the principal aim of the law, but these virtues, along with courage, belong to a time frame that does not admit the presence of mind. The law aims at an innocence that individual experience undercuts and historical time has already disposed of. The law preserves in its name a trace of the conditions without which it cannot succeed but during which it cannot exist.[6] By setting the law forward into a time when writing has already been invented, the Stranger arms it with mind and strips it of power. In order for the Stranger to get out of this paradox that he himself has devised, the virtues of the Cyclopean age must alter. The virtues cannot have mind in charge of them unless they have been infected by mind. The Stranger had already hinted at this when, in the eidetic structure of the good, he had made moderation second if it were with mind, and mixed justice with good sense and moderation. The experiential deviation from the law has its counterweight in the tardy revision of virtue by mind.

The Stranger had gained Clinias's acceptance of his proposal that the judge-legislator, who was not to kill anyone in a family at odds with itself, had to establish friendliness (φιλοφροσύνη) among brothers most of whom were unjust. He now argues that in Cyclopean times there was no civil strife, for those then were friendly with one another (ἐφιλοφρονοῦντο ἀλλήλους, 678e9). Isolation was as effective as legislation is supposed to be; but it is now shown that legislation was assigned the task of recovering friendliness among people who had forgotten the original terror and lived together with all the consequences of envy, rivalry, and ambition.

---

6. This is the hidden link in the *Statesman* between the shepherd as the paradigm for the statesman in the first part and law in its defectiveness in the second part.

The unequal distribution of wealth in the city, which goes along with an ineradicable scarcity, entails that the law must overcome the results of conditions without overcoming the conditions themselves. The Stranger will later set aside Socrates' solution of communism as simply impossible except for gods and the sons of gods (739b8–e5). If the law were capable of convincing everyone of the true ranking of goods, then perhaps it would not need any supplementary force to bring about a semblance of a forgotten past; but if that possibility is as remote as Socrates' communism, then the law would apparently have to devise a kind of terror that differs from the threat of cataclysm. The criminal law seems not to suffice for this purpose, although the Stranger admits that it is indispensable if they are not legislating for the sons of gods (853c3–7). He has already alluded to a divine fear as the most beautiful terror (671d1–2), and the theology of the tenth book seems to supply what is missing from the criminal law itself. Whether that theology, as it backs up the criminal law, upholds the eidetic structure of the good is another question.

The men of Cyclopean times were neither criminal nor artless. A god supplied them with the two arts of weaving and pottery for just such an unprovisioned life (679a6–b2). There was no Prometheus among them who had to steal fire from the gods and give them, instead of foreknowledge of their own death, blind hopes.[7] The Stranger denies that there had ever been a time when fire was unknown and the eating of meat involved a sense that as a prohibition has been broken that had to be broken, so sacrifice had to make up for its necessary transgression. The gods of civilized man were then still known to men in however an unsophisticated form. The Stranger is far less radical than the poets. "They were good," he says, "for whatever they heard was beautiful and ugly, they believed (ἡγοῦντο) in their naivete to be said most truly and were persuaded. No one knew (ἠπίστατο) how to suspect a falsehood on account of wisdom, as they now do, but in holding (νομίζοντες) the things said about gods and men as true they lived in conformity with them" (679c2–7).[8] The Stranger distinguishes between their lawful beliefs about gods and men and their convictions about the beautiful and ugly. His distinction recalls the difference between the genetic structure of law and the eidetic structure of the good. The primitive version of that difference was to interpret the

---

7. Cf. Aeschylus *Prometheus Bound* 247–254.

8. The difference in the phrasing—ἃ ἤκουον . . . ἡγοῦντο ἀληθέστατα λέγεσθαι and τὰ λεγόμενα ἀληθῆ νομίζοντες—means, I think, that they were aware in the former case that they heard the precepts they obeyed but were not aware in the latter that "the things spoken of" were possibly not the same as the beings.

difference between the divine and the human goods as the difference between gods and men. A disjunction between two kinds of beings was the original form of the Stranger's disjunction, which, though it had dispensed with any beings, had assigned being to the goods. They lived then in accordance with the difference between gods and men, and were obedient out of conviction to the difference between the beautiful and the base. The latter characterization seems to allude to the lawful ways that prevailed at that time. The absence of the conditions that would have encouraged injustice and insolence reduced the twofold character of the law in the genetic structure of law—the beautiful and the just—to the single element of the beautiful. The Stranger implies that men then had the noblest character (γενναιότατα ἤθη, 679b8). They lacked the wisdom to suspect falsehood in the differentiation of gods and men, and they lacked the experience that would have made them diverge from the law. The difference between knowledge and experience that now holds in cities is the foil to the difference between the ignorance and the innocence that then made Cyclopean man both law-abiding and incapable of discerning in the law the eightfold structure of good. Without gold and silver they could not know that wealth too was a good.

Clinias and Megillus react differently to the Stranger's citation of four lines from Homer (680c1–d3). Clinias finds him charming (χαρίεις), and some other parts of his poetry refined and civilized (ἀστεῖα), but he admits that like the rest of the Cretans, who do not indulge in the poetry of strangers, he does not know much of it. Perhaps, then, Clinias does not know how the Stranger has altered the meaning of Homer's verses by taking them out of context. Megillus, on the other hand, is familiar with Homer; he believes he surpasses all foreign poets, though his account is rather of an Ionian than a Laconian way of life. Homer is softer than Tyrtaeus; he does not celebrate courage or even patriotism as the only virtue. Megillus must know that truth-telling is not a conspicuous trait of Odysseus. He also seems to be aware of what the Stranger had to do to Homer in order to get him to bear witness to his logos. It was through mythology, he says, that Homer imputed wildness and cruelty (ἀγριότης) to what was old (τὸ ἀρχαῖον) in the life the Stranger described. Savagery is the mythological equivalent of isolation. It is impossible to say whether Megillus means that cannibalism expresses poetically paternal rule, in which the father swallows the sons and tries to cancel generational succession, or merely that the poet makes an image of the absence of community in the eating of strangers (cf. 953d8–e4). If Megillus hints at the second possibility, he would imply that the sociality of the city goes along with a certain openness to strangers. That was amply proved in his own case. For us, however, it is hard not to think of the Spartan practice of the expulsion of strangers (ξενηλασία), and the Stranger's rebuke of the Spartan and Cretan way of life, which he said was closer to that of an army camp than of those who are settled in towns (ἄστη).[9] The Spartans and Cretans did not individually rub down and tame (ψήχων τε καὶ ἡμερῶν) their savage and vexatious young (ἀγριαίνοντα καὶ ἀγανακτοῦντα), but kept them grazing in a herd (ἐν ἀγέλῃ νεμομένους φορβάδας, 666d11–e7).[10] Is Megillus, then, acknowledging the implication of the Stranger's story, that bestiality is a political phenomenon and not to be ascribed to prepolitical life (cf. 766a1–4)? In any case, the Spartans' admission of foreign poetry seems to make up in part for their occasional exclusiveness. Homer is the way into Spartan history.

If one reflects on Clinias's ascription of charm to Homer, and Megillus's acknowledgment that mythology bears witness to logos, it seems that the two interlocutors have split between them two of the three criteria the Stranger laid down for the judgment of the imitative arts. The Stranger will soon say of the verses he cited about the Cyclopes as of those he then quotes from the *Iliad* that they "have been spoken somehow according to god and according to nature," for Homer like the rest of the poetic genus "touches on, with the help of the Graces and Muses, many things that come into being according to truth" (682a1–5). Homer seems to be on a par with learning (μάθησις), for which, the Stranger had said, if charm goes along with it, truth completes its rightness and benefit (667c5–7). The benefit of Homer lies in his confirming the Stranger's story and connecting a hypothetical beginning—the flood—with the Dorian invasion. Homer seems to negotiate between the Stranger's apparently arbitrary choice of a widespread disaster and the Spartan past with which Megillus is familiar. This fortunate collapse of the hypothetical into the real seems to be behind the Stranger's praise of Homer's verses as spoken in accordance with god. It is a kind of miracle that Homer should supply the three stages the Stranger needs in order to proceed from them to what might have happened in the aftermath of the Trojan War. What is in accordance with the nature of things fits providentially the intention of the Stranger to return to where he digressed into music and drunkenness. He

9. The ambiguous status of Sparta is indicated by the Stranger at 683a7–8, where he first calls the Dorian settlement of the Peloponnesus their fourth city, but then allows it to be called a tribe (ἔθνος).

10. Ἀγέλη alludes to the Spartan and Cretan name (ἀγέλα) for the bands in which boys were trained.

says that they have come back to the same issues "as if in accordance with god" (682e10). Mythology, as the image of things, gets rearranged in such a way that it proves to be what happened in truth and conforms with the intention of the Stranger. This coincidence of truth and intention recalls the Stranger's interpretation of the rightness of an image in light of the rightness of its intention. The Stranger, in placing his own intention as the fulfillment of Homeric truth, reveals that the forward movement from cataclysm to Dorian invasion has been in fact a backward reconstruction of the conditions that must have determined the beginnings of Sparta. Just as the flood puts the Cyclopes in time, so the settlement of Troy in the plain confirms the "uncanny forgetfulness" of the flood, since many streams, according to Homer, flowed down on the city from the heights above. The poet puts us in medias res, the Stranger accounts for the antecedents.

The Stranger did not have to cite Homer on the Cyclopes, but he did need him for Dardania and Troy if he were going to come back to Dorian institutions. A reflection that began on the late development of mind figured out a beginning that could pull Homeric mythology into its own hypothesis; by a second miracle a further reflection on the consequences of the hypothesis picked up along the way two lines from Homer that brought the argument into real time, and then by a third miracle the point the Stranger reached in real time matched the point at the start of his digression. It is as if mind, at the head of the eidetic structure of the good, made itself the principle of the genetic structure of law, not, however, on the level of the law's abstract schema, but in terms of the particular circumstances that led Sparta to retain only one part of the virtue of soul. The linkup between the eidetic structure of the good and the genetic structure of law occurs through the virtue that Clinias and Megillus had extolled and the Stranger demoted. It thus brings the discussion back to its very beginning, where Clinias, through his experience of the law, had discerned that the truth of things was war. This truth, the Stranger will soon demonstrate, is the truth of Spartan history (686a7–b2). The experience of Clinias the Cretan makes him mistaken about the truth of things and not mistaken about Sparta. This too is a kind of miracle. As the fourth miracle that punctuates the third book, one is led to ask whether Plato is suggesting through the charm of his mythology the possibility that a charm of this kind could belong to the nature of things. Is his imitation of things an imitation of a grace in the being of becoming? The order in disorder, which was the principle of the symposium in speech, would thus have a counterpart in cosmology. This is a suggestion that emerges from the way in which the Stranger has gone from music to gymnastic; but it could just as easily be ascribed to what was false in his poetry.

The Stranger traces the beginning of legislation in the following way. After the Cyclopean era there came to be the tribe or flock (ἀγέλη), as if of birds, in which the eldest ruled, since they took the rule of the father and the mother in the isolated family as their model. Subsequently, they made larger communities and farmed on the foothills of their mountain dwellings. They built walls to protect themselves from beasts and thus, without intending to do so, made a single, large, and common household (680d7–681a3). Then, however, differences among the households became conspicuous, for the peculiar traits of the elders were imprinted on their descendants, since their previous isolation over many generations ensured the persistence of their own inclinations. The more orderly descended from the more orderly, the more manly from the more manly, and they severally had their own ways in regard to the gods and themselves. It is unclear whether the Stranger means that as the manlier households had more warlike, so the more orderly had more pacific gods. In any case, once the households had come together, each with its own laws, which they severally preferred to those of the others, it was necessary for them to choose public officials (κοινοί), who would look at the customs of everyone, pick those they most liked, show them to the leaders of the various peoples, and give them the opportunity to choose from among them. These public officials were legislators, but they were not the rulers. They set up the rulers from the quasi-kings of the tribes, and only ruled during the transition to either an aristocracy or monarchy.

The very sequence the Stranger has set up does not allow him to merge the legislator with the ruler, for the rulers have a power that antedates the common laws, and the common laws are not designed to establish a principle of rule but to make an amalgam of the laws that each tribe has. Since there is no other principle of rule except the paternal, on which the rule of the eldest is based, there cannot be a claim to superiority by any of the rulers. The Stranger thus somewhat artificially postpones conflict and war to the third phase that Troy represents. All the species of regimes and political events converged on that era. If the Stranger means that political life as we know it was essentially complete at the time of the Trojan War, there must have been many rapid changes after the second phase that Dardania typifies. War must have become common, and, if one can infer anything from the context from which the Stranger quotes Homer, civil strife as well. The two lines are from a speech of Aeneas to Achilles; Achilles had asked him, "Does your heart

urge you to fight me in the expectation that you will rule over the Trojans? Not even if you kill me, will Priam for that reason place the office
in your hands. He has sons, and he himself is sound and not witless"
(*Iliad* XX.179–183; cf. XIII.458–461). The earliest legislation, then, lagged
far behind the political. However crudely, it reflected, in distinguishing
between gods and men, the eidetic structure of the good, and, in dividing
the noble from the base, the genetic structure of law; but it did not yet
handle the competing claims to rule within the city. It aimed at uniformity and had no way of founding difference (cf. 684a3–4, b7). The legislators established the rulers; they did not make that act of establishment
part of the law they proposed. The quarrel between ancestral and natural
right, with which the *Iliad* begins, was not yet a problem for the law.

2   THE DORIANS

The return to where the Stranger digressed is not a complete return.
Whereas in the eidetic structure of the good, laws would, if rightly formulated, make men happy, now the issue is what changes in the law would
make a city happy (683b3–4). Whether it is as reasonable to call a city
happy as it is to call it good had not been answered satisfactorily by Socrates, when in the *Republic* Adimantus had objected that the soldiers
were wretched though just—Socrates had thus inadvertently confirmed
through his city in speech the opinion he was urged to refute—and Socrates had replied that he was out to make the city as a whole happy and
not just a part (419a1–421c7). The happiness of a city, in any case, might
radically differ from that of a citizen, for freedom and greatness or empire
seem to make up the two elements in a city's happiness (cf. 742d2–d7;
962e4–6), and whoever of the citizens partake of them would either destroy the city or live an illusory happiness.[11] The third book will end
with Persia and Athens representing as great a split between empire and
freedom as possible; but the Stranger will argue that these two political

---

11. In Aeschylus's *Persians,* the ghost of Darius advises the Chorus to enjoy each
day as it comes, but they sing instead of Darius's conquests, which they link with
their own former happiness: ἦ μεγάλας ἀγαθᾶς τε πολισσονόμου βιοτᾶς ἐπεκύρσαμεν
(840–842, 852–853). Socrates never ascribes either justice or happiness to his best city
in speech or its citizens when he summarizes its structure and excellences at the beginning of the *Timaeus*; Critias follows suit insofar as he grants old Athens justice
but not happiness, which he reserves instead for the kings of imperial Atlantis (*Critias* 112e3; 121a8–b7); consider *Republic* 373d4–10 in light of *Critias* 110e3–6. Critias
is likewise silent about the moderation of old Athens; compare *Critias* 110d1–2 with
Timaeus 18b3–5.

principles can never be balanced except providentially. The city in itself is self-defeating. The laws, one can say, are meant to check this self-defeat of the city from infecting its citizens. We already know from Clinias what happens when the laws do not exert such a check.

Immediately after the Stranger mentions that the inhabitants of the three kingdoms the Dorians established in the Peloponnesus swore they would aid the kings if anyone tried to destroy any of the monarchies, the Stranger himself swears by Zeus (683d10–e3). He swears in the midst of a question of how a monarchy or any rule is destroyed; and he answers that they have encountered a little before an argument that established that no rule is ever destroyed except by itself. Megillus has not forgotten the argument, and the Stranger wants it to be confirmed more by the truth of what happened in deeds than it ever could by an argument that was possibly empty and vain (683e7–684a1). Now the Dorian oath implied that those who promised to uphold it would never alter of themselves, and if they did the gods would punish them. Oaths anticipate the preservation of a self-identity over time that no circumstances can ever affect. The allusion, then, the Stranger makes to speeches they met with a little while ago (ὀλίγον ἔμπροσθεν) is partly to the very oaths sworn by the Dorian conquerors of the Peloponnesus.[12] They obliged themselves to be constant regardless of necessity. Everything was subject to their will (cf. 687c1–8). Their oath, however, proved to be ineffective. They must, then, have been punished. If the Stranger is suggesting that he will find real evidence for this aspect of the premise of oath-taking, he seems to recall at the same time the original argument of Clinias,[13] who was willing to defend the view that the concept of self-defeat was entirely unproblematic. He had made his view more plausible by finding its best confirmation in cities, in which the victory of the better over the worse or the demos (τὸ πλῆθος) was rightly called a victory of the city over itself (627a5–10). The Stranger now implies that they will not have an empty dispute about the self-contradictory language of Clinias, but they will encounter facts that give some coherent version of Clinias's view. We are now really back at the beginning. It seems, then, that the Stranger must

---

12. I know of no other passage in Plato where ὀλίγον ἔμπροσθεν alludes to something just said, but a similar phrase occurs in Herodotus, τοῦ περ ὀλίγῳ πρότερον τούτων μνήμην ἐποιεύμην (4.16.1), whose reference is four lines back; cf. 4.79.2, which goes back six lines; and Plato has phrases like οἱ ἔμπροσθεν ῥηθέντες νυνδή with a reference no more than six lines back (717b2).

13. This is the suggestion, according to England (361 note 1), of F. H. Dale. The apparently superfluous τὸν αὐτὸν λόγον at 684a1, which Badham wished to delete, is appropriate if it refers to the logos of Clinias.

develop an argument that, in making sense of self-identity, does not fall into the paradox of Clinias and, in assigning some responsibility to the will, show the workings of some kind of rational theodicy. The Stranger's own oath certainly suggests that he has something of the kind in mind.

The first Dorian kings swore they would not make their rule more violent as time went on and the royal family would abide by what they had sworn to. The three peoples of the three kingdoms swore, in turn, if the rulers lived up to their oaths, they would not try on their own to overturn the monarchy or ally themselves with others who might attempt to do so (684a2–b2; cf. *Critias* 120a7–b2, c6–d3). The kings were surely improvident not to anticipate the possibility that their original circumstances might not last. Would not the same degree of force appear to the people excessive if their conditions were to improve? The Stranger alludes to this difficulty when he compares the peoples' demand that they be allowed to accept the laws voluntarily with the implausible injunction of patients to their doctors and trainers that they submit with pleasure to the treatment and cure of their bodies, for he adds in the latter case that one often must be satisfied if health can be restored without great pain (684c1–10; cf. 720a4–6). The Stranger does not say whether the kings had the ability to teach or persuade the peoples of this limitation on their volition. The division of the conquered area into three had the advantage that two cities could always combine against the third if it were unjust; but the Stranger does not add that no provision could have been made against an unjust alliance of two against one. Unanimity of king and people in any one city poses a threat to another city in which king and people are divided. The Stranger's way of formulating the oath leaves it unclear whether it was contemplated that there could be an association between a king and his people stronger than the presumed solidarity of one people with another or one king with another. The three cities seemed to have no structure apart from the common laws and a lawful king. Equality in the distribution of land and the absence of old debts made it easier to establish laws, so that initially there were no cries of outrage—"The immovable rights of property are sacrosanct!"—but the Stranger again does not make it clear whether equal and unencumbered lots were guaranteed for the future despite the inevitable fluctuations in fortune of individuals. What was missing from the oath was an articulation of what exactly would constitute an injustice against either king or people. In short, even on paper, the three kingdoms had not foreseen even the most obvious of contingencies; and it can only cause surprise that Megillus is puzzled as to what went wrong and what the Stranger could possibly believe was at fault in the original arrangements (685a1–5).

Megillus finds the Stranger's question difficult. Easy or not, the Stranger replies, they have to consider and examine it, for otherwise their original determination to go through their journey painlessly, "by playing an old man's sober game about laws," would have to be given up. It is certainly not obvious why the failure of Dorian institutions was an indispensable issue for either journeying easily or disporting themselves soberly. The exposure through Clinias of the failure of Dorian laws was, one would have thought, sufficient; that the same kind of exposure has to be done for the political setting of those laws seems superfluous. The fairy tale the Stranger makes up about Sparta is no doubt as playful as the symposium in speech, but in what way is it sobering? What is gained in getting at Megillus after putting Clinias in his place? If one analogizes their journey to gymnastic and their discussion to music, in which they succeeded in separating these two arts from one another, it would seem that the exercise of their wits on something as real as Spartan history would contribute to the recombination of body and soul. Such a recombination is necessary if there is to be an account of the genetic structure of law; but the fancifulness of the Stranger's history precludes the very possibility of their recombination. One would have imagined that the perfect choral dance would be that in which the virtues of soul come to be in time, and then the city with its laws would develop into an appropriate setting for the protection and fostering of those virtues; but such a harmony between soul and city lay shattered as soon as the Stranger chose to make a mockery of the real rather than project an ideal story. The story he prefers has an ending in failure that suddenly turns around into a complete success not despite but because it was a failure. A tragic conclusion is the happiest of events. Megillus is asked to applaud the ringing down of the curtain on utter ruin. The tragedy and comedy of life dissolves into something new and strange.

The extravagance of the Stranger knows no end. He now claims that the three Dorian cities were designed not only for their own mutual protection but also for the protection of all the Greeks, who feared the still formidable power of the Assyrian empire, of which Troy was a part and in trusting to which Troy had initiated the war (687a2–e5). The sons of Heracles, who had set up the three kingdoms, were thought to have arranged a force superior to the Trojan expedition, for just as the Heraclidae were better than the Pelopidae, so their army, which had defeated the Achaeans, proved the superiority of the Dorians. Megillus accepts without question an argument that the Stranger himself had checked him from using in the first book, when he had cited Spartan prowess on the battlefield as a proof of the superiority of their institutions to those of all barbarians (638a1–2). The Stranger sets Megillus up for the fall by piling on the human and divine supports the Dorians believed they had (685e6–686a6). He even goes so far as to assert that they would have been irresistible in war had their original intention (διάνοια) been realized in the unitary consonance of the triple alliance (686b2–4); but he gives the show away by effecting through "a slight zeugma," as England puts it, an identity between plan and deed—γενομένη γε ἡ τότε διάνοια καὶ συμφωνήσασα εἰς ἕν—as if all it took to be powerful was to imagine it.[14] The Stranger thus grants an ideality to the original Dorian arrangements not in order to have harsh reality wipe it out but to bring to light the utter spuriousness of its very ideality. We have been led along with Megillus into accepting the greatest evil for the real good of the city. Megillus believes that one could not look elsewhere than at laws and regimes that preserve or destroy beautiful and great things (686b8–c3).

Megillus's remark about beautiful things, which the Stranger soon echoes, connects Spartan history with the problem inherent in the genetic structure of law. The genetic structure of law was primarily concerned with the beautiful and the just; but the city, without which there cannot be law in the strict sense, rests on an irresolvable tension between empire and freedom, or between what makes it big and beautiful and what makes it just. "Do all we human beings," the Stranger asks, "just as we ourselves did just now, inadvertently suppose, whenever on any occasion we believe we see the occurrence of something beautiful, that it would have accomplished amazing things had only someone just known how to use it beautifully in some way or other, and now perhaps would we be thinking neither rightly nor naturally, no less than, in general, everyone else about everything else, whatever it is that they think of in just this way?" (686c6–d4). The error to which all human beings are prone, and for which the Stranger laughs at himself because he has just fallen for it, is to look at the collapse of a grand scheme and immediately imagine what would have been if knowledge had been properly employed. The contrafactual application of knowledge is not of knowledge of ends but of means, for the specious grandeur of the failure obliterates the real consequences of its imaginary success. In the case before them, the Dorian alliance, had it not dissipated almost at once, would have succeeded in maintaining its own freedom and the enslavement of everyone else, and they and their descendants would be doing forever among all human be-

---

14. England, 368: "The *plan* was that of a confederacy; and the *carrying out* of the plan involves the existence of the confederacy, and it is with this that, in sense, συμφωνήσασα agrees."

ings, Greeks no less than barbarians, whatever they should desire (687a2–b2). The Stranger uses the Dorian settlement, whose utopianism was shown by their oath, in order to come back to the position of Clinias, who had loosely put together the truth about all human things with victory in war. Victory in war can be squared with the premise of eternal warfare only if the victor ends up with a universal empire, in which its own freedom is first at the expense of everyone else's and finally at the expense of its own. Rome is the perfect illustration of this movement.[15] What alone can prevent so calamitous a success is incompetence, luck, or the knowledge of the eidetic structure of the good. The city, in developing from imperfect conditions, assumes a character that is independent of what must inform it if it is not lucky enough to be incapable of defeating its neighbors or subduing completely the people it conquers. Sparta had the Messenians as its sobering constraint (cf. Thucydides 4.80.2–3), Rome had Carthage until it wiped it out and precipitated its own loss of freedom. The eternal tyranny Clinias believed constituted happiness necessarily follows in the train of the Roman achievement. A happiness belongs to the fulfillment of the city's twin principles that necessarily makes its citizens' happiness precarious. The citizen must pray that the city not achieve what it sets out to obtain, but he is hardly in a position to counsel its defeat. The oath the Dorians swore and soon broke was subjectively punished and objectively rewarded. They were taught a lesson about the will that they were not in a position either to understand or appreciate. It was no doubt, as Aeschylus says of the divine law "by suffering understanding," a violent grace of the gods.

The necessarily late installment of the eidetic structure of the good raises this question: What prevents the city, prior to the coming to light of that structure, from abusing instrumental reason to doom itself while imagining it was accomplishing its manifest destiny? Is intelligence apart from good sense necessarily ineffective, and does it ultimately trip itself up before it can realize Clinias's eternal tyranny in an imperialistic form (cf. 687c5–7)? The Stranger started off the present era of political life with a cataclysm; it effectively buried all the advanced arts of the previous era and hence destroyed along with them the universal empire that might have been the culmination of a very long interval of technological progress (cf. 689c8–d1). The cataclysm now seems rather convenient, not to establish, as we were led to believe, a smooth transition from the Cyclo-

---

15. Cf. Tacitus *Agricola* 24.3 *saepe ex eo [Agricola] audivi legione una et modicis auxiliis debellari obtinerique Hiberniam posse; idque etiam adversus Britanniam profuturum, si Romana ubique arma et velut e conspectu libertas tolleretur.*

pes to Sparta, but to guarantee that what Megillus believes would have been wonderful had it happened did not happen, and, if disasters of the same kind belong to the nature of earthly things, could never happen. The imperfect beginnings of political life have as their background the imperfect conditions on earth that have to be pronounced to be good if without them an eternal nightmare is otherwise always in the offing. A cataclysm, however, unlike the failure of an imperial design, is not something that anyone could pray for. Is the point of the Stranger's comparison of our thoughtless wishes to Theseus's prayer to Poseidon that he destroy his wrongly suspected son Hippolytus (687d1–e4), that no citizen of Atlantis, however much he was endowed with good sense, could have prayed to Poseidon to make his country vanish beneath the waves before it set out to conquer the rest of the world? As he presents the comparison, the Stranger surely lets Megillus draw a more consoling conclusion, that the failure of the Dorians was tragic; but we as spectators are meant to rejoice purely in the tragedy as tragic, without the least trace of resentment, and not because the manner of its representation has enchanted us.

Now that the argument has come around to the eidetic structure of the good as the model in light of which the laws are to be laid down, the Stranger seems to be indifferent whether Clinias and Megillus regard him as being playful or serious. His indifference points to the difference between his playfulness, for which good sense must prescribe failure if the alternative is a ruinous success, and his seriousness, which only has to leave it at not praying for everything to turn out as one wants if one does not possess mind. Mind thus looks as if it has been put in charge of the city, but only in the limited sense that the legislator must try to instill good sense in the city and eradicate folly (688e5–8). Mind deputizes the laws to rule in its place, and the laws in turn bring in opinion, which the Stranger does not now characterize as being true (689a5–c3). He calls it the greatest folly whenever anyone does not love but hates anything opined to be beautiful and good and loves and embraces what is opined to be base and unjust. The Stranger does not demand that one love what is just. Yet the contrafactual imagination, when faced with the prospect of eternal empire, loved what seemed beautiful and good and embraced injustice. In going back to his former understanding of education as a process of bringing about a consonance between feelings and reason, the Stranger seems to ignore the resistance the nature of the city itself puts up to separating the unjust from the beautiful. In his second formulation, in which the Stranger labels the dissonance of pain and pleasure with rational opinion the ultimate and greatest dissonance, he explains that the feelings belong to the demos of the soul in just the way the demos and multitude belong to the city. This politicization of the soul assigns at first the locus of the city's desires to the people, but when the Stranger rephrases this, he says that he calls it folly whenever the soul sets itself in opposition to sciences, opinions, or logos. If, then, the soul without qualification is nothing but the feelings, the city must be the demos, and the blame that implicitly attaches to the people for the ruin of the Dorian alliance has to be extended to the city as a whole. The Stranger, moreover, is as incapable as Socrates was of making soul and city exactly parallel. He speaks of sciences, opinions, or logos as the natural rulers of the city, but he does not speak of laws as the city's natural rulers. Instead, he now speaks of the people disobeying the laws and their rulers and matches it with the presence of beautiful speeches in the soul that do no good; but he had started out by speaking of hatred of the beautiful and love of injustice as the decisive factors for gauging folly. The demos is outside the range of beautiful speeches, effective or not. Finally, if the demos is comparable to the feelings, it is all but admitted that the consonance at which education aims is never achieved politically, for that consonance was called complete virtue, and the demos can at best be on the way to a consonance that if realized would effectively make both the laws and the rulers vanish.

The slips and slides in the Stranger's argument, which leads to the conclusion that the rulers must partake of wisdom, and this wisdom is the most beautiful and greatest of consonances, leave it obscure what wisdom is supposed to do, and how it is related to law (689c6–e2). In this entire discussion the Stranger has been silent about mind. The Stranger lists seven claims to rule, of which the sixth, knowledge and good sense, was the first in the eidetic structure of the good. Its demotion, despite its having seemingly the greatest right, points directly to the role wisdom is to have in adjusting right to necessity. The seven claims to rule are these: (1) that of the father and mother, and in general of parents over offspring, which is everywhere a rightful claim; (2) what follows from the first, that of the nobles or wellborn (γενναῖοι) over the ignoble; (3) that of the elders over the younger, which goes along with the first two; (4) that of masters over slaves; (5) that of the stronger over the weaker; (6) that of the knower over the nonknower; (7) that of chance. Of these seven, the first and third showed up respectively in the Cyclopean way of life and its original extension; the second was a belief of the Dorians, who thought that as the descendants of Heracles they were better than the Achaean descendants of Pelops; the fourth was behind their subjection of the original inhabitants of the Peloponnesus; the fifth was embodied in their belief in their superiority in virtue because they had beaten the conquerors of Troy (685d6–e3); and the seventh was in the sheer dumb luck of Sparta to have twins born into the royal house (691d8–e1). What is conspicuously missing from the Stranger's history is knowledge and good sense. All the other claims are grounded in the development of political life since the cataclysm. They cannot be ignored, for good sense would cease to be sensible if it made the vain attempt to put itself in place of them. The weight that has to be attached to each one varies with the historical circumstances (cf. 711c8–e3; 744a8–c4). Obviously the Cyclopean right is the most powerful and least subject to another rule (cf. 754a9–c2), though the prohibition of incest, without which the city would lose its exogamic basis, shows how an adjustment already occurred between family and city prior to any interference by wisdom. The Stranger, then, has given a version of the past that illustrates the restrictions with which mind must deal even before it can dream of translating the eidetic structure of the good into the genetic structure of law. These claims always fall below the horizon of rational power. They are therefore easily overlooked by instrumental reason whenever it imagines what it could have accomplished had it only been in control of some glorious enterprise. The Stranger seems to suggest that these factors tend on their own, quite apart from the unforeseeable advent of cataclysms, to act as a brake on the realization of universal empire.

The six principles of rule, in diluting mind, dilute the operation of the good (cf. 712c8–d1). Right takes precedence over good. Divergence from the eidetic structure of the good is built into the necessarily circumstantial structure of ruler and ruled. This divergence is the political equivalent to the experiential divergence from law that tragedy and comedy represented; but it is not a divergence that can be overcome but at best harmonized with the intent of mind. The principles of this divergence are always in some kind of harmony insofar as they mutually limit the absolute claim that they severally put forward in their natural opposition to one another (690d3–5; cf. 714e6); but this kind of limitation leaves very little room for knowledge to make its own adjustments among them. It is misleading, then, for Clinias to single out might as a rule of necessity, for the rest too exert a compulsion on the structure of the laws. Knowledge alone is powerless to gain compliance, for it has to urge the nonknower to follow it, and the nonknower is by definition the demos of the feelings that cannot know that they do not know. Consequently, knowledge must form an alliance (cf. 645a4–b1). This alliance is with law, which Pindar had identified with force. The Stranger, in realigning law with the voluntary, does not deny that it may, in Pindar's words, "do violence to what is most just," for the most just would solely be in accordance with the dictates of knowledge (cf. 875c3–d2). Knowledge, however, must be content with being just one element among the claims of right, and acknowledge what the Argive and Messenian kings failed to do, that it is more than the whole if by way of wisdom it incorporates the measure of the mean (690e1–5). Law is the form in which knowledge will be present in the city, for law should be the prudent gentling of the imperious demands of every claim of right, including the right of knowledge (690d1–5).

Although the Stranger had ascribed to the demos of the soul the source of folly if it does not obey the laws and its rulers, he now has Clinias agree that in the case of Argos and Messene, it was their kings who went beyond due measure and in their seeming wisdom or folly destroyed everything (690d5–691a9). This contradiction, however, is only apparent, for the natural hierarchy in the soul undergoes a splitting effect in its political counterpart, where the seven claims to rule do not allow one to predict which of the six in any given situation will pass beyond the measure of the mean. Within the soul itself, the claim of the oldest to rule becomes in the theology of the tenth book the priority in becoming of soul to body, and the Pindaric claim of the natural superiority of force becomes the issue, into which the Stranger declined to enter at the beginning, whether the worse is ever stronger than the better (627b1–2). The relation between mind and soul in the soul is an unresolved perplexity in the Stranger's theology. There is, then, for the soul a simplification in the competing claims to rule; but in real time a complex tangle of claims occurs that necessarily obscures the natural structure of soul. For Sparta, there was over time an adjustment of the claim of birth, which a god arranged to be halved in power, to the sober power of twenty-eight elders, which the Stranger says occurred through a mixture of human nature and some divine power, and these two rules later received in turn the bridle of the ephors, who came close to being the equivalent of the seventh claim of chance (691d8–692a6). In the guise of the expression "human nature mixed with some divine power," the Stranger alludes to Lycurgus, who consulted Apollo at Delphi about legislation, and in referring to "the third savior," who moderated still further the Spartan regime, he alludes to Zeus, to whom the third libation at a symposium is poured. The Stranger could not have more beautifully encapsulated the way in which Dionysus has sponsored the setting for the examination of Cretan and Spartan laws. The symposium in speech, with its principle of order in disorder, becomes, in its translation into real time, the gradually acquired structure of Sparta, within which the random still acts as the ultimate source of stability. Sparta, however, does not just owe its stability to a regime where the second, third, and seventh claims to rule modify each other; its constant engagement in war with a subject population added a fourth constraint to the three that the regime itself had. In saying that Sparta was at war with Messene at the time of Mardonius's invasion of Greece (692d6–8; 698e2), the Stranger goes against the truth while confirming the insight of Clinias. The disparity that now comes to light, between the Spartan failure to establish lawful equivalents to the eidetic structure of the good, so that only the fourth of the virtues of soul is part of their law, and the Spartan success to ensure stability through a happy mix of the fruit of that virtue with a balance among three claims to rule, shows how the conditions, which ideally are to realize the eidetic structure of the good, compensate for the falling short of its realization. This disparity does not just show up in pederasty and the looseness of Spartan women, which the Stranger took as signs of the imbalance between Spartan resistance to pain and Spartan perviousness to pleasure, but in the exposure of Clinias as harboring the dreams of Polus and Callicles. The soul is out of control while the city in which that soul grew up is the model of self-restraint.

Sparta and Athens together managed to accomplish through war what the three cities of the Dorian alliance would have accomplished without war had someone been able to establish in Argos and Messene the same mixture of principles that Sparta came to enjoy in time (692b7–c7). Persia would never have attacked Greece had they not despised it; but the foresight that would have been required to do by knowledge what came to be providentially in Sparta seems not to be available, for one cannot say beforehand which claims to rule will at any given time be prominent. What one does know is that at no time will the sixth claim to rule ever have a clear field to translate the eidetic structure of the good into the genetic structure of law. This impossibility arises directly from the necessarily imperfect beginnings of political life, and makes it moot whether knowledge, were it to have its own way *per impossibile*, would be able to achieve stability.

3   PERSIA AND ATHENS

The Stranger concludes his account of the Dorians by saying that a city must be free, sensible (ἔμφρων), and friendly to itself, and this is what the legislator must look at in framing his legislation (693b4–5). He immediately adds that these three targets, which he now calls moderation, good sense (φρόνησις), and friendship, are the same. What startles one the most is the implicit identification of freedom and moderation, for moderation looks as if it is the contrary to greatness or empire, and what were at the start the twin principles of the city, which Megillus had endorsed, are now reduced to one. To be under constraint is to be free, for to be without constraints is to be the tyrant city of an empire, and to be an imperial city is to be itself subject to tyranny with the attendant loss of its own freedom. That moderation, in turn, is the same as good sense is perhaps too easy an identity; but their identification with friendliness is harder to make out. Friendliness had been the original goal of the judge-legislator, who was to reconcile the family at odds with itself; and it now seems to be the same as the voluntary submission of the ruled to the rulers.[16] Such friendliness had a natural basis only in the first claim to rule, for all the rest cause some degree of irritation, however unjustified: even the unlucky might be resentful of the winner of the lottery. The six obstacles to that consonance between feelings and reason, which was complete virtue, have now been shown to the would-be legislator, in the guise of the Stranger's mythological history, to be resistant to any a priori solution. It thus seems that the *Laws* should now come to an end, for without some fresh start in the real, nothing more can be said. Insofar as Clinias soon supplies that fresh start, the Stranger acknowledges that they are at a dead end; but Clinias does not come up with his proposal before the Stranger looks at the city from another angle.

The accidental coalition in Sparta of monarchy, oligarchy, and democracy, each in a watered-down version, seems to give the Stranger the opening he needs to take apart its two extremes and reexamine freedom and empire once more, as each is exemplified respectively in Persia and Athens. It is not obvious what the Stranger hopes to gain by going over the same ground in two cities rather than in one. The history is going to be just as mythical as it was before, and the elimination of the seven claims to rule, which made the mythology more palatable by laying out a template for the interpretation of the political history of any city, allows, it is true, for a clarity of principles but at the same time blocks the way to any useful application. It seems that we are given an eidetic structure of the city after we have been given its genetic structure. The fact that the Stranger first spoke of monarchy and democracy as the "two mothers, as it were," from which all other regimes have come to be will not deceive

---

16. In the *Republic*, the submission of the ruled to the rulers was moderation since those with knowledge—each member of the demos had entered the city with an art—had to acknowledge their inferiority to those whose education was solely based on opinion.

anyone into believing that a double genesis is being assigned to regimes; rather, they are the two principles of any city regardless of how a city has come to be constituted. This emerged plainly enough in the freedom and unlimited rule over others that the Stranger, along with Megillus, had imagined to have been the opportunity the Dorian alliance missed. The problem we have is twofold. First, what comes to light through the separation into species, each with its own embodiment in a barbarian and a Greek city, that was concealed in the contrafactual imagination of the Stranger and Megillus? And, second, what is the connection between the eidetic structure of the good and the genetic structure of law, on the one side, and, on the other, the genetic and eidetic structures of the city? Once the questions are put, a short answer immediately comes to mind. The eidetic analysis of the city brings out the connection between education, or the theme of the first two books of the *Laws*, and the origin of political life. This was missing in the genetic analysis, in which it was left as a puzzle how any reform of the defects in Dorian virtue would affect the admirable stability of Sparta. Education, in turn, was split at the end of the second book into gymnastic and music. Gymnastic and music turn out to be what determine the difference respectively between Persia and Athens, and gymnastic and music were the two arts upon which the separation within the eidetic structure of the good was based. In this way, the Stranger completes his account with everything in its place.

The history of Persia begins with a more principled mixture of monarchy, aristocracy, and democracy than that with which Sparta finished. They were free and masters of others, but they shared their freedom with the ruled and brought them into an equality with them; the soldiers were friends with their generals, and if anyone had good sense and was able to advise, Cyrus gave him license to speak and honored him. Persia exhibited a less class-structured regime than Sparta; rather, the aristocratic and democratic elements were distributed across the entire population without Cyrus having to dilute his rule in any way. Good sense was not restricted to a single group, and equality did not take the form of the lot. This sensible arrangement, however, could not last. Even when Darius restores Persian rule, he alters the way in which friendship is maintained. Equality is now tied in with the laying down of laws, and Darius, drawing the demos to himself by money and gifts, lawfully distributed the tribute, formerly paid to Cyrus alone, to all the Persians (695c10–d4; Herodotus 3.89.3). Darius silently drops the right of everyone to give advice. Wisdom is squeezed out as law comes in and the regime becomes more democratic.

Cyrus was constantly on campaign and left the education of his sons
to the women. As soon as education comes back as an issue, the family
and women return as well. It is the family of tragedy, with its incest
and fratricide, that shows up in Persia: Herodotus tells of Cambyses' marriage with his sister and murder of his brother (3.30–31), the Stranger
mentions only the latter (694b4). The Cyclopean way of life, with which
the Stranger had started his account, seemed to have entered intact the
larger communities of tribe and city; but now, in a barbarian setting, it
suffers from the imperial drive of Cyrus. The Stranger echoes the last
chapter of Herodotus's *Histories*, in which it is suggested to Cyrus that
the Persians abandon their small and harsh (τρηχέα) country and occupy
a territory more in accordance with their newfound grandeur, but Cyrus
rejects the proposal: "Soft men are wont to come from soft regions, for
the same soil does not grow (φύειν) wonderful fruit and men good at war"
(9.122.3). Herodotus adds that the Persians submitted to the judgment of
Cyrus and stayed where they were, for "they preferred to rule, dwelling
in an infertile country, than in sowing the plains be slaves to others."
The Stranger says that the Persians were shepherds, "offspring of a harsh
country" (τραχείας χώρας ἐκγόνων) that made them capable of staying
awake in the night and living out of doors; but once the household was
left to the women and eunuchs, a Median form of education took over
and corrupted them (cf. Xenophon *Cyropaedeia* 1.3.2–5). The initial failure, then, was the absence of gymnastic to take up the slack in the move
away from a nomadic way of life. This was something Sparta knew how
to keep artificially, since it was under the constant threat of the Helots'
rebellion (693b9–c4).

The corruption that necessarily follows in the train of imperial expansion shows up first in the imperial family. It takes power away from everyone else and within itself does what it wants. Domestic license feeds off
the lack of political moderation. The Spartan failure to instill moderation
on the same scale as they drilled in courage of a certain sort now looks
less serious, since moderation was built into its regime-structure and
made up for its absence in the soul. The Stranger had exposed its absence
in Clinias and lured Megillus into dreaming of its imperial equivalent;
but now the presence of immoderation in the imagination seems to allow
for the demotion of moderation from the high rank it held in the eidetic
structure of the good. It ceases to be praiseworthy in itself as it becomes
all the more indispensable for the rest of virtue. The principal reason for
its demotion is that moderation, on undergoing a translation from one of
four virtues in the eidetic structure of the good into one of two virtues
in the genetic structure of law, can no longer put forward a claim to rule

on its own. Moderation, when isolated (μεμονωμένη, 696d5), is nothing but law-abidingness. Moderation thus negotiates between the eightfold good and the duality of law and rule. So if Megillus had praised it, there would be no right to rule, and had he blamed it, he would have denied any limit to the various claims to rule. Moderation deserves an irrational silence (ἄλογος σιγή, 696e1). Its irrationality is due to its being the sound (φωνή) in the consonance (συμφωνία) between feelings and logos (cf. 696c8–10).

The Stranger managed to return to the goods through the accumulation of wealth in the expansion of Persian power, for wealth played no role in his account of Sparta (696a4–b1) and was the most conspicuous sign of the lack of moderation in Persia. Moderation, then, becomes the indispensable supplement of each set of goods, which the Stranger now divides in three: the goods of the soul, the goods of the body, and external goods (697b2–6). In restricting his own ranking to these three, while conceding to the actual legislator the assessment of everything after the three highest, the Stranger informs us of the placement of the seven claims to rule (696e3–697c2). Not one of those seven is to go higher than fourth, but which is to be the fourth and which the last is not up to the Stranger, Clinias, and Megillus to decide. They themselves are in some sense desirers of laws (νόμων ἐσμὲν καὶ αὐτοί πως ἐπιθυμηταί, 697a7), but they are not legislators. This beautiful solution, in which no longer any discrimination is made within each species of good, seems to put justice, as the mixture of every other virtue (631c7–8), at the top, so that its difference from justice as obedience to the law and the rulers is reduced to a minimum. The only hint that all is not well is the peculiarity that good sense shows up twice in the new ordering, once at the head of the virtues of soul and again among the seven claims to rule. Mind, it seems, has not yet found its place.[17]

To deprive the people of their freedom to an excessive degree, and to expand a despotic rule beyond what was appropriate, had the inevitable consequence in the Persian empire of creating mutual and pitiless hatred between former friends and reevaluating in deed the rank of wealth, so that everything else that was spoken of as honorable and beautiful became nonsense (697c5–698a3). This silent folly seems to be at the opposite pole from what occurred in Athens.[18] As the Stranger tells it, its ulti-

17. The expression ἔχειν νοῦν occurs at 701d9 of the city and as the equivalent of its being ἔμφρων and having φρόνησις (693b4, c3, e1). It is the Stranger's answer to Megillus's ἐχόντως νοῦν at 686e2.
18. If τὴν is retained at 698a9 (τὰ δὲ περὶ τὴν τῆς Ἀττικῆς αὖ πολιτείας), and not de-

mate corruption consisted in the universal pretense to wisdom that had
its origin in music (701a5–6). The Stranger thus sets up a nice symmetry
between the absence of gymnastic in Persia and the license of music in
Athens, so that they can point, by their extremism, to what would be the
fitting union of these two arts; but the evident absurdity of the causal
analysis in the case of Athens seems to be too high a price to pay for it.
That Athens should be the city in which simultaneously wisdom is the
highest good and everyone lays claim to it implies that the Stranger puts
together democratic freedom or utter lawlessness with the emergence in
a political setting of mind. Mind emerges out of total freedom from the
law. This too is folly, but of a very different sort from its Persian counterpart. Behind the opposition between despotism and freedom lies another
opposition between the lowest and the highest in the ranking of the eightfold good.

The Stranger works up an Athenian past, comparable in its soundness
to what he had done for Sparta and Persia. The fourfold gradation in
wealth, the reverence (αἰδώς) for the laws, to which the Athenians at the
time of Marathon and Salamis were enslaved, and the terror the Persians
inspired through the story of a dragnet they had cast over Eretria, from
which no one had escaped, combined to sustain a friendship among all
sections of the population. Shame becomes the Athenian trait; it bound
fast the coward, who was in the absolute majority among the Athenians—surely a sly poke at Dorian bravado—to defend the sanctuaries,
tombs, fatherland, relatives, and friends against the invader (698b4–
699d2). The Stranger now claims for Athens what had been in the first
book an image of either courage, once it had been extended to resist pleasure, or of courage and moderation together. Shame had been a lawful
dissolution of the evident difference between the virtues of courage and
moderation as they had been presented in the eidetic structure of the
good. The combination of fear and shame, or of two kinds of fear, that
made for Athenian moderation in the Persian wars helps to explain why,
in the genetic structure of law, the Stranger failed to ascribe explicitly to
courage the capacity to resist sudden changes in fortune.

At exactly this point, after he has heard Megillus's praise of his patriotic speech, and he himself has complimented Megillus, the Stranger

---

leted with England (whom des Places follows), and it refers back to διὰ τὴν σφόδρα
δουλείαν τε καὶ δεσποτείαν (698a6), then Athens and Persia are both characteristic of
pseudo-regimes, which equally display despotism and slavery but in different parts
(712e9–713a2): perfect freedom too is a form of despotism and slavery (cf. Gorgias
491e5–492a1).

pulls a switch and declares that the Athenian people were in the time of the ancient laws not slaves to laws simply, but they solely submitted voluntarily to laws of music (700a3–e7). The Stranger admits that he is only tracing the origin of lawlessness in Athens, and had it stayed within the theater it would scarcely have been terrible, but it spread, he says, from music until it had encompassed everything in the city. Even with this proviso, under which one would have to smuggle in the growth of the Athenian empire, the war with Sparta, and the effects of the plague, in order to get a somewhat more balanced picture of the causes of radical democracy in Athens, the Stranger's extravagance is hard to excuse and harder to defend.[19] It recalls nothing so much as the debate between Aeschylus and Euripides, with Dionysus as judge, that Aristophanes staged in the second half of the *Frogs.* Just as Dionysus went down to Hades in order to haul back Euripides to life, but had been led to see his error once he got there and heard what the squabble was really about between old-fashioned Aeschylus and new-fangled Euripides, so the Stranger, who went out of his way to bring Dionysus into Crete, seems to have second thoughts and pull back from the consequences of his musical innovation. Euripides makes it part of his defense that he gave speaking parts to everyone and thus acted democratically; he taught the people in the audience to chatter, think, see, understand, twist and turn, love to scheme, suspect evils, and be cunning in everything (*Frogs* 948–958).[20] Aeschylus recommends his *Seven against Thebes* and *Persians* for their equally didactic purpose of making the Athenians good fighters and eager to beat their opponents (1021–1027). He is particularly proud of never representing a woman in love (1044), just as if he had heard from the Stranger how the women ruined the Persian monarchy. The Stranger, in any case, deduces from the daring liberation of the demos from their betters in the theater their refusal to be enslaved to their rulers, their flight from the admonitions of their parents, their nonsubjection to the laws, and finally their scorn for oaths, pledges, and the gods (701b5–c2). At the very moment that most of the seven claims to rule vanish in Athens, the highest of the goods comes to the fore. The Stranger then pulls himself back and concedes that he has lost control of his speech, just as if it were a horse whose mouth were without a bit (ἀχάλινον στόμα). The same expression

19. Thucydides juxtaposes Pericles' praise of Athens at a public funeral with his own account of the plague, whose consequences were the increase in lawlessness, the belief that instant gratification was the sole good, and no fear of gods, whereas Pericles says nothing about the gods and asserts that Athens allows everyone to do as he likes without the disapproval of his neighbors (2.37.2; 53).

20. The phrase from "twist" to "scheme" is merely conjectural.

occurs in the *Frogs* (838): Euripides says it of Aeschylus.[21] The Stranger
goes on to say that he should not be carried violently along by the logos,
and thus fall, as the proverb has it, from an ass (ἀπό τινος ὄνου πεσεῖν), i.e.,
from a safe seat. This expression occurs in Aristophanes' *Clouds* (1273),
where Strepsiades, in berating his creditor, puns on the difference in seg-
mentation of ΑΠΟΝΟΥ, which can be taken as either ἀπ᾽ ὄνου (from an
ass) or ἀπὸ νοῦ (from mind).[22] Strepsiades' pun is in response to his creditor swearing by the gods, who, Strepsiades has learned from Socrates, are
not the Olympians but the Cloudesses and other cosmic beings. Mind,
then, returns to the argument in a funny way and leaves us completely
bewildered at what the Stranger's intention could be.

There seem to be several strands to the argument. One could begin
with the contrast between the wealth of the Persian royal family, which
allowed its members to do whatever they wanted, and democratic freedom that, in its musical form, allowed the Athenian demos to imagine
whatever it wanted. The earlier comparison of the demos to the feelings
would belong here. This consideration would imply that every regime
is a mixture of reality and imagination, and apart from the lowest good
everything else in the city belongs to the Cave: the Stranger had just spoken of money as being (οὐσία, 697 b6). One certainly has to be struck by
the fact that Athenian tragedy represents on the stage every conceivable
crime as occurring within royal houses. It pulls inside democracy its tyrannical and barbaric opposite. The ambiguity of the words "tyrant" and
"tyranny" in the language of tragedy is well-known. That the Stranger is
thinking especially of tragedy is indicated by two things. He traces the
corruption of the old laws to the mixture of musical species. One of these
was the mixture of dirges (θρῆνοι) with hymns, or songs for the dead with
prayers to the gods, and another was the mixture of paeans with dithy-
rambs, or songs in praise of Apollo with songs about the birth of Dionysus
(cf. 800c5–d5).[23] Both mixtures seem to be the models for the understanding of tragedy.[24] The Stranger, moreover, connects radical freedom with

21. The same phrase occurs in Euripides' *Bacchae* 387–388: ἀχαλίνων στομάτων
ἀνόμου τ᾽ ἀφροσύνας τὸ τέλος δυστυχία: The end result of an unbridled mouth and lawless folly is misfortune. The Chorus say this of Pentheus, who denies that Dionysus
is a god.

22. Aristophanic Scholia on this line, though neither those of R or V, refer to this
passage in the *Laws*, but they seemed to have read it with νοῦ and not ὄνου.

23. England (408) ingeniously suggests that "genesis of Dionysus" might possibly
mean a "Dionysiac product."

24. The third mixture of species the Stranger mentions, the imitation of songs
set to the flute by songs set to the lyre (700d7–8), seems to allude also to tragedy, for
Aristotle expressly says that the flute is not ethical but "orgiastic," has its capacity in

the common opinion that pleasure is the sole criterion of music. If pleasure is understood in this way, it would stand as far apart from its possible
consonance with the law as from the applicability of rightness (ὀρθότης)
to the judgment of the imitative arts, which required the notion of charm
as a supervenient pleasure on what is.

There are no doubt these threads in the discussion of music in Athens; but they do not suffice to answer the question why radical democracy as a political phenomenon is tied in so closely with the corruption
of music. The Stranger offers a clue just before he checks the wild career
of his logos. Next to the liberation from the judgment of the knowers,
there would come upon the Athenians, he says, "the freedom to refuse to
be enslaved to rulers, and following that freedom the freedom to flee the
slavery and admonition of father, mother, and elders, and when they are
near the end of the course, the freedom to seek to be disobedient to laws,
and at the finish not to be at all concerned with oaths, pledges, and gods,
exhibiting and imitating the ancient Titanic nature of legend, who on
their return to those regions lead a hard life and never cease from evils"
(701b5–c4). The vision of eternal punishment for Athens seems to
frighten the Stranger off and bring him back to his purpose in telling the
story of music. Apart from the ambiguity in the last clause—it could be
either the Titans or the Athenians who return to Tartarus—one is struck
by the expression "exhibit and imitate" (ἐπιδεικνῦσι καὶ μιμουμένοις), in
which both verbs apply no less well to the poets than to the audience (cf.
658b7). If, then, the utter lawlessness the Stranger describes fits either,
Athens represents, theatrically and in reality, the political counterpart to
the symposium in speech, in which the guests were allowed to get out of
control in order that the symposiarch might be the spectator of the ways
and natures of men. Without Athenian theatocracy there would be no
way to observe what is the nature of political life, or the way in which
the original Cyclopean way of life becomes Titanic once man enters the
city and becomes civilized. The barbarization of man lurks beneath the
surface of political man, not as an older stratum that comes to light in
the breakdown of the city but as that which lurks within political life
itself. What seemed to be, in the element of empire, the aberration of the
tyrannical family at its head, proves to be, in the element of freedom,

---

catharsis and not understanding, and makes speaking impossible (*Politics* 1341a17–
25); cf. Plutarch *De musica* 15: "The mixolydian mode is the mode of experience
(παθητική), suitable for tragedies. Aristoxenus says that Sappho first found the mixolydian mode, from whom the tragic poets learned. They took it, at any rate, and yoked it
with the Dorian, since the latter renders the magnificent and dignified, while the former renders the experiential, and tragedy has been a mixture through them."

the truth about the city itself. Our only access to this truth is through the poets, who could, in turn, have only shown it under democratic conditions and through the mixture of species. The Stranger thus has his account of gymnastic culminate in music. It is a music over which an unreformed Dionysus presides (cf. 700d5).[25] The counterpart, then, to a citizen proposing that his city fail in its imperial enterprise is an Athenian wishing that Athens exhibit everything he needs to understand political life. Athens embodies the experiential deviation from the law. It is the ultimate "justification" for the Stranger's failure to distinguish, in the pleasure-contest, between the exhibitor of tragedy and tragedy itself.

The Stranger ends by recalling the argument of the three books in reverse order: despotism and freedom, the Dorian settlement, the foothills of Dardanus and the settlement by the sea, the survivors of the cataclysm, the speeches about music and drunkenness, and whatever preceded them (701e1–702b3). All these items were designed to answer two questions: how would one best manage a city, and how would one best live one's own life privately. One can say that these two questions correspond respectively to the genetic structure of law and the eidetic structure of the good. Whether, however, their speeches have proved useful for this double purpose requires a test (ἔλεγχος). Clinias says he believes he knows what it is. He proposes that they make a city in speech. He thus reacts in somewhat the same way as Socrates had, who, when asked about the Stranger's second question, proposed in the *Republic* a city in speech that would answer the Stranger's first question. The implicit argument for Socrates' procedure was that if a good city could be founded, and its principle were discovered to be justice, one could conclude on the basis of the presumably perfect matchup between city and individual that justice in the individual would make for happiness. Clinias, however, starts with an awareness of the disparity between the happiness of the individual and the justice of the city, for that had been the point of greatest dispute between him and the Stranger. It is uncertain whether he is now willing to forego the dispute for the sake of the other purpose he wants the making of a city in speech to satisfy. He now informs the Stranger and Megillus that he was commissioned, along with nine others, to lay down laws for a new colony in Crete, and they were granted permission to choose either native or foreign laws. Clinias believes he might use their city in speech for the city to be founded. Clinias's two purposes

---

25. In the *Republic*, Socrates likens democracy to a supermarket of regimes (557d4–9), to which the founder of any regime, including his own, has to go, for only there would men of all sorts come to be (557c1–2).

make for an essentially unstable argument, for the particular end will interfere with the universal model that is to put the Stranger's speeches to the test. This kind of interference is characteristic of every Platonic dialogue, where the good as the interlocutor(s) conceive(s) of it does not square with the thrust of general arguments. Two gentlemen of Athens, who are the sons of famous fathers but otherwise undistinguished, want to know whether they are to teach their sons the art of hoplite-fighting, but when they consult Socrates, he turns it into the question, What is courage? This leads in that dialogue and similarly in every other dialogue to an experience of the argument that is not the argument in itself but the real argument. What is remarkable about the *Laws*, and perhaps unique to it, is that a character in the dialogue experiences the dialogue in such a way as to propose the embedding of his own experience of the dialogue within the dialogue.

Out of the argument of the action of the first three books of the *Laws*, the Stranger is to make another argument. A project in speech$_2$ comes to be out of the experience of a speech$_1$. It is to test the speech$_1$. The laws the Stranger devises are both conditioned and unconditioned. They are conditioned insofar as they must satisfy conditions over which he has no control, and they are unconditioned insofar as they cannot fit exactly the conditions Clinias has not foreseen or the Stranger has not asked about. The number 5,040, which the Stranger picks for its numerical properties, has nothing to do with the size of the population Magnesia will have. His laws thus duplicate within themselves the same mixture of particular and general that goes into the makeup of every other Platonic dialogue. The form, however, that this mixture takes in the laws of the *Laws* seems to preclude it from being a test of the argument of the first three books of the *Laws*. How can a universal logos be tested by laws that, in ceasing to be universal, still are not deeds? The Stranger remarked to Megillus, when he had suggested that the common mess and gymnastic exercises served equally for training in courage and moderation, that it is difficult in political matters for anything to hold alike in deed as in speech (636a2–5). He had then pointed to pederasty and the looseness of Spartan women as the consequences of the common mess. The deeds show up the mistakes in the law (cf. 683d8–684a1). If, then, a city in speech is to be supplied with laws, those laws cannot be tested before they are in fact established, and one can observe how they work over time: did they lead or not to the purpose for which they were designed, and did one law come to interfere with another (cf. 769d1–e2)?[26] Clinias's city in speech may

---

26. One may compare the challenge Socrates set his auditors at the beginning of

well supply a guide for the laws of Magnesia, but if the laws of Magnesia
are not the same as those of the *Laws*, they may not help the Stranger
out of his perplexity. Is he, then, to wait around for another generation or
two until Magnesia succumbs or not to the defects of Sparta, Persia, and
Athens (cf. 752b11–c5)? He would, moreover, have to know the lives of
its citizens inside and out if he were going to satisfy his second question.
It seems, then, that the *Laws* must contain within itself the evidence the
Stranger needs to put to the test his own argument. That evidence must
lie in the laws themselves. The laws of the *Laws* include within them the
temporal experience of the laws. It is right, I think, to call these laws
songs.

---

the *Timaeus:* they were to put in motion his best city in speech in such a way that it
would show off its distinctive features (19c2–8; 20b4–6). It was easy enough for Socrates to list how its warriors would behave toward its enemies in wartime (*Republic*
466e1–471c3), but it would be harder to resist the concession Glaucon exacted from
him that ruined the policy of the communized city (468b9–c9).

IV

LAW AND PRELUDE

1   People and Place

From that point in book 4, when the Stranger first proposes to start the legislation for Clinias's city, and Clinias wants there to be no further delay, to the actual start of the legislation in book 6, as much time has passed as the first two books occupied (712b1–3; 771a5). The preliminaries to the laws of an actual city are as extensive as is the prelude to law in general. The reason for this delay is not due to the amount of information Clinias must supply about the city, so that the Stranger may adjust his self-consistent scheme to the contingencies of the site, its history, and future settlers. All that is disposed of in the first few pages of book 4. The Stranger is perfectly aware that Clinias may find that the actual conditions do not coincide with all that his scheme requires (745e7–746d2; 747d1–e12). Indeed, the Stranger argues that his code with all its innovations could not be realized even approximately unless a tyrant were to be present with the legislator at the founding of the city, and he knows that Clinias finds tyranny too repugnant to step aside in favor of the sort of tyrant the Stranger specifies, even should he suppose that such a tyrant could be had for the asking, and that Clinias could resign his post and persuade his fellow commissioners to follow suit (711a5–7). The coincidence of philosopher and king was the minimal condition for Socrates' best city in speech to come down to earth from a pattern laid up in heaven, but the timely concurrence of a tyrant and a legislator does not increase the chances so greatly that the Stranger's concessions to the feasible make him any better off than Socrates was and hold out to Clinias any greater purchase on reality (739a1–e3; 807b3–c1). The lowering of the standard leaves the odds unchanged.

Even apart from this initial obstacle, which the Stranger apparently sets aside without explanation, there seems to be always something that puts off the beginning of the laws, despite Clinias's impatience to get started and the Stranger's own promises (718b5–c3; 723e5–8; 734e3–6; 768e2–3). The overriding reason for the constant postponements must be

due to Clinias's unawareness of the disparity between the eidetic structure of the good and the genetic structure of law, and of the way the sev-
enfold claim of right necessarily pulls on the eidetic structure, while the
experiential deviation from the law alters the genetic structure. The laws
cannot begin to be laid down before Clinias comes to realize what accom-
modations must be made if the Stranger's laws are to achieve a self-
consistency that seems to go against the grain of the very principles on
which the law depends and from which it cannot help but depart. It
seems, then, that the Stranger is not as intent on satisfying Clinias's demand for a paradigm for his laws as he is on putting together in a coherent
way all that his analysis has so far riven apart. Clinias's city is just the
most general particular the Stranger needs in order to hang his project on
necessity. Without it, he would have no occasion to distinguish between
conditions that belong to a place and its past and present and those that
inhere in the translation of mind and logos into law. The sacred associa-
tions (φήμη) of some topographical feature that may dictate the name of
Clinias's city are of a different order from the problem of putting into
experiential time an atemporal structure of good that no known being
comes even close to exemplifying (704a4–b1).

The Stranger often speaks of his exposition as a διέξοδος, or survey, in
which the necessity to go through the law one section at a time, so that
each section can fit between what preceded it and what is to come next,
requires that parts be treated apart from their being parts, and only when
the entire survey is done can they truly begin to become, on a second
pass, parts of a whole (768c8–d7; 820e2–6). This general difficulty of discourse seems to reflect the difficulty of "doing" eidetic and genetic structures together. Insofar as the successive items of discourse may be said to
imitate the genetic structure of law, they are incapable of simultaneously
fitting into the structure of parts that the manifold of the eightfold good
represents. The Stranger urges Clinias and Megillus to be on guard against
his violating the principle that he invoked in criticizing Cretan and Spartan law (705d3–706a4). Their laws looked to only a part of virtue, but his
laws are all to look to virtue as a whole and never to isolate a part from
the whole. It is surely not easy to figure out whether the Stranger has
maintained this principle throughout, and nowhere is the difficulty more
acute than in the very section in which he warns Clinias and Megillus to
be on their guard.

The conditions that hold for the site of Clinias's city—it is eighty
stades from the sea, has no close neighbors, needs hardly any imports,
and its terrain resembles the rest of Crete—satisfy the Stranger; but he is
distressed to learn that it has a good harbor (704b4–d2). In the rather

oblique argument that follows, the Stranger launches an assault on Athens, whose acquisition of a navy presumably led to the erosion of patriotic loyalty, and certainly promoted the rise of the demos, which supplied the manpower for the fleet. The Stranger's appeal to history seems to be as perverse as his earlier tracing of Athens' decline to musical innovations. The Stranger does not mention the empire. The worst possible conditions for the acquisition of virtue would be a city on the coast with a good harbor and in need of many imports (704d4–8). The Stranger could be describing Athens; but the description fits just as easily Socrates' "true city," which is probably on the coast and exports and imports on a large scale, for, as Socrates says, "it is pretty nearly impossible to found a city in a region where it will not be in need of imported goods" (Republic 370e5–7). The second-best regime of the Laws starts out with more favorable conditions than the best city in speech does; and even after the true city expands and subsequently shrinks, it keeps the artisans with which it began as citizens, and does not replace them, as the Stranger does, with metics, slaves, and foreigners. It might seem strange that the Stranger's city should have greater defenses against corruption than Socrates' city does, if one were not to consider that the Stranger's aim is ostensibly higher than Socrates'. Socrates wanted the core of the citizen body to have moderation and courage, and the education he proposed was not geared for either justice or wisdom. Justice was to follow from the structure of the city—each of the three classes was to mind its own business—and wisdom had to be added through a second course of education; but the Stranger starts out with the claim that partial virtue has no place in his legislation. In rejecting the conditions for Socrates' city, the Stranger also rejects the conditions for the possibility of a conversation about justice and the best city. Along with the less stringent demands of Socrates, the Peiraeus goes too. It is as if the Stranger were turning his back on both philosophy and the best regime. There is not going to be in his city any hotbed for revolutionary thought. The city needs him to get started, but it will never breed his like. Laws cannot be formulated that, as Megillus put it, could match through compulsion the spontaneous growths of Athenians as good as the Stranger (642c6–d1).

The Stranger had argued that cloistered virtue was particularly susceptible to the sudden intrusion of pleasure, against which it had built up no resistance, since it was without experience of its insidiousness; but now the Stranger wants the city to be closed to outside influences, which find their way most easily through a port, so that the ways of the people may be simple, straightforward, friendly, and immune to the desire for riches. The Stranger attributes a great deal to initial conditions and thereby denies to the legislator any special effort or skill on his part to counteract trends liable to overturn his laws. Friendliness had been initially the primary purpose of law, but now it seems to be built into the preconditions of the law, and all the legislator has to do is not work against the advantages he did nothing to create. The absence of ship timber in the territory of the city ensures that there is no native inducement to become a commercial or an imperial power. If they take to the sea, it can only be by the compulsory imitation of an enemy, who forces them to meet the threat of an invasion with a fleet of their own. It is precisely at this point, when Clinias does not understand what the Stranger means by the deleterious imitation of the enemy, that the Stranger declares that his laws will legislate only for virtue as a whole. The connection is obscure. The Stranger seems to be anticipating his later point, that no human being legislates anything, for the compulsion Persia put upon Athens to match them in naval power or perish made the greater democratization of Athens all but inevitable, if one does not accept the Stranger's preposterous suggestion that Athens should have preferred to surrender rather than rely on its navy, and Plataea, in completing the safety of Greece, would have been possible without Artemisium and Salamis. Minos, he remarks, could impose on Athens a harsh penalty, since Athens had no fleet at the time and could not build one. It was all to the good that it was compelled to remain a stationary hoplite force. That a powerful enemy either dictates savage terms if one is helpless before him, or else drags one willy-nilly into a response that in the long run might be destabilizing, seems to be sandwiched in between the Stranger's uncompromising position against laws not designed for virtue and the absurd assertion that ships allow one to hit and run and elevate flight into a noble practice that weakens the daring needed to fight and die in place.

It is enough to cite the Scythians, who baffled the Persians by constantly fleeing before them, and whom no one ever accused of cowardice, to cast doubt on the Stranger's thesis that lions would become deer were they to be trained in tactical flight.[1] Not even Odysseus's speech, which the Stranger quotes in part, supports him in context, for Odysseus there argues against the prudence of Agamemnon's plan to anchor off the coast for a night, since the Achaeans have already suffered too much not to pick up on Agamemnon's despair and flee (*Iliad* 14.65–102). Alcibiades, it is true, does say on the eve of the Sicilian expedition: "Our ships will provide security, either to stay if things go well or to go away" (Thucydides 6.18.5); but he hardly strengthens the Stranger's case, for the strat-

1. Cf. Plato *Laches* 190e4–c6.

egy of imperialistic expansion is not at issue. If sea power and cowardice always went together, then Minos should not have been able to lay down courage to be the only virtue and at the same time to extend his rule throughout the Cyclades and as far as Athens (Thucydides 1.4). It seems, then, that the Stranger's apparent elevation of courage at the expense of virtue is really an argument against the injustice of empire and its primitive form, piracy (cf. 823e2–4). He is urging the fusion of courage with moderation, and hence adhering to his program of virtue as a whole, since moderation is incompatible with the daring any departure from one's homeland demands. Indeed, in the same speech in which Alcibiades promised the safety of sea power, he declared that he knew for a certainty that a people as restless as the Athenians would be quickly destroyed were they to cease to expand, and "men live most securely if they least depart from their present ways and laws, even if they are worse" (6.18.7). The Stranger is making hoplite courage a matter of necessity, since for a landlocked city there is no place to run and hide. He tries to guarantee that no conditions either within or without will force the city to give a special place to courage. Courage drops easily to fourth place when no necessity has to exaggerate its excellence. Wealth too likewise drops to eighth when there is no opportunity to make money. The legislator does not have to put in laws against luxury if there are no luxuries to be had. The Stranger, then, is reflecting on how readily the city confuses necessity with morality and discerns something splendid in what cannot be helped. The structure of the eightfold good has a chance to determine the law provided the legislator does not have to cope with conditions that necessarily alter the rank of every good.

It would have been to Athens' advantage, the Stranger says, to lose many multiples of seven children if Theseus's only way of discharging Athens' debt to Minos had been the development of a navy (706a8–c1). This contrafactual mixture of fact and fancy is hard to make out. It was better that Theseus could bring "twice seven" youths to safety out of the Minotaur's labyrinth by means of Ariadne's thread than for him to retaliate by means of a navy Athens did not have and the timber for which Attica could not supply. The oddity of the case makes one wonder whether Plato is not alluding through the Stranger to his own *Phaedo*.[2] That dialogue starts with an account of why Socrates' execution was delayed—the sacred ship that went yearly to Delos in commemoration of Theseus's daring rescue had failed to return and all public executions

---

2. Cf. Ronna Burger, *The Phaedo: A Platonic Labyrinth* (New Haven 1984), 17–20.

were postponed until that time—and it ends with Socrates glowering like a bull (ταυρηδόν) as he asks for instructions about the poison he must drink (58a7–c5; 117b5). The setting of the *Phaedo* is a myth, in which Socrates leads the visitors to his prison—Phaedo names fourteen of them—out of the labyrinth of fear. He is a second Theseus with a novel remedy against an old enemy that he himself embodies. If one considers Socrates' refusal to flee in light of the sophists' homelessness that kept them safe, then the Stranger's recommendation of stubborn resistance unto death would refer to Socrates' rescue of philosophy from the mortal blow it would have suffered if he had got into the habit of constant flight. Socrates does after all liken his obedience to Apollo to his stance as a hoplite: he always stayed in line wherever his commanders posted him (*Apology of Socrates* 28d5–29a2). Socrates could have easily evaded execution by fleeing to a law-abiding city like Cnossos (cf. *Crito* 52e5–53a1); but had he done so, philosophy, for whose descent to the marketplace he bore alone the responsibility, would not have easily survived him. The Stranger, then, would be far from isolating courage from the rest of virtue; rather, he would be celebrating Socrates in an alien setting. His project to lay down every law in light of virtue would not be possible had Socrates not given up his life for the securing of the life of philosophy. That the Stranger virtually identifies himself later with Plato seems already to be hinted at (730a6). The *Laws*, one might say, is the *Republic* if it were staged out of town.

Clinias does not deny the Stranger's guess that, since the population in each city had become larger than its land could support, an invitation to settle the new city was extended to everyone in Crete (707e2–4); but the Stranger goes on to say that despite the uniformly Dorian character of the colonists, there is likely to be less initial friendliness among them than would have been the case had a single city, like a swarm of bees, been compelled to seek a new home. He argues that just as uniformity of dialect and laws impedes the introduction of new laws (for however bad the old laws may have been the people are comfortable with them, even if they were the cause of their ruin), so the very ease with which novelty can be introduced among a motley crowd is an obstacle to the rise of any esprit de corps, and a long time is needed to have the settlers fuse into one (708b1–d5). It is at this point, as if he foresaw the collapse of the city, that the Stranger remarks, "To found and legislate for cities is really and truly (ὄντως) the most complete and perfect achievement in point of manly virtue" (708d6–7).[3] The disparagement of human legislators,

---

3. Badham's facile τελεωτάτων, which England is inclined to accept, should be re-

which he was just about to voice, when he reflected on how disasters outside of human control have a way of altering laws and regimes, was held in check when he considered that chance was equally powerful in disease, in war, and at sea, but the arts that handle these different kinds of events do make a difference, and no one would want to dispense with them because they were not always successful. There is, then, an art of legislation and the Stranger presumably must have it, though he never uses the word νομοθετική; the closest he comes to it is to speak of the legislator who is dependent on or connected with truth (τὸν νομοθέτην ἀληθείας ἐχόμενον, 709c8; cf. 890d6–7). Νομοθετική does occur in the *Gorgias* and the *Statesman*. In the *Statesman* the law consists of written prescriptions the statesman leaves behind when he himself goes abroad; and in the *Gorgias* the legislative art, of which sophistry is its phantom image, knows how to bring about beauty and strength in souls. Νομοθετική, then, must be an art of writing that knows how to persuade and threaten on the basis of a complete knowledge of how the law affects the soul by whatever it encourages or forbids (cf. *Minos* 321d1–10). There is no guarantee, the Stranger now admits, that this knowledge will be effective. It needs the greatest degree of force if its own mixture of persuasion and force is to take hold. A tyrant of a certain type has to be available to the legislator if he is to overcome the resistance his laws are sure to encounter.

The Stranger draws this conclusion in an odd way. He appeals to the fact that the knowledgeable pilot, general, or doctor could formulate in a prayer what kind of luck his art would need if it were to get him out of a tight situation. If the sea were calm, anyone could steer; if the growth were benign, the doctor would not have to pray; and if the general had all the advantages, his strategy would be by the book. Book 4 began as if the Stranger were thinking about the best possible conditions, from which Clinias's city fell just a little bit short; but now he seems to imagine a crisis as the permanent given of all legislation that no one but the most skilled could even hope to master. Regardless of how favorable the geopolitical conditions may be, the legislator has to face a people either too set in its ways to change or too disparate to unite. There seems to be no comparable crisis built into other arts in which, though chance offers opportunities that only the skilled can exploit, their success does not always depend on beating the odds. In order for seamanship to be on a level with legislation, one would have to say not that there are occasions

---

sisted, since it breaks the connection with the later argument about the tyrant, who is already hinted at in the phrase πρὸς ἀρετὴν ἀνδρῶν.

that the most skilled pilot alone can handle but that the more furious the storm the better the voyage; and in the case of generalship, not when defeat seems certain is a victory secured, but that one courts the greatest risks to achieve something that could not otherwise be gained. In the case of legislation, however, the Stranger is saying that the best of all lawful orders occurs if and only if complete political upheaval precedes it. Only when things could not get worse can the legislator display his art; on all other occasions he must make so many compromises that the merest amateur could do as well. The Stranger seems to be applying the symposium in speech directly to the city, and whereas then the symposiarch could preserve order in disorder while he came to an understanding of the natures of men, now he has the tyrant with the whip hand standing by while the legislator lays out a pattern of law. Tyranny is a heady draught for a people to swallow on the off chance that they will wake up sober.

The criminal origin of a lawful regime appalls Clinias. If the text is sound, the Stranger asks for a soul in the grip of tyranny (τυραννουμένη ψυχή),[4] a soul that has not a trace of justice or lawfulness in it, but to which there belongs a natural moderation of a vulgar kind (δημώδης) that can be found even among beasts (709e6–710b3). The Stranger requires in addition that the tyrant be young, with a good memory, quick to learn, brave, and magnificent by nature. Clinias speaks of such a nature as an orderly tyrant (τύραννος κόσμιος, 710d7), as if he realized that the disorderly order of the symposium in speech were now in a single individual. The Stranger is curiously silent about how the legislator teams up with the tyrant; all he says is that inasmuch as any tyrant has the power to turn the ways of the citizens in whatever direction he wants most easily and quickly, the tyrant he proposes would present his own character as the model to be copied, praise those who succeeded in imitating him in their actions, blame those who failed, and dishonor whoever disobeyed his rules (711b4–c2). It is unclear what the legislator would supply. Does he simply write up laws that formulate the tyrant's nature? If precept follows emulation, justice as obedience would be built into the law; but the Stranger certainly implies that the thoughtfulness of mind (φρονεῖν) is not to be expected in his young tyrant. Does the tyrant lack knowledge of his own nature, and is this why the Stranger's account recalls the sym-

---

4. Τυραννευομένη ψυχή seems to be a compendious expression: Socrates says that the tyrant, whom many criminals in a democracy generate, is the one who has in himself the greatest and vastest tyrant in his soul (μέγιστον καὶ πλεῖστον ἐν τῇ ψυχῇ) (Republic 575c6–d1).

posium in speech? If the laws were to depict the tyrant's soul as he is, there would lurk inside every law-abiding citizen the tyrant, and the Stranger would have got no further than Clinias, who had earlier exposed his wish for eternal tyranny. Socrates too had finally admitted to Glaucon, in the myth of Er, that his ring of Gyges test would yield the same results even in the best city; but he then denied that those who partook of philosophy would make the same choice the holder of the first lot did (*Republic* 619b7–d1). The nature of those destined to be philosopher-kings matches for the most part the nature of the tyrant; but the tyrant is conspicuously lacking in one feature that Socrates assigns to them. The tyrant is not εὔχαρις (*Republic* 487a2–5). He is charmless. Clinias had ascribed charm to Homer, and the Stranger used it to designate the peculiar pleasure that images can bring. The tyrant is not playful; he is altogether in earnest. It might be the task, then, of the legislator, if the tyrant is lucky enough to meet up with him, to bring inside the law an element that is as certainly missing from the law's paragon as it is seemingly incompatible with the law itself. The Stranger is surely aiming higher than Socrates if he believes he can pull off what has all the earmarks of a minor miracle.

2   REGIMES AND LAW

In the face of Clinias's skepticism that even a tyrant could make a people over in a short time, the Stranger contrasts the feasibility of his proposal with what he regards as really difficult, the coincidence of the greatest power with moderation and good sense in one man, or, what is equally unlikely, the occurrence of divine *erōs* for moderate and just ways in the rulers of any regime (711c3–712a7). The Stranger argues against Socrates that for philosophers to become kings or kings philosophers is a more remote possibility than what Clinias finds so hard to accept.[5] In a sense, the Stranger is merely following out the strict implication of Socrates' own myth, which he has the Muses tell, according to whom if there is a continual cycle of regimes, the best city in speech follows tyranny as a matter of course (cf. *Phaedrus* 243e3–5). Clinias, in any case, knows nothing of this, and even after the Stranger's account, he still asks how the tyrant and legislator would get together; but the Stranger, rather than answering Clinias directly, says, "Let us try to attach a myth to your

---

5. Ritter comments at 712a (109) that one could even speak of a citation from the *Republic* here if the mention of the best laws did not argue against it.

city, and just as if we were ancient children, indulge in the make-believe (πλάττειν τῷ λόγῳ) of fashioning laws" (712a8–b2). The myth he means is his own solution, which he had just asked Clinias to accept as if it had all the authority of an oracular utterance (καθαπερεὶ μῦθός τις λεχθεὶς κεχρησμῳδήσθω), and his very first step in complying with Clinias's request to get started on the laws is to summon a god, who on hearing his prayer is to come in all graciousness and good will and join with them in arranging the city and its laws (712b4–7). The Stranger soon adds to his myth a second myth, that in the age of Cronus men lived happily under the rule of *daimones*, and laws are to be understood as their copies, for law as the distribution of mind (ἡ τοῦ νοῦ διανομή) is nothing but an anagram of δαίμονα (713a6–714a2; cf. *Cratylus* 398b5c1).

The sudden shift from a sober though radical possibility to a myth, so that Clinias can get over his extreme uneasiness about the tyrant, seems to mean that the Stranger has replaced the tyrant with a god, or, if one follows the Hesiodic story about Cronus, Zeus is the usurper or young tyrant whom the Stranger had in mind all along (cf. 859a4–6 with 861b6–c1). The nonmythical version of the Stranger's allusion would be that the legislator needs to have the absolute power a divine revelation would alone grant him if he is to have any hope of legislating against necessity. Book 4 would thus begin with a return to the start of the *Laws*, where Zeus was credited with the responsibility for Cretan laws. The legislator must be a poet of a very high order if he is going to be able to project his voice onto another and come forward as his own other's second-in-command.[6] That the Stranger got Clinias to accept Homer's version of a Cretan story already pointed to the only plausible way in which the legislator with all his art has to pray for the very worst conditions if he is to accomplish the best of lawful regimes. The union of wisdom and power in Socrates' logos thus undergoes in the Stranger's myth a split into two that then recombines in a phantom double in which persuasion and force seem to be apart but are really together. God, as the Stranger said, when he momentarily despaired of ever legislating anything, is everything, but art knows how to turn chance into an opportunity (709b7–c1). As long as the Stranger remains a stranger, and does not have to accede to Clinias's request to become a citizen of the new city (753a5–6), Clinias can become a ventriloquist and duplicate Minos's suc-

6. The Stranger shows how this is done at 861b1–6, where, in midsentence, aorist participles, which require a first-person plural finite verb, are picked up by ὁ παρ' ἡμῶν νυνδὴ ῥηθεὶς λόγος.

cess. The charm that is missing from the tyrant's makeup would belong instead to the legislator himself. The Stranger cannot be faulted if Clinias's inexperience in foreign poetry does not allow him to adopt this suggestion.

The Stranger asks either Clinias or Megillus to answer his question as to what kind of regime their countries have, and Megillus, who answers first on the grounds that he is the older (and thus confirms age as one of the seven claims of right), cannot give a straight answer, "for [Sparta] seems to me to resemble (προσεοικέναι) a tyranny—it is amazing how tyrannical the ephors have become in it—and sometimes it appears (φαίνεται) to me to look like (ἐοικέναι) the most democratic of all cities; but to deny in turn that it is an aristocracy is absolutely strange [Megillus means οἱ γέροντες or the Elders]; and there is besides a kingship for life in it, spoken of by us and all men as the most ancient of all" (712c6–e3). Clinias agrees that he too cannot say what kind of regime Cnossos has. The Stranger then explains that their regimes really and truly (ὄντως) partake of regimes, for the phantom images of every factional regime would not otherwise show up in them and allow their laws to look solely to war (714b8–c1). It seems, then, that the Stranger is about to recommend a mixed regime whose laws would look to virtue as a whole; instead, he declares "theocracy" to be the regime to which the principle "might is right" actually applies, and when this new label baffles Clinias, and he asks what god is truly the master of those with mind, he supplies a myth in order to justify this sudden turn in the argument. The mythical background for the Stranger's proposal involves a reversal in the order of time: Zeus is to be the agent for the restoration of the age of Cronus. The age of Cronus stands for the rule of mind. Mind retakes its throne through violence. In the seven claims to rule, the fifth was violence and the sixth good sense; and Pindar had identified the fifth with law. The Stranger seems to suggest that the two apparently opposed principles are as close together as θεός and δαίμων. The principle of might can be properly reassigned to the god or gods, who as "the mightier ones" (οἱ κρείττονες) really deserve the title (713a2–4; cf. 718a5; 917a1–3), and the principle of mind is the true meaning of *daimōn*. Pindar, then, was mistaken: law is not to be identified with just one of these two principles but is the weld between them. Law is the weld because it is always experienced against the grain regardless of whether it is the true embodiment of good sense or not.[7]

7. The Stranger alludes perhaps to the parodos of Aeschylus's *Agamemnon*, where, in the so-called hymn to Zeus, "whoever he is," the Chorus speak of the vio-

The myth speaks of a time prior to the cataclysm that started off the Stranger's account of Dorian history. The gist of that account was that political beginnings are always imperfect, and law always bears traces of its piecemeal development. Now, however, the Stranger needs perfect beginnings for men, the blessedness of whose life the law, without the resources of those times, must try to duplicate both in public and in private. Cronus knew that no human (ἀνθρωπεία) nature was capable of ruling human (ἀνθρώπινα) affairs on its own authority, but it would necessarily get swollen with injustice and insolence (cf. 875b1–c3).[8] Accordingly, Cronus set over men superior beings, the *daimones*, who excelled men by as much as men now excel tame cattle. The Stranger now seems to admit that the domestication of man, which his earlier myth, in white-washing the Cyclopes, had disregarded, is the primary task of the law (cf. 874e9–875a1); but surprisingly he does not now assign this task to the tyrant, whom he had made the legislator's assistant, but to mind. The principle behind the eidetic structure of the good comes to the fore at the very moment when the Stranger should have acknowledged that the disappearance of perfect conditions in the age of Zeus necessarily required a supplement to mind. Mind was too soft, he had said, to manage man all by itself (645a4–b1).

The Stranger seems to have abandoned the genetic structure of law entirely and attached law directly to the eidetic structure of the good, all of whose human goods, he had said, look to the divine goods, and all of whose divine goods look to their leader mind (631d4–6). This attachment can be done in a sense through an ambiguity built into the medio-passive of the verb πείθειν, for as a middle it means to obey, but as a passive it means to be persuaded. Whoever, then, is εὐπειθέστατος to the established laws is most obedient to them (715c2); but the Stranger would also want the citizens to be won over as far as possible to virtue (ὡς εὐπειθεστάτους πρὸς ἀρετήν, 718c8). Law, then, contains within itself either violence or mind, violence if "or else" accompanies every law, mind if it formulates a persuasive version of the eightfold good. The either/or of law, however,

---

lent grace (βίαιος χάρις) of the gods, for Zeus opened up a path for good sense (φρονεῖν), in authorizing the law, "by one's own suffering understanding" (τῷ πάθει μάθος), whereby "sobriety (σωφρονεῖν) comes even to the unwilling" (176–184).

8. The use of ἀνθρώπειος and ἀνθρώπινος in this passage, and the one that follows in book 5 (732e2–4), seems to be exactly the reverse of what the two suffixes ordinarily mean: "'Ανθρώπινος semble s'être toujours distingué d'ἀνθρώπειος; chez Thucydide, ἀνθρώπειος veut dire 'humain' en parlant des événements de la vie humaine (bonheur ou malheur), tandis qu'ἀνθρώπινος signifie 'conforme à la nature humaine.'" Pierre Chantraine, *La formation des noms en grec ancien* (Paris 1933), 203.

is misleading, for the threat in the law spreads throughout the law, no matter how rational the law may be, and blurs experientially the difference between force and persuasion. The most law-abiding of citizens can only be self-deluded if he pretends that the threat of a punishment he has never undergone has never affected him. Law wants to be the impossible togetherness of the necessary apartness of Persia and Athens as the Stranger understood them eidetically. This double aspect of law, whereby the tyrant of the Stranger's original proposal disappears inside the law, comes to light in one of the most extraordinary expressions in the entire dialogue. The rank of the magistracy, the Stranger says, to which a citizen is to be assigned, should be determined by the degree of his subservience to the gods (τὴν τῶν θεῶν ὑπηρεσίαν), and the greater the subservience the greater ought to be his rank (715c3–6; cf. 762e3–5). The Stranger defends his calling rulers (ἄρχοντες) servants (ὑπηρέται) to the laws, for he wants to emphasize as strongly as possible his opposition to the Thrasymachean thesis that whoever has the upper hand (ὁ κρατῶν) lays down laws in his own interest; but he does not apologize for the identification of laws with gods. This identification is due not only to the mythical doubling of the legislator, but also to the true significance of the second myth, that if a mortal (θνητός) and not a god rules a city, there is no possibility of an escape from evils and troubles (713e3–6). The Stranger's first attempt to translate the eidetic structure of the good into law involves the replacement of "the divine," which characterized the soul's virtue in his first account, with "gods." "The human" of that account thus becomes "mortal," and what was then apart gets put together through the notion of "deathlessness" (ἀθανασία), which is now said to be in us to some unspecified extent (713e8). Becoming, which made the genetic structure of law wholly separate from the eidetic structure of the good, can be discounted once "gods" usurps the place of "divine," and what does not die puts us in some relation to them. The ἔστι of the eidetic structure of the good yields to the ὄν of the prelude.

The establishment of a continuity within a substantial difference between gods and men allows the Stranger to formulate what Clinias will recognize as the first part of the first prelude to the laws (723d8–e7). That first prelude is divided in two by a discussion of prelude and law as well as by an example of the difference between prelude and law. The example is taken from the marriage laws. It thus reestablishes the genetic structure of law, which had been headed by marriage, and inserts it between the two parts of the first prelude. The marriage law interrupts what should have been a prelude based entirely on the eidetic structure of the good. This digression splits the gods, who determine the structure of the

first part of the prelude, away from the soul, which starts off the second
part (726a2–3). Man as a generational being gets in the way of binding the
most divine of human possessions, as the Stranger calls it, as closely to
the gods as the preeminence of mind in the law might have led one to
expect.

The Stranger's unofficial prelude is addressed to the assembled settlers, who Clinias is asked to imagine have come and are present (715e3–
6). The prelude falls into three sections. The first section concludes with
Clinias's affirmation that every man must conceive (διανοηθῆναι) of himself as a future follower of the god (715e7–716b9); the second and third
sections are without an interruption and end in the midst of the Stranger's speech (716c1–d4; 716d4–718a6). The first section is about thought
(διάνοια), the second about action (πρᾶξις). Each of the first two sections
is based on an ancient proverb. The first proverb is that the god holds the
beginning, end, and middle of all the beings (τὰ ὄντα), and on a straight
course of rectitude (εὐθείᾳ) he accomplishes a natural revolution. The
second proverb holds that the god is the measure of all things (χρήματα).[9]
The god of the first section is concerned with justice, the god of the second with moderation. The two virtues that were the goal of the genetic
structure of law now show up in the doubleness of the god. Insofar as the
god is the god of justice, he arranges for the punishment of those who fall
short of the divine law, while he guarantees the happiness of whoever
follows right (δίκη) in humility and due order (ταπεινὸς καὶ κεκοσμημένος).
The greatest crime is hubris, the belief that one can strike out on one's
own without a guide, and the greatest punishment is to be abandoned by
god, though if one takes on many followers who believe one is a somebody (τοῖς πολλοῖς ἔδοξεν εἶναί τις), one soon submits to punishment (δίκη)
and ruins oneself, one's family, and one's city. To depart from the path the
law lays out is to be lost, and in that wilderness in which man is nothing,
there is the god who, in holding all of time in his grip, is the agent of the
"or else" of the law. This god is the god of terror and hard to distinguish
from the tyrant (cf. 720c6). The Stranger immediately juxtaposes this picture with another, which is built up on the basis of the question, "What
action is dear to (φίλη) and in conformity with god?" Fear is followed by
love, or obedience by emulation. What is now at issue is becoming like
god: γίγνεσθαι did not occur in the first section of the prelude. To become

9. Χρήματα alludes to the Protagorean motto; but it is clear from what follows
that the Stranger means not beings but πράγματα, things with which we deal and are
of concern to us; cf. *Cratylus* 385e6–386a3 and *Theaetetus* 152a1–8 for the two different ways of handling Protagoras's χρήματα.

as like to god as possible is to be moderate (σώφρων); to be unlike god and at odds (διάφορος) with him is to be not moderate; but no punishment follows on this implied enmity, for no matter how great the dissimilarity is with god, likeness always entails difference.

In putting god in charge of the laws, the Stranger has briefly outlined the two possible forms religion can take, either a religion of law, in which man does what god tells him to do, no questions asked (cf. *Statesman* 294b8–c6), or a religion of imitation, in which man does what god does.[10] The unbridgeable gap between god and man in the first form shows up as the difference between god as the beginning, middle, and end of all beings and man as nothing; the possible nearness of man to god in the second form shows up in god being the measure of all things. If hubris is the sign of man's deviation from god in the first form, and hubris is the contrary of one kind of moderation, then the moderation to which the Stranger appeals in the second form is likely to be sanity, whose contrary is madness. The Stranger would thus imply that mysticism in some form is the ultimate consequence of emulation, and he deliberately blocks that way of descent into madness by speaking of measure and men of due measure (οἱ ἔμμετροι). Despite, then, the Stranger's apparently seamless joining of thought and action, these profound differences remain. It is the purpose of the third section of his prelude to cover the space between them. Not ancient proverbs but ancient practices back it up.

The third section is concerned with sacrifice and burial. These two actions are the pillars of definitional law. Definitional law says what man is or what he is not through his regular performance of some rite. Sacrifice denies that man is a god, burial denies that man is either a beast or carrion. Man is both soul and body, and there are gods. These two actions are the plainest evidence that law wants to be the discovery of what is. The double meaning of νομίζειν—to believe and to practice the lawful things—can be expressed together as follows: it is to come to believe through practice in the law's imitation of mind's divisions and collections of the beings. In Plato's *Minos*, Socrates' comrade brings up the differences in sacrifice and burial as proof that Socrates' definition of law cannot be true (*Minos* 315b6–d5). He does not realize that the verbs carry with them beings, whose nature is determined by the verbs. The comrade is more impressed by the fact that the Carthaginians sacrifice human beings than that they sacrifice, and by the fact that the Athenians have altered in time the way they bury the dead than that they bury them. He

10. Cf. Leo Strauss, "On the *Euthyphron*," in *The Rebirth of Classical Political Philosophy* (Chicago 1989), 197–198.

does not realize that at the same time man is everywhere being defined by these two verbs, he himself is defining Greeks over against barbarians, and insofar as some Greeks, according to him, also sacrifice human beings, he is defining civilized man. He is also unaware that man is defined temporally through sacrifice and spatially through burial, since he says that some Carthaginians sacrifice their own sons to Cronus or Time (Χρόνος), and his main evidence for change in burial custom concerns whether the corpse was put in a pot prior to its being carried out or it was buried in the house and not outside the city.

After the Flood, "Noah built an altar to the Lord, and took of every clean animal and of every clean bird, and offered burnt offerings on the altar of the Lord" (*Genesis* 8.20). This is the first sacrifice of flesh after Abel's. God then said to Noah and his sons (9.1–6):

> The fear and dread of you shall rest on every animal of the earth, and on every bird of the air, on everything that creeps on the ground, and on all the fish of the sea; into your hand they are delivered. Every moving thing that lives shall be food for you; and just as I gave you the green plants, I give you everything. Only you shall not eat flesh with its life, that is, its blood.[11] For your own lifeblood I will surely require a reckoning: from every animal I will require it and from human beings, each one for the blood of another, I will require a reckoning for human life.

> Whoever sheds the blood of a human,
> by a human shall that person's blood be shed;
> for in his own image
> God made humankind.

God connects the permission for man to cease to be a vegetarian and eat flesh, which entails that man is now a terror to all other animals, with the prohibition of murder, for man was made in God's image. The connection is obscure. The permission to shed blood is bound up with the prohibition to eat blood, whose identity with life reidentifies man, in his being the image of God, with life simply. Man is not flesh. He is therefore not to be eaten. As a definitional law, the prohibition against cannibalism lies concealed in the prohibition against murder that follows on man as a political being. Man is defined through what he does. The definition nec-

---

11. Cf. pseudo-Justin Martyr, *Quaestiones et responsiones*, 145: ἵνα καὶ ἐν τούτῳ χωρίσῃ ἡμᾶς ὁ θεὸς τῆς τῶν θηρίων ὁμοιότητος, τῶν σὺν τῇ βρώσει τῆς σαρκὸς λαπτόντων καὶ τὸ αἷμα ὧν τὰς σάρκας ἐσθίουσιν.

essarily involves a translation of man, who is noetically defined at his creation, since God is neither male nor female, into a corporeal equivalent, since law is necessarily concerned with behavior and not thought. God's address to Noah both begins and ends with the exhortation to be fruitful and multiply; but his own reflection, after he has smelled the pleasing odor of Noah's sacrifice, was, "I shall never again curse the ground because of humankind, for the inclination of the human heart is evil from youth" (8.21).

That the bad man is defiled (μιαρός) and unclean in respect to his soul (ἀκάθαρτος τὴν ψυχήν) indicates the shift from thought to action in the Stranger's account. The soul can be understood within the law only corporeally, and the holy and unholy among men be distinguished by some image drawn from the body.[12] The gods too are separated by left and right (717a8); but at this point, when the Stranger is about to string all the divine beings along a vertical line passing from heaven through the earth to what is below, he surprises us: "First [πρῶτον μέν], we assert, as for the honors, those which [are] after the Olympians and the gods who maintain the city, one would hit most rightly the mark of piety [εὐσέβεια occurs now for the first time], should one assign the even, second, and left [honors] to the chthonic gods, and [honors], which are the upper ones and match the former, to those just now mentioned first" (717a6–b2). In this awkward and puzzling sentence, the Stranger alludes to how burial, in the genetic structure of law, was the replacement for good sense (φρόνησις) in the eidetic structure of the good, and was said to complete the regime. Burial then expressed the separation between body and soul, with no union between them, that characterized as well the structure of the eight-fold good.[13] Now, however, once the gods supply a possible link between them, it is necessary that the gods who are second be put in speech first

12. Out of the more than seventy references in the *Laws* to cleanliness and pollution, this is one of two in which uncleanliness is an aspect of soul; the other refers to whoever plots a murder but does not commit it with his own hand: unlike the murderer he can be buried at home (871e8–872a7). Likewise, ἱεροσυλία involves the soul only when it is extended to cover matricide or patricide (869b1–4); cf. Angelos Chaniotis, "Reinheit des Körpers-Reinheit des Sinnes in den griechischen Kultgesetzen," in: *Studien zum Verstehen fremder Religionen,* ed. J. Assman and T. Sundermeier, vol. 9, *Schuld, Gewissen und Person* (Gütersloh 1997), 142–178.

13. In the *Gorgias,* Socrates, in making sophistry be the phantom image of the art of legislation and rhetoric of justice, starts from a division between body and soul in both the true arts and their spurious counterparts that forbids the rejoining of body and soul and thus precludes the possibility of an architectonic art of man as a whole. The *Laws* works out the consequence of this split for legislation; but it differs from the *Gorgias* as well as from the *Republic,* neither of which has the word ἔμψυχος, by employing it seven times (first at 782c8).

in order to remind us of what has been lost, no less than gained, in this tentative translation of the genetic back into the eidetic: once "gods" replace "divine," εὐσέβεια is the most obvious way to render φρόνησις. There is, in any case, no ἔπειτα δέ [in the second place] that can properly come after the πρῶτον μέν with which he began; instead, he says, "after these gods the man of good sense (ἔμφρων) would sacrifice to the *daimones*, and after them to heroes." Heroes are now mentioned for the first time. Private shrines, lawfully consecrated to the gods of one's fathers (πατρῷοι θεοί), follow next, and after them the honors paid to parents both alive and dead (cf. 869b1–4; 930e7–931a8). It is religiously right (θέμις) to pay them back in old age for all they have done when one was young, and to believe that the three kinds of good one has—of substance (οὐσία), body, and soul—are due to them and must be spent in service to them, with the highest priority being given to the lowest of the goods and the lowest priority to the best. The injunction to yield to angry parents, who imagine they have been wronged, and the mention of Nemesis as the messenger of Right (Δίκη), who watches over any thoughtless words a son may utter against his parents and punishes them severely, make it clear that justice, insofar as piety belongs to it, is the main element in this account of action; moderation comes in only with regard to the burial of the parents, when the most moderate of tombs is said to be most beautiful and a rough measure is supplied: it should not fall below or rise above what one's forefathers did in burying their parents. A due measure (τὸ μέτριον) of expenses should also be paid yearly to the dead in order to keep their memory fresh.

More than half the third section of the prelude is devoted to parents. It comes closer to being part of a law than a prelude, but since it does not yet have legal penalties attached it is still an exhortation. The poet, whose guise the Stranger will assume, finds another fault in it; but at the moment, one has to be impressed how obedience and emulation, fear and love, thought and action, mortal and immortal, what is above the earth and what is below it, body and soul, justice and moderation have all been woven together in such a way that the disparity between the eidetic structure of the good and the genetic structure of law has all but disappeared. What seems to be decisive for this virtual disappearance is burial. Its primacy in the structure of definitional law was already implicit in the ostensibly first position the Stranger assigned to the chthonic gods. The inclusion of heroes in the series of deathless beings, without any special verb, such as ἐναγίζειν, to distinguish them (cf. Herodotus 2.44.5), also suggests it. Whether one is to infer that what appears to be a spatially

vertical line, which binds the whole together, is really the temporal continuum of past, present, and future is obscure; but the Stranger does seem
to draw a horizontal line immediately afterwards, on which he places our
relations to those who are spatially either closer to or more distant from
us: offspring, kinsfolk, friends, fellow citizens, and strangers. The survey (διέξοδος) of these relations belongs, he says, to the laws themselves
(718a6–b2). This proves to be a mistake, for the very same sequence
shows up in the second part of the prelude (729a2–730a4), and what is
more, in that part of the prelude that deals, the Stranger says, with all
practices that are divine (732d8–e2); the human (ἀνθρώπινα) practices that
follow and conclude the prelude of the laws concern pleasure and pain,
"for we are conversing with human beings, not gods, and what is most
human (ἀνθρώπειον) by nature are pleasures, pains, and desires, from
which of necessity the mortal animal in its entirety simply hangs in suspension, as it were, with the greatest earnestness" (732e3–7). The last
section of the prelude's second part thus brings back that which most
distinguished the genetic structure of law from the eidetic structure of
the good, pleasure and pain. At the same time, that last section also
brings back the divine puppet, by whose strings the gods were jerking us
around in either play or earnest. At this point the reader too should feel
somewhat dizzy, as he realizes that the Stranger has no intention of wip-
ing out the distinction with which he started, between the eidetic structure of the good and the genetic structure of law, but he still wants to
preserve them while he rearranges their elements.

3   Double Law and Prelude

The Stranger distinguishes between what belongs to law proper and what
the legislator ought to say even though it does not fit the form of a law.
This distinction seems to be prompted by a reflection on a difference
within the law that the Stranger himself has just made (718b2–c3). In
assigning to the law the horizontal dimension of a man's relations to
other men besides his parents, he speaks of the law as partly persuading
and partly punishing by violence and right (βίᾳ καὶ δίκῃ) whosesoever
character does not submit to persuasion. The Stranger thus indicates that
the threat in the law can only in a sense be called persuasion, and consequently most of what Clinias will call a prelude, that which concerns the
honoring of the gods and the caring for parents, is not strictly speaking a
prelude, since it heavily relies on threats for compliance. The splitting of

god between an agent of justice and an exemplar of moderation needs a preface that the tenth book presumably supplies; but the tenth book itself follows on the criminal law and presupposes the failure of the Stranger's own effort at lawful persuasion. One wonders, then, whether every law must necessarily infect its own prelude, and only what the Stranger now recognizes as a prelude, their own discussion about law, can truly be called a prelude. When, in any case, the Stranger incorporates into the second part of his prelude all that he had initially relegated to the laws themselves—in accordance with his revised plan not to begin the laws until he has gone through what was still left out (718c1–3)—he manages to use the language of exhortation—shame, moderation, and reverence— as long as he is speaking of one's relations to children, kinsfolk, friends, and fellow citizens, but when he concludes with the faults committed against strangers, he threatens the transgressor with an avenging god (729e3–730a2). The prelude of the law takes its bearings necessarily from the law, for right interferes with the disjunction the Stranger wants between violence and persuasion.[14]

The Stranger raises the issue of prelude and persuasion when he realizes that the first part of his prelude might make its audience, if their soul is not absolutely raw and savage (ὠμὴ ψυχή), more amenable and tamer, but he does not rate its effect very high, since there are few who are eager to be as good as possible in the shortest possible time (718d2– e1). He then quotes six lines from Hesiod's *Works and Days* (287–292), where Hesiod, in addressing his great fool of a brother, separates the rough and steep path of virtue from the smooth and near way of vice. In the passage that precedes this, Hesiod had urged his brother to hearken to Right and forget Violence, for Zeus ordained the former as a law for men, whereas among the beasts there is no Right, and they are ordained to eat one another (274–278). Right shows itself primarily as the prohibition against cannibalism and bestiality; it is, therefore, as definitional law, connected with the knowledgeable speaking of right (280–1). Accordingly, Hesiod speaks of his own understanding and good will (ἐσθλὰ νοέων) when he calls his brother a fool (286), then distinguishes the absolutely best man, who understands all things on his own (ὃς αὐτὸς πάντα νοήσει),

---

14. In the *Timaeus,* Socrates distinguishes between Timaeus's prelude and subsequent law or tune (29d5–6). If one makes use of the Stranger's differentiation between them, Socrates would imply that Timaeus cut "necessity" out of his prelude, and Timaeus later admits that he did so (48e2–49a4). See further D. Daube, "Covenanting under Duress," *The Irish Jurist* 2 (1967): 352–359; reprinted in *Talmudic Law* 1 (Berkeley 1992): 23–31.

from the good man who obeys the good speaker, and declares that whoever neither thinks for himself nor listens to another is useless (294–297). From the position of mind, then, the Stranger wants to appeal to Hesiod's second group, to which Hesiod can only hope his brother belongs, but like Hesiod he knows that the difference between what negatively defines man and what makes man good is not readily established through law. "Not a beast" is not the same as "rational animal" (cf. 874e7–875d5). The word Hesiod uses to characterize his brother as a fool is νήπιος, whose literal meaning was thought to be "not speaking" (Hesychius s.v. νηπύ- τιον.). It is all to the good, the Stranger says, if the greater good will that his prelude might induce in his audience will make them more capable of understanding (εὐμαθέστερον).

What Hesiod says both before and after the lines the Stranger quotes shows up in the effect his own speech has had on him and which he wants to make public (719a4–5). He is reminded of the poets, whose ignorance of the possible harm of their speeches had led to their dismissal from any position of authority, but whose powers of persuasion the legislator now needs.[15] In addressing the legislator, the Stranger adopts the voice of the poet; he even goes so far as to say "I" while speaking as the poet (719a7). The poet argues that while the legislator can say only one thing about one thing, he says many things about the same thing, for he always speaks from within his characters and has them say what suits each of them (cf. 916d6–e6). The poet, then, is persuasive because each soul-type has its own type of speech; and if the legislator wishes to speak persuasively, his speech must likewise come from within the main type or types he believes his audience consists in.[16] The Stranger, however, in addressing the assembled colonists, had made the god the measure, despite the fact that he urged that the proper measure be observed in burial; but it is precisely in death that the incommensurability of man and god is most manifest. The legislator can threaten from on high in the name of the god who holds the beginning, middle, and end of all the beings, but he must abandon the god who is the measure of all things if he wants to come down to earth. The mortal, which the god himself established, is itself the obstacle to the application of a divine measure. Contrary to

15. For a straightforward opposition between law and poetry, see Lycurgus *In Leocraten* 102: "The laws on account of their vehemence do not teach, but they enjoin whatever one must do, but the poets, in imitating human life, by their selection of the most beautiful of deeds, help with logos and demonstration in persuading human beings."

16. Cf. *Phaedrus* 271c10–272b2.

what the Stranger maintained, when it comes to burial, man is the mea-sure.[17] The poet says that the legislator's measure (τὸ μέτριον) and the hu-manly commensurate would seem to coincide in only one case, if a man with a measure (μέτρον) of wealth, who was moderate (μέτριος) himself, were to recommend the mode of his burial; in all other cases, the legis-lator could ensure compliance with whatever measure he chose, but it would not be agreeable to either the wealthy woman or a man who works for a living (cf. 955e5).

The poet implies that even if the legislator's measure were in fact the same as the man of measure, it would not be due to the same considera-tions, for the legislator would have to claim that his measure were a de-duction from the god of measure, even though it could not possibly be so deduced,[18] while the measure of the mean can vary within a wide range for all those who are men of due measure with moderate means. The law is going to be most irritating as soon as it prescribes a number, for the soul never experiences anything numerically, and the translation from the measure of the mean to the arithmetic measure is always an illusion of art. In trying to get around this criticism of the poet the Stranger uses another model. He recalls the difference between two kinds of medical treatment, one of which comes closest to the gentle remedies for which children would crave (720a2–6). Although the Stranger mentions in pass-ing that gymnastic too maintains the same difference (720e3), his elabo-ration of the medical model implies that law starts from the premise that man is sick, and his restoration to health is its primary purpose. The Stranger does not work out the first step of this implication: if the law is to be persuasive, it must first persuade us that we are sick. It turns out, moreover, that the law is incapable of duplicating the treatment free phy-sicians offer the free. They first learn from their patient and his friends what the trouble is, then teach as far as they can what the cause and the cure are, and only after they persuade do they prescribe (720d1–e2). The persuasion does not go so far, the Stranger suggests, as to give a reason why the measure of the dosage and the number of its frequency must be what they are, but only that a certain course of treatment must be under-gone, consists in so many steps, and will last for so many days. Accord-ingly, the legislator, in persuading, will divert attention away from the

17. This implication of the poet's criticism emerges when the Stranger formu-lates the rule for dedications to the gods: "The man of measure (τὸν μέτριον ἄνδρα) must dedicate measured (ἔμμετρα) gifts to the gods" (955e5–6).

18. When the Stranger later deduces a measure from his theology, he does not draw its strict consequence, that there should be no burial at all (959a4–d2).

specific prescription and stress instead the need to follow a certain way. This answers one objection of the poet. It is more important to put the law's patients in the mood to take its advice than to convince them that the law has chosen the right numbers; but the law cannot conduct a dialogue with the citizens. It cannot be what his own model demands that it be, a dialogic cure of the soul: the Stranger himself belatedly admits that this is the case (857c6–e5). The Eleatic Stranger calls the cure the art of soul-purification, which Theaetetus believes is not an ideal version of Socrates' maieutics but a form of sophistry (*Sophist* 226b1–231b8). The law could copy only very crudely what the Eleatic Stranger calls the sophistic art noble by descent. The law addresses a crowd inexperienced in education (722b7). Should the law become truly dialogic, it would face two insuperable difficulties. If the law reasons soundly, it cannot allow everyone who does not follow its reasoning to disobey the law; and if the law does not reason soundly, it cannot allow those who see through it to disregard its provisions. In the *Crito*, Socrates, as if he were the Stranger's poet, makes the laws of Athens speak to him and, contrary to their very nature, argue with him; but he has the good grace to pretend that the buzz of the laws drowns out everything else. Socrates does not correct, for example, their first egregious blunder; it concerns the marriage of his parents and his own birth (50d1–3). In order to excuse their mistake, we are forced to say that the laws in this case at least speak poetically.

The brutal treatment the slave assistants to the free physicians accord their slave patients corresponds to the law as it has been formulated up to now; and nothing the Stranger proposes is going to alter this tyrannical aspect of the law (722e7–723a2). The free citizens are going to be addressed collectively as free and as slaves, with no sure criterion for their distinguishing who is who (cf. 777b4–c1; 919e3–5). The explicit cut the law makes between slave and free is overlaid with another cut that the law insists upon but cannot enforce. The law seems to be of a duplicity that the poet cannot rival; he at least always declares when he is changing masks; but the law speaks out of both sides of its mouth at once. Indeed, in his first example, the Stranger doubles the law and inserts what he will call the prelude inside the law; he does not put it, as he later suggests it should be, before the law. A man of thirty-four whom the insert at last persuades to marry knows that he has only a year before the penalties kick in; and a man of twenty-one, should he find the insert equally convincing, has to keep his impatience in check for five or ten years. One wonders, then, what the poet can contribute to the law, since the Stranger seems not to need his services for drawing the distinction between prelude and law. If, however, one looks back to what started the Stranger's reflection, the quotation from Hesiod, one realizes that precisely if the ways of virtue and vice are as Hesiod portrayed them, then the legislator must summon the poet to invert the perspective of time. He must put the future ease of virtue up front and slide the length and steepness of the road into the background; and the incurable woe Right inevitably inflicts on vice in the end must be indexed in the present and all the glamour of vice painted over. The Stranger, then, is criticizing the poet for telling the truth and ruining the law, for his own educational proposal had also been to load the pain of virtue onto vice and make it as unattractive as possible.

The poet's exercise of phantastics, in alliance with the legislator, suggests another way in which the poet might prove useful. The poet implicitly questioned the legislator for equating the god with the measure of human things. He thus indicated that if the legislator wants to maintain the measure of the mean he must adjust the god to it and not the measure of the mean to the god. The poet would start not with "the god" but with the Olympian gods; they would supply the divine types that the human types could be encouraged to emulate. They would be generated out of the human and thus be deviations from the straight aspiration the Stranger's prelude had assumed. He had started at the top and did not take into account the refractive index of the human. The poet could truly make the laws into the gods of which the best of the citizens would be the most obedient servants. The Stranger himself had pointed the way to this when he turned to practice and put Olympian gods, *daimones*, heroes, and the gods of the fathers on the same scale of worship. The poet is merely asking whether sacrifice could not have its counterpart in the dianoetic imagination. The Stranger had ingeniously gone from the deathlessness in which mind partakes to the continuum of the deathless beings from the Olympian to the chthonic, but he had not given shapes to those beings. The Stranger will later assign one of the twelve districts of the country to Plouton (828c6–d5). Plouton there stands for the principle that no communion of body and soul is at any point superior to their dissolution. He stands simultaneously for the patriotic death, the eidetic structure of the good, man's most profound ignorance, and philosophy, which Socrates in the *Phaedo* had said was nothing but the practice of separating body and soul.

The Stranger chooses to exemplify the difference between a single and a double law with the marriage law, for the legislator would lay it down as the first law, since he will put the natural beginning of becoming in the first position in his ordering of the city (720e10–721a8). The verb to marry is law-laden. It carries with it just as much a discovery of what is as sacrifice and burial do. Through it man and woman become husband and wife. They become husband and wife if and only if they are not in the line of relations the law forbids. The Stranger, however, is silent about incest. He jumps over the necessarily exogamic character of any non-Cyclopean way of life. His law appears less definitional and, at the same time, more natural than it is. When the Stranger actually starts the laws, the marriage law ceases to be first: the sacred and holy things initiate the laws (771a5–6). The city does not now figure in the reasoning a man is to be induced to follow. Everyone, he is told, conceives a natural desire for immortality; and the immortality that belongs to the human race, insofar as it is always one and the same and congenital with all of time, thus binds together the eidetic with the genetic. The law that, in the Stranger's second myth, partook in its entirety of deathlessness through mind (713e6–714aa2), has now been time-indexed and at its beginning given a beginning that imitates the god who holds the beginning of all the beings. The range that "the deathless" occupies is the mean between "the divine" and "the god." The marriage-prelude thus stands outside the prelude of all preludes but still belongs in between its first and second parts. Marriage has its proper though eccentric place between sacrifice and burial.[19] The prospective groom is told that to achieve renown and not lie dead without a name is also a desire of the same kind as his.[20] While the prelude undercuts the belief that the buried dead are something, it cannot but denigrate any other way of self-perpetuation, as it holds out the illu-

---

19. In *La scienza nuova seconda*, ed. F. Nicolini (Bari 1942), sections 8–12, 333, Giambattista Vico makes the three principles on which he establishes his science the three customs of religion, marriage, and burial, which are found no less among barbarous than among civilized nations. All three are to be traced to what he calls *l'impossibile credibile*, or the identification of bodies with minds (section 383), which is in turn nothing but his interpretation of Tacitus's saying, *fingebant simul credebantque* (*Annales* 5.10). This is the golden thread that runs through Vico, *una da essi stessi finta e creduta divinità* (sections 13, 376), by means of which he can distinguish between *coscienza* and *scienza*, and assign the former to philology, which observes the genetic, or the *l'autoritá dell'umano arbitrio*, which is the source of *la coscienza del certo*, and the latter to philosophy, or the eidetic, which contemplates reason, which is the source of *la scienza del vero* (sections 137–38; cf. 321, 324). What his hieroglyphical frontispiece already implied, Vico finally admits, is that the diachronic has to be understood synchronically (section 446).

20. Diotima, on the other hand, carefully distinguishes between the two kinds of desire, and says of those who turn to sexual generation that they are pregnant corporeally and are supplying for themselves, "as they believe," deathlessnes, memory, and happiness for all of time (*Symposium* 208e1–5).

sory hope of greater substance in the perpetuation of a family name. The double law seems to be most persuasive when, if one refuses to marry, it gives the purpose of the yearly penalty: "in order that one may not imagine that living alone brings one profit and a life of ease" (721d3–4).

The Stranger alters his understanding of how persuasion and force are to show up in the law when he notices that all legislators up to now have not only failed to relieve the willful tyranny of the law in any way but have omitted something else that the laws also need (722c2–4). The conversation the Stranger has had with Clinias and Megillus from dawn to high noon supplies this second omission. It consisted of preludes to laws (722d2).[21] These preludes certainly showed that Clinias and Megillus were sick, for Clinias derived from his experience of Cretan law the insight that war was the nature of things, and Megillus had dreams of universal empire and Clinias of eternal tyranny. It would seem, then, that if their morning talk and walk, from which they are now resting in a very beautiful spot, corresponds to the conversation free patients have with their doctors prior to treatment, then from this point forward the Stranger is going to prescribe the cure. The laws of the *Laws* are a regimen for Clinias and Megillus to follow. They are a translation of the Stranger's instruction about law into recipes of persuasion. The first such recipe is book 5, in which Megillus never speaks and Clinias voices his assent only at the end. The Stranger thus indicates how he understands Clinias's proposal to test the argument of the first three books through the founding of a city in speech. This founding in speech represents not only how a general argument undergoes particularization but also how the double and triple voice of dialectic changes into the single voice of rhetoric. This difference between *dialogos* and *logos* does not mean that the dialogic part was free of persuasion and the logos part is to be free of instruction (cf.723a7), but it does distinguish between what the doctor and the patient have severally to do. The causal account the Stranger has given does not have to be reproduced by Clinias in its persuasive image. One can say more precisely that just as the second part of the prelude in book 5 is a prescription for the soul without the logos of μουσική of the first two books, so the second half of book 5 is the third book without the logos of γυμναστική. The poet of the first three books is about to deliver a monologue.[22]

21. One could say that the relation between the Declaration of Independence and the Constitution of the United States exemplifies the difference between prelude and law, and how the two are and are not bound together.

22. É. des Places observes that the corrective μὲν οὖν at 728a2 is unique in contin-

The Stranger shifts from the model of the double law, in which the persuasive element is inserted between the ordinance and the penalty, to a separation of persuasion and threat on the basis of a reflection on his own series of preludes to laws. The double law suggests that obedience to the law and understanding of the law are thoroughly mixed together (722c1); the separation implies that one obeys only after one has understood the reason or reasons for one's obedience. But law does not and cannot wait. It is already in effect before its possible persuasiveness can be effective. The Stranger's preludes altered Clinias enough to have him invite the Stranger to partake in a preliminary form of legislation. The Stranger suggests that all codes need similar preludes; but if they are to be at all like his preludes, they must always be postludes, for Clinias and Megillus were exercised in other ways before they underwent the first round of the Stranger's treatment. If the Stranger's laws were to have a prelude of comparable length, they could not precede the habituation to the laws themselves, for they would then be arguing and cajoling before the citizens were born, and the Stranger's preludes would be Socrates' noble lie, according to which the rulers, the soldiers, and the entire city were completely molded, raised, and educated within the earth (Republic 414d1–e3). The preludes cannot be performed before the songs are known by heart, and they would be superfluous if they merely confirmed what the laws had already drilled in. Even if one assumes, with Clinias, that the Stranger restricts the general prelude solely to the address that he has begun but not yet finished (723a4–b2), the new colonists are all Dorians and inured with principles no less at odds with the Stranger's principles than Clinias and Megillus were. The preludes, then, must be always postludes and at least partial demolitions of the structure and meaning of the laws as experienced.[23] The Stranger goes so far as to suggest, if one takes him literally, that either the children start reading the Laws or their instructors start teaching it to them between the ages of ten and thirteen (811d5–e1). The law must be truly deadly if its antidote has to be given so soon after its ingestion. The Stranger calls preludes ἀνακινήσεις (722d5),

---

uous narrative (as is the syllogistic οὖν at 731c6); but the conclusion he draws is not warranted: "à vrai dire, le passage, comme tout le Vᵉ livre, pourrait être transposé en dialogue par questions et réponses." These particles are rather signs of arguments conducted by the Stranger with himself in shorthand.

23. Insofar as Aristotle assumes for the principle of the Nicomachean Ethics that it is the moral man to whom he is speaking, the relation between virtuous habituation and his account of the virtues reproduces the Stranger's song and postlude (EN 1095b2–13). Indeed, Aristotle takes on the guise of the nonce legislator after the law when he establishes as virtues what before him were not acknowledged to be virtues and consequently had no names.

literally re-motions, or the setting in motion again of once settled things. The preludes are designed to restore the law after the experiential deviations from the law have taken hold of the soul. Oedipus tells Jocasta after he hears her account of the oracle Laius once received: "How a wandering distraction of my soul and re-disturbance (ἀνακίνησις) of my mind hold me in their grip" (Sophocles *Oedipus Tyrannus* 727).

V

PRESCRIPTIONS

I   KNOWLEDGE AND IGNORANCE

Any address to a crowd inexperienced in education, the Stranger had acknowledged, severely limited its persuasiveness (722b5–7); but he ended the fourth book with the remark that it is appropriate and mutually most advantageous for the legislator and his audience to have mastered education as far as they can while they reflect on the eidetic structure of the good (724a7–b2). It would seem that the first part of the prelude, which set the god in his double form apart from the divine, was not to be part of any education. The Stranger refuses to anticipate book 10. This refusal confirms the way in which the Stranger's exposition of the laws is constantly subject to revision. Now that preludes are officially a part of the law and apart from the law, the educational element in persuasion has increased. The second part of the prelude links up with its first part through "gods" and "divine." Soul is declared to be the most divine of all one's possessions after gods, "being most one's own" (οἰκειότατον), or, more literally, "closest to home" (726a2–3). Gods, then, have ceased in some way to be strictly "beings" and become merely the most divine of things. They belong now to one's most intimate possessions. When we say "our god" or "our gods," we are employing, if one thinks in terms of Greek syntax, the genitive of belonging and not the dative of possession. The Stranger seems to have slid them together. The license to do so comes from his summary of the first part of the prelude; he says it was about gods and the dear forefathers (οἱ φίλοι προπάτορες), or, as he had called them earlier, gods of the fathers (πατρῷοι θεοί, 717b5). "One's own forefathers" could also be a translation of οἱ φίλοι προπάτορες.[1] However

---

1. In the *Euthydemus*, Socrates is caught in a trap he foresees but cannot avoid. Dionysodorus asks him whether he has Zeus of his fathers (ἔστιν σοι Ζεὺς πατρῷος;) and he admits he has altars and shrines that are of the family and of the fathers (οἰκεῖα καὶ πατρῷα); he then corrects Dionysodorus and says Ζεὺς πατρῷος is called among Ionians Ζεὺς ἕρκειος καὶ φράτριος; but he grants that Apollo, Zeus, and Athena are his (ἔστιν γάρ σοι, ὡς ἔοικεν, Ἀπόλλων τε καὶ Ζεὺς καὶ Ἀθηνᾶ) and would be his gods

else one may choose to palliate the expression "the most divine of possessions after gods"—the laws after all had been said to be the gods—there
is a sense in which the Stranger has taken to heart the poet's criticism
and accepted the need to speak in the measure of men. The gods are, as
it were, the most perfect versions of ourselves.

Soul is at the crossing of the vertical dimension of the deathless with
the horizontal dimension of the mortal. The second part of the prelude
is going to work out the ways in which it occupies that central position.
The killing of animals in sacrifice and the burying of the dead show that,
as far as practice goes, the soul is already implicit in the continuum of
the gods, *daimones*, heroes, and ancestors. The high rank of the soul is
not a given; to indulge the soul is not to honor it, for only if one makes
it better from worse does the soul obtain honor as a divine good. The
seven ways of indulgence that the Stranger then gives amount to a negative characterization of the eidetic structure of the good. What runs
through the indulgences is ignorance parading as knowledge. They are all
forms of pseudo-wisdom or δοξοσοφία (cf. 732a4–6).[2] The first indulgence
occurs to everyone as soon as he becomes a boy, when he believes he
is competent to know everything. The Stranger seems to allude to the
experiential deviation from the law that comedy represents. The second
indulgence is never to blame oneself for one's own faults and mistakes,
but to believe that others are responsible and oneself error-free. In the
first table of divine goods, justice followed moderation, now it follows
good sense. The third and fourth indulgences belong together; they are
opposed respectively to moderation and courage, for the third consists
in the gratification of pleasures contrary to the speech and praise of the
legislator, and the fourth does not work at enduring the toils, fears, and
pains the legislator praises but gives way before them. The fifth consists
in ignorance of one's own ignorance and maintains that life is worth living at any price: "The soul believes that the things in Hades are bad, and
one does not strain against the soul by teaching and proving that it does
not know whether the things of the gods there are not naturally the greatest of all goods for us" (727d2–5). This error is the most important of all,
since it does not acknowledge the separation of body and soul that was

---

(οὗτοι σοὶ θεοὶ ἂν εἶεν). Socrates is then forced to agree that they are animals (ζῷα), and
since he had earlier admitted that all those animals that he could give away, sell, or
sacrifice to whatever god he wanted were his, he could do the same with his gods
(302b4–307a3).

2. This is the first of three discussions of δοξοσοφία; the second crops up in the
discussion of criminal law (863c4–6); and the last is the main opponent to the theology of book 10.

central for the eidetic structure of the good; Hades is now the invisible bond between them. The sixth error promotes beauty at the expense of virtue, with the false claim that body is more honorable than soul, "for nothing earthborn is more honorable than Olympians, but whoever opines otherwise is ignorantly unaware (ἀγνοεῖ) of how wonderful is the possession that he neglects" (727e1–3). The seventh is to desire the acquisition of money whenever it is ignoble (μὴ καλῶς), or not to be ill at ease in acquiring it, "for all gold on and under the earth is not equivalent in worth to virtue" (728a4–5).

Every human being, the Stranger then sums up, does not know that in all these cases he is disposing the soul, the most divine of possessions, most dishonorably and disgracefully. An inversion of the beautiful and good things that the legislator enumerates and orders occurs in the practice of bad and ugly things. The Stranger then speaks, as one would expect, of right (δίκη) and thus completes the fusion of the good that belongs to the eidetic structure of the good with the just and the beautiful that belong to the genetic structure of law. What the Stranger has been trying to do is to transform the neutral verb "to honor" (τιμᾶν) into a law-laden verb: "Virtually no one of us honors rightly, but we all believe we do" (727a1–2; cf. 728d4–6). He thus admits that his two structures, the eidetic and the genetic, have been established against the common opinion of his audience. This emerges most plainly when he speaks of right (δίκη). What is just and right, he says, is beautiful, but what is called right is in fact punishment (τιμωρία) for evil doing (728b2–c8), which consists in an assimilation to the bad and flight from the good, but virtually no one reckons (λογίζεται) that this is the greatest punishment. Hardly anyone experiences the experience that attends on injustice, for whoever does not undergo punishment is wretched without knowing it, and whoever does get punished and perishes serves as a deterrent to others but remains to the end in ignorance of his own badness.[3] Self-knowledge, then, is the burden of this section of the prelude. It requires paradoxically both a knowledge of the better and the worse in one's own makeup and a knowledge of ignorance. The Stranger, in turning from the gods to the soul, summarizes Plato's *Apology of Socrates*.[4]

The next topic concerns the human goods (728e9–729a2). It denies

3. For this interpretation, see T. J. Saunders, "Notes on the *Laws* of Plato," *Institute of Classical Studies*, supplement 28 (1972): 18–21.

4. Verbs of knowledge and belief occur fourteen times in this passage: ἡγεῖσθαι four times, δοκεῖν and εἰδέναι twice each, ἀγνοεῖν, γιγνώσκειν, δοξάζειν, λογίζεσθαι, οἴεσθαι, and ψεύδεσθαι once.

honor no less to perfect health than to excessive wealth. It thus shows that the prelude cannot be a prescription that anyone can follow for his children, and as for oneself, rather than sickliness being something one would deliberately induce, it must be the acceptance of a condition that diverted one to higher things (cf. 732c6–d3). In the *Republic*, Socrates mentions, along with his own *daimonion*, the continuous ill health of Theages, which checked him from a political career and led him to philosophy (496b6–c76). The structure of the eightfold good thus undergoes a change; it now adds evil to the goodness of certain goods, but inasmuch as it cannot assign a measure to the evil, it remains outside the law. At the same time as the human goods complete the soul's relation to the individual, the plan of the entire prelude becomes clear. It began with man's relation to the deathless, continued with soul, body, and external goods, whose central issue was the formula of tragedy, whether it is best not to be born, and two more sections will now comprehend all divine practices: the first deals with one's relations to others, the second with the opinion others have of oneself (cf. 733a1). One could then formulate the four sections, not altogether inexactly, as follows: (1) soul in relation to god; (2) soul in relation to itself; (3) soul in relation to other human beings; (4) others in relation to soul. The third section extends from one's own children through one's relatives, friends, fellow citizens, guest friends, suppliants, and strangers. It tells one how to behave toward them in terms of one's own inner disposition. The fourth section, though the Stranger says it is about what sort one is oneself (730b3), really handles the showing of oneself to others, since it has to do with praise and blame. Truth (ἀλήθεια) is first and means trustworthiness (730c1–d2); the second is three varieties of justice (730d2–d7); the third the open sharing of one's virtue (730e1–731b3); the fourth the balance between waspishness and gentleness (731b3–d5); the fifth is deference to others and opposed to self-love (731d6–732b4); and the last is the suppression of excessive laughter and tears in the face of sudden good luck or misfortune (732b5–d7).

Several things are notable in the Stranger's formulation. Truth as truthfulness obviously takes over from good sense in the eidetic structure of the good (cf. 729c5–6); justice is still in second place and includes the benefiting of others; and moderation and courage are separated and intertwined in the issues of self-love and chance. So far, then, the Stranger has fulfilled his promise not to legislate anything that does not look to virtue as a whole, but admittedly only if one leaves aside his complementing virtue with piety. The Stranger it seems, cannot move forward without needing what the eidetic structure of the good and the genetic structure of law did not prepare us for, the theology of book 10. Another change, which may not be unrelated, is that the soul is now something more than mind and desire; soul is to be of a noble anger (θυμὸς γενναῖος), and the highest type of just man is spirited or thumoeidetic (θυμοειδής) (731b2, 7). Since the Stranger goes on to say that everyone must be equally gentle (πρᾶος), he casually inserts here the structure of the soul that Socrates, without giving as he admitted a precise account, went to such lengths to elaborate in the *Republic* (435b9–d5). Socrates had begun with the watchdog as the perfect model of harshness and gentleness together; but though he said the watchdog was philosophic in both ways, he was forced to recant and assign gentleness solely to the philosophic (*Republic* 375d7–376c6; cf. *Timaeus* 17d8–18a7). How the thumoeidetic and the philosophic converge and diverge may be said to be the nerve of the *Republic*. In the *Laws*, the Stranger first says that whoever helps the magistrates in punishing the unjust is the great and perfect man in the city, and he ranks him higher than either the nonwrongdoer—in *Republic* terms the man who minds his own business—or whoever prevents the unjust from acting unjustly; but the Stranger does not ground these differences in nature. After he distinguishes between generous competition and resentful denigration, however, he argues that it is impossible to escape from the unjust who are either stubbornly or incurably unjust unless one never lets up on their punishment. The Stranger implies that the fierceness required is hardly separable from resentment; one has to gentle one's anger and hold it back in all cases where the unjust are curable, and only let it go against whoever is incorrigibly bad. Gentleness is a consequence of knowledge; one has to know that no one is willingly unjust and injustice is one of the greatest evils (731c2–d4). This knowledge is subsequent to indignation, which is not naturally allied with any knowledge of injustice. This knowledge, moreover, would not suffice for just punishment, for one would also have to know how to detect the incurable and perhaps be oneself the physician of the soul. Could one always trust even in that case that the ineffectiveness of one's treatment was the same as incurability? Callicles claims that Socrates has not turned him around, but does that mean that no one could? The Stranger seems to be preparing the ground for the enigma of book 9: how a Socratic principle can be the foundation of criminal law. The gentleness Socrates ascribed to his guardians was due to their natural friendship even with those fellow-citizens who were intent on mischief (see also *Republic* 470c5–9). In the criminal code of the *Laws*, citizens are punished for many crimes more severely than metics, strangers, or slaves.

The paradox with which the *Laws* began was the notion, which Clinias introduced, of being superior and inferior to oneself. The Stranger's prelude confronts the paradox head-on (731d6–732b4). The soul as the cause of one's life is to be discounted and the soul as the possible recipient of good to be praised. The eidetic structure of the good is used as an engine to dissolve the self from whatever goods belong to it. To love oneself is to believe one is something without the good. It is to be in Hades. This greatest of all errors puts what is one's own ahead of the good, the beautiful, and the just. It is to mistake opinion for wisdom. Opinion is always one's own opinion. It necessarily lacks the transparent anonymity of knowledge. The sole knowledge that is one's own knowledge is the knowledge that one knows virtually nothing. It is to know what one does not know. The knowledge of ignorance is virtually the all-encompassing theme of the Stranger's second prelude. The second prelude virtually summarizes the argument of Plato's *Lysis*.

Just before the Stranger turns to the human, he speaks of hope; but hope does not figure in the subsequent analysis of pleasure and pain (732d8–734e2). Hope is to diminish the vehemence of afflictions, and the imminence of evil is to color the presence of good (732c6–d3). Since the god, one's own *daimōn*, and the *daimones* determine one's fortune, hope and fear cannot strictly belong to the human. The Stranger distinguishes between what we want and do not want, on the one hand, and, on the other, the kinds of lives that are available to us. There are according to him only eight available to us; to believe there are others is due to ignorance and inexperience. There is the moderate life, the thoughtful life, the courageous life, the healthy life, and their four opposites (733e3–6). The contrast in the difference between the moderate life and the licentious turns on the difference between "pleasantly" and "pleasure," so that if one wants to live pleasantly it is impossible to choose the life of intense pleasures and pains.[5] The Stranger, moreover, had said that the life we want is any life whatsoever in which, with a multitude of great and intense pleasures and pains, the pleasures surpass the pains; but it now turns out that there is no life of this kind. The Stranger means that though it might happen for a life fitting this description to befall someone, he could not have chosen it, for he would have chosen a life out of his own control and consequently the intense pain of his insane desires must always outpace their satisfaction (cf. *Gorgias* 491e5–492a3). It thus seems that the immoderate and insane life is not choosable, any more than the life of sheer terror or the life of utter stupidity is open to us. The choices we make are determined by other considerations and always

---

5. Cf. Seth Benardete, *The Tragedy and Comedy of Life* (Chicago 1993), 98–99.

presuppose some virtue.[6] The only pair of lives the Stranger does not mention is the just and the unjust life. Clinias had expressed a preference for the life of the tyrant and a repugnance against tyranny. Does the Stranger now exclude the life of injustice because he had himself voiced the legislator's wish for a certain type of tyrant? Or is he assuming what he had recently declared, that no one can willingly choose injustice? The life of justice is equally set aside perhaps because the distress the thumoeidetic man feels at injustice and the pleasure he secretly takes in punishment are beyond any calculus.

2 THE REAL AND THE IMAGINARY

The completion (τέλος) of the prelude should herald the start of the song (νόμος); the prelude ought to give the keynote of the regime; but there is not and cannot be any one law of the regime. The Stranger hastens to correct himself: "But rather in truth there surely must be an outline of the laws (νόμοι) of the regime" (734e3–6). Nothing of the sort happens. One might suspect that the surreptitious introduction of a Socratic principle and a Socratic understanding of soul might have something to do with the postponement. The Stranger will soon take up Socrates' proposal of communism and deny that it is feasible, even though such a city is still to be the paradigm for the laws (739a1–e7). The Stranger seems to have got himself into a fix. He had rejected an account of the regime-structure in the name of a theocracy, and his second prelude had then pitched virtue so high that everyone had to be either a Socrates or at worst Socrates' guardians. There is now a crisis of rule. This crisis shows up in an image taken from weaving, which the Stranger seems to borrow from the *Statesman,* and he then follows it up with an image of the city's population as a herd, though he admits that it ought to have come earlier in thought. The inverse structure of the *Statesman,* which went from herding to weaving, prepares the way for an abbreviated account of the *Republic.* One cannot but be reminded that the myth of the age of Cro-

---

6. Burnet's construal of the difficult ὑπερβαλλόντων (734c7), as England reports it, points to these other considerations: ὡς τῶν μὲν (sc. τῶν ἡδέων) τῷ φίλῳ ἡμῖν ὑπερβαλλόντων . . . τῶν δ᾽ αὖ (sc. τῶν λυπηρῶν) τοῖς ἐχθροῖς (ἡμῖν ὑπερβαλλόντων): "on the grounds that the pleasant things exceed by their dearness to us, and in turn the painful things exceed by their hatefulness to us." "He finds," England says, "a suggested distinction between what is pleasant generally and what is pleasant to the individual *by being especially adapted to his nature.*" See also T. J. Saunders, "Notes on the *Laws* of Plato," 25–27.

nus, a version of which separated the shepherd from the weaver in the *Statesman*, preceded the Stranger's address to the assembled colonists. There are allusions, then, to two dialogues in neither of which does the law occupy a central place. Both the philosopher-king and the statesman rule without it.

The distinction the Stranger now makes between warp and woof, in light of which the rulers are to correspond to the greater strength and solidity of the warp-threads, and the ruled to the softer and just equitableness of the woof-threads, implies that the prelude is addressed to the rulers and the laws proper are to be addressed to the ruled. The rulers are to be moved solely by honor and disgrace, the ruled by rewards and punishment.[7] The prelude is designed to be a test of the undifferentiated settlers. Whoever responds favorably to its exhortation belongs to the rulers, whoever does not belongs to the ruled. The image of warp and woof implies as well that as persuasion is to force and as free are to slaves, so the eidetic structure of the good is to the genetic structure of law. Unfortunately, the Stranger does not work out his image in a clear manner; it would have run smoothly had he said, "Just as the warp and woof must be different if they are to be woven together, so in a like manner the rulers and the ruled must also differ if there is to be one city or one regime." Instead he says:

> Just as [in the case of] any weaving together or maybe any other web whatsoever (καθάπερ οὖν δή τινα συνυφὴν ἢ καὶ πλέγμ' ἄλλ' ότιοῦν), it is not possible to make woof and warp from the same [threads], but it is necessary for the genus of the warp-threads to be superior in point of virtue—it is strong and has obtained a certain solidity in its twistings, but the woof is softer and enjoys some just equitableness—on the basis of which (ὅθεν δή) there must be a proportional discrimination in just this way between those who will rule the magistracies in the cities and those in turn who are confirmed and tested with a slight education. There are, in fact, two species of regime, the establishment of magistracies for each [magistrate], and the assignment of laws to the magistracies. (734e6–735a6)

---

7. Cf. Helvetius (quoted by A. V. Dicey, *Lectures on the Relation between Law and Public Opinion in England during the Nineteenth Century* [London: Macmillan, 1905], 458 note 1): "Moralists ought to know that as the sculptor fashions the trunk of a tree into a god or a stool, so the legislator makes heroes, geniuses, virtuous men, as he wills: . . . reward, punishment, fame, disgrace, are four kinds of divinities with which he can always effect the public good."

The Stranger breaks the construction of his sentence twice; he begins with accusatives that have no verb to govern them, and he replaces "so in a like manner" with another connective (ὅθεν δή). The consequence of the first inconcinnity is that the difference between warp and woof is given but not the way in which they make up the web, any more than one can figure out from the difference between rulers and ruled how magistracies and laws form a single regime, for the second inconcinnity prevents the restoration of the required sense and keeps the two elements of the city apart. We know from the *Statesman* that warp and woof can reflect the difference between courage and moderation, and politically the difference between the martial and the judicial elements of the city, but they could only do so because the statesman was their weaver.[8] Here there is no statesman. The Stranger's decision to replace the double law with prelude and law forces the regime to unravel. He too has turned his regime into a faction, in which the stronger make the weaker do what is just. The tyrant still casts his shadow over the purported theocracy. The vertical element of rule and the horizontal dimension of law, which is the political translation of the difference between the eidetic structure of the good and the genetic structure of law, do not consist together. It is mainly for this reason that the laws cannot be laid down before the Stranger devises a way to tone down the dissonance he himself created.

The Stranger's first solution is wholly imaginary. He remarks that only a tyrant could be ruthless enough to carry out the culling of a herd; he dismisses out of hand the possibility Socrates himself needed, of a rhetoric that would persuade everyone over ten to leave on their own (*Republic* 540a5–541a7). A legislator without tyranny is reduced to the gentlest of remedies; it is euphemistically called a deliverance (ἀπαλλαγή), but really means "good riddance to bad rubbish." The Stranger informs Clinias that Cnossos would be the city most suited to the new legislation if, as he had surmised, the new settlement mostly consists of the havenots (707e3–4); but, as it is, the legislation is going to be imposed on the possible offscourings of every Cretan city, and Clinias's first task will be to scoop out the dregs or divert them somewhere else. The Stranger can do in speech what Clinias can never do in deed (736b4–7). With the utterance of perfect imperatives—πεπεράνθω and ἔστω συμβεβηκυῖα —they have won over the good and dismissed the bad. The bad, he says, have been tested over time, by means of every form of persuasion, to show

---

8. Aristotle, in citing this passage, remarks that Plato failed to say how the rulers will differ from the ruled (*Politics* 1265b18–21).

their true colors. If Clinias had not put up so much resistance to the Stranger's original proposal, when he had despaired of ever finding a way either to convert a homogeneous swarm to new laws or to fuse together a heterogeneous crowd, the selection from the applicants to the new colony would have been the tyrant's first act, and the prelude to the laws would have been the end of the laws. The law as a means to reconcile the majority of the bad with the minority of the good would have become superfluous. Such a rearrangement, however, at which the Stranger now hints (735a7), would not have sufficed. Once the tyrant carried out the selection, the Stranger could have proceeded directly to the number of the citizens and the laying out of the country; but had he done so, he would then have had to have pushed forward the issue of communism. He prefaces that issue with the observation that it would surprise anyone who was not reflective and experienced in legislation that the city they are going to found is second in comparison with the best. Because it is so unusual, he would not expect it of any legislator who was not a tyrant (739a1–6).[9] The legislator-tyrant would then come very close to being Socrates' philosopher-king, and at least the communistic part of his proposal would become feasible. But if, then, we were to finish this extensive contrafactual, all the property arrangements of book 5 would go, and we would be left with its penultimate item, the demand that everything in the city be based on modular 12, and the sciences of number, plane and solid geometry, harmonics, and of circular and noncircular motions be studied as part of a liberal education (746d3–c2). These sciences are the same as those that Socrates proposed in book 7 of the *Republic*. They were meant to prepare the way for the rule of philosopher-kings. The revision, then, of the Stranger's present way thus points up two things: how the second-best regime always trails in the wake of the best simply, and how the *Laws* is haunted, ever since book 3, by the problem of beginning. These two things seem to be not unconnected. It is because the best is always out of reach that one is always getting started (cf. 728c9–d3).

No sooner does the Stranger declare what is to be done as already done than he comes down to earth with a bump and reverts to a piece of good luck he had earlier discovered in Dorian history (736c5–6; cf. 684e3–5). Unencumbered property is the lasting foundation of any political order; everything the Stranger has said so far presupposed what he had taken for granted. He has been going forward on the basis of a condition that, if it were not in place, would make him either a fool or a reluctant participant (737a7–b4). The Stranger seems to be straightening out his

9. For this translation, see L. A. Post, *AJP* 75 (1954): 206.

own crooked path, for this too should have been put up front along with the weeding out of the colonists; but, as it is, this indispensable advantage proves to be inferior to the abolition of all private property. The Stranger now goes out of his way to imagine what one would do if one had to handle a city where it was as impossible to cancel debts and redistribute property as it was to let the burdens of poverty remain as they were. His solution seems fantastical.[10] The agitators ought to be large property owners with many debtors, and over a long period of time they ought to cancel the debts and redistribute their own property. Their principle of action would be that poverty does not consist in making one's property less but in making one's insatiety more (736e2–3). When the Stranger reformulates the principle, and says it is the only way out, one begins to see what he means. It is nonavariciousness joined with justice (τὸ μὴ φιλοχρηματεῖν μετὰ δίκης). His agitators, then, who can belong to any so-called regime, must have been animated by a divine love (θεῖος ἔρως) of moderate and just practices; and that, he had said, was really difficult and rarely happened in a long time (711d6–e7). It was not to be compared with his own prayer for a young tyrant of a certain type. The Stranger, it seems, even when he has clear sailing, must take his bearings by the *Republic*.

The Stranger admits that only a thorough inspection of the site of the future city can determine how many men, if they live soberly, the land can support, and whether the maximum number suffices to defend the country against its neighbors and help out any who are unjustly attacked (737c6–d6). He grants that there might be a discrepancy between the two numbers, and only an initial expansion at the expense of a neighbor could bring them into line. A variant of this problem confronted Socrates' city, which under Glaucon's demand had expanded in order to satisfy his craving for luxuries; but when Socrates had eliminated Glaucon's taste for the superfluous and put the city of fevered heat on a crash diet, he did not shrink its territory, for the guardians could not live the life of the true city if there were no surplus to support their unproductive virtue. The Stranger does not make it any easier for himself. He picks a number out of thin air that seems to require, as Aristotle says, a huge number of metics, slaves, and foreigners to sustain so idle a population (*Politics* 1265a13–28). Socrates' city had at least its artisan-businessmen as part of the citizen body; but the Stranger does not allow any contamination of

---

10. Cicero, however, tells a story about Aratus, who succeeded in reconciling the dispossessed with the present owners of their estates, that might indicate its feasibility; but Aratus had outside resources and had to persuade that money be accepted for property (*De officiis* 2.81–82).

his people. Fifty-nine numbers go evenly into the number he picks, 5,040, but the Stranger does not use most of them in his calculations, and on occasion he has to use others. The Stranger thus juxtaposes his knowledge of a number that has very pretty arithmetical properties of no significance with his ignorance of the real nature of the territory and its population. He is deliberately working in the dark on a blueprint that necessarily falls short of the best. It looks like an impossible project. How can what is only in speech borrow so haphazardly from what is in deed and still be a self-consistent plan? Even if Clinias will have to make compromises all along the line, he can still, the Stranger insists, build on his scheme (745e7–746d2). The Stranger allows that every number he proposes might have to be altered in practice, but that the set of prescriptions still holds. The Stranger himself, however, had objected, when he assumed the guise of the poet, that law and number go together, and if the slots for the numbers remain blank, one no longer has law but exhortation or prelude, and prelude is only for those who have no need of laws.

The Stranger seems to be squeezing himself into a tight corner. An "ideal" number, whose properties the proper authorities must come to know at their leisure, must be accommodated to the number of gods the founder of the city discovers to be already in place. None of the sanctuaries, temples, altars, or statues ought to be dislodged, regardless of whether local traditions or foreign influences led to their consecration (738b2–d2; cf. 848d1–5).[11] The Stranger implies that 5,040 has so many factors that there can hardly be any number of gods, *daimones*, and heroes that does not already divide evenly into it, or, if their number falls short, suitable additions can readily be made (cf. 759a8–b4); but primarily, we are led to believe, he must be thinking of the convenient matchup between the twelve districts, into which he is going to divide the territory and the city, and the twelve Olympian gods, to each one of whom one district is to be consecrated (745d7–e2; 820b7–c2). The Stranger, however, never does assign these gods to their parishes; rather, the only god who has a parish assigned to him is the chthonic god Plouton (828c6–d1).[12] The number twelve, then, must refer primarily to the months of the year (758d5–7; 771b3–6), and the reflection on earth of the celestial order is

11. Wilamowitz compares the Stranger's proposal to Clisthenes' preservation of the old cults when he made the new demes and tribes (*Platon* [Berlin 1919] II, 398).

12. Ritter mentions this peculiarity, along with the absence of any further assignment of gods to the districts, and the primacy of the months of the year for the number 12 (131 and note).

embodied in the lunar calendar. Had the Stranger chosen a multiple of 365, he would have lost some integral factors, but he would have gained the number of days in the solar year, on each one of which some magistracy is to sacrifice (828a7–b3). The apparent coincidence of old traditions with the latest in number theory (5,040=7!) is an illusion. The real purpose of the sacred is not the concrete illustration of scientific knowledge but the light (φῶς) it provides for knowledge by acquaintance (738d7–e8). Friendly feeling, which regular gatherings at the temples promote, is once more said to be the greatest good for a city. No distrust of old stories, whether apparitions (φάσματα) of gods occurred or inspiration from them was reported, should detract from the usefulness of what persuasion established. Here are the clearings where one shows oneself to be not counterfeit but simple and true, and where one learns to detect those who are out to deceive.

Just before the Stranger is going to rule out communism, he suggests that its principle—the things of friends are in common—and corollary—everything is out in the open and there is no place to hide—can be made up for by the proper exploitation of the sacred. In order to duplicate what one cannot really achieve, one is to abide by the principle, "Do not budge what cannot be budged." This principle (μὴ κινεῖν τἀκίνητα), to which the Stranger plainly alludes, pertains to everything that is sacred. The Stranger's very next move, however, violates it. In the ancient game of checkers, the last move of utter desperation is to move one's piece from the line called sacred (739a1). The vindication of the sacred involves its playful violation. Although the sacred saturates the second-best city, and the city retains as well the natural privacy of eyes, ears, and hands, it still must look to the nonsacred city, where holy matrimony is newly defined as whatever is most useful (Republic 458e3–4). The Stranger suggests, then, a ready formula for converting the paradigm of the best city into its second-best approximation: Find the sacred equivalent to all that is rational in it. But even if one grants that the Stranger has found in the light of sacred festivals a likely match to the transparency of communism, there cannot be comparable elements throughout the regime without, as the Stranger later admits, establishing secret police everywhere and thus destroying what he wanted to preserve (807e2–808a7). The Stranger indicates how loose the fit between the paradigm and its closest copies must be when he remarks that he has to leave it up to Clinias whether he chooses the first, second, or third-best regime, "or whoever else at any time should be willing, in approaching the models, to assign to himself, in accordance with his own temperament, whatever he likes of his own fatherland" (739b4–7; cf. 681c4–d1).[13] It is not easy to say why the *Laws* should not now be at an end. There would seem to be not one but an infinite variety of third bests, modelled on the second best, all of which would have traces in their institutions of wisdom and justice combined, but none of which could claim that it had done any better than conform with the whims of its legislator and the conditions he could do nothing about. Everyone knows that the Stranger is going to adopt large chunks of Athenian law.

"A city and regime are first and its laws the best, wherever the ancient saying comes to be (γίγνηται) throughout the city as far as possible; and the saying is, 'Really and truly (ὄντως) the things of friends are (ἐστί) in common'" (739b8–c3). The best city is a matter of becoming, friendship just is. The friends of the saying are two, the city is one to the extent that the laws can make it so (cf. 739d6–7). Friends must still have what they share, in the best city no one has anything to share. The principle of the best city contradicts the aim of the best city. Its model is the single individual and not two friends (cf. *Republic* 462c10; 464b2): "It has removed from life everything that is generally spoken of everywhere as private, and has contrived as far as possible, by hook or by crook, for even the naturally private things to have become common, for example, for eyes to be thought (δοκεῖν) to see, for ears to be thought to hear, and for hands to be thought to act in common, and for everyone, in turn, in joy or in pain at the same things, to praise or to blame as one" (739c5–d3). Not only, then, does it seem impossible to discover in speech a stable basis for a regime of the second rank, but the best, if it is in itself inconsistent, cannot be that against which it is to be measured. If, however, one looks back to the Stranger's account of choral songs and dances, where to perform well in them was to be well educated, then the law has the same aim as communism, to put in concert the opinions and feelings of everyone in the city, from the start to the very end of life (cf. 659c9–e3; 994c1–d2). The citizens, through doing the same things as they hear, end up by seeing the same things: the shadows on the wall of the Cave. The commonality of opinion (νομίζειν) communizes the dianoetic imagination (740a3–b1). The law, then, simply reproduces the contradiction at the heart of the best city, for while it casts over the city a strict uniformity of opinion, it declares the sanctity of the private. It protects the family as it weakens it by prohibiting incest and demanding devotion to a common mother. If friends are those who are willing to stand in for one another,

13. On this third, see O. Apelt, *Platons Gesetz* (Leipzig 1916), vol. 1, 244 note 78; 252–253; 259 note 82.

then the law takes over this principle in the form of substitutability: everyone under the law is the same as any other. The law, in its impersonality, aims at the equivalent of friendship. The "other I" of friends becomes equality before the law (cf. 757a5).

"Let them make the distribution (νεμέσθων) [of earth (γῆ) and houses] with some such thought (διάνοια) as this: he who obtains this portion must believe (νομίζειν) it common to the whole city, and since the country (χώρα) is the fatherland (πατρίς) he must treat her with greater respect than children do their mother, by the degree to which she, by being a goddess, has become the mistress of things that are mortal, and he must have the same thoughts (διανοήματα) as well about *daimones* and the gods who are in place in the country (ἐγχώριοι θεοί)" (740a2–b1; cf. 877d5–8; *Republic* 414de2–6). The earth is and is not the country, the mother is and is not the fatherland,[14] the part is and is not the whole, the gods and goddesses are and are not one's own. One's lot, the Stranger says, which made the distribution (ὁ νείμας κλῆρος), is a god (741b5). The law, in making divisions in deed that it wants to wipe out in thought, cannot but induce experientially a denial of everything it wants to be believed. Unlike the situation in the best city, there is going to be nothing in the second best that confirms its stories. The noble lie gets debased.

The rest of book 5 is equally concerned with means to equalize the unequal (741a7–b1). Training in mathematics wakes up the sleepy and naturally stupid; it leads to improvement against nature by divine fortune (747b3–6; cf. *Republic* 526b5–10). The arithmetical measure, for which every one is a cipher, is to work with the law against any show of difference. Despite the fact that moneymaking is strictly curtailed, the commensuration of the incommensurate and the uniformization of the non-uniform that lawful currency (νόμισμα) establishes remains the intent of the law and lawful ways (cf. 918a8–b6).[15] It would be better, the Stranger says, for each colonist to come with an equal amount of money, but as this is impossible, there will be instead an equality of opportunity, with honors and magistracies apportioned out "as equally as possible by

14. The tyrant, Socrates says in the *Republic* (574d4–8), "just as he was then punishing his mother and father, will in this way again, if he can, punish his fatherland (πατρίς), . . . and so he will have and take care of his formerly dear fatherland and, as the Cretans say, motherland (μητρίς)." On the confusion about the status of real property in the *Laws*, see W. G. Becker, *Platons Gesetze und das griechische Familienrecht, Münchener Beiträge zur Papyrusforschung und antiken Rechtsgeschichte*, vol. 14 (Munich 1932), 131–133.

15. Demosthenes (24.213) reports a saying of Solon: "Just as private individuals had invented money to be currency (νόμισμα) for the sake of private transactions, so laws (νόμοι) are the currency of the city."

means of an unequal but proportionate measure" (744c3). The twelve sections of the country are so divided that those with poorer soil are larger and those with richer are smaller; and each of the 5,040 lots are divided in two on the same basis, and whoever has one half of his lot right next to the city, which is founded as near as possible in the center, has his other lot on the border of the country, and the same ratio is maintained for every other divided property. Each of the twelve sections is also to have the same number of rich and poor (745b3–d7). The neatness of the first distribution seems to be a recipe for disaster over time: if the country police carry out the improvements the Stranger recommends (761a6–b6), how will the lots remain equal? It is one thing to stem the growth of excessive wealth, it is another to avoid resentment at apparent inequality. Even in the first distribution, some will have the two halves of their lot contiguous. Mathematical training of a rather high order is required if everyone is to figure out for himself that appearances are deceiving; but, as the Stranger says, illiberal pettiness is thought to be a concomitant of exact calculation (746e3–c3).[16]

In looking back from the end of book 5, one sees that the Stranger's proposals can be divided between, on the one hand, that section of the second part of the prelude which involved the self and its extension through property to whatever could be called one's own, and, on the other, that section that was devoted to selflessness and sharing. These two sections are thus reflected in the law's attempt to embrace the self-contradictory structure of the best city in speech. The Stranger has also managed to translate the vertical line of deathlessness, which characterized the first part of his prelude, into its spatial dimension by consecrating the city and all its parts to the gods, to whom in turn he has given a habitation and a name. The Stranger, however, throws off the spell of his own construction and labels it a dream: he was molding a city and its citizens out of wax (745e7–d2). It would *never* be the case that all the indispensable conditions would coincide: the men will refuse to comply with the restrictions, and the country and the town will not be susceptible to his measures. The Stranger then answers his own charge:

> In each of the things that is going to be, I suspect this is the most just: The exhibitor of the paradigm—what sort the undertaking ought to be—should not omit any of the most beautiful and truest things, but whoever finds any element in them impossible, he should swerve

16. See further, A. Rameil, *Die Wirtschaftsstabilität und ihre Problematik in Platons Gesetzesstaat* (Munich 1973), 18–19.

aside from it and not do it, but whatever of the rest is nearest to the paradigm, and whatever appropriate action bears the greatest natural kinship to it,[17] he should contrive for this to come into being, but it is most just to allow the legislator to complete and finish off his wish list, and once it is done, then examine together with him what of the proposals fits and what of the legislation is an obstacle; for it is surely true that in all cases even the craftsman of the most paltry thing, if he is to be worthy of regard, must produce self-consistency (τὸ ὁμολο-γούμενον αὐτὸ αὑτῷ).[18] (746b5–d2)

The Stranger seems to take back everything. If neither the land nor the people can put up with what he has outlined after the prelude, what can be salvaged? Are the elements of his plan so detachable from one another that Clinias can pick and choose and put into effect one or two and ignore the rest? If self-consistency is the prerequisite for the blueprint, as Clinias later acknowledges, when he almost bites his tongue for momentarily interrupting its completion (805b3–c1), the Stranger must be aiming at a higher generality than the framework he appears to be setting out. There must be a structure of law as such that can be formulated regardless of any set of laws in which that structure is embedded.

The Stranger then proceeds to illustrate the self-consistency of his plan (746d3–e3). He reverts to the number twelve, whose factors and multiples up to 5,040 will yield not only the number of fratries, demes, and villages, but the order of armies in battle and on the march, coinage, weights, dry and liquid measures. The Stranger never again refers to fratries, but if kinship groups are meant, then even generation is to be subject to number. All utensils, he continues, should also be standard-ized, and one should not shrink from it in fear of the reputation for small-mindedness. The universal principle (κοινὸς λόγος) that the legislator should maintain (νομίσαντα) is that numbers in their divisions and com-plexities are useful for everything (746e3–747a5). The essence of the law

17. Taking τῶν προσηκόντων πράσσειν with ὅτι and συγγενέστατον as parallel to ἐγγύτατα with K. Schöpsdau, "Der Staatsentwurf der Nomoi zwischen Ideal und Wir-klichkeit," *RhM* 134 (1991): 142 note 16.

18. The expression τὸ αὐτὸ αὑτῷ ὁμολογούμενον occurs in the *Phaedrus* (265d7; cf. *Timaeus* 29c6) as a partial characterization of Socrates' first speech about Eros; it be-longs to one of two species of speech; whereas one species "in a synoptic view brings things scattered everywhere into one look (ἰδέα), in order that by defining each thing it may make plain about whatever it wants to teach," the other species is able to di-vide things species by species at their natural joints and not break off a mere part (μέρος). The first species, then, presumably gains its clarity at the expense of the natu-ral articulation of a whole. Socrates' first speech is clearly divided into sections on the goods of the soul, the goods of the body, external goods, and pleasure.

is to be found in the specious identification of the measure of the mean with the arithmetical measure. The *esprit de géometrie* parades in it as the *esprit de finesse*. In the *Statesman*, the Eleatic Stranger had begun by putting the political art together with arithmetic and all other arts stripped of actions (258d4–6); and the consequence of that understanding of "theory" (τὸ γνῶναι) was to make the statesman conform with the paradigm of the divine shepherd, whose grazing (νέμειν) of the human herd in the golden age survives now under other conditions in the law. The Athenian Stranger, in redefining law on the basis of the myth of the golden age, seems to have been preparing us for the same conclusion. It is no wonder, then, that the poet was the first to object to the Stranger's procedure. The poet is wholly indifferent to the arithmetical measure. The speeches he puts in the mouths of his characters are commensurate with them, and precisely for this reason there are no numbers in them.

The legislator, however, cannot avoid either number or the irritation it causes. The Stranger's solution is to turn the argument completely around and reassess the function of number. Number is not so much an instrument of the law as it is the single most important element in education. The Stranger implies that even if Clinias has to dispense with modular 12, and thus give up the self-consistency of the paradigm, what he must preserve at all cost are the mathematical sciences. It is the task of other laws and practices to rid souls of the illiberality and love of money that might otherwise accompany the learning of these beautiful and appropriate subjects (747b6–c2). The Stranger strongly suggests that wisdom depends on mathematics, and if elsewhere, as in Egypt or Phoenicia, it has turned out that so-called criminal wickedness (πανουργία) has arisen along with it, though he cannot say whose fault it was—the legislator perhaps was no good, fortune was harsh, or nature—he knows that it cannot be ascribed to mathematics. The Stranger warns Clinias that some regions are better than others, and no sensible legislator would legislate against the conditions he cannot alter. These conditions include divine influences—temples ordained by Ammon, the Egyptian Zeus, or sacrifices from as far off as Etruria might still remain on the spot (738b6–c5)—and they can work for or against him. It is possible, the Stranger concludes book 5, that the place Cnossos has chosen is cursed, and whatever led to the former migration might still be as malevolent. Clinias accepts the advice and thereby admits he knows nothing of the site. "The god," the Stranger later says, restored the city of Magnesia (919d4; cf. 946b6).

VI

ON GETTING STARTED

I BEGINNINGS AND MAGISTRACIES

At the beginning of the sixth book, the Stranger raises in quick succession four problems of beginning. If the city is just getting started, (1) how can anyone have proved his competence to rule? (2) how can the electors choose properly if they have not been raised in the ways of the laws? (3) how can there be an authority to maintain the new laws in the face of the distress they will initially cause? and, finally, (4) where is one to get the authorities to start off the new enterprise? The Stranger introduces these problems, which admit of more or less imperfect solutions, with a more general issue. This issue resumes a topic that stood in the way of the Stranger following up at once the prelude with the song (734e3–735a6). Other considerations then flooded in with a higher priority: there was a ceiling on the regime if either the legislator was not the tyrant or there could not be institutional means for the elimination of the private, and the sacred and numerical devices had to be relied on instead. Now that the Stranger returns to the magistracies, he proposes to handle, not the two species of regime—magistracies and laws—but rather two species within the first of those species—magistracies and the laws to be assigned to them (751a4–b2). The laws themselves are once more postponed.

If cities have good laws, the Stranger remarks, but the magistracies set over them are unsuitable, not only are the laws of no use, to say nothing of the laughter that would result, but cities would incur the greatest injury and ruin from them (751b5–c2). If the laws are only on paper and no one is there to see to their compliance, the laughter is easy to understand; but the injury and ruin are not as obvious. Is any departure from good laws worse than disobedience to bad laws, and the blight on the ideal necessarily deadlier than corruption of the rotten? The Stranger must be proposing something really risky if even that which falls far short of the best carries with it such dangers (cf. 752b5–6). If the magistracies and the laws are not to be mismatched, the laws, one would imagine, should be given first, for the magistracies must be adjusted to them and not the laws to the magistracies. The Stranger's own way denies this apparently self-evident principle. He sets up the magistrates independent of the laws they are to administer. The problems he raises have nothing to do with the laws of the *Laws* but apply to any new founding whatsoever, provided that a people do not just move elsewhere with their laws intact. The Stranger, then, seems to be working out the consequences of his own image of warp and woof, and arguing that, if any adjustment is to be made, the woof of the laws has to comply with the greater virtue and education in the warp of rule; but the Stranger in fact does not set the magistracies higher than the laws. A mixture of monarchy and democracy determines the general structure of the magistracies, and great care is taken to insure that the indifference of chance mollify the resentment of the demos (756e9–10; 757e4; cf. 759b5–7). Knowledge, experience, and education qualify by law the right to hold some magistracies, but virtue and good sense never. The Stranger grants that there are two kinds of equality, and the regime must, for the sake of friendship, hit upon a mean between masters and slaves, on the one hand, and, on the other, the good and the bad; but despite the fact that the assignment of the unequal to the unequal produces all goods, no matter how small its contribution may be, the Stranger does not establish any procedure for the perfect and precise kind of right to prevail anywhere in the city. The equitable and the indulgent (τὸ ἐπιεικὲς καὶ σύγγνωμον) are like a shard broken off from the just itself, but their use is unavoidable if there is not to be civil strife (757c6–758a2). Indeed, the Stranger employs six out of the seven claims of right, in various measures, when he determines the lawful qualifications for rule;[1] but those six claims were supposed to be decisive only below the horizon of the eidetic structure of the good. Now they are conspicuously in first place, and the eidetic and genetic structures, with which the Stranger began, have disappeared. The magistracies are built to last; their very indifference to higher considerations is designed to support the delicate threads of the law. The magistracies constitute a structure within the law that reflects a deviation from the law. They are there to fall back on, they are not there to set one straight.

---

1. The right of the mother and father is to determine the relation of Cnossos to the new city (754a9–b7); Cnossos is to claim the privilege that goes along with its greater antiquity (752e4); ancestral priesthoods are not to be disturbed (759a8–b1); priests are to come from pure households (759c2–6; cf. 751c7); the right of age in various degrees holds in all magistracies; the right of the stronger shows up in the greater weight given to those of higher property assessments; the right of masters over slaves is later admitted to be a conundrum (777b4–c1); and chance of course is inserted into the elections at various points.

Once the Stranger poses the first problem, Clinias believes it would be pretty nearly impossible for the election of magistrates to be faultless (751d6). In posing the problem, the Stranger does not indicate that the first magistrates are as little brought up in the new laws as are their electors; he stresses the electors' lack of education and unfamiliarity with one another (751c5–d5). If the founders were superior in understanding to the first settlers, it would be perhaps an advantage, after the laws have stamped everyone with the same character, if that discrepancy were somehow to be preserved; but this ceases to be a possibility once the Stranger declines to become a partner in the regime (753a5–8), and Clinias is the sole conduit between the *Laws* and Magnesia. Everything is going to be filtered through him. He is to guide his fellow Cnossians as they put into effect laws that are at least as repugnant to them as to every Dorian who is enrolled, and they are to decide on their own whether the practices of the new citizens are in conformity with the intention of the laws. The Stranger washes his hands of the real business of founding after he insists that Cnossos cannot just pay ritual heed to its obligations (752d3–7). Magnesia is never going to get off the ground. Even should one suppose that by some miracle the first magistrates were devoted to the letter of the law, and the law was so clear that no ambiguity in their reading of it could arise, it would take nearly eighty years before everyone in the city had lost every trace of other laws; but by that time the contamination from the past would have altered the ways of the people, and it is certainly possible that not even the Stranger, were he by some miracle to return, would then recognize the laws he laid down. Who would realize that the common mess in timocracies preserves a trace of the communism of Socrates' best city?

That the beginning is more than the whole of the work is proverbial, and, the Stranger says, all of us praise a beautiful start; but, he continues, it appears to him that it is in fact more than half, and no one has adequately praised the coming to be of a beautiful start (753e6–754a2). On the basis of his own inadequate suggestion now, whose difficulties he acknowledges (754b1–2), we can say that no one has ever praised such a start because it has never occurred. The Stranger himself had noted the absence of mind at the beginning of the becoming of mind, and the absence of the whole of virtue at the beginning of cities. All the same, he says, just because they cannot devise a faultless beginning, that cannot be an excuse for either him or Clinias to back out of the project (751d8–752b3). Just as Clinias cannot renege on his promise to the Cretans to found the city, so the Stranger must live up to his promise to help Clinias "along the lines of the present mythology." The Stranger then adds, with that odd playfulness he has shown throughout, "At any rate I would not willingly, in speaking a myth, leave it headless, for should it wander everywhere like that it would appear grotesque (ἄμορφος)."

> Clinias: You have spoken most excellently, Stranger.
> Stranger: Not only in speech, but as far as I can I shall do it as well.
> Clinias: Let us act (make) in just the way we are speaking.
> Stranger: This will be done, if a god is willing and we master old age
>   to this extent at least.
> Clinias: Well, it is likely that he is willing.
> Stranger: Indeed, it is likely. (752a5–b2)

The Stranger catches us up into real time and wonders aloud whether either he or Clinias will live long enough to do what they promised. Clinias could no doubt die before he translated the laws of the *Laws* into the laws for his city, and it is even more likely that he might not survive the ordeal of migration and supervision of the laws; but the Stranger cannot possibly foresee his dropping dead on the road, or, if he did, that the story he is telling would wander off like a zombie and not know where it was going. If we suppose that Plato is at this point speaking through the Stranger, and he is imagining that he might leave the *Laws* unfinished, why did he not just put it into his will that the *Laws* in that case was not to be published? And once he had finished the *Laws,* why did he not cancel these lines? What does it mean, in any case, to galvanize back into life an ordinary expression for completing a story—putting a head on a tale—so that the Stranger can express his reluctance to have the *Laws* haunting the world? What is so misshapen about the *Laws* so far that the Stranger should indulge in this pun? The problem of beginning belongs with the problem of ending. If a solution is not found, the necessarily imperfect inauguration of the regime could put a stop to the Stranger's storytelling; but the first problem is one of deed and the second of speech, even if the Stranger says that it too is a doing. The Stranger has to let the man on the spot handle many things; he cannot be expected to hold his hand whenever he meets with a practical problem. If, however, the Stranger has a problem of his own, it must concern the fate of the *Laws* as written. Once it is published, it is going to roam wherever chance takes it. When anyone meets up with it, he is going to be as little educated in it as the first colonists, and whatever the tradition may be in which the *Laws* is caught up, its magistrates are as likely to be as untrained as Clinias. The *Laws* is fated, if it survives, to go headless into the world, to be read in countries more distant from Athens than Athens is from Crete. If Homer has not made much headway in Crete, Greek poetry is unlikely to accompany the *Laws* anywhere else. The delicate fabric of the *Laws* cannot make it without the support of far stronger but cruder arrangements. The magistracies the Stranger outlines give one version of the kind of support the *Laws* needs.

The first hint that the Stranger is going to propose the *Laws* itself as a teacher's manual is bound up with the way to overcome the resistance that inexperienced men will put up to the laws (752b10–c6; 811b8–e5): "Only if *we* should remain (μείναιμεν) somehow or other for as long a time as the children need to get a taste of the laws, are adequately raised with them, have become used to them, and share with the whole city in the election of offices." "We" must refer not only to Clinias and his co-founders, who are all to be enrolled in the new city, either by persuasion or by the application of the measured violence Cnossos has at its disposal (753a1–b1), but also to the Stranger, whose abiding presence can be secured only through writing and not through any degree of force. His presence is admittedly going to be a phantasm. It is a sign of the riskiness and ridicule the Stranger is courting that the *Laws* may end up as either itself a children's story or the model for more than one such story, for the reality of the regime will never live up to it; but only if the *Laws* can form the taste of the young can the direction that Cnossos, as the guardian of the laws, will impart to the colony be somewhat thwarted. The inevitable dissonance between the education and the laws, which is merely the institutional equivalent of the difference between prelude and law, does not necessarily do any harm. The *Laws* , as the lawful departure from the law within the law, is the novel replacement for tragedy and comedy as the traditional expressions of the experiential deviation from the law. The *Laws* can travel farther than the twin choruses of Dionysus.

The Stranger discusses twelve offices (cf. 946a6); they divide into three groups of four offices each. The first group structures the polis itself, the second the country, and the third the education and its failure. The third group constitutes the institutional structure of the double law:

City	1 Law Guardians	2 Generals	3 Council	4 Prytany
Country	5 Priests	6 Country Police	7 City Police	8 Market Police
Double Law	9 Music Stewards	10 Gymnastic Stewards	11 Minister of Education	(12) Law Courts

Nocturnal Council

One sees at a glance that just as the guardians of the law, the priests, and the supervisors of music contests form a group,[2] so the army officers, the country police, and the supervisors of gymnastic contests do too. Eleven of these twelve offices initiate business, but the law courts do not and only in a sense are, as the Stranger says, magistracies, though all the other magistrates are in a sense daily administrators of right (767a5–9). Even though a city is not a city without law courts (766d3–4), they do not fit perfectly at the moment into the unfolding of the Stranger's plan (768c3–8). They anticipate the breakdown in the effectiveness of education to eliminate criminality and that of sacred festivals to overcome enmity. That twelve is the master number of the regime but only eleven magistracies support the regime on the primary level either foreshadows the need for the nocturnal council or indicates to what extent failure is built into the second-best regime. Failure first shows up in the Stranger's scheme in the most elaborate presentation of any magistracy. The country police are divided in their duties between seriousness and play, and in the serious part there is for the first time punishment in the form of beating: anyone has the right to beat anyone who while on country service is found to have been absent without leave from the common mess for a single day or night (762c2–d1). The beating to be inflicted on the country police precedes the discussion of beautiful slavery (καλῶς δουλεῦσαι), on which every man is to preen himself (καλλωπίζεσθαι) rather than on beautiful rule (762e4–5). In town, only the slave and the foreigner are beaten for an act of injustice, but the native gets off with a fine (746b4–c4). The central authorities lose much of their power in the country and at night among armed men.

2   SUCCESSION

The magistracies invert the true relation of warp and woof. In embodying the slave aspect of the law, they are indispensable as long as there is law and regardless of what the laws are. So much is this the case that the offices for music and gymnastic contests are given, but the offices of education in music and gymnastic are not, even though the Stranger begins with a set of divisions that requires their establishment (764c5–d5). One

2. That the reviewers of all twelve magistracies are to be priests of the Sun and Apollo (957a5–6), and that the priests and sacristans are to care for all foreigners concerned with musical sights and sounds (953a3–b4), confirms the Stranger's intention to place the priests in this vertical group.

might say that the displaced law courts are the substitutes for them. Out of the thirty-seven guardians of the laws one of them is always to be the minister of education. If the Stranger hopes that Clinias will be the first elected to the post, he would have good reason to doubt whether the magistracies for music education will ever be filled (766b1–c1). The minister of education is spoken of as the last magistrate (765d4); and provision is made after him for what should be done if any magistrate dies in office (766c2–5); but to this fitting conclusion there is added another note, apparently misplaced, about the death of the guardians of orphans (766c5–d2). The issue of temporal succession is raised just before the Stranger speaks of the law courts, and how the precise articulation of trials (δίκαι) would most rightly be at the end of legislation (768c6–8). The law courts are in fact completed toward the end of the legislation (956b4–958c6), but they are not the last item: "Next there is this: for a man so born and raised, who begot and raised children, dealt with contracts in a measured way (paying the penalty if he had wronged anyone and getting back compensation from others), and grew old in fateful compliance with the laws, for him there would be a natural end (τελευτή)" (958c7–d3). Not the law about death but the death of a citizen concludes the laws. Two wholly different orders of time are made to coincide in speech.[3] Whatever may be the ultimate significance of this coincidence, funeral arrangements, which the genetic structure of law had already laid down as the end of the regime, are put at the end of the legislation: "All burials of the dead and nonburials—of patricides, temple robbers, and everyone of the kind—have been established previously through laws, so that legislation would be pretty nearly at its end for us" (960b1–5). The Stranger, however, does not let the end of life be the end: "In pretty nearly all cases it is not the accomplishment of something, any more than it is its acquisition and founding, that is the end (τέλος), but once one finds completely (τελέως) the means of preservation, only then must one hold that all that has to be done has been done, but prior to that the whole is incomplete (ἀτελές)" (960b5–c1). The nocturnal council is really the end, and its task is endless.

The synchronic structure of the magistracies cannot be completed without the intrusion of the diachronic. The diachronic shows up in three ways: in human life, in institutions, and in the Stranger's own exposition: "Let the arrangement of trials have been told to wait around for us at the

3. For their coincidence, one may compare 772c1 with 772c3, where the "end" of the legislator (τέλος σχόντος) is juxtaposed with the end of corrections, subsequent to his death, in his legislation (τέλος ἔχειν).

end (πρὸς τῷ τέλει), but the establishment of all the other magistracies has received pretty nearly most of their legislation; but it is impossible that the whole obtain precision and clarity about each single thing in particular and everything in general throughout the city and its entire political administration until the survey (διέξοδος) from the beginning takes separately the second, the middle, and all the parts and arrives at the end (πρὸς τέλος)" (768c8–d7). The law courts force the Stranger to look forward to the end, but this prospect involves him in the perplexity of time: only after the survey of the whole can the parts be properly fitted into the whole, but once the Stranger starts all over again he must start all over again, for no part will be completely finished as a part before the next part will be completely finished, and so on, for only after the whole has been completed with all its parts can the parts of the whole be complete. The endlessness of the Stranger's task proves to be the next topic; it makes the Stranger hesitate once more and delay for a moment his turning finally to legislation (768e2–3). Just as that part of the law that seems to be all of the law declares publicly the impossibility of the law's fulfillment—it is assumed as a matter of course that prior to death everyone has either been in the wrong or been wronged at least once—so the ambiguity in the structure of law courts—though they are not magistracies, it is not easy to deny indisputably that they are magistracies—has plunged the Stranger into the problem of parts. Since parts can be handled if and only if they are not handled as parts, it is inevitable that the problem of preservation, with which the nocturnal council deals, and for which it then seems the law courts were the dummy, coincides with the problem of virtue and its parts. Only at that point is "virtue" for the first and last time in the *Laws* in the plural: the Stranger insists that the competent ruler of the city as a whole must possess more than the vulgar or popular virtues (αἱ δημόσιαι ἀρεταί, 968a2).[4]

What the Stranger has previously said, Clinias now says, meets with his approval; more precisely, it is entirely to his mind (κατὰ νοῦν); but the Stranger, by the attachment of the beginning (ἀρχή) of what he is to say to the end (τελευτή) of what he has said, has spoken in a still more friendly way (φιλίως) (768e4–7). For Clinias, κατὰ νοῦν and φιλίως express his expe-

---

4. The Stranger underlines the significance of this single plural by his expression at 688a7 (πρὸς μίαν ἀρετὴν οὐσῶν τεττάρων), which all but states that the virtues are four. When the unity of virtue becomes a problem, the phrase the Stranger uses, ἐν ἕκαστον ἀνάγκη φάναι, τεττάρων γε ὄντων, has εἴδη as the subject (963c6). In the *Republic* "virtue" is twice in the plural; the first time they are "all the rest of the so-called virtues of soul" that probably lie very near to the virtues of body (518d9); the second time, in the myth of Er, they are the virtues of ancestors (618b1).

rience of the Stranger's complaisance indifferently; but for us the two
expressions reflect the intention the Stranger had ascribed to education:
it is to begin in pleasure and end in mind.[5] The Stranger discerns at once
what Clinias has inadvertently expressed: "Well, then, up to now we
must have played through (διαπεπαισμένη) the thoughtful and childlike
play of old men (ἡ πρεσβυτῶν ἔμφρων παιδιά) beautifully" (769a1–2). Clinias then interprets the Stranger by way of an opposition: "It is, then, the
seriousness of the [real] men (τὴν σπουδὴν τῶν ἀνδρῶν), as you seem to be
making clear, that is [really] beautiful." Clinias means that the beautiful
manner of their own playful performance in speech will find its real-life
match in the beautiful deeds of the citizens from whom they themselves
are now at two removes. The contrast between adverb (καλῶς) and adjective (καλήν) recalls the Stranger's distinction between "to sing and dance
beautifully" and "to sing and dance beautiful things" (654b11–c1). The
Stranger, in any case, is not as sure as Clinias about the meaning of their
play; he explains it through the example of painters, whose business is
thought to admit of no limit (πέρας) in the case of each of their paintings
(ζῷα): They touch up and retouch to such an extent that it is thought
their ordering and adorning would never stop, "so as for the paintings (τὰ
γεγραμμένα) no longer to admit of the possibility of continual progress
toward the more beautiful and more brilliant" (769a7–b3).[6] The Stranger
applies this example to the business of the legislator, who needs a continuous line of successors to correct his mistakes, fill in his omissions, and
restore his writings. Legislation is never at an end. It duplicates human
life that also has no end (τέλος) except in death and burial. Clinias be-

5. For the way in which κατὰ νοῦν and φιλίως do and do not coincide, one may
compare how the Stranger first speaks of a young man of twenty-five trusting to have
found a mate κατὰ νοῦν ἑαυτῷ καὶ πρέποντα and then of how he must seek τὸ πρέπον
καὶ τὸ ἁρμόττον (772d5–e3; cf. 859a3–4). Note that κατὰ τὸν αυτῶν (!) νοῦν (802c4) alters
its meaning as one either makes it reflexive with I. Bekker or not.
6. The precise meaning of the clearly technical terms χραίνειν and ἀποχραίνειν
is unknown; in Timaeus's Lexicon, ἀποχραίνειν is said to mean to blend colored surfaces into one (cf. Plutarch's φθορὰ καὶ ἀπόχρωσις σκιᾶς of Apollodorus's technique [De
gloria Atheniensium 346A]); in [Aristotle] De coloribus 796a24 ἀποχραίνεσθαι is used
of changes in the color of fruit as it ripens; and in the Republic it occurs in Socrates'
description of pleasure: "Is it not necessary that they also associate with pleasures
mixed with pains, phantom images of true pleasure and shadow-painted (ἐσκιαγραφη-
μέναις), taking their hue (ἀποχραινομέναις) by the position they have alongside one another, so as for each of the two [pleasure and pain] to appear intense, and among the
senseless engender frenzied desires for each other, and they are fought over just as Stesichorus says the phantom image of Helen in ignorance of the true was fought over by
those at Troy?" (586b7–c5). The context here suggests that the Stranger alludes to the
difficulties involved in perspectival coloring: the painter has to brush on colors up
close that will appear right at a distance.

lieves that the play of children and the play of old men are on either side of the serious business of mature men; but the Stranger implies that only in their own case, in imitating in play children who imitate in play the seriousness of men, is the picture of human life complete. They are the φάντασμα of an εἰκών of that which is in time. The diachronicity of man becomes synchronic only in play.

The Stranger seems to rely for his argument on Clinias's ignorance of painting, for he claims that a painter works on only one painting his entire life and has to designate a successor to make sure that the painting will be as beautiful as possible and not deteriorate over time, but rather keep on getting better, since his own mortality and the weakness of his art will put a check on the ever brighter sheen of his work (769b6–c8). This seems absurd (cf. 956b2).[7] Endless fiddling spells ruin for either picture or law. It is certainly not what the Stranger advises his successors. In the first law, he allows ten years for experiential adjustment to the law, but it is to be unmovable thereafter unless all the magistrates, all the people, and all the oracles of the gods consent unanimously to alter it (772a4–d4). The Stranger, moreover, tells his successors that he is supplying only an outline (περιγραφή) of the whole and omitting everything trivial, and they must fill it in (770b5–8). If the laws of the *Laws* form just an outline of the law, the Stranger cannot have colored it, and those who come after him have to find the pigments, grind them up, and apply them. Let us then suppose instead that the Stranger ascribes to the writing of law a temporality that truly holds for those who experience the law. The law could remain the same and still appear to change as a man experienced it in the course of his life. The genetic structure of law could thus culminate in the eidetic structure of the good without there being in the former any of the elements of the latter as each of them really is. Once it is admitted that the laws might be written perspectivally, the poet's objection, that the legislator has to say only one thing about each thing, does not have to hold. As Clinias has already shown us, they are experienced perspectivally even if they are not written perspectivally. The difference, then, between prelude and law might be only a crude version of the experiential manifold of the law, and the *Laws*

---

7. Pliny, in his preface to his *Natural History* 26–27, does explain the imperfect used by painters and sculptors (e.g., *Apelles faciebat*) as indicating that their art was always under way and incomplete, and they would have corrected the faults of their works, each one of which was presented as their last, had not fate interrupted them; but this seems to be a misunderstanding of the Greek imperfect ἐποίει or ἔγραφε, which signifies rather "So and so was the maker," "So and so was the painter"; cf. Jacob Wackernagel, *Vorlesungen über Syntax* (Basel 1926) I, 181.

itself, in its constituting the whole of the law part by part, might be imitating the alterations the citizens undergo in time. That criminal law occurs before civil law in the Stranger's presentation could be closer to the order in which the law comes to light experientially than to the order of the law in itself: Justinian puts the two "terrible" books on criminal law almost at the end of the *Digest*.[8]

The legislator seems to be caught in a difficulty from which he cannot extricate himself. He would be extraordinarily foolish, the Stranger says, not to revise his laws in light of his experience of them (769d1–e2); but since the habituation to the laws takes precedence over any possible defectiveness in the laws, they cannot be constantly subject to revision without ruining their primary purpose. To tinker with the laws is one thing, to improve them on the scale the Stranger seems to be talking about is another (770e7–771a4). The Stranger, moreover, is "at the sunset of life" (770a6), and he has no intention of becoming a resident alien in Magnesia and observing Clinias's secondhand version of his own proposals. The *Laws*, as far as he is concerned, completes the laws. The Stranger wants his successors to agree with him, Megillus, and Clinias, that they must look to one chief point in any emendation of the law: "Regardless of whether the nature of the inhabitants is male or female, young or old, every intensity of seriousness will have strained and been directed throughout their entire life toward this—how in the world would a man be becoming good (ὅπως ποτὲ ἀνὴρ ἀγαθὸς γίγνοιτ᾽ ἄν), with the virtue appropriate to a human being (ἄνθρωπος), whether its source is some practice, way (ἦθος), possession, desire, opinion, or some teachings (μαθήματα)" (770c7–d6).[9] The juxtaposition of "becoming" with "good" is nothing else than the union once more of the eidetic structure of the good with the genetic structure of law, and the list of sources, from practice to knowledge, encompasses the range from moderation and justice to mind.

8. *De confirmatione digestorum* 8a: *et post hoc duo terribiles libri positi sunt pro delictis privatis et extraordinariis nec non publicis criminibus, qui omnem continent severitatem poenarumque atrocitatem. quibus permixta sunt et ea de audacibus hominibus cauta sunt, qui se celare conantur et contumaces existunt: et de poenis quae condemnatis infliguntur vel conceduntur, nec non de eorum substantiis.* The Greek version does not apply any epithet to the two books.

9. The enigma the Stranger hands on to his successors recalls Socrates' reply, just before he introduces the "third wave," in defense of the best city in speech as a paradigm: "Do you, then, believe," he asks Glaucon, "that a painter would be any less good, who on painting a paradigm of what sort the most beautiful human being (ἄνθρωπος) would be, and assigning everything in an adequate manner to the painting, cannot show that it is also possible for a man (ἄνδρα) to become of that sort?" (*Republic* 472d4–7). The painter cannot be faulted for not showing the possibility of a human being who is neither male nor female.

The Stranger, then, tells his successors, just before he turns to the laws, that the starting point of the discussion in the *Laws* is to be their guide; but he does not leave it at a mere rehearsal. He confronts them with a triple problem: the becoming of a good man, the virtue of soul of a human being, and the male and female nature of young and old.[10] The virtue of soul of a human being belongs to the eidetic structure of the good; but the temporal and natural differences of male and female and of young and old belong to the genetic structure of law; and these differences cannot possibly be preserved in the becoming of a good man, especially if ἀνήρ has the same meaning Clinias gave it when he contrasted the beautiful seriousness of men with the thoughtful play of themselves as old. The simultaneous acknowledgment and suspension of time and nature, habit and mind, which the Stranger's thoughtful play had fully realized, cannot have, it seems, a counterpart in the serious life of the city. The laws of the city are the impediment to the *Laws*.

3   MARRIAGE

In starting off the laws, the Stranger harks back to where in book 5 he first introduced the number 5,040 (771a5–c1; 737c1–738c8); but whereas earlier he had merely set the number and the sacred side by side, now they are inextricably linked, since the months of the year are invoked to justify the consecration of each of the twelve months to a god or a child of a god. Every city, the Stranger claims, assigns a special place to 12; but 5,040 is a better choice than any other, since 12 divides it evenly, and 11 can be treated as a factor if one either subtracts two from it or adds nine. Earlier, he had recommended 5,040 since every number up to 10 divided it; but now he cannot enhance its cosmic significance without pointing out its defect. The defect admits of a "small cure," but it is small only practically. The Stranger calls its arithmetical explanation a myth: 5,038

---

10. At the beginning the Stranger, in speaking of education, said that if children were educated well they would become good men (γίγνοιντ᾿ ἂν ἄνδρες ἀγαθοί), and *once they had become good* (γενόμενοι δὲ τοιοῦτοι), they would conquer their enemies in battle and do everything else beautifully (641b6–c2; cf. 644a7–8). In the new formulation, there is still the present progressive of γίγνεσθαι but no longer the aorist; but in book 7, those men and women who *became* conspicuously good (διαφανῶς γε-νόμενοι) are to be praised once they are dead (802a1–5). That the man who is to be perfect (τέλεος) must in being good pursue a life of good reputation (950c4–7), while the human being who is perfect has, in addition to the virtue that depends on education in pleasure and pain, good sense and true opinions (653a5–b1), helps to set apart ἀνήρ and ἄνθρωπος.

is also an even number, but otherwise it has nothing in common with 5,040. Within the factors of 5,040, eleven stands for the concessions the Stranger had anticipated would have to be made to already existing local temples and sacred precincts. It is the emblem of non-self-consistency within the Stranger's self-consistent plan: he has to omit at least one Olympian god if he is to make room for Plouton. Nothing is going to work out exactly right. The get-togethers for sacrifices then served one purpose only—to promote knowledge by acquaintance and friendly feeling; now they are also for the sake of gratifying the gods and of casting the spell of the holy over the nakedness of the marriageable youths and maidens. The choral songs and dances they perform are occasions of play (παιδιαί) for a serious end (σπουδή). The decently naked is the Stranger's substitute for the communism of women in the best regime. Reason and timeliness (λόγος καὶ ἡλικία τις) will offer plausible excuses (εἰκυῖαι προφάσεις) for nonadherence to the laws otherwise in effect (cf. 775b5–6). As soon as the genetic structure of law is initiated, deviations arise along with it. The reasonable demand that there be no mutual ignorance (ἄγνοια) among the citizens runs aground on the shame that must bar the pure "theorizing" of the young (θεωροῦντάς τε καὶ θεωρουμένους) (cf. 925a2–5).

The Stranger's advice to the prospective groom seems as unnecessary as it is useless (772e7–773e4). He recommends that wealthy families not intermarry, as if he were afraid that the property restrictions, whereby no family can have more than a certain amount of movable goods, would prove ineffective, and an oligarchical tendency built into the regime was liable to grow (cf. 926a9–b2). He also recommends that orderly families marry into the more reckless ones, as if he were unaware that if this blending could be achieved it would be ruinous, since the uniformity of disposition would be closer to blandness than to virtue. He urges those who know themselves to be either too sluggish or too hasty to blend with their opposites, as if their self-knowledge were not enough to counterbalance a natural bent. It is not easy, the Stranger says, to realize that a city must be like a mixing bowl, in which the wine of madness enters at the boil, but a sober god chastens it. The city, then, must contain a slightly intoxicating brew; water alone is not "a good and measured drink" (cf. Philebus 61c4–8). There is a ferment in the law-abiding city that the laws, for all their sobering influence, do not and are not to water down. The symposium in speech is to be not just in speech. "Virtually no one," the Stranger goes on, "can discern the occurrence of this in sexual generation." He thus takes back his own recommendation and leaves marriage exactly where it was before he gave the prelude. The city needs but cannot have knowledge of the "nuptial number." The principle on which the

Stranger relied was that mutual attraction resides in similars, and opposites do not attract. A spurious physics leads to a hopeless policy, a genuine physics would lead to no policy at all. One may suspect that the plausible thesis "wealth marries wealth" has spilled over into a rule of nature. The Stranger, in any case, ends up by advising the father to enchant his children into a greater equableness, and reproaching him if he himself shows an excessive zeal for greater wealth. The prelude to the marriage law is bound to have little or no effect. It resembles rather a brief warning to the Stranger's successors: once the fractioning of the city occurs along the lines the Stranger foresees, harsher remedies might have to be introduced and be too late. The law is incapable of handling inequalities of either a natural or quasi-natural kind.

The position of women shifts constantly in the Stranger's laws. One assumes at first that 5,040 is the number of men who have lots in the city; but the women become finally "citizenesses" (πολίτιδες) in book 7 (814c4), without it ever being made clear whether the men are to be halved or the city to be doubled in size (cf. 923d8–e1). The intention of the marriage laws is to bring women out into the open as far as possible (cf. 781a1–5, c6–8). They too are to have a common mess, and their resistance to drinking in common is to be overcome, but the Stranger draws the line at public intercourse, though only such a provision would ensure that no one in the years of procreation ever generates while drunk (775b4–e4). The Stranger starts out with the grand proposal that husband and wife always be sober, but he ends up with the wish that at least on the wedding night they not get drunk. They are to believe that, whatever the state of their bodies and souls, it gets wiped off directly onto their offspring. Will parents blame themselves for every defect in their children? Bride and bridegroom are not to be distracted in undertaking a common action; and there should be female supervisors who every day for at least twenty minutes discuss among themselves whether they have seen any infraction of the sacrifices and rites of marriage (784a1–e1). These women have the right to enter the house of a married couple for no more than the first ten years of their marriage; and such a right certainly includes spot inspections at night. No sooner, however, does the Stranger list the punishments for anyone, man or woman, convicted of any irregularity, whether it be a mistake or due to folly, than he withdraws all the regulations: "If the majority act in a measured way in matters of this kind, let the laws lie buried in silence and cease to be laws" (784e7–785a1; cf. 783b8–c1). Laws are always for the disobedient minority: *quicquid multis peccatur inultum*. So either the Stranger gives up the regulation of private life entirely or he proposes the spread of such terror in a disorderly population that it would necessarily be self-defeating.

Every lot has two houses, not, as we were led to believe, to equalize the distances everyone would thus be from the central city, but to keep the in-laws from interfering with the bride and bridegroom, and, one has to add, to make it easier for the city's officials to poke and pry into what relatives would otherwise protect from outside inquiry (775e5–776b2). There is an internal exile of the newly married couples, all of whom form the first line of defense in depth against invaders, and who, in defending the fatherland, are defending the fathers. The Stranger's official reason for the measure is the satiety that otherwise comes with uninterrupted intimacy; there cannot be bonds of friendship unless there is longing. The communized city, then, is fundamentally opposed to friendship, and the Stranger, in designating it the model, has to work against its realization in the extended family if he is going to achieve community in the city. In passing on the torch of life from the past to the future, the private is privileged.

The private shows up in one of its more recalcitrant forms in slaves. It is not just that "we" in general speak for and against their usefulness in just the way we experience them (776b5–c2), and consequently hold no consistent view about them, but the Stranger too finds slaves to be particularly enigmatic, for they are ourselves insofar as laws are strictly laws and rule us by way of threats. The Stranger allows there to be a class within the city that exemplifies for the citizens what it once meant to live under laws, and what it would now mean for them should the preludes fail to replace the laws entirely. Since the city cannot afford such a replacement, the city attempts to duplicate itself within each master, so that he can show what he is when he has complete discretion. Slavery is a device to test those who are genuinely just, and really and truly hate injustice, for there is no other way to put Gyges' ring on everyone's finger (cf. Xenophon *Cyropaedeia* 5.2.9). The creature man is simply peevish and hard to handle, and when it comes to the indispensable discrimination—to separate in deed slave and free—he appears reluctant and ill-disposed (777b4–c1). The city cannot redistribute the slave and the free in accordance with nature; the philosopher had to be king in order for Socrates to correct the vagaries of nature; but the city must enforce whatever distinctions the law confirms and hope that at least some of the privileged can prove their right. A city without slaves promotes vanity and bestows on everyone the unearned badge of justice; a city with slaves has within its structure the equivalent of the symposium in speech: it discovers the just and shames everyone else. Freedom, then, would be the intoxicant in the mixing bowl of the city that the law must dilute but still maintain above the level of small beer.

The Stranger now admits that the order in speech is not the order in deed (778a9–c1). First things are never first. Marriage was first in the genetic structure of law; but it could not have been first if they were engaged in laying out the actual city. Housing ought to have been much earlier; indeed, the arrangement of the sacred precincts, the housing of the magistrates, and the law courts really belong to an earlier phase of the founding. The Stranger goes out of his way to mention those law courts that are to handle cases of homicide in which the penalty is death (778c4–d3). In deed, the failure of the law follows immediately on the end of the prelude and precedes the laying down of any law. The template of the second-best regime becomes third best as soon as one turns to its realization. Before the founder posts the law about the making of life, he will begin by making the taking of life conspicuous. The orderly progression from marriage to the grave, which the genetic structure of law had outlined, and which the Stranger seems now to have finally begun to fill in, belongs to the order of making in speech, which, the Stranger implies, allows any piece of the puzzle to be crafted at any time the speaker pleases, and does not have to convey along with its production the meaning it has as a part. Once more the law courts are out of place. Their displacement carries in its train the issue of the city walls; if they are allowed to be built, the country police would prove to be absurd (778d3–779b7). The prominent position of the country police was principally due to the beatings they deserved if they were unjust and insolent. Criminality lurks at the heart of the law regardless of the disorderly order of the Stranger.

Through the difference between "in speech" and "in deed" in the case of housing, the Stranger is led to the issue of the city walls. The private and the public are put together in speech. The Stranger then naturally connects the demand that the newly married men still share in the common mess with the general observation that law cannot be limited to public things. The obstacle to law and order is woman. She is naturally more secretive and thievish than man.[11] The natural inferiority of the female in point of virtue brings more than twice the mischief to the city. A disorder exists in the constitution of the family that only its abolition

---

11. The thievishness of woman seems to be an allusion to the making of Pandora in Hesiod *Works and Days* 67 (ἐν δὲ θέμεν κύνεόν τε νόον καὶ ἐπίκλοπον ἦθος) and 78 (ψεύδεά θ' αἱμυλίους τε λόγους καὶ ἐπίκλοπον ἦθος).

could presumably eradicate. We are, then, not at the beginning of the law when we are at the beginning either in speech or in deed. The Stranger now goes back to his own beginning, the Dorian practice of the common mess and the license of Spartan women. This return takes the Stranger further back into "prehistory," where cannibalism and incest were part of the Cyclopean way of life. If, the Stranger reasons, there have been so many changes in the ways of human beings over a very long period of time, women too can be altered to fit into a more orderly and political life. The Stranger thinks he would be howled down if he raised this possibility elsewhere, but with the common mess already in place, he has a chance to propose its extension. The common mess, which Clinias had implicitly claimed to be a deduction from an insight by a divine legislator, is now given a completely human origin. "*A war legislated*" the practice, or it was "some other business with the same power among a small population when an overwhelming want held it in its grip," and "once they had tasted it and were compelled to use it they decided that the lawful practice made a great deal of difference for security" (780b2–c2).

The Stranger "rationalizes" myth; but he does not now appeal to the Amazons, whom the Sauromatian women exemplify in reality, in order to show how almost anything is possible (804e4–805a3). Instead, he picks up the start of his own potted history of the Dorians, but now admits that the human race may not have always existed (781e5–782a3; cf. 676a1–b8). Alterations in climate are likely to have brought about many changes in animals, and along with the rise of cities and their destruction all sorts of changes would have occurred in food and drink. The Stranger hints at some theory of evolution. The story that vines were not always, any more than were olive trees and grains, allows one to infer that men were originally carnivorous and ate each other in just the way other animals do now (cf. Plutarch *de esu carnium* 993 C–D). Human sacrifice, which "we see even now surviving among many," consecrates a former necessity. It brings under law what once was lawless, and expresses necessity as atonement. The gods now exact what once could not be helped. Human sacrifice, however, establishes only one end of the range of eating habits; the so-called Orphic way of life establishes the other end, in which cows are not tasted and animals not sacrificed, but only cakes and fruits steeped in honey are the pure offerings to the gods; and "on the ground that it is not holy to eat flesh and stain the altars of the gods with blood, they cling to everything without a soul and abstain from all ensouled things" (782c2–d1). What is now barbaric was once a necessity, and the gods evolved along with all other changes. The Stranger's allusion to Dionysus and Athena, and his mention of Demeter and Persephone, turn the Olympian gods into the founders of a less savage way of life that elsewhere has advanced much further. "Orphism," however, does not represent a higher stage in moral progress; it is merely a mythical way of explaining the greater availability in some regions of a vegetarian diet. Morality is concerned with the orderliness of human life, and from that point of view the Cyclops's cave, in which Odysseus found everything to be in place, represents the peak at which law aims (*Odyssey* 9.219–223).

The central thread in the Stranger's apparently stray remarks is hard to pick out. The argument seemed to go off course at the moment the Stranger was confronted with the question how the first year of married life was to be lived (779d7–e7). He was even willing to give it up in midstream if Clinias and Megillus decided not to hear it, though as far as logos goes (λόγου γ᾽ ἔνεκα), the logos about the entire political order would in that case fall short of its goal (781d3–6). On his return to the issue of marriage, after a digression as essential to logos as irrelevant to deed, bride and groom, he says, ought to pay attention in their partnership of making children (783d8–784a1). "To pay attention" is literally "to apply the mind" (προσέχειν τὸν νοῦν), but the Stranger does not demand of them to have mind (ἔχειν νοῦν), though he says it is applicable to other common actions. The question the Stranger raises so delicately is how to combine mind and desire, even though Eros, as Hesiod says, overcomes the mind of all gods and men (*Theogony* 120–123). Moderation in eating has been achieved in Doric regions through the common mess, and the Stranger had proposed how moderation in drinking could be maintained in the symposium; but moderation in sexual relations seems to be beyond any regulation as long as it occurs in private.[12] In bringing this issue back to the beginning of man, the Stranger calls our attention to the problem of definitional law. Man was once no different from beasts; when necessity let up a little, and plants were domesticated, men defined bestiality not as a characteristic of what man once was but of what man would become were it not for law. Definitional law arose out of a misinterpretation of

---

12. If England's emendation ὡς for εἰς is accepted at 783b5, then the advance of the speeches (προϊόντων τῶν λόγων), on the same course (οὕτως) "as when we had earlier come to the common mess," would refer to the way in which the symposium in speech had been involved in that discussion and how it will be involved in the discussion of upbringing and education in book 7. The ordering of human life in regard to food, drink, and sex, which men resist having exposed (τὰ ἐπίπροσθεν αὐτῶν), induces the Stranger to propose legislation for them and then, with the laws as a cover (αὐτὰ ἐπίπροσθεν ποιησόμεθα), to delve more deeply into them; see T. J. Saunders, "Notes on the *Laws* of Plato," 46–49. In book 7, he begins with an admission of the limits to such legislation, and in book 8 proposes that when it comes to sex the usual veil be kept in place.

necessity once necessity disappeared. We know from Clinias that once the necessity for the common mess vanished it obtained a meaning that did not originally belong to it. Incest, then, was once a necessity of the Cyclopean way of life; when men began to live together, the necessity for exogamy was concealed under a reinterpretation of a former necessity: to commit incest is to transgress the human. Incest and cannibalism, then, took on a new look; interpreted as the unconstrained satisfaction of *erōs* and hunger, they came to characterize bestiality (cf. Aristotle *Politics* 1253a33–37). The desire for drink, however, cannot be made to fit into this scheme. Wine belongs to "civilized" man, and thirst for it cannot be understood as an original constituent of man as beast. Although the secret drinking of women led to the Stranger's digression on the three most powerful desires and needs of human beings, drinking is out of place. Only as a *representation* of man's originally disordered state, both individually and socially, does it fit with the prelaw conditions that cannibalism and incest signify. Thirst, in short, regains a place on a par with the two other desires only through the Stranger's own speech about the symposium in speech. The symposium in speech offered a new interpretation of Dionysus, and, as the sponsor of comedy and tragedy, the indispensable associate of Apollo and the Muses. Poetry's representation of Oedipus and Thyestes is of the essence of definitional law. The Stranger wants the Muses and the gods of gymnastic to quench the increase and influx of the three forms of desire: they are to constrain them by terror, law, and the true logos (783a4–b1). Terror and law show up together in tragic poetry. The true logos, however, would involve the uncovering of definitional law as misrepresentations of necessity, and the putting together of *nous* and *erōs* in a new way, or philosophy. "The true logos," according to the Stranger, was possible only for an individual (645b1–8).

VII

EDUCATION

I Unwritten Law

Once the Stranger alludes in a cryptic way to the prohibitions of incest
and cannibalism, it is inevitable that the issue of unwritten law arise, and
the question how writings, even if they do not carry sanctions with them,
can penetrate as deeply as customs and ways that hardly anyone is inclined to resist, but whose significance hardly anyone is aware of or can
express. In going back to the beginning, the Stranger has uncovered a
layer of law and order that he needs but cannot reshape so as for it to
conform perfectly with what his written laws are to induce. He wants to
rewrite unwritten law. What has made man man antedates what is to
make man capable of being informed by the eidetic structure of the good.
Book 7 represents the issue structurally in the following way. The end
(τέλος) of education is stated twice. The first comes after the mathematical training culminates in a true astronomy, and the Stranger says, "Well,
then, *we must at this time declare that the lawful ways in regard to
education* in matters of learning [mathematics] *are complete*" (ἤδη τοίνυν
χρὴ φάναι τέλος ἔχειν τά γε παιδείας μαθημάτων πέρι νόμιμα) (822d2–3). The
second comes shortly afterwards when the Stranger has treated hunting
at some length: "Now, then, *we must at this time declare that **all** the
lawful ways in regard to education are complete*" (νῦν οὖν ἤδη πάντα χρὴ
φάναι τέλος ἔχειν τά γε παιδείας πέρι νόμιμα) (824a20–21). This doublet
looks at first as if it represents the duality of soul and body that originally
showed up in the eidetic structure of the good; but the measured praise
of hunting is designed to have hunting make (ἀποτελεῖ) souls better or
perfect them (822d3–5). Nothing is said about the body. Hunting is not
only the completion of all educational laws and not just a supplement to
them, but it is meant to illustrate as well unwritten law, which goes beyond obedience to the law and reveals which citizens deserve perfect
praise (τέλεος ἔπαινος) in point of virtue (822e4–823a6). The Stranger,
then, ends book 7 with the same theme with which he began it. Even
though it looks as if the course of education is ascending from gymnastic

to the highest kind of music, it is rounded off by something that brings us back to the beginning. The beginning concerns the motions of body and soul, and the end deals with two kinds of motion: the first is about the real regularity of apparent irregularities in the movement of heavenly bodies, the second is about the hidden tracking of the irregular motions of beasts (cf. 763b7). Hunting is the first topic that articulates the law perfectly. It consists of three parts: a partial discovery of what there is, a praise and blame of certain kinds of hunting or prelude, and a law with prohibitions and permissions. Since its divisions include man among the hunted, it fulfills the aim of the unwritten law in presenting in its prelude an understanding of the bestiality of man as hunter and hunted, and attaches that aim to the highest sciences of being. The second completion of education is all of education; but since this law carries no penalties, its completeness makes, as the Roman jurists would say, for a *lex imperfecta*.[1]

The Stranger begins with the obstacle private life puts up to the prevalence of the public law. Small and frequent departures from the intent of the legislator, which are not manifest to all, make it as impossible as it would be indecent to apply to them the penalties of the law; but since men get gradually accustomed through them to transgress the written law, the legislator has no choice but to speak about them by way of instruction and admonition. The Stranger himself imitates the obscurity of these experiential deviations from the law. What he has said so far, he admits, looks like things spoken in darkness; but he wants to make them plain by bringing specimens (οἷον δείγματα) into the light (788c2–4). Such exposure is contrary to the very nature of unwritten law. Since its formation is imperceptible and nonuniform, it shows the degree to which, before it comes to light as a custom, the common opinion about the good and bad of pleasure and pain, to which the Stranger had given the name of law, has been violated in the darkness of individual experience. From this point of view, written law, no matter how detailed it is, is always in outline, and the colors have to be applied, not by the successors to the first legislator, but by the people themselves. They do not, however, correct and restore, but botch and alter the picture. The apparent stability of tradition is a perspectival illusion: if the legislator stood next to his painting he would see nothing but indistinct and indefinite shapes that were always on the verge of smudging the lines he had drawn so carefully.

The Stranger wants to add a protogymnastic that begins in the moth-

---

1. Cf. Ulpian *Liber singularis regularum* 1.1 in I. Baviera, *Fontes iuris romani anteiustianiani* (Florentiae 1940), 2; see further David Daube, *Ancient Jewish Law* (Leiden 1981), 78–92.

er's womb to the protomusic that nurses already practice. This protogymnastic presupposes that the right upbringing would try to make bodies and souls as beautiful and good as possible (788c6–d2); but the Stranger's own prelude had recommended that for the body a mean be struck between health and sickness, strength and weakness, beauty and ugliness, for otherwise the extremes would foster either reckless vanity or illiberal humility in the souls of the young (728d6–e5). The right upbringing must violate the true policy, for if the Stranger is right, present-day practices, through negligence, are closer to the true policy than his own recommendation. What looks rational from the beginning is from the end contrary to reason. The Stranger's recommendation could become the fashion if the "right" people took it up, and nurses followed suit out of snobbery. Unwritten law operates initially by way of emulation. It thus differs from preludes, whose persuasiveness is backed up by the threat in the law. Unwritten law, as the Stranger presents it, requires at the start a doubly correct insight: the indissoluble connection between the right conduct of private life and the stability of legislation, and the strict deduction from that principle to the Stranger's protogymnastic (790a8–b6). The Stranger does not say whether the fashion can be sustained once it becomes custom and the masters cease to understand why it was originally instituted. He had observed at the start that people in Athens, with nothing better to do, carry around fighting cocks under their armpits or in their arms, and had inferred that all bodies, provided they are suspended at their ease, are benefited by motion, regardless of whether they are carried on horseback or on ships. At the beginning, strong nurses, without a thought in their heads, would be carrying their charges on long walks. If the weaker nurses came to use babycarriages instead, would anyone realize that it was not just the constant motion but the cradling in the arms that made a difference?

The extension of a protogymnastic to a protomusic has already been anticipated. Mothers quiet restless babies not by stopping all motion but by rhythmically rocking them, and as they do so they sing to them (790c5–e6). In the lullaby "Rockaby, baby," the action of the singer reproduces the words of the song: as the bough breaks and the cradle falls in the song, so the baby in deed is suddenly dropped and as suddenly caught. A regular motion and song are imposed on the irregular motion and wails of the baby, and they induce in turn a real terror from without from which the baby is at once relieved.[2] Even for older children there is the same

2. The verb the Stranger uses for this kind of terror, δειμαίνειν, is frequent in tragic poetry but never occurs, for example, in either Xenophon or Aristotle. In Plato,

kind of enactment. One sometimes says to a child, "I am going to eat you up," and goes through the motions of total consumption. The fear of vanishing into nothing is thus allayed. Behind the Stranger's argument is the thought that the self is the self through the insideness of mind (ἐν-νοεῖν), or the awareness that mind depends on the outside. The Stranger therefore connects lullabies with Corybantic cures, in which the sounds of flutes from the outside dominate the sounds of flutes heard within. The terror within is a madness that consists in the disappearance of any difference between inside and outside: one loses one's mind or is outside oneself (ἔξω ἑαυτοῦ) when there is nothing outside but everything is within. One becomes sane or is restored inside oneself (ἐν ἑαυτοῦ) when there is again a distinct inside. The restoration to the world and its security is made through a shaking (σεισμός) that pulls the ground from under one's feet.[3] It induces the feeling of security precisely because the insecurity is outside. The terror, then, is that there is no ground for one's being, for the annihilation is coming from within. The cure consists in attaching the terror outside oneself to a god to whom one can sacrifice and appease. The god then proves to be gracious through the alteration of disordered motions and cries into ordered dances and songs. The child's prayer

---

the verb and cognate noun are distributed unevenly: once in the *Phaedrus*, four times in the *Republic*, eight times in the *Laws*. Cephalus says the old are full of terror (δεῖμα), and that if one of them finds many injustices in his life, he wakes up often in the middle of the night, as children do, in terror (δειμαίνει) and lives in evil hope (*Republic* 330e2–331a1); and the Stranger later says that the story goes that a man killed violently, if he had lived in the pride of freedom, gets angry when he is newly dead at the doer, and with himself filled with fear and terror (δεῖμα) on account of the violence of his own experience, when he sees his killer occupying his own customary haunts, he is afraid (δειμαίνει), and in his own distraction, with the killer's memory as his ally, distracts as far as he can both the doer himself and his actions (865d6–e6; cf. 933c2). In the phrase μνήμην σύμμαχον ἔχων, England (407) says, "there is the germ of tragedy." Δεῖμα occurs twice in Thucydides, first about the matricide Alcmeon, to whom an oracle hinted that there was a possible release from his terrors (2.102.5), then about the fears and terrors that befell the Athenians on their retreat from Syracuse (7.80.3). One might add that in Galen δεῖμα and δειμαίνειν each occur once, and on both occasions he is discussing the melancholic, who according to Hippocrates desire to die and fear death (*De symptomaton causis* [203 K]; *De locis affectis* [191 K]).

3. In *King Lear*, Edgar cures his blind father Gloucester of despair by persuading him that he has survived a suicidal leap off a cliff. Edgar tells him that the "poor unfortunate beggar," as Gloucester calls him, who parted from Gloucester at the top of the cliff was "some fiend; therefore, thou happy father, / Think that the clearest gods, who make honours / Of men's impossibilities, have preserv'd thee." Gloucester then says: "I do remember now; henceforth I'll bear / Affliction till it do cry out itself / 'Enough, enough,' and die. That thing you speak of / I took it for a man; often 'twould say / 'The fiend, the fiend.'" (Act 4, scene 6, 73–79.)

"Now I lay me down to sleep" is based on a similar kind of original terror and offers as solace the same kind of Corybantic relief.

After the suggestion of how a gymnastic in motions would induce a protocourage in very small children, which would contribute greatly to a part of virtue of soul, the Stranger turns to peevishness or irritability (τὸ δύσκολον) or its absence as another not small part of the bad or good condition of soul (εὐψυχία).[4] He observes that luxury is commonly believed to produce in men an ill-tempered disposition, with a hair trigger on their anger, which exceedingly trivial occasions set off; but an exceedingly strict and savage enslavement perfects in men a humility, illiberality, and misanthropy that make them unsuitable partners in a common life (791d5–9). It utterly baffles Clinias how the city could nurture those who do not yet understand language, and, when the Stranger explains, he chooses complete indulgence of the baby's whims. The Stranger appeals to the way in which nurses figure out what a baby hates and desires through its tears and cries, and infer that they guessed well from whatever brings silence.[5] The Stranger opposes the cheerful (ἵλεως) to the peevish and mournful (θρηνώδης), who is full of lamentations (ὀδυρμοί) more than the good man should be (792a8–b2; 947b5); and he remarks that everyone by a kind of divination addresses the disposition of god as ἵλεως (792c8–d4). What in a god is graciousness is in him who is to be divine (θεῖος) cheerfulness. What no one would call the peevishness of a god if he does not support a human request is precisely to be said of anyone who flies off the handle at the slightest frustration of his will. The Stranger does not have a way to hit upon the mean between gentleness and savagery, but he playfully suggests that women are to maintain a graciousness (εὐμενές), serenity (ἵλεων), and gentleness (πρᾷον) throughout their pregnancy (792e2–7). The unenforceability of his suggestion makes it playful.

What the Stranger prescribes for the good condition of soul, neither to be precipitous toward pleasures nor to live on the assumption that one will ever be free from pains, has no counterpart in any practice or exercise. Like any other mean, it is easier to formulate than figure out what counts as excess or defect. Unwritten law has set up a manifold of norms that seems to embed the mean in the way of life of a people without there being any ground for it except its antiquity. The Stranger, in connecting his theme with unwritten law, is forced to confront the difficulty that if

---

4. For the double meaning of εὐψυχος, see Aristotle *Topics* 112a32–35.

5. The Stranger's description recalls what the nurse, in Aeschylus's *Choephoroi* (749–760), says of the baby Orestes, when she was a soothsayer of his needs and he was a senseless thing (τὸ μὴ φρονοῦν) and could not speak (οὐ γάρ τι φωνεῖ).

a novel code of laws needs the support of unwritten law, it is relying on the ways of the fathers, whose customs are the old mortar that must and cannot bind together the spanking new bricks of the regime (793a9–d5). On the front line stands the harshness of law itself, behind it the apparent rationality of persuasive preludes, but below the preludes and out of sight lies a complex set of ways, which cannot be either uprooted or reshaped. That there seems to be a difference between the left and right hand is emblematic of what the deceptive reasonableness of unwritten law can accomplish. We have become lame in our hands, the Stranger says, by the folly of mothers and nurses (794d8–e2). His remark brings us back to the criticism he had leveled against the comparable lameness in Spartan and Cretan law, which failed to balance training in aggressive courage with training in defensive moderation (634a1–4). The Stranger is now once more at the beginning, but at a more literal level. Ambidexterity comes up as an issue immediately after a lack of balance can be discerned between the way in which babies are habituated against terror and improperly inured to discontent. The ancient ways of Greece are out of kilter. Despite the Herodotean claim that the Greek polis has melded Scythian freedom with Asiatic art, and the Homeric gods strike a mean between the rationality of Persian impiety and the excessive religiosity of the Egyptians (cf. Cicero *de re publica* 3.14), the Stranger seems to be demanding a new blending of foreign ways. Scythian ambidexterity and Sauromatian equality of men and women are to enter into a reconfiguration of unwritten law. This revision requires as well an appeal to an Egyptian art (799a1–2), and later to a version of the cosmic gods of Persia, so that one begins to wonder whether the Stranger is setting out to propose a total rebarbarization of Greece in order that the foundations of law can accommodate an entirely new project of laws in an adequate manner: the laws are to be outside of any historical or geographical horizon. When Socrates asked his nameless comrade, "What is law?" or, "What is the law?" he added a so-called ethical dative ἡμῖν (for us), which indicated that a horizon-free definition of law was scarcely possible (*Minos* 313a1). The laws are always going to be our laws. The Stranger does not so much disagree with Socrates as raise the question what would be entailed if law were to start off on the right foot.

2   CONSECRATION

When there has not yet been any socialization outside the family, there are still elements of gymnastic and music in the first three years of a

child's life. Once the children gather in the twelve villages, they spontaneously invent games, which the nurses supervise, while other officials
supervise them. Here begins some form of punishment (κολάζειν), designed to check insolence but, just as in the case of slaves, mild enough
not to impart resentment. From the age of six, the girls and boys are
separated, and, though both are given over to lessons (μαθήματα), the boys
get a complete course of military instruction, and the girls only if they
like (793d7–794d2). Here begins the Stranger's gradual incorporation of
the female population into the city. The female represents in his discussion all that no one knows about human nature before the law has concealed it. A variety of customs suffices to cast doubt on the naturalness
of one's own, but it does not suffice to decide whether a Scythian custom,
which teaches one how to shoot the bow with either hand, is not as much
a distortion as the asymmetry inbred among the Greeks. The advantage
ambidexterity brings is of the same order as the advantage the legislator
derives from not keeping half the population out of political life (805a4–
b2). Everyone over time becomes comfortable with the ways of his tribe,
and, just as in the case of a change in diet, the initial disagreeableness of
new ways shortly disappears (797a9–798b4). Unwritten law, then, seems
indifferent, unless one insists on calculating everything in terms of utility. It would make no difference whether, in Amazons taking to the field
or in Spartan women fleeing panic-stricken to temples (814b4–5), the female was better revealed for what it was, unless the city must require
that no one be a hindrance to its defense. Greater efficiency in the use of
the city's resources decides policy but settles nothing. Just as the fact that
a poor country is compelled to execute thieves, whom a richer country
might readily let off with a lighter sentence, and that a populous country
might be able to afford to ignore conscientious objectors, tells us nothing
about just punishment, so the greater arc in open country that Scythian
archers on horseback can cover by the use of both hands does not explain
why it should serve as the model for the handling of the bow among
Cretans, who on their terrain have not much use for horses. The Stranger
recommends ambidexterity for hoplite fighting, but it would seem to be
a piece of useless virtuosity: how could a hoplite detachment switch their
shields and spears in the midst of battle without exposing themselves to
the greatest danger?[6]

The difference between the left and the right hand, as it is now main-

---

6. If Thucydides is right, that hoplite formations tend inevitably to veer to the
right in order to protect the exposed side from danger (5.71.1), could the Stranger
mean that ambidexterity would overcome at least partially this tendency?

tained in Greece, shows up in the words used for the right and left. The word for the right (δεξιός) means dexterous and clever, and the Stranger had spoken of the incapacity of Spartan and Cretan courage to stand its ground against the dexterity of seductive pleasures (πρὸς τὰ δεξιὰ καὶ κομψὰ καὶ θωπευτικά) (634a1–4). The right has a single name, the left many. It recalls the difference between the singularity of ἀρετή and the many words for vice. The three most common words for the left are ἀριστερός, εὐώνυμος, and σκαιός. The first is a compound of the superlative of "good" and the comparative suffix -teros, which indicates a separative difference. It is clearly a euphemism for the sinister character imputed to the left. The second term announces itself as a euphemism, for εὐώνυμος means "with a good name." The third also means ill-omened, unlucky, and awkward, and in prose hardly ever is to be taken literally.[7] The consequence, then, of the cultivation of the right hand at the expense of the left has been its transference into language. The Stranger himself had used "left" to designate things connected with the chthonic gods (717a8). He had done so at the very moment he spoke of them first but declared them second. If, then, the Scythian practice of ambidexterity gets installed in Clinias's city, the language of things must change. The awkward and ill-omened must be given new labels. No longer could it be said of Ajax that had not a god afflicted him he would not have gone leftward (ἐπ' ἀριστερά) in his mind (Sophocles Ajax 182–3), and the sinister meaning of Laius's name—λαιός is another word for "left"—would disappear. It is in language, then, that the unwritten law most comes to light, and nowhere more so than in everything that pertains to men and women.[8] If the Stranger has his way, the manly (ἀνδρεῖον or ἀνδρικόν) would lose the entire range of its extended meaning, and the Stranger himself, under the new customs, would not be able to speak of "the womanish and slavish ways of nurses" (790a6; cf. 935a1; 944d3–e2; 949b3).[9] His proposal to distinguish between songs appropriate to females and males would have to be entirely rephrased, since the orderly and moderate would no longer characterize the female once training had canceled entirely or blurred sufficiently their supposed differences (802e8–11). The Stranger, then, uses the issue of ambidexterity to get at the broader question whether all

7. Plato once lets it have its literal sense—Socrates is discussing the way of division (Phaedrus 266a1)—but it involves him in an awkward omission of μέν.

8. In the Cratylus, Socrates briefly indicates the relation between law and language (388d9–e3).

9. In the Timaeus, men who are cowardly and unjust become women before they are given an erōs peculiar to women: "womanish" precedes "woman" (90e6–91a4).

habits and ways can be neutralized, so that no biases that could skew the higher education of body and soul would show up in the initial colorlessness of unwritten law. Such a neutralization would amount to hindering, as far as possible, the accretion of superfluous beliefs around the ways of a people. Burial would then not give rise to stories about ghosts and the terrors of graveyards; but the Stranger admits that it would be a hopeless task to persuade men, abashed in their souls by waxen figures hung at their parents' tombs, to ignore them (933a5–b5). The majority of human beings, he says, live in terror (δειμαίνοντας) (933c2).

Apart from the possibility that the Stranger is hinting at the rationalization of all unwritten law, his isolation of a custom from the way of life of which it is a part poses the following difficulties: Can the alien be grafted successfully onto a native growth, and, even if the graft took, would it not change the fruit in an unknowable way? Are not ambidexterity and the equality of men and women of a piece with nomadic conditions and the nondivision of the arts?[10] The experientially seamless web of custom can in this way be picked apart, but the nest of the magpie is still a jumble. The Stranger seems to be intent on making his task hopeless, for the more he cuts away from the way things are, peers more deeply into the unregulated, and uncovers there the endlessness of change, the more he makes the exceedingly strange and noncustomary (τό γε σφόδρα ἄτοπον καὶ ἄηθες) the basis for the unchangeable law. Everyone, and not just infants, are to live "as if they were always sailing" (790c8–d2; cf. 813d3; *Timaeus* 89a5–8). Everything has to be shaken up for the sake of settling down. It is the undiluted application of the symposium in speech to law. The flooding in of the theme of unwritten law (ὁ ἐπιχυθεὶς λόγος) brings on a constant flow (ἐπιρρέοντα) of stable (μόνιμα) habits that are to be altered and rearranged (793b2, d5). The Stranger's attempt to stabilize the written law through the writing up of the unwritten law is not only paradoxical in itself but contrary to his own concession that his survey of the laws will keep him from the small things; but now nothing is too small for him even if it is an obstacle to maintaining a synoptic view of law (793c5–d5). A sign of the instability the Stranger has deliberately introduced is his declaration at one point that gymnastic, which had been postponed since the end of book 2, is now perfectly complete (παντελής), only to announce much later that gymnastic has then absolutely achieved its limit (πάντως ἤδη πέρας ἔχει) (796d6–8; 834 d8–e2). The first declaration leads to an admission that, though he believed he had

---

10. Cf. Mildred Cable, *The Gobi Desert* (London: Hodder and Stoughton, 1942), 169, on the Mongol family.

said everything there was to say about the gifts of the Muses and Apollo, still he had not said what should have been stated first to everyone: games belong to music (796e4–797a9). The subsequent revision of music leads to a return to gymnastic, under which there then falls tragedy and comedy (813b1–817e3). These crossovers, with which the changing status of the female is connected, culminate in the double ending of education, where hunting crowns astronomy and advanced mathematics.

The Stranger's new account of play is not without its puzzles. He had noted earlier the spontaneity in the invention of games when children get together (794a2); he now argues that revolution begins in the playground, when everything old-fashioned is disparaged, and only if the same people are always playing at the same things in the same way and enjoying the same games (παίγνια) can the lawful ways laid down in earnest (σπουδῇ) remain at rest (797a7–d2).[11] The young (οἱ νέοι) are susceptible to the new (τὸ νέον), and regardless of whether the innovator proposes a change in color or shape, the result is always harmful to the city. It would seem, then, that the Stranger must be proposing that τὸ ἀρχαῖον νόμιμον can and must be taken literally: it does not mean "the old and lawful way," but "the lawful way of the beginning (ἀρχή)," for the conservation of everything old, just because it was old, would doom the Stranger's project from the start. Clinias certainly takes it in this way (797d1–6); but the Stranger goes on to describe how any departure from the usual, whether it be in climate, diet, thoughts, or natures of souls, has a way of becoming in time the usual again, and it is characteristic of every soul, if the laws remain unchanged, and every memory is lost of things ever being different, to revere them and fear to alter anything of what has once been established (797d9–798b4). Any conservatism is built on change, and there never is a state that is good because it always was. The brevity of the Stranger's account of gymnastic, which he finished off in less than two pages, is now easily explicable. The longer account was book 3, in which the history from the cataclysm to the collapse of the Dorian dream showed that the beginning was destined to be always a defective beginning, and one never starts from scratch. In returning to that argument, the Stranger takes back the strict conclusion one could draw from his present condemnation of novelty in children's games, and restricts its ap-

---

11. The Stranger's expression, ταχθὲν μὲν γὰρ αὐτὸ [τὸ τῶν παιδιῶν γένος] καὶ μετασχὸν τοῦ τὰ αὐτὰ καὶ ὡσαύτως ἀεὶ τοὺς αὐτοὺς παίζειν (797a9–b2), is highly unusual, since it recalls the language normally employed of the beings that are always (e.g., *Phaedo* 78c6, ἅπερ ἀεὶ κατὰ ταὐτὰ καὶ ὡσαύτως ἔχει), or of celestial motions (cf. *Laws* 898a8–b1), and can hardly be found elsewhere in Plato; contrast Timaeus's description of health (*Timaeus* 82b2–5).

plicability to songs and dances that imitate better or worse human beings
(798d1–e7). The Stranger has brought us back again to the beginning.

It is not immediately obvious why the Stranger took the long way
around through children's games to link up with his earlier citation of
the Egyptian way of consecration. The return, however, involves an innovation that leads to a crisis in the Stranger's endeavor. This crisis elicits
from Megillus a protest on behalf of the human race, but neither he nor
Clinias experiences the crisis itself. The Egyptian solution provokes the
crisis. It provides for all songs and dances to be consecrated, first with an
arrangement of the festivals throughout the year, and to what individual
gods, children of gods, and *daimones* they ought to be dedicated; then certain officials are to arrange what song must be sung at the several sacrifices (θύματα) of the gods, and with what kind of choral dances they must
celebrate the sacrifice (θυσία) at the time; finally, all the citizens, in performing a common sacrifice (θύσαντας) to the Fates and all the other gods,
must, in pouring a libation, consecrate the songs to each of the gods and
other divinities (799a4–b4). The Stranger has never mentioned libations
before, and sacrifice rarely; neither had occurred in his first account of
Egyptian ways. He used θύειν first in book 4 (716d6), and in book 5 θυσία
and θῦμα (738e3, 741 c3); but on no occasion before now were sacrifices
assigned in principle to definite gods.[12] Only by such an assignment can
the charge of impiety be brought against anyone who, after introducing a
nonsanctioned song or dance, refuses to accept his official banishment
from holy places. Impiety is now mentioned for the first time. Piety was
the target one would hit if one were to distribute honors rightly to the
Olympian and chthonic gods (776a6–b2); but no distribution had then
been made that declared which gods were to receive which honor at
which time and which place. Consecration puts an end to generality. If
the pyrrhic dance is to be sanctioned, then Athena, with the full panoply
of the hoplite, comes along with it as its sponsor and the universal object
of emulation (796b6–c4; cf. *Critias* 110b5–c2). In Socrates' myth in the

12. Critias, in describing what he takes to be the reality in old Athens of Socrates' mythical city, does not refer to sacrifice, despite the prominence of priests then
and Socrates' mention of it now (*Timaeus* 24a4–5; 26e3), and the close association of
the guardians with the temple of Athena and Hephaestus (*Critias* 112b4), but when
he turns to the story of Atlantis, where the temple of Posidon has a barbaric form
(116c9–d2), he first mentions sacrifice in general (113c1), and then speaks at length
of sacrificial rites to Posidon (119d7–120c1). Josephus has Moses ask God not to be-
grudge him knowledge of his peculiar (ἴδιον) name, "in order that when sacrificing
he might invite him by name to be present at the sacred rites" (*Jewish Antiquities*
II.275). *Exodus* 3.13 is silent on this point. Perhaps the Biblical God is called holy because he is a this and there are no other gods.

Phaedrus, Hestia is the only god who has never seen the hyperuranian beings; she is still a god despite the fact that nothing connected with a logos has informed her (247a1–2). There is no "idea" of "this place." The holy is an immobile this.[13] Euthyphro, then, was right, after all, to answer Socrates' question about the holy and the unholy in just the way he did: "I am saying that the holy is just the same as what I am now doing" (*Euthyphro* 5c8).

In one sense, the Stranger's survey of the laws is now at an end. "Gods" have functioned up to now as beings over against human beings, just as "divine" had started out as distinguishing goods of the soul from human goods. One could appeal to gods and the divine as long as one did not link them to any ceremony in which it had to be stated to whom one was praying and sacrificing (cf. 871c3–d2).[14] The verb "to sacrifice" belonged to definitional law and implied that there were beings of a certain kind before whom other beings of a different kind performed certain actions on other beings of a certain kind; but with the consecration of each song and dance to a certain god, the definitional law takes on its particular form that fuses together "human being" and "of this tribe." It is for this reason that the Stranger had just implied that "the natures of souls" were no different from bodies, and they underwent the same distress at any change but then settled down and conformed with whatever customs lasted long enough to wipe out any memory of another way of life (797e2–798b4). What had been a speck on the horizon, when the Stranger urged that whatever holy places and rites were already in place should be left undisturbed (for he could make use of them for fostering the friendship of the new settlers), has now blotted out everything that lets itself be formulated. The holy is the content of the unwritten law, and it forbids the determination of the human apart from the ways it has prescribed. Aristotle illustrates the lawfully just of political right with

---

13. Hestia is the first god whose name Socrates discusses in the *Cratylus*, for that is to begin in conformity with the law (401b1–2); it is to her that a presacrifice (προθύειν) prior to all gods is made (401c6–d3). There seems to be behind the connection of Ἑστία with ἔστι the graphical resemblance of ΟΥΣΙΑ with ΘΥΣΙΑ. The cosmological counterpart to Hestia is Timaeus's χώρα, which can properly be addressed as τόδε and τοῦτο, since as a here for me (τόδε) or a here for you (τοῦτο) it does not partake in the likeness-character of any apparent something (*Timaeus* 49e7–50b5).

14. Herodotus distinguishes the original Pelasgian practice of sacrificing to nameless gods, whose common designation (θεοί) signified that they put (θέντες) all things in order, from their subsequent adoption of the names of Egyptian gods. The next step was the reworking of the Egyptian gods through Homer and Hesiod, who renamed them, assigned offices and arts to them individually, and indicated their shapes (2.52–53).

several examples. One of them is the sacrifice of a goat but not two sheep, another is the sacrifice to Brasidas (*EN* 1134b22–3; Thucydides 5.11.1); but Aristotle does not add—and this is decisive—there is no sacrifice at all unless it is of something to somebody. The poet, who the Stranger imagined objecting to his first prelude because his prescription of the measured lacked a number, knew what lay in store for the Stranger.

At exactly this point in the argument, though Clinias does not object to the extension of the charge of impiety, the Stranger urges them to "experience what we deserve" (πάθωμεν τὸ πρέπον ἡμῖν αὐτοῖς). He likens their experience to a man, whether alone or with others, whether young or old, who on coming to a crossroad would not rush down one path without first questioning himself and everyone else where the road was leading. So too they must pause and confirm the present solution to their perplexity; but they do not have the time, for they must now go to the end (τέλος) of the laws and not be thwarted from attaining the limit (διαπεράνασθαι) that the order of the present laws requires: "Perhaps, if a god should be willing, this survey (διέξοδος) too as a whole, once it reached its end (τέλος), would indicate adequately the present perplexity" (799e1–7). Let us delay the answer to the question, Where does the Stranger come to the end and resolve the perplexity? and ask first, What is the perplexity? The Stranger states it in the fewest number of words: "Let this oddity, we say, have been passed as a common opinion: Songs (ᾠδαί) have become for us laws (νόμοι)" (799e10–11). At the very moment this resolution is decreed, the Stranger has destroyed at a stroke his entire project. If songs are now laws, if, that is, the pun in νόμοι has ceased to be a pun, but νόμος has become univocal, and it is no longer possible to speak of political laws as "really and truly" (ὄντως) being laws (722e1), then unwritten law is now as much law as the written law, and everything else that formerly did not belong to the system of threats in the law is the law. Persuasion has vanished into terror. Nothing does not have its assigned penalty. Everything is now part of the canon. The Stranger's attempt to make "holiday" the original of which "holy day" would be the copy has failed. Punishment prevails everywhere. "Let no one," he says, "utter a sound (φθεγγέσθω) contrary to the public songs, sacred rites, and the entire choral song and dance of the young any more than [anyone is to contravene] any other law whatsoever" (800a4–6). The Stranger's failure to insert an equivalent to the words in brackets amounts to the cancellation of the Dorian law of laws, which gave permission to the old, out of the hearing of the young, to speak against the law (634d7–e6). There are now no longer any preludes.

The total silence imposed on any dissonant voice anywhere has the effect of making everything in the city of deadly earnest. There is to be no play in the law. The Stranger could not avoid starting this discussion of the Egyptian art of consecration with children's games if he were to face the paradox of Hestia who, as if she were also elsewhere, was one of the three gods on the city's acropolis (745b7). The Stranger has allowed himself to go on, even though he is either still stuck at the crossroads or else has come to the end, because he has not stated what the songs and dances are and to which gods they are to be consecrated; but this is only a smokescreen, for once the real founders settle these issues, they have settled everything else and left no room for the *Laws*. He had granted a triple role to the unwritten law: it provides the clamps between the laws, the central supports of the laws, and the envelope of the laws (793b4–c3). Now, however, that it has taken over all of the law, he is out of room and out of time. His solution is to restrict his reforms to six templates (ἐκμα-γεῖα) that are directly related to the gods; but no sooner does he declare that the arrangement is at an end than he plunges once more into the crisis that he had only put off (802e11–803a1). The first template effectively gets rid of tragedy (800b8–801a4). Tragedy is silenced once the Stranger counters it with auspicious speech (εὐφημία). Auspicious speech is to surround a sacrifice when the sacred victims are burnt in accordance with law. A son or brother who spoke tragedy's kind of blasphemy on such an occasion would spread despair (ἀθυμία) and evil forebodings in his father and relatives; but now publicly, in virtually all Greek cities, after a magistrate has sacrificed, a number of choruses come, "and stand-ing not far from the altars and sometimes right next to them, they drench the sacred victims with every kind of blasphemy, harrowing the souls of the audience with the most mournful (γοωδέστατοι) words, rhythms, and harmonies, and whoever best succeeds in making the city, which has just sacrificed, burst into tears, that chorus carries off the prize of victory." The Stranger allows that if the citizens have need of these particular ex-pressions of pity (οἶκτοι), then they should be restricted to unclean days, and choruses ought to be hired from elsewhere, just as now there are pro-fessional mourners who accompany the dead "with a Carian Muse" (cf. 947b3–6).

The Stranger once more proposes the rebarbarization of Greece. He wants to break the connection between the pity of tragedy and the gods (cf. 960a1–2). He had been after tragedy from the beginning of book 7, where he had juxtaposed the lullabies that calmed the terrors of babies with their threnodies of discontent that nurses learned only how to in-

dulge, and the Stranger himself had nothing to offer except the measure
of the mean. That childish frustration of the will now comes back in the
form of tragic pity. It is directed against the gods and expresses the necessary consequence of their serene existence: "It is best not to be born."
The innermost terror of tragedy is suicide. It is no wonder, then, that the
Stranger wished pregnant women to be serene. He was not joking. He
now wants to separate terror from pity, by restricting the latter to funereal
songs that do not intrude on public celebrations. Such an antitragic separation, however, breaks the continuous linkage he had forged in the
first prelude between the Olympian and the chthonic gods. The Stranger
wants to quit speaking of burial practices as quickly as possible. He does
not want to regulate them at the same time that he is concealing their
experiential deviation from the law. Once he had introduced consecration
as the universal cure against change, he let in the holy in its haecceity,
and that meant the songs and dances of tragedy, whose burden contradicts
the intention of his own laws. He can clean up the sacrifices and put out
of sight the tears of things to which tragedy gave a final form, but he
cannot either overcome those tears, as his dismissive indulgence of them
admits, or seemingly invent on the spot a superior form for them. The
sign of the Stranger's perplexity is that his formula for the first template
is "εὐφημία, " and the genus of song is to be absolutely εὔφημον; but ordinarily the formula would mean "Silence," and the genus of song "silent."
Inasmuch as the second template is assigned to "prayers to the gods to
whom we on each occasion sacrifice" (801a5–6), in what can the auspicious and nonwhining speech of the first song or law (νόμος) of music
consist (cf. 821d2–4)?[15] From the prohibition of oaths in all cases where
a great profit is thought to be at stake (949a5–b4), are we to infer that in
the first template there is to be no swearing by the gods? Silence before
the gods means that the gods do not have to be named.

The third song or law of music adds a further difficulty (801a8–d7).
Poets must realize that prayers are requests from gods, and they should
particularly make sure that they never unwittingly ask for what is bad as
if it were good. Who makes up the second song if not the poets, and how

---

15. For the close connection between the injunction "Let there be εὐφημία " and
prayer, cf. Aristophanes *Thesmophoriazousae* 295; *Wasps* 860–874. In the *Phaedo*
(60a3–4), Xanthippe ἀνηυφήμησε and said the sort of things women say on those occasions; but the verb means, "to cry εὐφήμει," and has thus reversed in practice the
εὐφημία of sacrifice: at the end Socrates rebukes the men for bursting into tears and
bawling, and says he heard that one ought to die ἐν εὐφημίᾳ (117d7–e2). Custom
has sanctioned for the women a formal outlet of grief that it has denied the men.

do those prayers differ from the third?[16] Now Clinias too has some trouble
in following the Stranger; and only on his third attempt does the Stranger
clarify his meaning: the poet is not to make anything contrary to the lawful
things of the city, whether they be just, beautiful, or good. The Stranger
thus puts together the good of the eidetic structure of the good with the
beautiful and just of the genetic structure of law. He implies thereby that
the second template consists solely of the goods of the eidetic structure,
and the third template either combines or identifies them with the morality of the law. The poet, then, can commit one of two grave faults: he
might either separate morality from the good or reassign the goods of
either the second or third template to the fourth, in which hymns and
praises of the gods are sung (801e1–2). If the poet follows the Stranger's
own lead and interprets "divine goods" as "goods of the gods," he cannot
interpolate into the second song any request from the gods that would be
suitable for a human being to utter. He might even declare that only the
heroes, who along with the *daimones* are in the fifth template, are properly praised, inasmuch as they alone are endowed with both divine and
human goods; but he could not then couple those praises with prayers
(801e2–4). Though he reminds Clinias that neither silver nor golden
wealth (πλοῦτος) is to dwell and be established in the city (801b5–7), he
fails to remind him that wealth was a good only in the eidetic structure
of the good, and the separation of body and soul, to which he now alludes
in the word "established" (ἱδρυμένον) and later confirms when he has
Plouton be the god of the twelfth month, was the principle of the eidetic
structure of the good and not of the genetic structure of law.

The sixth template is reserved for songs in praise of the dead (801e6–
802a3); but while the Stranger's first formulation is free of ambiguity—
the songs are for those citizens who have the end (τέλος) of life—his second is not: "To honor, moreover, the living with praises and hymns is not
safe (ἀσφαλές), until someone runs through his entire life and puts on it
a beautiful end (τέλος)." As England says, "We must imagine a pause or
break of some sort after ἀσφαλές," if we are "to save the author . . . from
saying 'we must not praise *living* people before they are *dead*.'" There is,
however, no pause or break, and the living are to be praised when dead.

---

16. England's solution (264) is to deny that the second song has any need of a template and assign to the second the content of the third, and Ritter's (191–192) is to
supply from the third the good of the second, and let the third add something new.
Ritter is surely mistaken, against Susemihl, to insist on the strictly subsidiary importance of οἷς θύομεν ἑκάστοτε.

It is entirely in accordance with Solon's dictum, "Call no one happy before he is dead," since that too denies the possibility of the knowledge of happiness to whoever lives a happy life. The continuity between immortal and mortal that the Stranger had proposed in his first prelude, so that there was hardly a break between the chthonic gods, the ancestral gods, and dead parents, seems to have taken on another guise. The Stranger, in any case, within a very short interval revises his statement about those who are to be praised. They are at first those who, having proved to be obedient to the laws, have accomplished in their lifetime beautiful and laborious deeds, whether of body or soul; but in the second formulation their end itself must be beautiful, and they themselves conspicuously good men or women.[17] "Good" now seems to have resumed its older sense of "brave" (cf. 922a1–5).

The Stranger concludes the order of his musical laws in utter confusion (802a8–e11).[18] He demands that songs suitable for females and males be distinguished—and thus increases the number of templates from six to twelve—but he declares that the orderly and moderate (τὸ κόσμιον καὶ σῶφρον) is the natural inclination of the female, and should as such be transmitted lawfully and rationally (ἔν τε τῷ νόμῳ καὶ λόγῳ). If the primary intention of the law is already manifest in the nature of women, then he cannot go on to recommend a uniformity in the education of girls and boys, for the law if successful would diverge from reason, and if reason prevailed, with the support of nature, the law would become a dead letter. The Stranger himself must be puzzled, for though he proposes to explain next how the tradition and instruction of music are to be handled (803a1–3), he is diverted, and when he gets back on track, he first says that the gymnasia and schoolhouses in the city and areas for field sports outside have already been laid out, only to take it back at once and say they are

---

17. The triple γε μήν in such short order (801e1, e6, 802a1) seems to underline the difficulty of distinguishing properly the fourth, fifth, and sixth templates.

18. The extraordinary anacolouthon at 802c7–d3 shows how deeply the Stranger is entangled in poetry. He begins with a clause that strictly must apply to those brought up in either kind of music, the severe or the sweet (ἐν ᾗ [μούσῃ] γὰρ ἂν ἐκ παίδων τις μέχρι τῆς ἑστηκυίας τε καὶ ἔμφρονος ἡλικίας διαβιῷ), but he continues as if the clause held only for the moderate and ordered Muse, so that one is forced to rewrite in one's head the clause (along the lines of Stallbaum's construe) in order for ἀκούων δέ to have its proper contrast. The reason for the anacolouthon is to remind us of what the Stranger had said, that men get used to anything in time, and the mature and sensible age is not a privilege of the education in the more austere music. It would at this point defy the best poets to figure out what the wishes (βουλήματα) of the legislator were and how they were to conform, in their choice of the beautiful poetry of the past, with the intention of his wishes (κατὰ τὸν αὐτῶν νοῦν). The Stranger implies that they would simply follow their own taste.

now to be stated lawfully and rationally (τῷ λόγῳ μετὰ νόμων) (804c2–8). That the problem women pose has thrown him off course he indicates by making equality in the education of male and female his next law (804d6–e4). The woman question, however, seems to trigger the Stranger's erratic course rather than suffice by itself to be the sole cause of his distraction. He introduces it with a simile:

> Just as the shipwright, at the beginning of his building, lays down the keel (τὰ τροπιδεῖα) and outlines the shapes (σχήματα) of boats, so I too, in trying to articulate the shapes (σχήματα) of lives in conformity with the ways (τρόποι) of souls, appear to myself to be doing the same thing, really and truly (ὄντως) to lay down their keel (τὰ τροπιδεῖα), rightly considering this: if we live in what manner and with what ways (τρόποι), shall we best carry on our life (βίος) through this sail of life (ζωή)? Well, then, though the affairs of human beings do not deserve much seriousness (σπουδή), still all in all it is necessary to be serious; and this is not a lucky thing (εὐτυχές). (803a3–b5)

The Stranger puts himself on board a boat he has not built and has no intention of building. In his case, the boat has long been launched and is sailing to an unknown destination. He is at the sunset of life. As for everyone else, he is going to stop at the keel. The Stranger is concerned only with the ways of souls and not with the shapes of lives. He is not the captain of anyone's life. He had started the seventh book with the building of the house of the law whose supports the unwritten law was to supply. Now he is at sea, and has no intention of making life watertight. He is concerned only with the beginning. At the beginning is play or παιδιά. His proposal to consecrate play turned play into its contrary. He was compelled to be serious (σπουδάζειν) and eliminate play (παίζειν). Now he takes it all back:

> I assert that there should be seriousness about the serious, not
>   about the not serious, and by nature god deserves all blessed
>   seriousness, but a human being has been contrived to be, as we
>   said before, a kind of toy of god, and really and truly (ὄντως) that
>   has been the best part of him. So every man and woman must
>   go along this way, and, in playing the most beautiful possible
>   games, live through his life, with a conception contrary to what
>   they think now.
> Clinias: How?
> Stranger: Now they believe no doubt that serious affairs are for the
>   sake of games, for they believe they must arrange well the

things of war, which are serious, for the sake of peace. But, as I
now realize (ἄρα), that which we claim to be the most serious
thing—it is play (παιδιά)—has not been, is not, and will not
be by nature in war, nor does war ever contain an education
(παιδεία) worthy of our regard. (803c2–7; cf. *Epistle* 7, 344c1–d2)

The most important things are the least urgent things. The Stranger now
reaffirms that the experience of little children at puppet shows is solely
in conformity with the truth about man; but the needs of the city have
to deny that truth, and the Stranger, in bowing down to those needs, has
outlined a program that would subvert that truth. He could hold onto it
as long as "religion" was not the left hand of his "theology."[19] The seriousness of play cannot survive its consecration. Megillus discerns in the
Stranger's words the expression of the utter contemptibility of man; but
that contempt is the Egyptian experience of the sacredness of everything
except man (cf. *Minos* 319a5–8); it is not the same as the puppet or wonder (θαῦμα) of man in play. The Stranger characterizes a life lived in play
by three participles: "sacrificing, singing, and dancing" (803e1–2). Such a
life makes it possible to win the gods' graciousness and beat the enemy
in battle. He has given, he says, the types of singing and dancing designed
to accomplish this; but as for the third, he quotes from Homer: "Telemachus, some things you yourself will think of in your mind, others a *daimōn* will suggest, for I suspect that you were born and raised not without
the will of the gods" (804a1–3). The Stranger quotes the words Athena
addressed to Telemachus, whom she accompanied in disguise from Ithaca
to Pylos, where they have found Nestor at the beach performing a sacrifice to Poseidon (*Odyssey* 3.1–28). Nestor's son Peisistratus will soon tell
Athena, as he offers her a cup from which to pour a libation and pray,
that all men have need of gods (3.43–48). The Stranger applies Athena's
words to his own case. The colonists are to think that what he has said
has been adequate, but "the *daimōn* and god will suggest to them sacrifices and choral dances, to whom severally and when they are to celebrate
in play and appeasement and live their life in conformity with the way of
nature, being puppets for the most part, but partaking to some small degree in truth and reality" (804a5–b4). The Stranger pulls back from any
suggestion about sacrifices; he restores purity to his theology and thus

19. The distinction between theology and religion determines the structure of
the *Euthyphro*, the first part of which is controlled by the problem of the "ideas," and
the second by that of prayer and sacrifice: ὁσιότης and εὐσέβεια occur only in the second part (the former seven times, the latter once). One may compare Sextus's separation of the issue of god(s) from that of sacrifice (*Pyrrhoniae hypotyposes* 3.218–222).

grants that Megillus's interpretation of his words is not incorrect (cf. 871c3–d2; 958d4–6). Man becomes contemptible at the very moment the divine becomes the holy. There is no truthful revelation (cf. 893b1–3). It was an inescapable necessity that made the Stranger propose that necessarily spurious translation; but now he has looked away from it toward the god and through that experience looked down on man. He asks Megillus's forgiveness (804b7–c1). His subsequent error, on resuming his legislation (τὸ δ' ἑξῆς τούτοις), so that he declares that schoolhouses and playing fields have been laid out when they had not, seems to reflect his second disorientation, this time in turning back toward man (cf. *Republic* 516e3–7). The rationality he demands of law (τῷ λόγῳ μετὰ νόμων) does not consist with the local. The compromise he then reaches between his sudden looking away and his equally abrupt return is to propose the equality of the sexes. The piety of women supplies the link between his two experiences and his proposal (814b4–5).

3   THE *LAWS*

The indifference of right and left, no less than of male and female, will soon culminate in the indifference of day and night, and along with it the Stranger will recommend the *Laws* itself, which has been going on since dawn and is now more than half a day old, as the model writing for purposes of instruction. Of all the twists and turns of the dialogue this is perhaps the most astonishing. It belongs to a shift in the perspective from which the Stranger now examines education. The teachers and not the pupils are the focus of his attention (cf. 813b1–2).[20] The teachers are all strangers, hired for pay, to teach everything that pertains to war or music (804c8–d3). The Stranger, one might say, arranges for the multiplication of himself throughout the city. They cannot presumably be the models for emulation, however strictly they comply with the rules that all foreigners must obey. They are to be a permanently eccentric element in the structure of the city. Whatever their pupils learn from them cannot be either local or patriotic, but solely subject to an art that is independent of local conditions. The entering wedge into the universal is compulsory public education of all boys and girls. At the beginning of the book, the Stranger suggested some regulations of mothers and nurses; now he deprives the fathers of any say in whether their children are to be educated or not

---

20. Of all the instances of "teaching" in the *Laws*, a third are in book 7 (17); and twenty-six out of a total of thirty-five μάθημα are in book 7.

(804d3–4). He assimilates the regime more and more to the best city in speech and calls a halt only when the city would have to be completely communized and lose every trace of privacy (807b3–808a3).[21] The substitute for the slogan "The things of friends are in common" is "Knowledge is to be shared." Its teachers are to have nothing in common with the city.

The Stranger makes an extraordinary recovery from the oppressiveness of consecration, but not before he meets resistance from both Clinias and Megillus. Clinias is the first to react. The Stranger has just said that it is most senseless for the legislator to halve a city's strength when he could double it if the women were to learn the same things as the men. Clinias at first grants, rather grudgingly, that it would be an error, but then for a moment feels overwhelmed when he reflects on the many departures he has heard from the regimes with which he is familiar. The Stranger's support of the old-fashioned, to which, Clinias said, he and Megillus were most kindly disposed (797d1–6), has put him off balance, now that the Stranger has just drawn its ultimate consequence in the insignificance of man; but Clinias rather magnanimously recovers his composure: "But just as you spoke utterly in tune, for you ordered us to allow you to go through the logos, and once you had gone through it well, we were on that condition to choose what seemed best (τὸ δοκοῦν), so you have made me now on my own rebuke myself because I said that" (805b4–7; cf. 746b5–d2). The self-consistency of the Stranger' plan has just come into conflict with Clinias's prejudices, and, almost simultaneously, he rebels and experiences his error. Clinias undergoes the equivalent to the Stranger's own experience of looking away toward the god and realizing the paltriness of man. Clinias's experience of guilt and self-punishment represents the unrealizable goal of the law: the experiential deviation from the law—in this case the formal rule the Stranger was granted to carry through his project without regard for local conditions—is to coincide as nearly as possible with a self-delivered reproach in favor of the law and against one's own objection. Clinias suspends his present experience in light of a distant end. He thus does not support Megillus when the Stranger disparages the Spartan handling of women and urges

---

21. One should note the verbal parallelism—emphasized by the positions of τέλεον and τελέως—of the need for the legislator to be complete (τέλεον) and not a half (διήμισυν) and, if he is not, of his leaving behind instead for the city half of a pretty nearly completely happy life (σχεδὸν τελέως εὐδαίμονος βίου) (806c3–7). The Stranger thus encapsulates the major difficulty in Socrates' conception of the applicability of happiness to the city as a whole. The completion of the legislation does not entail the completion of a single life for the city (cf. 816c7–d2).

him to let the Stranger speak freely, "until we go through the laws in an absolutely adequate manner" (806c8–d2).

The Stranger believes it is his next task to describe the way of life of the citizens (806a4–7), even though he has not yet finished the children's education, and the law itself has not educated the minister of education adequately (809a6–b1). The Stranger casually remarks that no citizen practices any art, and farming has been entirely handed over to slaves, so that the only common practice left to the citizens is to eat together at the end of the day, though the men and women still dine apart (806d8–807a3). As everyone notices, Glaucon's objection to Socrates' true and healthy city, where everyone has an art and no one is idle—that it is no better than a city of sows—truly applies to this city, and the Stranger echoes Glaucon in saying that if everyone is just being fattened, then they deserve to be torn apart by another animal that courage and toils have worn down to nothing but sinew and bone. The Stranger makes the citizens into Socrates' second class of warriors and thus confronts Adimantus's question: What are they doing with their lives when they are not fighting? The Stranger has got the children up to the age of six, and when he resumes their education he takes them up to sixteen (809c7–810a2), which is the earliest age for the girls to marry, but the men do not patrol the countryside before they are twenty-five and may not marry before thirty. What are they doing in all this time? If one lets oneself be swayed by the drift of the Stranger's talk, one might be led to suppose that they do nothing but study and practice, whether it be for gymnastic or musical competitions. The second chorus of Apollo consisted of those up to thirty, but the Stranger does not say for how long the children belong to the first chorus of the Muses (664c4–d1). They are in any case more likely to become muscle-bound than eggheads, for advanced mathematics is not for everyone (813e35–7; 818a1–7).

If, of course, one were to factor in an average life expectancy of forty, which one now calculates to have held in ancient times, the Stranger's silence would not be as surprising, but the Stranger assumes a lifetime of three score and ten or more throughout, and perhaps under the favorable conditions he has outlined this span would not be uncommon. The puzzle therefore remains: What are the immature doing? One can presume that the grown-ups are almost entirely occupied in political and domestic tasks (808a7–b3). There are all those slaves, metics, and foreigners to supervise, to say nothing of the bad citizens whom the wide-awake magistrates terrorize at night (808c2–4). Although from the outside the city looks like twelve agricultural communities, none of the masters know the art of farming. They live the life of farmers, but they never handle a plow.[22] They know how to rule without having learnt a single one of the arts whose artisans they control. This seems to be the recipe for disaster. We learn in book 8 that the citizens do possess an art, an art that needs much exercise and many lessons (μαθήματα), which they use to preserve and enjoy the common order of the city (846d2–7; cf. 770d3; 812e7–9). Virtue, then, is knowledge, and all the training in lawful habits was nothing but preparation for something else. At the end of book 1, the Stranger had praised the symposium for its great usefulness in getting to know the natures and conditions of souls; he assigned that knowledge which the symposiarch alone possessed to the political art (650b6–9). He had then carefully distinguished this use of the symposium from its possible advantage in education in virtue (652a1–b1). Are we now to suppose that the Stranger has extended the franchise to such an extent, and the popular virtues have fallen away and become knowledge? The nocturnal council seems to have intruded much too early. He does say at any rate that whoever, with due regard for his health, is to the highest degree a caretaker of living and thinking (τοῦ ζῆν καὶ τοῦ φρονεῖν) stays awake for the longest possible time (808b6–c2). No one, he says, is worth anything asleep, any more than one who is not alive (808b5–6).[23]

Just before the Stranger turns to the education of the minister of education, he speaks of the bestiality of the young, which, sharpened by an inchoate rationality, requires the greatest number of constraints. While they are receiving instruction as if they were free, they incur chastisement for any infraction as if they were slaves (808d8–e7). Curiously enough, the minister of education also has to go back to school, for the Stranger goes out of his way to use the term for elementary education (παιδεύειν), and he has "the law itself" educate him (809a6–7). When Socrates asked Meletus who educates (παιδεύει) the Athenian young and makes them better, he would not allow his first answer, "the laws," but insisted on knowing what human being, who in the first place knew the laws, did so (Apology of Socrates 24d10–e2). Now, however, at this crucial point, the Stranger evades Socrates' question by first animating the law, and then, on reflection, giving in form at least Meletus's very answer, the Laws! A book, or a series of books, is going to be the educator of the

22. Cf. M. Piérart, Platon et la cité grecque: Théorie et réalité dans la constitution des "Lois" (Bruxelles 1973), 79, 476.

23. Despite its theme, book 7, which is also the longest book, has the fewest instances of ἀρετή with five than any other book except the ninth on criminal law with three. Book 11 also has five, book 8 six, book 6 nine; the rest are all double digit. The root of "just" (dik-) also occurs the least number of times in book 7 (eight); book 8, which has next to the fewest, has eighteen.

minister of education. It is going to bear very little resemblance to the laws of the city, but it is to be in the hands of the city's instructors, who are to be hired from abroad if and only if they agree to have the *Laws* as their manual (811e5–812a1).[24] The Stranger has devised a posthumous screening of the teachers: there might not be a single candidate for many generations. He has the good grace to say, in concluding the section on writings and their teachers, "Let this be my myth and let it come to an end (τελευτάτω) in this way" (812a1–2).

What seems to distinguish the section on writings from what precedes and follows it is the absence of their consecration. It has been stated, the Stranger says, just before he turns to nonmetrical writings, how the choral songs and dances are to be chosen, corrected, and consecrated (809b3–6; 813a1), and, after he divides dances into various kinds, he says that the legislator must consecrate them and prohibit any tampering with them (816c1–d2), but in the intermediate section on writings there is not a word about consecration any more than there is about their revisability. The *Laws* falls into this gap as the paradigmatic writing. The Stranger is not exactly clear about why, as Clinias puts it, he is really and truly (ὄντως) in a state of perplexity about it (810c5–6). What further sets writing apart is that no subject matter is assigned to it. It comes between the templates of choral song, on the one hand, and, on the other, dances, mathematics, and astronomy, but the Stranger never says what should or should not be taught from books. The Stranger then adds the question whether reading and writing should be taught at all, as if he had not assumed from the start, once he had made laws in the strict sense be written laws, that the laws were available to all and not the province of a few officials (809e3–7). It seems, however, that if reading and writing are not taught for more than three years, the proficiency of the general population would be low, and only the most gifted would attain a level of knowledge on their own that would make the laws, let alone the *Laws*, accessible to them. When, moreover, the Stranger does finally overcome his reluctance to touch on what puzzles him, he drops the issue of prose, with which he started, turns exclusively to the writings of poets, and poses the question whether whole poets or anthologies should be learnt by heart (809b6, 810b4–7; 810e6–811a5). The issue becomes whether vast learning (πολυμαθία) makes one good and wise, and the only clear point the Stranger makes is that everyone would concede that not every writing ever published is first-rate.

24. Cf. G. Picht, *Platons Dialoge "Nomoi" und "Symposion"* (Klett-Cotta 1990), 33–38.

The lameness of this conclusion makes one realize that books can be read anywhere, and unless the slaves of the house become spies for the city, or the house itself can have a voice of its own (807e6–808a7), the sanctity of the private opens the door to subversive literature. Why, then, did not the Stranger just propose a general censorship along the lines Socrates laid down, and whatever was in conformity with the laws would be allowed and whatever was not would be forbidden (cf. 957c4–d6)? The Stranger had not, however, started out with a Socratic theology, according to which the gods were the causes of all goods and they themselves entirely beautiful. If one uses the language of Varro, Socrates replaced, at the beginning of the best city in speech, the gods of the poets with the gods of the philosophers in order that the gods of the city might not get a foot in the door and interfere through the holy with the education of the guardians. The Stranger, however, had started with a distinction between body and soul and divine and human goods, and only when he confronted head-on the problem of change did he tack on a religion that he then left entirely in the hands of the city.[25] He had left, in other words, the gods of the city to the city. He knows, moreover, that Clinias, like all Cretans, knows very little of Homer or any other foreign poet, so he can hardly expel what has not yet got in without spoiling an innocence that is hardly uncorrupt (cf.886b10–d2).[26] The Stranger, then, seems to be imagining what would happen if he and not Homer were at the beginning, and he and not Homer were the educator of a new Greece. What if philosophy and not poetry started off civilization? Would it be possible to redraw the distinction between barbarism and civilization, so that the double origin of Greece in the *Iliad* and the *Odyssey* could be grounded philosophically? The *Iliad* is about a man who learns that he needs the gods if he is to be who he is, for only they support the distinction between body and soul and demand the return of Hector's body for burial. It is Achilles who realizes that the soul is something, after all, in the house

25. Augustine says that Varro, who borrowed his threefold theology from the pontifex Q. Mucius Scaevola, separated "civil theology from mythical theology, cities from theaters, temples from the stage, rites of the pontiffs from songs of the poets, as if he were separating beautiful things from ugly things, true from false, serious from playful, and what was to be sought from what was to be spurned," though he knew that the latter depended on the former and reflected it as if in a mirror (*De civitate dei* 6.9). Augustine also reports that Varro wrote that he would not have placed divine things after human things, as he did in his *Antiquitates,* had he been founding a new city, but would have started with the gods of the philosophers (4.31; 6.4).

26. Valerius Maximus records that the Spartans banished the poetry of Archilochus because they feared it would damage the morals of their children more than it would improve their minds (6.12.*ext.*1).

of Hades (*Iliad* 23.103–4). So decisive is this theme for what we call humaneness that Vergil had to end the *Aeneid* with the killing of Turnus and leave in the dark whether his corpse was ever given back. The *Odyssey* is about a man who traveled very far, saw the cities of many men, and knew their mind. It is a story about the way and the obstacles to wisdom. Despite Vergil's combination of the *Odyssey* and *Iliad* into one book, there is no Odysseus in his story. Aeneas is renowned for his piety, and Vergil was not at the beginning of Rome.[27] Achilles' justice and Odysseus's wisdom set the course for Greece. If the Stranger has doubts whether he can duplicate Homer's achievement on his own, his hesitation to broach the issue of writing is perfectly understandable (cf. 858e1–859b1).

The Stranger is very pleased when he glances back at his own speeches all collected since dawn, for they suit the bill and have been spoken "in a manner absolutely like a kind of poetry" (811c7–d5). The *Laws*, up to this point at least, blurs the difference between poetry and prose, and fits the hearing of the young better than anything else the Stranger has learned or heard. The young are to hear a story about how their laws came to be, how their legislator began in error, how he refused to accept many arguments, and how he and his colleagues filled in, left out, corrected, and altered on their own authority what an unknown Athenian had left behind. If the Stranger has his way, these Dorian children are going to grow up, to an even greater extent than Megillus had, with a second fatherland (642b6). They are going to hear a story about their laws, inside of which there is an outline of laws declared to be gods and fundamentally flawed (715c4). Just as the gods of Homer are and are not the gods of the city, so the *Laws* is and is not their legislation. The *Laws* is the basis of their education, it is not something they are to obey.[28] Once the *Laws* is the paradigm, the Stranger is willing to let the minister of education add other pieces of prose and poetry, and he urges in particular the transcription of any speeches as yet unwritten that he finds not unlike the *Laws* (811e1–5). He proposes, in short, the writing down of Socratic speeches. Clinias is not so sure: "We are, apparently, proceeding according to the supposition and are not stepping outside the supposition

27. All the same, Vergil seems to be imagining something similar to the *Laws* for Rome, when he assigns to a Carthaginian singer a Lucretian kind of poetry, and to Anchises in Hades a Platonizing teaching (*Aeneid* 1.740–746; 6.724–751).

28. Timaeus proposes lessons to counteract the effect speeches, spoken in public [i.e., the laws] and in private, have on those with bad constitutions in bad regimes (*Timaeus* 87a7–b4). These regimes would be according to Socrates all known regimes, which merely vary in the extent of their badness.

of the speeches; but whether we are right in regard to the whole or not, it is perhaps difficult to insist" (812a4–6). Clinias is no doubt troubled as much by the violation of the Dorian law of laws the Stranger casually introduces—the young are going to discuss the laws with foreigners—as by the finality (τελευτάτω) of the Stranger's pronouncement about the myth, for it seems to deny a rethinking of this part at least in light of the whole. He may also be thinking that the criminal law, which must soon be tackled, could not possibly be suitable for the young to hear: that the laws could continue to educate despite the presupposition of criminal law, that the education in the law has failed, has the air of a paradox (cf. 857c6–e5). Clinias, in any case, could hardly have guessed that the Stranger was going to propose the abolition of Cretan pederasty or offer a new theology. The Stranger accepts the reasonableness of Clinias's qualms. He says that whether it is right or not to have the *Laws* as a textbook must wait "until we come to the end (τέλος) of the entire survey of laws" (812a8–9).

4 IMITATION

The theme of instruction requires a review of gymnastic (813a5–b2). It allows the Stranger to denounce once more Spartan women, whose behavior at the time of the battle of Leuctra helped to spread the opinion that the human race was the most naturally timid of all beasts (814b4–7). If the women are trained, the Stranger implies, the influence of religion will be kept in place (cf. 909e5–910a6). This time Megillus does not protest, and Clinias concurs with the Stranger's elevation of women to citizenesses (814b8–c5).[29] The review of gymnastic also lets the Stranger reveal a gap in his remarks about wrestling, which, and though the gap is the biggest part of wrestling, he cannot even now make up for, since "it is not easy if a display in the body and a pointing out in speech are not simultaneous" (814c6–8). The book had begun with the impossibility of putting into law all that the legislator had to say, but now the Stranger implies that there is something unsayable in the unwritten law itself: the comportment of the body defies description, yet defines a people as unmistakably as a signature. There is a limit to logos. The name for this limit is the ἄλογον or ἄρρητον, the irrational. The Stranger is going to match the disgrace of Spartan women with the disgrace of all Greeks,

29. Cf. C. Mossé, "Dénomination de l'Athénienne dans les plaidoyers Démosthéniens," *Ktema* 10 (1985): 77–79.

who do not know about the incommensurability of certain magnitudes, but who are sunk in the nonhuman and swinish ignorance of strict Pythagoreanism, for which no magnitude cannot be expressed as a ratio between two whole numbers (819c7–e1). Body and motion resist the power of number. The poet's demand that the legislator translate everything he certifies to be measured (μέτριον) into a number cannot be carried out. The resistance to translatability raises the question whether the Stranger's insistence on eliminating differences, whether they be of left and right, female and male, or night and day, was not meant to point to this mathematical issue, and that it is here where one would have to begin with the asymmetry of nature: its order, if it has one, may not necessarily show itself in a way that the city can readily use. Maybe the possible equality of the right and left hands does not entail that there is not a hidden bias in the spatial orientation of things. To be face to face with someone is not the same as facing oneself in a mirror. Nature too might be lame.

The sixty-year-old singers in the chorus of Dionysus signal the return to gymnastic. They deal with rhythms and harmonies that suit the imitations of the experiences of soul, and are to make sure that the notes of the lyre match the words of the song and are not sounding crosswise to them (812b9–c7). The Stranger rejects such complexities not on the grounds that they are untrue to the experiences of soul but because they make learning too difficult for the young, who have only three years to master what they should know. In the copy of the experiences of soul there is possibly a simplification of their reality. The ratios of shorts and longs in the rhythms, and the ratios of intervals in the scales, together with the logos of the words, are to accomplish an enchantment of the souls of the young, by which they are being summoned through imitations to follow along in the acquisition of virtue. This singing has its counterpart in dancing, which is in turn to impose a shape on the movements of the body that unavoidably accompany the movements of the soul (815e4–816a6). The Stranger begins his classification of dances as if they could all be fitted into a regular scheme of bifurcations. The first division separates the imitation of more beautiful bodies in light of the august or majestic (τὸ σεμνόν) from the imitation of uglier bodies in light of the paltry or insignificant (τὸ φαῦλον), and both the paltry and the august divide again into two more species.[30] The august divides into the

---

30. The august (σεμνόν) means almost everywhere in Plato the pretentious, and the verbal denominative (ἀπο)σεμνύνειν in the active to magnify and claim a divine sta-

serious pair of war and peace, and the pyrrhic or martial dance splits into
an imitation of either defensive or offensive actions; but the peaceful
dance does not lend itself at once to a comparable division, for the disputable part of it has to be cut apart from what is indisputable and suitable to law-abiding men. The disputable dances, which go by the names
"Nymphs," "Pans," "Silenuses," and "Satyrs," are Dionysiac or Bacchic
celebrations and imitate these beings when drunk;[31] they cannot be labeled either peaceful or martial, for it is not even easy to determine what
they mean or want (βούλεσθαι). They are, the Stranger decides, not political and can be left wherever they are lying.

In returning to the unwarlike Muse, the Stranger labels the whole
genus a celebration of the gods and their children when one is under the
impression (δόξα) that one is faring well; and the genus can be divided
between the greater pleasures that result from an escape from toils and
dangers into goods, and the gentler pleasures that accompany the preservation and increase of previous goods. Even though there was a place for
them in the genetic structure of law (632a2–b1), there are to be no imitations of noble men who in facing adversity fail (cf. 732c1–d7; cf. Republic
399a5–b3). There is no representation of defeat (cf. 813d3–5). The Stranger's divisions seem to have betrayed him into covering over human experiences. Still, however, he has to fill in the two blanks on the paltry side of
dancing, but he supplies only one, comedy. Does he then imply that tragedy belongs in the one empty spot? Tragedy would thus be the imitation
of the experiential opinion that either there is never an end to toil and
danger or there is a total and permanent loss of goods, and if the tragedies
we have are any guide, no one behaves in a dignified manner under either
circumstance (cf. Republic 605c10–606c1). If the term "paltry" (φαῦλον) is
meant to recall Megillus's rebuke of the Stranger—that in treating man as
a plaything and a puppet he had disparaged (διαφαυλίζεις) the human race
too much—then tragedy would be one way of responding simultaneously
to Megillus and the Stranger. Despite, however, the neatness with which
tragedy would then fill out his own scheme, the Stranger seems at the
same time both to preclude this assignment and suggest it. Although he
separates the playthings (παίγνια) of comic laughter from the seriousness,
whether it be of the tragic poets themselves or their themes, he casts

---

tus for something or in the middle to give oneself airs; with the exception of Socrates'
Laws (Crito 51b1), only Hippias uses σεμνόν without irony (Hippias Maior 288d3); cf.
Gorgias 502b1 (of tragedy); Statesman 290d8, e7; Philebus 28b1, c3, 7.

31. Wilamowitz, Platon II, 401, wants to read the nominative for κατῳνωμένους,
in order to get rid of drunk gods and ruin Plato's thought.

doubt on it by inserting a parenthetical, "as they claim" (817a2). The Stranger, moreover, had confessed that he did not know whether man as puppet was the gods' plaything (παίγνιον) or had been put together for some serious purpose (σπουδῇ). There is, then, a place for tragedy on the paltry side; but it can also be lurking under the disputable category of the Dionysiac (βακχεία), for the Stranger, in saying that those dances imitate the drunk, could be describing the Laws. The Laws certainly began as a distant imitation of a drunken revel, and it has scarcely lost its character as a symposium in speech despite the not entirely deceptive appearance of a greater sobriety it has gained in the meantime. We have only to remember the Stranger's provocation of Megillus when he solemnly recommended the high seriousness of play. It looks, then, as if tragedy and the Laws are disputing for a place on either the left or right side of dance, and to settle which belongs where would come close to understanding why the Stranger now says that they are the makers of the best and most beautiful tragedy.

The difficulty of placing either the Laws or tragedy in the Stranger's scheme can best be seen if one considers that the Stranger puts under the Bacchic the dances called Silenuses and Satyrs, both of whom are present in person in Satyr drama. Satyr drama seems to be in-between comedy and tragedy and possibly the origin of both. Socrates too seems to belong there, for he himself likens Alcibiades' drunken praise of him to a satyric and silenic drama (Symposium 222d3–4). The Stranger, moreover, connects these Bacchic forms of dance with rituals of purification and initiation. He thus brings us back to the prototragedy he had found in the lullaby and Corybantic rites. The original bestiality of man, whether one takes it historically or genetically, would make the nonpolitical genus to which the Stranger relegates these dances more indicative of the theme of the Laws than the civilized forms he welcomes into the city. The Stranger had already removed the pity of tragedy from the vicinity of the holy and restricted it, if the city were to need it, to the mourning for the dead. Does tragedy, then, in ceasing to be political, belong with the Laws on the edge of the city? The understanding of things is always eccentric to the things themselves.

It would seem that divisions generate asymmetries all by themselves (cf. 878b4–6). Clinias had begun with the assertion that war was real and peace but a name; and although the Stranger had instructed him that war and peace were two, and war was for the sake of peace (628c6–d1), he now suggests that this duality was a fundamental myth of the city; fighting to victory in war was to be coupled with winning the gods' graciousness, and both of them were the result of play, and play was the life of peace

regardless of whether one was at peace or at war (803e1–4). Dancing, however, begins with the distinction between the martial and the peaceful.
The return to gymnastic is a return to the primacy of war for the city: the
Stranger had put play under music. He now starts out with a distinction
between beautiful and ugly bodies; but he immediately adds a manly
soul to beautiful bodies entangled in violent toils, and a moderate soul
engaged in good fortune and moderate pleasures. Ugly bodies and ugly
thoughts belong to comedy, but an ugly body with beautiful thoughts,
which was Alcibiades' understanding of Socrates, is another possible combination. When, moreover, the Stranger turns to peaceful dances, he contrasts the greater intensity of pleasure the cowardly and immoderate man
experiences with the lesser degree of the orderly and brave; but he does
not do the same for the experiences of war, so that one could distinguish
the reaction to such stress on the part of the moderate and the brave.
Would one of them experience greater pleasure in offense and the other
in defense? If the text is sound, the Stranger speaks of the imitation of
the imitation of offensive actions (815a5–7). He seems to be alluding to
the double distance at which such gestures stand from the act of killing,
for if there are to be no dances of noble dying—the Stranger might thus
hint that it does not exist on the battlefield (cf. 944c6–7)—the thrust of
the sword, the cast of the spear, and the shot of the arrow are, when
represented, without their intended object and do not show what is involved when a blow goes home. In any case, the double character of the
pyrrhic compels one to ask whether there is also a double form of comedy, one of offense, which Socrates describes at great length in the *Philebus* (48a8–50a10), and another of defense, which is designed to thwart
or deflect the barbs of an Aristophanes.

The Stranger admits that the serious things cannot be understood
without the funny things, and as the thoughtful person (φρόνιμος) needs
to observe both, so the virtuous needs to recognize both, so that he does
not inadvertently do or say laughable things, *if there is no need* (μηδὲν
δέον). Tragedies, it seems, may be read but not performed, and slaves or
hired foreigners are to perform comedies. These comedies are to be constantly changed, in order, presumably, to hinder the duplication of a
comic type in the city by dint of repetition (816d3–e10).[32] The slaves, who
in the city represent the actions of men solely subject to the law as threat,
are now on the stage to represent funny things. Is comedy to ridicule the

---

32. Cf. W. Theiler, *Untersuchungen zur antiken Literatur* (Berlin 1970), "Die be-
wahrenden Kräfte im Gesetzesstaat Platos," 253 note 1.

law, and thus shame the spectators into taking their own bearings by the preludes alone? The Stranger himself had suggested a funny scene. The slaves were to say to themselves: "What a disgrace! We, of all people, have to wake up our mistress! What a slugabed! What an Oblomov! She ought to wake us up! If we had our way, the whole house would sing in her ear: 'Sleepy head! Slugabed! The police are knocking at the door! And we summoned them!'" (807e6–808a7). The Stranger did not know whether he should call it a practice or a law that the free are always to be the first who are awake and stirring about. If it is to be a law, the slaves become the masters; if it is to be a practice, the slaves must show up their masters only on the stage. Would the audience laugh and say, "It couldn't happen here?" Would, in fact, its very impossibility make them indifferent to the message and, on the very next night after the show, sleep through dawn? The Stranger composes the following reply to the tragic poets:

> Best of strangers! We ourselves are the poets of the best and most beautiful tragedy possible. Our whole regime, at any rate, has been put together as an imitation of the most beautiful and best life. It is this, we assert, that is really and truly (ὄντως) the truest tragedy. Now you are poets, but we too are poets of the same things. We are your rivals in art and competitors for the most beautiful drama. The true law [song] alone has the nature to perfect and complete this. That's our hope. So do not imagine that we, just like that, would any more allow you to fix your stages in the marketplace and introduce actors with beautiful voices, speaking more loudly than we do, than grant you permission to harangue the children, the women, and the entire crowd [cf. 658d3–4], and though you speak about the same practices you do not say the same things as we do, but generally most of them are the sheer contrary. We would, you know, be pretty nearly completely crazy, and every other city whatsoever would be too, should it permit you to do what you now say, before the magistracies had decided whether you have made sayable things and suitable to be spoken publicly or not. Now, then, sons and offspring of the soft Muses, first we have to show your songs, in comparison with our own, to the magistrates, and if it is evident that you are saying the same or maybe better things, we shall grant you a chorus, but if not, friends, we could never do it. (817b1–d8)

The Stranger seems to have conceded a lot to Megillus, who protested when he had maintained that play and not seriousness was proper to man; now the most beautiful and best life is a tragic life, and the Stranger is the maker of such a life in an image. He competes with the tragic poets and exhibits the truest tragedy. The tragic poets miss the truth about the tragic life. That truth seems to be contained in the first place in "the best and most beautiful life possible," for this is once more a formula for the impossible union of the eidetic structure of the good with the genetic structure of law. For tragedy, the experiential deviation from the law points to suicide;[33] for the Stranger, it points to the eidetic structure of the good. Tragedy would have failed, then, not in discerning the character of lawful justice and moderation, but in not setting them up against the structure of the eightfold good and its leader mind.[34] Oedipus, with the double meaning of his name ("Know-where" and "Swollen-foot"), comes the closest to representing the eidetic and the genetic, the first of which is displayed in Oedipus's solution to the riddle of the Sphinx, and the second in the twin prohibitions of incest and patricide. Those prohibitions were holy, and Oedipus's discovery of man was necessarily a violation of the holy; but Sophocles could not point out the arbitrariness of the translation of the divine into the holy, and thus could not distinguish, as the Stranger had, between sacrifice, on the one hand, and, on the other, singing and dancing (cf. *Oedipus Tyrannus* 863–910).[35] Oedipus's life was tragic because he could not will to be who he claimed to be once he knew who he was. For tragedy, the best life is the political life, but it is best not to born, for the political life is the criminal life; for the Stranger, the

---

33. Consider Sappho fr. 85 Lobel (137 B): τὸ ἀποθνήσκειν κακόν: οἱ θεοὶ γὰρ οὕτω κεκρίκασιν· ἀπέθνησκον γὰρ ἄν. See further David Daube, "The Linguistics of Suicide," *Philosophy and Public Affairs* 1 (1972): 387–437. He points out that it is in Greek tragedy that one first finds an explosion of terms for killing oneself, and that the *Old Testament* has no special term for it, and neither the *Old* nor the *New Testament* prohibits it.

34. Plato's *Apology of Socrates* illustrates structurally the truest tragedy. In the first part, Socrates stands in for man in general in light of his interpretation of Apollo's oracle (23a7–b4); in the second part, through his *daimonion*, Socrates is just himself and not everyman. The first part deals with ignorance, the second with virtue. The moral of the first part seems to be suicide, that of the second, for which Achilles is the model, heroic defiance of man's fate. This tragic structure becomes philosophy once ignorance yields to the knowledge of ignorance, and the human good is to converse each day about virtue and everything else Socrates examines (38a1–7).

35. The word πόλις disappears from the play after its last occurrence in this stasimon (880), but afterwards its negation ἀπόπτολις occurs (1000), and ἄστυ (1378, 1450). If one follows up on O. Apelt's suggestion (*Platons Gesetze*, vol.2, 526 note 94), that the preludes are meant to be the equivalent to the choral songs of tragedy, then the three personages of the *Laws* are the actors in the drama, with the peculiar consequence that the Stranger is the tragic poet who has now come out from behind the scene and is on stage throughout.

truest tragedy is that political life is too serious for it to be a life of play.[36] The *Laws* itself is the true law. It is the in-tune song (ἐμμέλεια) of the out-of-tune (πλημμελές), or the orderly disorder of the symposium in speech.[37] It alone has been able to make the truest tragedy.

5 FALSE APPEARANCES

The last two lessons differ from everything that has preceded them in one respect: they are to be detached from the law if it turns out that a proof cannot be given that there are irrational magnitudes, and that the sun, moon, and planets cannot be shown to travel in circular paths (820d8–e7; 822c7–10). If neither were true, the Greeks would not be ignorant swine and uttering false reports against the gods, and the first end of education would end with the Stranger's claim to have been the poet of the truest tragedy. What the Stranger now proposes has nothing to do with tragedy, even though there is a sense in which astronomy, as a science of bodies in regular motion, falls under a theoretical gymnastic (cf. *Timaeus* 40c3–d3; *Erastai* 132a5–b3), and the replacement of the Olympian gods with cosmic gods, which is first broached here, alters how one is to understand the holy. "We [Greeks] say," the Stranger says, "we should neither examine the greatest god and the cosmos as a whole nor meddle in the investigation of their causes, and we say it is not even holy" (821a2–4; cf. 966e4–967d2). Since phrases like "Being mortal think mortal thoughts" strike us as typically tragic, there seems to be a connection, after all, between the Stranger's rivalry with tragic poets and his assertion that it is altogether dear to the gods as well as advantageous to the city to learn something as beautiful and true as his proposed astronomy (821a7–b2). In reverting to the gods of the barbarians (Aristophanes *Peace* 406–411; cf. Plato *Apology of Socrates* 26d1–3; *Cratylus* 408d5–e1), the Stranger frees himself from any restrictions on examining the gods and

36. Polybius, in speaking of the Roman use of religion (δεισιδαιμονία), praises the ancients for inculcating fears of the unknown, opinions about Hades, and "tragedy of this kind" in the people (6.56.11).

37. Pollux (4.99) and Athenaeus (XIV.28 [630 D–E]) assign the dance called ἐμμέλεια to tragedy, but the Stranger gives it to the peaceful (816b4–c1). Athenaeus goes on to say that in his own day (second–third century A.D.) the pyrrhic dance remains only in Sparta, elsewhere it is the Dionysiac, in which, now that there are no longer wars, the dancers hold thyrsi instead of spears and hurl them at one another (631 A–B).

their causes. He does not explain what advantage the city would obtain from the sort of investigation he proposes. When he first suggested the rudiments of astronomy, its purpose was to keep the lunar and the solar years together, so that the fixed days of festivals would not occur in the wrong seasons, and to make men more thoughtful about them; but there was no suggestion that the gods to whom the city was to sacrifice were the divine beings who fixed the calendar (809c6–d7). Now, however, that a mathematical model is proposed, which would also involve a causal account, the Stranger runs the risk of demonstrating to the city that the moon shines by reflected light, and Anaxagoras was right to say that it was earth (*Apology of Socrates* 26d4–6; *Cratylus* 409a8–b1).

The account the Stranger gives of astronomy does not match the high importance he attributes to it. It seems to be a placeholder for the theology of book 10, in which an argument for the priority of soul to body is given, and the cause of all motions traced to soul. Once the soul is in place, it is not clear whether astronomy, no matter how perfectly it proves the circular motions of heavenly bodies, can maintain its present rank. If order is always better than disorder (806c4–6), it still might be the case that there is order and order, and the confinement of the paths of the planets to circles might not be most revelatory of the true order of things. The apparent commensurability of all magnitudes has to yield to a proof of their incommensurability, and the Stranger suggests at least that surfaces and volumes might have a counterpart to linear incommensurability (cf. Ritter, 220–6). What the Stranger implies is that once there is a way to rationalize the irrational, the apparently chaotic becomes as orderly as the natural numbers, and there is no evident limit to what mathematics can represent as ordered. The discovery of irrational magnitudes simultaneously discloses the possibility of ever higher orders of order and demotes the circularity of celestial motions as being a privileged image of mind. Linear incommensurability is universally unknown among the Greeks, but it is not clear why they are worse off in their ignorance. The Stranger seems to imply that their ignorance makes them falsely draw the line about the necessities (ἀνάγκαι) against which not even a god fights. These divine necessities emerge in a sentence that begins with another kind of necessity—what of mathematics all the citizens must at a minimum (ἀναγκαῖον) know. A precise knowledge of arithmetic, plane and solid geometry, and astronomy cannot be expected of everyone: "But it is impossible to discard what is indispensable or necessary (ἀναγκαῖον) in them, and it seems as if the one who first uttered the proverb about the god looked at these things, and said, 'It is evident (φανῇ) that even a god shall not ever be fighting against necessity,' at least, that is, against those necessities that are divine, since of human necessities, at least, at which the many are looking when they say something of the sort, that is the most foolish of all speeches by far" (818a7–b6).

Human beings cannot be human if they do not know that gods do not resist certain necessities. There is a necessity for them to know what constitutes necessity for gods: "I imagine, if someone did not do (πράξας) these necessities, and in turn did not come to understand them, he would never become a god for human beings, any more than a *daimōn* or a hero would prove to be the sort to care seriously (σὺν σπουδῇ) for human beings, and a human being would be far from coming to be divine should he be unable to recognize one, two, or three, or in general odd and even, or be altogether ignorant of counting (ἀριθμεῖν), and be unable to count and classify (διαριθμεῖσθαι) night and day, in his inexperience of the revolution of moon, sun, and all the other stars" (818b9–d1). If human beings were swine, a god of a different kind, as Xenophanes suggested, might be possible; but once the Stranger requires that the incommensurability of certain magnitudes be known if human beings are to be human beings, then the minimal condition for human beings becoming divine passes beyond the knowledge he first lays down, since the capacity to count and awareness of the circuits of the heavenly bodies do not entail that knowledge. Man must first know how to count day and night as two and then as one (cf. *Epinomis* 978b7–d1). He must first see the two visible parts of the day before he comes to understand their invisible unity. Up to this point he does not have to do anything; but once he begins to do geometry, he must act. These actions consist in constructions, which Socrates says are as laughable as they are necessary (μάλα γελοίως τε καὶ ἀναγκαίως) (*Republic* 527a6). From these constructions there arises the proof that if the two legs of a right-angle triangle are equal, the square on the hypotenuse is equal to the sum of the squares on the two sides; and from this proof the question about the commensurability of the hypotenuse with the length of the side first comes to light. It is, I think, this kind of geometrical construction to which the Stranger alludes with his mysterious πράξας. If a god does not do these constructions, it is impossible for him to know these necessities or be a god for human beings, for without the proof of the irrationality of √2 he would believe what man knows to be impossible, that odd can be even.[38] To know these necessities

38. Ritter's interpretation of πράξας, that a god must be the maker of a self-binding necessity (211–214), seems to me as impossible as England's modification of

is a necessity; it is nothing very grand or beautiful; but not to know them is to be absolutely contemptible (παντάπασιν φαῦλον) (820b4–c6). The Stranger echoes Megillus, who thought that the Stranger was expressing his absolute contempt (παντάπασι διαφαυλίζεις) for man when he said that man partakes in truth to some small extent. Megillus had not known the half of it.

6   HUNTING

Two lessons precede hunting. If they were removed, hunting would be placed right next to the Stranger's claim to have made the truest tragedy. If they are indispensable, hunting becomes the first example of the difference between what the legislator praises or blames and what the legislator makes into law. The Stranger thus recovers what his proposed consecration of everything threatened to banish, for even though young and old were to learn mathematics as a game, there was still a necessity to learn it. Now, however, the unwritten law is restored, to which no penalty is attached if the young prefer to go fowling or fishing rather than stick to the daylight hunting of four-legged beasts without the use of nets and traps; but it is a curious consequence of the bestowal of praise on one kind of hunting that, despite the Stranger himself proposing it, no penalty is attached to those who disobey and do what is explicitly prohibited (823c8; 824a10–19). There are no numbers in this law.

It is easy enough to see that hunting is just as much a placeholder as astronomy, for as astronomy stood in for theology, so hunting stands in for philosophy or dialectic, for the curious juxtaposition of the issues of mathematical sciences and of tragedy cannot but remind us that in the *Republic,* after tragedy has been banished, it is replaced by these same sciences, which Socrates then crowned with philosophy. What is even more curious is the Stranger's indulgence in a set of divisions, seemingly lifted from the *Sophist,* in order to determine what is to be praised or blamed and what is to be allowed or prohibited. The key to what he is doing lies in the fact that the law as he presents it uses hunting in the literal sense, but praise and blame extend hunting and the hunted to in-

---

it, that god creates in us "the faculty of realizing mathematical necessity" (311), since in either case ποιήσας would be needed. England also has to separate artificially πρά-ξας from μαθών, as well as god from *daimōn* and hero. The significance of construction for Plato also shows up in the *Statesman,* where the Eleatic Stranger's distinction between πρακτική and γνωστική cannot hold up once mathematics' reliance on construction is recognized (258d4–e7).

clude actions and beings that implicitly would cover almost all of the things that are. The extensions thus allow us to reconsider the bestiality of man and link up hunting with the definitional and unwritten laws that originally separated man from beast and god from man. The entire range that man occupies first comes to light in hunting. It is the Stranger's first foray into law as wanting to be the discovery of the beings, and it prepares the way for what the Stranger has long postponed, the question of *erōs*. He extends the meaning of *erōs* along with the extension of "hunting."

Unwritten law belongs to that part of speech that the law does not claim for its own. Law always preserves an older part of a language and aims at freedom from ambiguity.[39] Law wants to have no similes and no metaphors;[40] but the extension of nouns and verbs so as always to be taking in almost everywhere more ground than their root sense warrants seems to be native to speech and occurs not only for the sake of economy, but because men notice the resemblance among things that the law does not and cannot acknowledge. The double meaning of νόμος is at the heart of the *Laws*. The experiential deviation from the law shows up in speech itself, and only if speech were to be made holy could these drifts in meaning be contained, but only to a degree, for even with such a consecration another kind of speech would grow up beside it and be the depository of everything the law forbade. The Stranger had had the tragic poets put their question to the legislator in this way: "Are we to bring and drive (φέρωμέν τε καὶ ἄγωμεν) the poetry?" (817a5–6). The phrase φέρειν καὶ ἄγειν usually refers to the laying waste of a country, in which the first term

39. The most conspicuous case of archaic language occurs in homicide law, where κτείνω rather than ἀποκτείνω is used; Plato follows this practice in the *Laws* (about thirty times). Only in the *Euthyphro* is there a comparable frequency of the uncompounded form. Thucydides' use of κτείνω and ἀποκτείνω is worth examining: first at 4.96.8 the uncompounded form stands in for the compounded; at 3.66.2 the Thebans distinguish the two. Of the ninety or so occurrences of the Ionic dative plural in -οισι and -αισι, eighteen are before the beginning of the laws proper at 771a5 (i.e., about three-sevenths of the whole). Clinias speaks the first two (625c2, d2).

40. The Stranger first points to this literalism of the law when he criticizes choral producers for transferring the word εὔχρως to song and gesture (655a4–8). Cicero *Topica* 7.32: *saepe etiam definiunt et oratores et poetae per translationem verbi ex similitudine cum aliqua suavitate. sed ego a vestris exemplis nisi necessario non recedam. solebat igitur Aquilius collega et familiaris meus, cum de litoribus ageretur, quae omnia publica esse vultis, quarentibus eis quos ad id pertinebat, quid esset litus, ita definire, qua fluctus eluderet; hoc est, quasi qui adulescentem florem aetatis* [τῆς ὥρας καθάπερ ὀπώρας (837c1)], *senectutem occasum vitae* [ἐν δυσμαῖς τοῦ βίου (770a6)] *velit definire: translatione enim utens discedebat a verbis propriis rerum ac suis;* cf. Fritz Schulz, *History of Roman Legal Science* (Oxford 1946), 98. Since *eludere* means to deceive by trickery and in law to evade a law by a dodge, Cicero's criticism of Aquilius is particularly telling.

designates the carrying off of all movable goods, and the second the driving away of all livestock. The poets are in the vanguard of nonlawful speech, for they see more deeply into the experience of things. To keep them out only slows down the reshaping of speech, it does not stop it. Τέμνειν καὶ κάειν can mean in the devastation of a country slash and burn, or, in the curing of a patient, cut and cauterize. If one were to superimpose the first sense on the second, one could say that the phrase then expresses the experience of the patient and the action of the surgeon simultaneously.

The Stranger starts his analysis of hunting without distinguishing it from anything else; but if one has recourse to the *Sophist* (219c2–e2), hunting and competition belong immediately to mastery, or the gaining of the upper hand (χειρωτικόν), and ultimately to acquisition, and hunting is distinguished from competition by its being secretive (κρυφαῖον), whereas competition is out in the open (ἀναφανδόν) (cf. 731a3–5). The secrecy of hunting comprehends the hiddenness of both hunter and hunted. The analysis of hunting precedes the Stranger's ordinances that pertain to training for war and competition (cf. 633b1–2). Hunting (θήρα) comprehends not only the hunting of beasts (θηρία) but also of human beings, whether it occurs in war or in friendship, and whether it is praised or blamed. "Hunting," then, in defiance of the "beast" (θήρ) lurking within it, denies any difference, as far as the action goes, between beast and man.[41] The swinishness of man, insofar as he does not know about irrational magnitudes, is juxtaposed with the bestiality of man, which shows up, despite his lawful hunting of the undomesticated swine, in war. The experience of men in war leads them on their own to the edge of the recognition of themselves as beasts of prey, which Homer steps over and shows them for what they are: "Antilochus darted forward like a hound, which jumps up at a wounded fawn, and as the fawn shoots out from its lair, the hunter hits it on the mark and loosens its limbs, so against you, Melanippus, Antilochus, staunch in battle, shot out in order to strip you of your armor, but Hector took note of it: he came running

---

41. It is the Stranger's silence about the tameness or not of man that most distinguishes his set of divisions from the Eleatic Stranger's, for when he divides hunting on land into hunting of either tame or wild animals, Theaetetus doubts whether there is a hunting of the tame, and the Stranger offers him several possibilities, that man is either tame or wild, some other animal is tame, or there is no hunting of man, and Theaetetus decides, "Just as I believe we are a tame animal, so I say there is a hunting of human beings" (*Sophist* 222b2–c2). The Stranger then puts under violent hunting the arts of piracy, enslavement, tyranny, and all of warfare (222c5–7).

through the battle line to oppose him, and Antilochus did not remain, stout warrior though he was, but he shuddered and looked like a beast that had done an evil—it killed a dog or a cowherd who was guarding cattle—and took to flight before a crowd of men could gather" (*Iliad* 15.579–588). The city may want to cut away warfare from hunting, for its laws about burial may want to say that man is not carrion, but the actions of war put a strain on the law that only a poet may be able to relieve. The city wants to separate the thefts of piracy from stealing up on the enemy, but the act itself, as well as the disposition that alone makes the act possible, does not admit of such refinement (cf. Xenophon *Cyropaedeia* I.6.27–28). Experience sides with dialectic and holds that "he who clarifies the art of hunting through the art of the general is not more august (σεμνότερος) than he who shows it through the art of lice killing, but he is for the most part more vain" (*Sophist* 227b4–6). Jacob committed fraud twice, once to get his brother Esau's birthright and later to win his father's blessing (*Genesis* 25.24–27.40). Esau was a hunter, born red and hairy; he had a craving for venison and once, on coming in from the field exhausted, asked "to gulp that red, red dish" his twin brother had prepared. All he got was lentil soup, but Jacob must have known how to duplicate the smell and looks of the real thing, just as later Rebecca had him dress in the skins of Esau and herself prepared a savory Isaac loved and Jacob's brother knew how to prepare. The hunter was almost a beast, the smooth and quiet man who lived in tents was a master of disguise.[42]

The Stranger separates the hunting that admits of praise from that which carries blame; but he seems to speak so carelessly that one cannot be certain whether the distinction applies only to the hunting of men in friendship, to the hunting of men in general, or to hunting simply.[43] This carelessness is not his, but belongs to the experiences of men, whose discernment no more readily distinguishes pimps from honorable go-betweens than it does Socrates from sophists, though it claims at times

---

42. Cf. David Daube, "How Esau Sold His Birthright," *The Cambridge Law Journal* 8 (1942): 1–6; also his *Studies in Biblical Law* (Cambridge 1947), 193–200.

43. "Just as the hunting of the aquatic [beasts] is extensive, so is that of the feathered extensive, and that which characterizes the huntings of the land [footed] animals is very extensive, not only of beasts, but it is also worth keeping in mind the hunting of human beings, both [τε] that which occurs in war, and [δὲ καὶ] the hunting in friendship too is extensive; one admits of praise, one of blame" (823b1–7). The resumption of the construction with hunting in friendship, after it has been broken off with the hunting of human beings, makes the last phrase ambiguous. The diacritical problem that hunting poses foreshadows the problem of the unity and manyness of virtue. It is in a sense the same problem.

to find a charm in the bribery of lovers that it withholds from other forms of flattery (cf. *Theaetetus* 149d5–150a7; *Sophist* 222d7–e3). The law pretends to know nothing of this. It declares what it wants and believes that is what it means (cf. 719a7–b2; *Minos* 316d8–e1). The written law wants to enjoin and prohibit certain things; and just as it cannot add "or else" without arousing speculation, however idle, about the source of its certainty that one cannot get away with its violation, so it must make one suspect about whatever it prohibits that it is somehow attractive in itself, and were it not for the law one would be naturally inclined to it. The Stranger now exaggerates to the point of absurdity this antinomianism concealed in the law. He addresses the young: "Friends, would that neither any desire (ἐπιθυμία) nor *erōs* for hunting at sea ever seize you, any more than for hooking and in general for the hunting of beasts in water by means of lobster pots that do the work of an idle hunt for men who can be either awake or asleep" (823d7–e2). The Stranger wants to keep the young awake, and not engage in practices that could be done in their sleep; but he expresses this laudable aim by implying that one would fall into laziness through the passionate desire to be an angler. His devout wish begins to make sense when he couples it with another: "And, in turn, may not the longing (ἵμερος) for piracy occur to you, any more than for the capture of human beings at sea, and thus make you into savage and lawless hunters; and may not theft in town or country graze even the surface of your mind" (822e2–5; cf. 831e8–832a2). The closeness of piracy and highway robbery to the ordinary ways of warfare, which had even shown up in his divisions, threatens the law-abiding civility of soldiers. What thus seems to be a fanciful extension in speech of an absurdly remote possibility in deed turns out to go to the heart of the law. The breeding of lawless desires cannot be kept apart from the inculcation of the law. The Stranger concludes his wish with this: "And, in turn, may not a wily *erōs* (αἱμύλος ἔρως) for the hunting of feathered things occur to any of the young" (823e5–824a1). The word for "wily" or "wheedling" occurs once elsewhere in Plato; Socrates uses it of the lover who, having convinced the beloved that he is a nonlover, is about to make a seemingly lawful speech (*Phaedrus* 237a4).[44] One is forced to wonder, then, whether,

---

44. It first occurs in the epic poets of wheedling speeches, whether of Calypso, Zeus, or the first woman or woman in general, and in tragedy of Odysseus or nonviolent devices: *Odyssey* 1.56; Hesiod *Theogony* 890; *Works and Days* 78, 374, 789; Sophocles *Ajax* 388; Euripides fr. 715.1; *Rhesus* 498, 709; Aeschylus *Prometheus Bound* 206; cf. Pindar *Nemean* 8.33.

just as legitimate warfare and lawless piracy approached one another in the former condemnation of the desire for angling, so the *erōs* the Stranger wishes to ban does not lie very far from the winged Eros Socrates wished to promote in his second speech, which, he declared, was the same speech as his first (*Phaedrus* 252b8; 262c5–d2; 264e7–266b2). However this may be, the first half of book 8 deals with warfare and pederasty.

VIII

THE FIRST END OF THE LAWS

I WAR GAMES

On the longest day of the year, in the month of June, while the sun is setting, after they have been on the road for more than thirteen hours, the Stranger proposes that the last month of the year (late June to early July) be dedicated to Plouton. He proposes that 420 of the citizens live in a district dedicated to Hades. His proposal follows a separation of festivals into those that women alone can attend from those that men can join. One of the most common of exclusively female festivals was the Thesmophoria. It was dedicated to the mother and daughter pair, Demeter and Persephone, who in Athens were called the Lawbringers (*Thesmophoriō*), and of whom Persephone was said to be the wife of Hades (Aristophanes *Thesmophoriazousae* 296). The arrangement of what sacrifices are to be assigned to what gods is not the province of the Stranger; their legislation requires the assistance of oracles from Delphi, and, with Clinias's approval, the Stranger restricts his own task to their number. He makes an exception, however, of Plouton, but he does it in such a way that one cannot tell whether he has properly performed the separation he proposed: "And further the chthonic [gods], and all who must be designated celestial gods and whoever else attends them [the celestial], must not be mixed together but separated, by making a lawful assignment of them to the twelfth month of Plouton; and martial human beings must not be vexed at a god of this kind, rather, they must honor him on the grounds that he is always the best for the genus of human beings, for there is no case, as I would assert speaking in earnest (σπουδῇ), where the community (κοινωνία) of soul and body is better than their dissolution (διάλυσις)" (828c6–d5). Syntactically, the phrase "the lawful assignment of them" includes the celestial gods, from whom the sense requires that it be separated. The same kind of confusion occurred when the chthonic gods were first introduced in the prelude: they were said to be second but were put in first place, and, syntactically, the second place was left empty (717a6–b2). The principle the Stranger lays down to justify his interpolation of

Plouton among the twelve gods holds for the entire city and all its citizens; the 420 occupants of his district have no special relation to the god.[1] Is the Stranger suggesting, then, that each of the other eleven gods is to embody severally some single principle applicable to the whole city? This would be the political equivalent to Socrates' erotic myth in the *Phaedrus*, in which different kinds of souls follow different kinds of gods, who lead them to a glimpse of the hyperuranian beings. It seems, however, that the principle he does enunciate allows for no other; at least there seems to be no room for the second of the two principles of the first prelude—emulation of the gods—though it might be thought to follow from the first—enslavement to the gods.

The puzzling note with which book 8 begins continues. No sooner has the Stranger implied that either philosophy is the only life or the tragic formula holds and it is better not to be born than he asserts that their city, given its leisure and freedom from necessity, must live well, "just as a single human being." For their living happily the prime necessity is neither to wrong one another nor be wronged by others, and though the first of the two is not very hard, it is very hard to acquire the power not to be wronged: "It is not possible to gain it perfectly (τελέως) unless one becomes perfectly (τελέως) good" (828d8–829a6). The Stranger supplements the first principle with another that seemingly contradicts it. The first states at its crudest that the highest good is the patriotic death, the second that the city has the opportunity to live the good life if its citizens are perfectly good, and they cannot be perfectly good if they suffer any injustice. Even if the Stranger had already affirmed that the central doctrine of the city is the immortality of the individual soul, and the good life begins after death if and only if one proved to be perfectly good in this life, it would still not suffice to explain the apparently Calliclean teaching that one must do all in one's power to protect oneself from injustice, for, were the afterlife in question, to have the power not to do an injustice would be decisive (cf. *Gorgias* 509c6–510a5). The crude version of the second principle is that at all times the citizens must go around armed to the teeth, but the Stranger had criticized Sparta and Crete for being nothing more than armed camps and hardly cities at all (666e1–2;

---

1. Pausanias says that the Eleians are the only people he knows who honor Hades (6.25.2). The Stranger's interpolation of Plouton recalls in Aeschylus's *Oresteia* Athena's introduction of the Furies into Athens, where they have never been before. They are not the pre-Olympian gods who take up residence but the very latest gods, whom Athena cleverly persuades to become gods to be worshipped and preside over all human affairs, and inside of each one of whom lies Clytaemestra, who originally invoked them, concealed in a dream they could not interpret.

cf. 708a2). If, on the other hand, one had recourse to Socrates' distinction between harm and wrong, and could assume that the Stranger meant harm by injustice, then he would be saying that if one is perfectly good one cannot be made worse by another, and to be killed, exiled, or deprived of citizenship might be unjust actions but they have no power to damage the goods of the soul (*Apology of Socrates* 30c9–d6). On this interpretation, in which the experience of injustice would have a double sense, the second principle would be easily reconcilable with the first, but only if the practice of dying and being dead were the core of the first principle. As it is, the Stranger urges the raising of a standing army in the middle of Crete. He gives no thought to the folly of Cnossos were it either to permit its colony to be so permanent a threat or to count on the Stranger's assurance that it is rather easy to be just.

The Stranger does not put as high a demand on the city as he does on its citizens. He drops "perfectly" in the city's case and says it only has to be good if it is to have a peaceful life (829a6–8). For the city to be good requires that it train during peace for war. At first, the Stranger proposes that the city en masse go on maneuvers once a month for at least one day, beautiful games be devised that imitate real battles as vividly as possible, and compositions of praise be recited for whoever seems to be best in the contests as in his whole life, and whoever is not is to be blamed (829b2–c5). The Stranger does not make it clear whether everyone who does not receive a badge of merit is to be blamed: later, he seems to recommend that they be the butt of nonrancorous and playful ridicule (936a2–5). He certainly allows for a lack of refinement in these compositions, for their poets can be only those past fifty who have done a beautiful and conspicuous deed themselves, regardless of whether they have any poetic talent or not. Gymnastic now steals a march on music and runs the risk of holding its best warriors up to unintended ridicule. The Stranger then declares that the soldiers, who include men and women, are "the prizewinners of the greatest contests" (ἀθλητὰς τῶν μεγίστων ἀγώνων), a phrase that echoes Socrates' about the guardians (ἀθληταὶ τοῦ μεγίστου ἀγῶνος), before they were demoted to auxiliaries (*Republic* 403e8).[2] On the basis of a strict analogy with boxers, the Stranger pro-

---

2. The context in which a similar phrase—"prizewinners of war"—recurs in the *Republic* (422b4) is not irrelevant. Adimantus has just asked how their city could fight against a great and wealthy city, and Socrates suggests several ways, more ingenious than plausible, the city could employ. He does not say that it could not be wronged because it was perfectly good (427e6–8). The Stranger's untimely denunciation of moneymaking puzzles Clinias (832b5–7). Why has not the Stranger, like Socrates, congratulated the city for the ease with which it will defend itself against its un-

poses daily campaigns for some part of the troops without arms, and once
a month everyone is to undergo a greater imitation of the real thing, with
weapons only slightly less dangerous than those used in combat, but sufficiently deadly to keep terror (δείματα) alive in a game (παιδιά). The legislator must anticipate that some will be killed, and so must provide for
the killers to be automatically acquitted of murder and cleansed of bloodshed in a lawful way (830a3–831b1). The Stranger sees no difficulty in the
loss of a few men and women, for the legislator is to believe that others
no worse will grow up to replace them. The Stranger gives no numbers.
We do not know what he would regard as acceptable losses, but they cannot be too low if "fear is not as it were to die." To hit the right balance
between what the city can afford and what the city must spend to maintain fear needs the nicest discrimination on the part of rulers whom the
Stranger in this crucial case must leave on their own. It recalls the need
to balance the number of warriors needed for defense against the number
of colonists a modest way of life would sustain, which the Stranger likewise could not determine without an inspection of the site (737c6–d6).

The Stranger introduces an odd misalignment between practices "if
we were boxers," and practices of the citizen-warriors. In the model case,
"we would not, in fear of the laughter of the thoughtless, lack the daring to hang up a lifeless phantom (εἴδωλον ἄψυχον) if we had no partners
to train against, any more than we would, if we were isolated and
complctely out of everyone ensouled and everything soulless, to pitch
ourselves to fight really and truly (ὄντως) our own shades (σκιαμαχεῖν)"
(830b5–c3). The Stranger speaks the language of Hades. On the other
hand, the laughter the legislator would incur should he follow this practice could not consist in the absence of partners, but only in the funny
need to split the city into two factions, who are to fight one another as if
they were engaged in real warfare. The city is ordered to be at odds with
itself. The "enemy" one faces today is one's real friend, and if one kills
him one is not guilty of murdering a fellow-citizen. Does the Stranger
also have a remedy for relieving the distress at killing a friend (cf. 865a5)?
In a populous country, the death of a temporary "buddy" will no doubt
be readily forgotten; but in a city whose first aim is the cultivation of
friendly feeling, is one's friend, whom more likely than not one has to
have killed face to face, to be no more to one than a lifeless dummy, or is
one to imagine that one is sending one's own shade to Hades? Rivalry is
no doubt an incentive to excellence, but deadly consequences are not

---

trained enemies, and instead gone off on a tirade that can only alert everyone to the
danger this new foundation poses?

easy to contain. Adrastus, we recall, was the innocent cause of two unintended deaths, and though from the first of them he was purified in a rite pretty nearly the same as the Greek, and for the second Croesus forgave him, still, "in acknowledging himself to be the most weighed down with misfortune of all the human beings he knew," he slew himself over the tomb of his second victim (Herodotus 1.45.3).

The Stranger offers two causes why no city nowadays engages in war games to the extent he recommends. The first is due to the insatiable love of making money, the second to the fear in any city in which a faction rules to distribute arms to those it keeps enslaved.[3] If the city without faction gains, along with a greater base for its army, a greater capacity to expand, the Stranger's preference for a state of neither perfect health nor perfect beauty would apply even to the unity of the city itself. Things are better for being a little bad. The consequence of the first cause is to make those who are naturally orderly into merchants and shipowners, and those who are naturally brave into pirates, robbers (whether of temples or houses), the bellicose (πολεμικοί) and tyrannical (831e4–832a2). The Stranger implies that his citizens, without any outlet in commerce, will be martial (πολεμικοί, 828d2) without being bellicose (πολεμικοί); but he does not explain how the absence of private interest will keep them in check, simply because the structure of the regime does not allow for any expansion. He certainly allows for colonies (923d2, 925b4–c3). Before he incorporated the women fully into the city, he had them be the orderly by nature (802e9–10); now that they are part of the army, are they effective enough to stop a takeover of the regime by the generals and officers? One would like to know whether the under- and over-aged, who would all to some extent be out of shape, could prevent the part on active service from usurpation. The city is fully militarized but not militaristic. The principle of its life is fundamentally timocratic, but it does not reward politically the recipients of its honors (cf. 921e5–922a3). There are, how-

3. A. W. Gomme, in discussing the unsuitability of hoplite fighting, given the character of most of Greek terrain, illuminates the Stranger's proposals: "the hoplite system was in all states, for the hoplite class, a thoroughly democratic one; and the fact that every man could supply his own armor and weapons . . . helped the Greek view of the relationship of the citizen to the State: a citizen contributed to the needs of the state when called upon, he was not taxed by a superior government; and there was no need for the state to possess a large store of arms which might fall into the hands of ambitious men and be as dangerous to normal well-ordered public life as (it was felt) would be a professional military class"; which, Gomme had earlier remarked, would be needed to train troops in light-armed strategy; *A Historical Commentary on Thucydides* (Oxford 1945), vol. 1, 14–15; Herodotus 7.9β.

ever, to be no contests or prizes for those who compete without armor (833a4–9; 834c7–d1). Just as no one can win any competition without realizing that his medal is a promissory note for the battlefield, so no one can lose without foreboding. It is never to cross the minds of the medal-winners that they deserve to rule. Ever since the Stranger got rid of gymnastic by the time he finished book 2, he has been slowly letting it trickle back in by drips and drabs, first when he claimed it was perfectly complete (796d8), only to reopen it once he brought in women (804d6), and then to return to it again in a discussion that included comedy and tragedy (814d8), and, after all lessons had been ended, to continue it in the supplement on hunting; now at last he stamps it with a limit (834e2). Music, which had been his primary concern as "the first legislator" (835b1), seems to have been overwhelmed by gymnastic.[4] The extent of its defeat can be stated very simply: there are gods of war but none of peace in Magnesia (943c6).

Gymnastic was to music as courage was to moderation, and it was the looseness of Spartan women and the prevalence in Crete of pederasty that most obviously showed the lack of moderation in their laws and ways. We are therefore shocked to learn that the Stranger's remedies are completely ineffective, and the test of the first three books, which the device of a city in speech was to supply (or so Clinias thought), has proved to be their refutation. Neither the educational inculcation of moderation nor the institution of virtual equality between the sexes has done anything to solve the problem that initiated the *Laws*. The union of moderation and courage has not taken place, and the Stranger's city is now nothing but a more efficient and more dangerous Sparta. It is always on the prowl. The Stranger has already made sure that the Helots who forced a kind of moderation on Sparta would not fulfill that purpose here (cf. Thucydides 8.24.4, 40.2). The most reasonable excuse the Stranger could offer for his apparent indifference to the remilitarization of Magnesia would be that, once he proposed in a final manner (τελευτάτω) to make the *Laws* the core of all nonspecialized instruction and put it, along with everything else of either music or gymnastic, into the hands of foreigners, the laws are in order, and he could afford to let the city slide backwards into the ordinary conditions that beset cities. His realism would be inseparable from his idealism: criminal law and theology are the topics of the next two books.

4. Cf. M. Vanhoutte, *La philosophie politique de Platon dans les Lois* (Louvain 1954), 28–29.

2   ERŌS

Had the Stranger proudly asserted that his proposals would instill chastity among the young and cut down adultery among the married women, we would have had to take his word for it, for the genetic structure of law had made it one of the first items on its agenda (631e3–632a2). It is true that we had been warned that something was amiss when he failed to cover in his outline of choral dances the representations of sudden reversals of fortune from good to bad, and left the tragic poets waiting in the wings until they proved their superiority to his own tragedy. The terror that was missing in choral imitations was more than made up for by the terrors of mock battles, but pity had been banished to back alleys and did not show its face in public (cf. 960a1–6). Once the Stranger revealed what divine necessities really were, he turned to human necessities, first in making the city almost into a war machine, and now in facing the desires Glaucon called fiercer than geometric necessities (*Republic* 458d5). The vehemence with which the Stranger denounced the love of money disturbed both Clinias and Megillus. He seemed to them to be tongue-tied in hatred and incapable of giving the second cause for the failure of cities to practice war in peacetime (832a7–b7). If, however, the love of money is, as the Stranger later says, the most powerful of all desires among most men (870a1–6), one wonders whether the idle predators the Stranger has created are not in need of an even more severe chastisement than the one he delivered to the greedy. He has held out the possibility of their renewing on a smaller scale the empire of Minos, restricted as they would be for the moment, in the absence of a navy, to the conquest of Crete. The lifelong hunger of the soul that he detected in natures of the moderate and brave, who are unfortunate but not necessarily ungifted, has not been sated in his own city. He had said that their regime was put together as an imitation of the best and most beautiful life; he had not said it was of the most just life.

The Stranger has silently arranged for his city to be another Rome, with the prospect of its becoming in time a commercial empire; but now he turns to another form of desire, as if Ares and Aphrodite did not always go together, and there were some special difficulty that his city faced, which he is in a unique position to solve. His own solution, however, turns out to be second or third best, while the difficulty is especially his own. "In the best possible case," he says, "the work belongs to a god, if it were possible in some way or other for the commandments themselves to be from him, but as it is [it is impossible], there is probably a need of some daring human being, who in honoring frankness will say what seems best for city and citizens, and, in the presence of souls in a corrupted state, order and arrange what is fitting and harmonious for the regime as a whole, while contradicting the greatest desires, without one human being as a helper, but all alone following logos alone" (835c1–8). The Stranger now declares for the first time that divine revelation alone could persuade, and no semblance of it, even if an inspired poet invented it and everyone else repeated it, would do. This is a task beyond the unwritten law. The poets have held up the crime of Oedipus in such a way that most human beings, "*although they are transgressors of the law*" (838a5), willingly keep away from intercourse with even beautiful siblings, but the crime of his father Laius has not had any effect on suppressing pederasty. The stories belong together, but no one holds that the son killed his father justly though unwittingly for his crime,[5] though they do sense that his own self-blinding perfectly matched the uncovering of his mother's nakedness. In one case they discern the pattern of right, in the other they behold a curious coincidence. The highest achievement of unwritten law is to establish the conviction that its violation brings about self-punishment: the law does not have to step in and correct a wrong that the wrongdoer himself acknowledges. The Stranger knows he cannot devise a story that will carry the same persuasiveness once it passes beyond the sacredness of the family. For this he needs the direct intervention of the god, who will not tell a story but announce a law, "or else." He admits, in other words, that the persuasiveness of the god is a form of terror.

Although the Stranger's account comprehends all sexual relations, he concentrates on pederasty, ostensibly on the grounds that it is a defect peculiar to Spartan and Cretan institutions, and did not antedate the time of Laius. Pederasty is now part of the unwritten law, with elaborate ways of courtship in Crete that could not easily be uprooted (cf. Strabo 10.21).[6] The Stranger puts off enchanting Clinias and winning him over to his own view to another occasion beyond the span of the *Laws* (837e5–6; cf. 842a7–8). The first of the two arguments the Stranger offers against pederasty appeals to its nonexistence among beasts, the second to a piece of

---

5. A. Diès, in his note on 836c2, does supply the connection: "On sait que Laïos passait pour avoir été l'instituteur de l'amour contre nature: un oracle lui avait, en effet, prédit qu'il serait tué par un fils."

6. Cretan pederastic courtship involves an imitation of a rape insofar as the rape is announced beforehand to the friends of the beloved, who can at the time reject the lover as unworthy, and the use of violence after the capture, which lasts for no more than two months, suffices to release the captive and allows him to seek his revenge. Although Strabo begins by opposing rape to persuasion, the description shows how force has taken on through law a persuasive aspect.

reasoning that, in recalling the purpose of the law, knocks down most of the legislation the Stranger has so far proposed. In examining any legislation, one is to ask the question, Does it or does it not bear on virtue? The marriage laws cannot pass such a test, even if it is unholy to deprive oneself of immortality (720c6–8). The city needs new citizens, and men feel the need to partake of immortality, but in neither case can one find any promotion of virtue. The legal age for marriage has been set for the men much too late if virtue was to have been its purpose by way of channeling desire (cf. *Republic* 460e1–461a2). The argument against pederasty is applicable across the board to any erotic relation: There is nothing manly in the soul of the seduced, and nothing moderate in the soul of the seducer (836d5–7). In order to divert this general argument to pederasty in particular, the Stranger must rely once more on the conventional picture of the female as passive, and disregard his own suggestions of how to make women manly. He argues soundly that scarcely anyone, "with the true law in mind," will lay down laws in favor of pederasty, for the survival of the city, the soundness of the family, and the promotion of virtue would have to be his chief concern. If, however, either gaps in the law allow for its growth, or a part of the law, like the common mess, even fosters it, it cannot easily be suppressed or prohibited without upsetting the very structure of the law in some unforeseeable way. The Stranger grants that the control of desires is especially urgent in a city where the illiberality of toil is not there to quench hubris, and the lives of the citizens are spent in sacrifices, festivals, and choruses (835d8–e2). Just as the law had to treat hunting in its literal sense, so the law must deal with *erōs* in the same way, and now that the *erōs* for money has been given no outlet, and the law cannot acknowledge any experiential or linguistic extension to *erōs*, all its vehemence has been confined into the narrow channel the law in its obstinate purity has defined. The Stranger's laws, for all their show of order, can do nothing to check sexual license. Education was supposed to make everyone into a desirer and lover (ἐπιθυμητήν τε καὶ ἐραστήν) of becoming a perfect and complete citizen (643e5). The dream has been dreamt.

The Stranger starts from first principles and almost at once becomes obscure (836e5–837d7). He wants to look at "the nature of friendship (φιλία), desire (ἐπιθυμία), and so-called ἔρωτες." He says they are two, and another third species (εἶδος) is out of both, but a single name, in comprehending them all, produces every sort of perplexity and obscurity: "We no doubt call like to like in conformity with virtue and equal to equal a friend (φίλον), and in turn [we call] also a friend that which is in need of that which is in a state of wealth, being contrary in genus, and whenever each of the two becomes intense (σφοδρός), we name it ἔρως " (837a6–9).

There are so far four kinds of friends, but if one takes into account that the first friend is masculine in gender and the second neuter, there would be eight all told.[7] If, however, one follows Diotima, only the second kind, in its neuter form, is ἔρως, and it is the desire for the good, whereas what most people call ἔρως is the desire for the generation of one's own (or oneself however understood) in the beautiful (*Symposium* 205d1–206b8). However this may be, the Stranger at once throws everything into confusion, in accordance apparently with the principle that "divisions generate asymmetries all by themselves." He assimilates friendship of the second kind to ἔρως of the second kind, for he says it is terrible, savage, and rarely admits of community (τὸ κοινόν). The Stranger seems to forget that the original problem was to bring about a friendship between a minority of the good and just and the majority of the bad and unjust (though he has certainly not forgotten the nature of the majority [838a4–5; 840d1]), and there is no way for this fundamental aim of the law to be fitted into these categories. The first kind of friendship from likes is gentle, shared, and lasts through life; it sounds as if it could be the flattering version of Aristophanes' praise of male homosexuality (*Symposium* 191e6–192b5). Certainly, the friendship of husband and wife cannot belong to the first kind (cf. 839b1; 840e1), even though the Stranger drops the condition "in conformity with virtue"; for if there is a tendency for male and female natures to follow the lines of the difference between manliness and moderation, then their friendship would be at best complementary even if not contrary, but in any case not readily squeezed into the Stranger's kinds. What happens to the first kind if it becomes intense? If some couple does share in this kind of ἔρως, are all marriages that do not live up to it to be dissolved?

The Stranger uses the two carelessly defined kinds of friendship to produce the third, and the third is meant to correspond to the ordinary experience of ἔρως: it combines the desire to behold at a distance with the desire to join into one, or the awareness that the beloved is already complete with the awareness of one's own radical incompleteness, which induces in turn the realization simultaneously that one could only be completed if the beloved, against the lover's own initial conviction, were also incomplete and could be completed *per impossibile* by the lover. The

7. One could regularize the Stranger's schema as follows: both types of friendship would divide into body and soul, and each of those four would divide again into mild and intense. These eight, four of which would be kinds of ἔρως, would then be combinable in various ways. A consecrated story that would praise some and denounce others seems impossible.

Stranger's description recalls nothing so much as the white and black horses of the *Phaedrus*'s myth. He says that the third kind is, in the first place, not easy to understand: "What would one want with this kind of ἔρως for oneself?" Such a lover, moreover, is dragged in contrary directions and is himself perplexed, when the one urges him to touch the bloom of youth (ὥρα) and the other forbids it.

> The one is in love (ἐρῶν) with the body, hungers for its bloom (ὥρα) just as if it were ripe fruit (ὀπώρα), and assigns no honor to the state of the soul of the beloved; but the other treats the desire (ἐπιθυμία) of the body as incidental, and sees (ὁρῶν) rather than "seethes" (ἐρῶν), and with his soul he is really and truly (ὄντως) in a state of desire (ἐπιτεθυμηκώς) for the soul, believes the body's satiation of the body to be hubris, and in shame and awe of the moderate, manly, magnificent, and thoughtful would want to be always pure with the pure beloved, but the ἔρως mixed out of both of these is the one we have described as third.[8] When there are so many kinds, should the law hinder all of them and keep them from occurring among us? Or is it not clear that we would want the ἔρως that is of virtue to be in our city, which desires (ἐπιθυμοῦντα) the young to become the best possible, and we would hinder, should it be possible, the other two?[9]
> (837b8–d7)

The Stranger has managed to transfer to Eros the principle for which Plouton stands: body and soul are completely apart and their dissolution superior to their community. There is not a word about the beautiful. The beautiful is reduced to a season of the year, and the body of the beloved is the ripe fruit of autumn. There is not a word about pleasure. What the body lover wants is a pseudo-restoration of his own youth in a more perfect form. He wants to reverse and cancel time. His experience is rooted in an acute sense of the passage of time; he is aware that man in his perfection is ephemeral, but he refuses to admit that he cannot seize the day. The experience of which he cannot make heads or tails is thus completed by the radical separation that the lover of the soul effects; but the second lover, who succeeds in making death the truth about Eros, has to lie through his teeth, for his shamefaced reverence for manliness, modera-

---

8. With the omission of τρίτος for the sake of clarity.

9. In the pseudo-Platonic *Definitiones*, purity (ἁγνεία) is defined as caution against committing errors toward the gods, or the natural service to the honor of a god (414a12). The beloved, then, is a god, in accordance with the *Phaedrus* (251a1–7), and the lover honors him by making him better (722a2–7).

tion, magnificence, and thoughtfulness cannot be either the beloved's or his own. Since justice is not included in the lover's reverence, he reminds one of the youthful tyrant, with the tyrannical soul, for whom the Stranger had the legislator pray (709e6–710b2). The beloved is just a boy, and if he is already the equal of the lover, there is friendship; if he is inferior, the lover must be painting a picture of the future, when all of these things will be his. The Stranger began with a distinction between virtue and need; he then replaced it with soul and body. It would then follow that the soul has no needs; but if soul desires soul, it does have needs, although the Stranger cannot say what they are except by falling back from seeing at a distance to communion (ἀγνεύειν ἀεὶ μεθ' ἀγνεύοντος) without ever saying how that could happen. The desire of the lover must consist in wanting the young to be as good as possible; his desire is not of soul by soul but a desire to transmit his own excellence to another who is potentially good. He would therefore have to begin by instilling in the beloved the desire to be good, and this desire must belong to the second kind: the lover must be wealthy, the beloved be in need: the παιδικά of the legislator is the tyrant. Behind the desire for the good of another's soul is the desire for a future equality. It is a form of generation, involves the separation of body and soul, and stands in absolute opposition to the marriage law.

The Stranger does not even try to frame a law that would incorporate the ἔρως he wants, for it would require an education in the *Phaedrus* and *Symposium* that even if they were part of the curriculum could not have the backing of the law. The law must promote lawful generation, but it cannot consecrate marriage if it despises the union of body and soul (cf. *Phaedrus* 250e3–251a1). The Stranger says he has an extremely easy way to prohibit pederasty; but he does not face the difficulty of condemning Laius in a story that condemns and acquits his son. Euripides wrote a play in which Laius fell in love with Chrysippus and said: "I am not unaware of any of the things for which you rebuke me; but nature compels me despite my judgment" (fr. 840 N). Laius expresses what the Stranger called the third kind of ἔρως. It is of an entirely different order from the crime of Oedipus, which does not seem experientially to be a version of ἔρως. Incest is a fulfillment of a dream in which there is the experience of no constraints (*Republic* 571b3–d4). It is the formula for the soul's rebellion against the city and all its laws. Pederasty does not have this character. If it were to be charged with the same horror, every child would have to be one's own sibling, and the city become one holy family; but when Socrates proposed the elimination of the family, he had to introduce artificial ways to check the rise of so many Oedipuses and lift the barrier against incest between brother and sister (*Republic* 461b9–e4), for were he to keep it in place, everyone would know to whom they were really related, and the purpose for which communism was instituted would fail. It is one thing to make the mother holy, it is another to consecrate the son.

A curious feature of the Stranger's account of ἔρως is that its language is all agricultural. After ἔρως had been applied to hunting, ἔρως is either of the pederast, who desires ripe fruit and sows on rocks and stones, where his seed will never take root, or of the adulterer, who does not keep off the field of the female in which he would not wish his seed to grow (838e8–839a3; cf. 841d3–4).[10] Even the young man who denounces the Stranger is full of seed (839b4). Coming as this does before the Stranger turns to agricultural law, where the same language returns in the literal sense, the shift from an older society of hunters to a newer society of farmers, with vestiges of an older way of life, could not be more plainly indicated. One is also forced to wonder whether the law, despite its intention to be always literal, must not poeticize ἔρως if it is to succeed in its handling of it. Must the law not interpret love entirely corporeally if it is to consecrate certain kinds of it? All of this language is known to us from tragedy: Danaus warns his daughters against the lust of beasts and men for the fruit (ὀπώρα) of their virginity (Aeschylus *Suppliants* 996–1005); Deianeira speaks of Heracles as a cultivator of the soil who sows and reaps a distant field (Sophocles *Trachiniae* 32–3); Creon says there are other fields his son can plow (*Antigone* 569); and the Chorus ask how the furrows of the father could have been silent so long about Oedipus (*Oedipus Tyrannus* 1211–2).[11] The hunger of the pederast, however, for the autumn's fruit is not consistent with the laws of harvest, for the stranger who is traveling the roads, if he desires to eat fruit, is not forbidden (845a5–b2); but to take in secret (λάθρᾳ) pears, apples, and pomegranates is as little disgraceful as to get away with (λανθάνειν) sexual intercourse (845b7–c1). The Stranger is no doubt, in juxtaposing these laws, being playful, but it was the necessity to consecrate play, if the un-

10. Timaeus also uses the same language but as imagery, but it is still inconsistent with his notion that there is a double desire, on part of male and female, to generate (*Timaeus* 91c7–d3).

11. The Stranger's use of ὀπώρα for youthful beauty is also known from Pindar (*Isthmian* 2.5); the context is the difference between the ancient poets, who celebrated their own beloved without pay, and the modern poets who, like Pindar himself, are devoted to the Muse who loves gain, and whose songs have silver faces and are sold overseas, for they celebrate victories in contests. Local erotic poetry has been replaced by the universal poetry of honor and glory.

written law were to be stabilized, that made him experience the nonseriousness of man. The language of tragedy becomes ridiculous when it becomes the language of the law. According to the Stranger, Ὀπώρα is a goddess (844d5).[12]

The Stranger believes that the combination of three provisions would accomplish most of what he wants. He will appeal to the ambition of the young, that they should rival and surpass famous athletes who were chaste as long as they competed, and not believe that certain gregarious birds, who wed for life, are better than human beings; he will urge the desire for the beautiful ways of the soul; and he will consecrate marriage so as to instill a fear of touching what is forbidden. The Stranger promotes a contest against pleasure in which none are to receive any prizes if they win. They are promised happiness instead; but this myth with which they have been enchanted from childhood does not suffice by itself (840b5–c3). It does not suffice because ἔρως is not experienced in the same way as other desires are; if it were, the ordinary lover would not be perplexed about what he wanted, he would know at once that it was pleasure. The fear of the gods must therefore supplement ambition; but in doing so it combines persuasion with threats and undermines the youthful citizens' superiority to athletes who, inferior though they are to themselves, have prevailed over desires they are unable to withstand without it (840c6–9). Once the Stranger promulgates the fear, he cannot expect that the young will retain a belief in their competitive edge. What they will make of the model drawn from birds is hard to conjecture (840d3–e2). The Stranger has to speak of their unions in the language of men: the birds are bachelors and pure until they procreate, and they then live holily and justly for the rest of time in the first agreements of friendship. The birds, like the athletes, do not need the gods to live holy, pure, and just lives. The Stranger adds finally the desire for the beautiful ways of the soul (841c4–6). This corresponds either to what he said was a very rare occurrence—a divine ἔρως by the powers that be for just and moderate practices (711d6–7)—or to the official description of the best kind of ἔρως but not to its truth, for its truth fits Socrates and hardly anyone else. Socratic ἔρως seemingly prevailed over sexual pleasure all by itself, though one has to add that he did have three sons.

---

12. Aristophanes has Ὀπώρα as an attendant of Peace (*Pax* 523), and at her wedding, with which the play concludes, indulges in a double entendre about her (1346–1350). D. Daube, *Roman Law* (Edinburgh 1969), 57, discusses the obscene use of *arare, aratio,* and *aratiuncula* in Plautus; it shows the ease with which the high and the low can change places.

If the citizens still cannot rise above pleasure, corrupted by all other Greeks and most barbarians, and seeing and hearing that disorderly Aphrodite has the greatest power, the Stranger suggests diverting her strength by an equivalent to bodily toils, the freedom from which occasioned the Stranger's original perplexity how to handle such idle youths (841a6–8). A second degree of rightness could be achieved if shamelessness consisted solely in getting caught and not in the indulgence in sexual pleasure; to get away with it would then be beautiful (841a8–b5). Now this compromise, even if it does not stimulate desire rather than reduce it—it is after all a point of honor to get away with it—is nothing but the unwritten law as it now prevails almost everywhere (cf. *Philebus* 65e9–66a3). What, however, truly astonishes is that the Stranger adds his three provisions to the second-best solution: "In this way the beautiful and the shameful to the second degree would be laid down as law by us, with a second kind of rightness, and three genera, in circumventing one genus, would *force* (βιάζοιτ᾽ ἄν) *those who are corrupt in their natures*, whom we address as inferior to themselves, not to transgress the law" (841b5–c2). When it comes to the erotic, there is no prelude; everyone is already corrupt and the uncorrupt an illusion of the pure lover; and its law differs from law in the strict sense only because no penalty is attached except an acknowledged shame. Perhaps, the Stranger suggests, we would be thought to legislate rightly should we deprive anyone caught in adultery of the city's praises, and make him really and truly (ὄντως) a foreigner (841e2–4). The Stranger does not know whether the law is one or two laws (841e4–5). He had offered one of two possibilities that they could *perhaps force* (τάχα ἄν βιασαίμεθα). The first was no sex outside of marriage, the second was no male homosexuality, but some kind of disgrace for adultery in holy matrimony. If secrecy is sanctioned in the second case, it is sanctioned in the first; but since the Stranger has not proposed any penalty in the first case, he has omitted even the penalty of disgrace if the second possibility should prevail. The Stranger remarked that it would be best by far if his combination of three provisions with the second level of the beautiful were in place in all cities; he did not say that Clinias's city would be more capable than any other to implement his mythical prayers.

3   AGRICULTURAL AND COMMERCIAL LAW

The laws that handle the sustenance of the people are for the most part well laid out. They are divided between the twelve farming communities and the foreigners, metics, and slaves who are the makers and retailers of all tools and materiel. Some laws are said to be borrowed from other legislators (843e3–844a2), and many others are too trivial for an aged legislator to bother with (846b5–c3). What more disturbs is that there are arrangements for avoiding the petty annoyances among neighbors, which can easily build up into a "huge bulk of hatred" (843b8), as if the Stranger had once more forgotten that friendly feeling was the most immediate task of the legislator, until one recalls that he had omitted the neighbor in his prelude, when he put on a distance scale how the citizen was to behave toward everyone from his own offspring to the stranger (729a2–730a9). Indeed, the very first time the Stranger had mentioned the neighbor, he was dealing with the country police, who were to guard their own district, "not only on account of enemies but also on account of those who claim to be friends," and what they were to do if a neighbor were wronged (761d6–e1). Now Zeus ὁμόφυλος has to be invoked and used as a threat in order to prevent the moving of the boundary stone between lots, and Zeus ξένιος has likewise to be called as witness against whoever moves a marker of foreign territory (843a4–5).[13] Zeus ξένιος had also been invoked in the second prelude (729e6–730a2), but it had not then been necessary to apply the same kind of threats to so-called friends. The boundary stone (ὅρος) is the basis for distinguishing (ὁρίζων) between friendship and enmity (843a2). Although neighbors always have grounds for a quarrel,[14] the Stranger's scheme of equal lots is bound to exacerbate this inherent tendency, for anyone who perceives an advantage in another's lot, whether it be in resources or yield, would be likely to compensate for it by an encroachment of his own. Once one gets away from the education and turns toward law, the citizens of Magnesia are like everyone else: the city now has a name for the first time (848d3). If, moreover, the reader happens to forget that they in fact are not farmers, though the Stranger, if the text is sound, now calls them that (843b2; cf. 761d2), any more than they are beekeepers or shepherds, but that slaves are doing all the work (806d9–e2), one would easily get the impression from the way in which the laws are formulated that each of the citizens is himself liable to move

---

13. Cf. E. Klingenberg, *Platons* ΝΟΜΟΙ ΓΕΩΡΓΙΚΟΙ *und das positive griechische Recht* (Berlin 1972), 7; he notes that the punishment from the gods (843a8) is not translated into law (10); contrast 881a8–b2; 913d4–914a5.

14. How friendliness is to be maintained if, as is likely, it is one neighbor who denounces another for having greater wealth than the law allows, and who gets half the surplus besides, is not explained (745a3–4). If it went to the gods, the resentment might be less (cf. Herodotus 1.89.3); but then there would be no gain in repute for those who voluntarily gave up their surplus (757c1–6).

a boundary stone, encroach on a neighbor's land, alienate the bees of another, graze his flocks in another's pasture, or dam up a neighbor's water supply. In borrowing from older laws the Stranger appears to have forgotten that they can no longer be literally understood. His citizens are not living the life of peasants; Glaucon could not take as violent an exception to them as he did to the farmers of Socrates' true and healthy city. They are devoted to one thing only, the care of virtue, and virtue is a single art that they study and practice in the precise sense (ἀκριβῶς) (846d1–847b2).

The Stranger does not allow any artisan to practice more than one art, or even to rule over artisans of an art other than his own, for human nature is incapable of doing more than one thing well in a finished and precise way, and every one of the artisans is to be compelled to be one and not many. That each of us is one was the hypothesis behind man as puppet (644c4); the necessity to be one through art now replaces it. The unity of the self consists solely in knowledge; once precision in production and product is demanded, the wholeness of each man is to be found in one skill, despite the almost infinite divisibility of which art is capable. The strictness with which the artisans are to be treated is no doubt designed to prevent the easy accumulation of wealth on the part of some entrepreneur, who could otherwise recruit under one roof many artisans of many different skills; but the restriction also seems meant to be a model of what the citizens themselves are supposed to be. They are not to be severally fragmented into many occupations. In particular, music and gymnastic cannot, under these conditions, be two, even though they cannot be the kind of one that χορεία, or song and dance, initially was. They cannot be one without destroying the entire program of the Stranger—the prelude had already stated that the principles of gymnastic and music were of different orders (728d6–e5)—and they cannot be two and at the same time be the basis for virtue as a single knowledge. This is the bombshell of the Laws. It shatters everything. Immediately after the Stranger wished that the city could have only the ἔρως for virtue, he turns around and asserts there is only the τέχνη of virtue. It is easy enough to say that there is a Platonic formula for their possible identity, ἐρωτικὴ τέχνη, but we are hardly in a position to know what the importation of Socrates' unique knowledge into law would mean. As it is, the city the Stranger has constructed requires the deduction we have drawn, for with everyone else equipped with a single art, it is scarcely possible that the rulers could be wholes themselves on some other principle.

Socrates had found it impossible to preserve the single principle of right with which he started if he were going to assign a structure to his city. He had to sacrifice the principle—no one was to enter the city unless he had perfect knowledge of a single art—for the sake of a class structure that interposed between knowing artisans and knowing rulers a class of warriors whose purpose was to be the embodiment of the lawful opinions of the city.[15] They were the core of the city and bound its other two elements together precisely because they did not know, for no knowledge but only myth could ever complete the nature they were to have. The Stranger, on the other hand, did not start with any structure—he had rejected the very notion of a regime in favor of law—and endowed his citizens with a double education that seemed to be subordinate at all times to the principle of the eidetic structure of the good. It thus seems that the surprise of book 8 was inevitable, particularly after the city was so strongly skewed toward the gymnastic side at the beginning of the book, and it was subsequently admitted, albeit silently, that music was inadequate to resist the primary force behind the experiential deviation from the law. The Stranger had proposed to conceal antinomian *erōs* by law. The criminality of man, which he had mentioned in order to point to man's surprising compliance with the unwritten law, is going to be the theme of the next book. It begins with the admission that, though it is somewhat disgraceful to have to deal with the topic, it cannot be avoided: neither are they themselves descendants of gods nor are they legislating for the descendants of gods (853c3–6). The principle of the criminal law is going to be a version of the Socratic thesis that virtue is knowledge. It is that thesis that the Stranger has now slipped inside the laws about artisans.

The Stranger believes that old and beautiful laws about water supplies do not deserve to be diverted elsewhere in his speeches (844a1–3). He cannot bother to channel them off to one side (παροχετεύειν) as if he could do better.[16] This inauspicious pun, as if he might otherwise be thought to be contaminating the clarity of his own reasoning with alien laws, seems to foreshadow the subsequent disorder in the arrangement of the agricultural laws. After the Stranger has finished with the laws about the water supply, with the provision that whoever disobeys the order of the magistrates must pay double damages and submit to the penalty for resentment (φθόνος) and peevishness of soul (δύσκολος ψυχή), and has turned to the

15. The importance of this becomes clear if one compares it with what Critias reports of Egypt and old Athens, both of which are said to approximate to Socrates' best city in speech and conform with the principle "one man/one job"; but the principle, in being more strictly applied than even Socrates would, destroys the possibility of there being any structure (*Timaeus* 24a2–c3; *Critias* 110c3–6).

16. See E. Klingenberg, op. cit., 63, for this translation; but he wants to put 845d4–e9 before 844d4–845d3, and thus regularize the water laws (63 note 16).

goddess Ὀπώρα of autumnal fruit and concluded her laws, in turn, with the provision that whoever is caught picking certain fruit, if he is free and under thirty, is to be beaten but not wounded and cannot bring a suit for the blows he received, but if he is older than thirty, he may, like the stranger, eat the fruit on the spot, and if he disobeys the law, he is to run the risk of not being allowed to compete in the contest for virtue, if anyone reminds the judges at that time of his disobedience—after all this, the Stranger turns back to the corruption of the water supply, which, unlike earth, sun, and winds, is readily poisoned (845d4–9). This divergent law comes after a series of laws that have linked virtue, insofar as it is not identical with knowledge, with agricultural law, and somewhat grudgingly granted the stranger some leeway in his compliance: if the stranger touches fruit that has been set aside for storage, and he does so in ignorance (ἀίστωρ), although he gets off with a warning and instruction on the difference between "noble" fruit that can be taken and "rustic" fruit that cannot, his slave is beaten (845b1–7). The principle "Ignorance of the law is no excuse" precedes the digression that includes a provision about how to deal with water that witchcraft (φαρμακεῖαι) has poisoned. That the Delphic laws of the priestly exegetes, who unlike all other priests and priestesses hold their office for life, and in whose election Delphi must assent (759c6–e2), are to determine how such water is to be purified proves that witchcraft and not mere poisoning of wells and cisterns is involved. The "poisoner" pays damages, but he is not punished for "superstition." If "superstition" is not a vice, and it is hard to see how it could be once Opora is a goddess, and its regulation would have to pertain both to him who believes he can poison a well in this way and the other who believes that he has succeeded, then the flourishing of such opinions in the city, which the Stranger will later admit are beyond the capacity of the legislator to uproot (933a2–c7), seems to be indistinguishable from the ways in which virtue and vice are ordinarily formed. They too may be nothing but superstitions or inseparable from superstitions. The Stranger, in any case, firmly sets his face against that possibility once he turns to the metics and slaves, each one of whom is solely one on account of the one thing he knows perfectly.

IX

CRIMINAL LAW

I HARD CASES

The ninth book begins in error. The error is due to the Stranger's conform-
ing with "the natural arrangement of laws" (853a1–3) rather than with
his own project, the education of the citizens (857e3–5). He slipped out
of his course and into the rut of ordinary legislation because he was entering on the criminal law, the need for which presumes that education has
failed to soften a few hard-shelled seeds (853b4–d4). Clinias pulls him up
short when he notices that the Stranger's unqualified penalty for theft—
double the value of what is stolen regardless of whether it is in a public
or private place—does not square with the Stranger's first capital case—
temple robbery—to say nothing of the variety of circumstances for which
the legislator must provide (857b4–8; 854d1–e6).[1] The difference between
prelude and law seems to justify the Stranger's error. The criminal law
cannot admit of a prelude, for persuasion is at an end once the criminal
law holds sway. The Stranger, however, does offer a prelude addressed to
the would-be sacrilegious. Unlike all the other preludes so far, which experientially come after the laws they precede in written form, this prelude is the first that strictly precedes the song of the law. It is designed
to deter those who are already set on breaking the law and need more
than threats to alter their resolve. It is the model for the prelude that
occupies most of book 10, which addresses the young who are on the way
to atheism. Inasmuch as both groups are believed to be open to persuasion, they represent an element in the city the city cannot afford to lose.

The Stranger praises Clinias for knocking him back from his headlong
course and reminding him of his earlier insight that, as far as he can
tell from the present, legislation has always been elaborated incorrectly
(857b9–c4). He can thus start again and abandon legislation for education:

---

1. For this interpretation of δημοσίᾳ (857b1), see D. Cohen, "Theft in Plato's
Laws and Athenian Legal Practices," *Revue internationale des droits de l'antiquité*
29 (1982): 127–130.

as the educational primer for the city, the *Laws* encompasses even the criminal law. We had thought that Clinias's hesitation to approve of the Stranger's proposal to turn their conversation in its written imitation into elementary education in advance of the completion of the laws was due in part to his doubt whether criminal legislation was suitable for the young. At the very point where, it seems, the citizens must be handled as slaves, the Stranger finds a way to keep them free. Slaves and strangers are most likely to display human weakness; the citizens are to be taught the nature of human weakness. When the Stranger returns to public law at the beginning of book 12 the penalty for public theft is death (942a1–4). Sacrilege, it seems, has in the meantime extended its range,[2] and one might at first suppose, along with an admission of the probability of citizen-crimes, that the theology of 10 is responsible; but the Stranger never connects the sacred with his theology, and nothing consecrated in the city can trace its support to the gods: τὸ ὅσιον and τὸ θεῖον are apart. Despite this separation, books 9 and 10 still hang together not only because they handle criminality, but because they propose a psychology, with which the Stranger apparently could dispense as long as he was not dealing with the recalcitrant element in the city and in man. The simple mechanism of pleasure and pain, along with the golden chain of reason, was originally enough for elementary education.

The last business of the eighth book had been assigned to the market police (849a3); and from this point of view, that trials and suits (δίκαι) should follow in the ninth book seems to conform, as the Stranger says, with the nature of the legislative order (853a1–30): in the scheme of the magistracies that the Stranger outlined in the sixth book, the market police complete the second tier of magistrates of the city as a geographical entity, and the law courts complete the third tier. The eleventh book, however, begins with the Stranger remarking, after the punishments for impiety have been laid out, that the next item is the suitable arrangement of contracts (913a1–2). The civil law, which is the overarching theme of the eleventh book, should surely precede the criminal law. What the law-abiding are to do should not come after what the criminals must suffer. Indeed, there is nothing in the Stranger's first sentence in book 9 that augurs the priority he is about to accord to criminal law. If book 9 switched places with book 11 and book 11 came after book 8, book 10 would still come after 9 and thus precede book 12. Theology would then be right next to the laws of burial and the nocturnal council, or the two

---

2. The phrase πατρίδα συλῶν (942a2), in recalling περὶ τῶν συλώντων τοὺς θεούς (864d1), and in its use of πατρίς, clearly puts this crime under ἱεροσυλία.

themes of the *Laws:* the former would be in accordance with the genetic structure of law, the latter in accordance with the eidetic structure of the good. That sequence would then echo the sequence in book 7, which first ends with an education in mathematical cosmology, and then ends a second time with an education in hunting.

The neatness of this scheme must have been suspect to Plato. We are meant to question our anticipations of his intention. To begin with the criminal law is to look forward and backward. In looking forward it is to argue that the civil law too depends on the psychology that the criminal law seems alone to require, and in looking backward it is to confess that book 8 declared the failure of education. The Stranger has not converted a Dorian city from courage to moderation, and the criminality inherent in *erōs* has not been cut out or cut back. Criminal law therefore must be in its proper place once the Stranger has already admitted that failure and now declares his embarrassment for discussing criminal law. The sequence the Stranger chooses shows that he has incorporated into his outline of law the experiential deviation from the law. As the Stranger presents the issue of criminality, it would not follow apparently that there should be laws to handle the occasional departure from the education and mores of the city. The various magistrates should be capable of handling hard cases without any guidelines and be solely subject to review by higher authorities (853b4–c3):

> It is in a sense disgraceful even to lay down as many laws as we are about to do, in the kind of city that we assert will be well governed and will obtain every kind of rightness in regard to the practice of virtue. Even to claim that in a city of this kind anyone is born (ἐμφύεσθαι) who is destined to share in the wickedness (μοχθηρία) of everyone else in regard to the greatest things, so as to forestall, threaten, and legislate, if anyone of this kind comes to be, and for the sake of averting their occurrence and, if they do occur, for the sake of punishment, to lay down laws for them, on the grounds that they will occur, is, as I said, in a sense disgraceful.

The Stranger presents criminal law as if it were designed for the criminal, but it is in fact designed for the law-abiding. It is not the number of crimes that occur but the number of crimes that could occur and do not that measures the effectiveness of deterrence. The criminal law keeps intact the innocence of the law-abiding, which they themselves are led to believe education supports all by itself. The Stranger therefore has preserved in the preposterous order of criminal law first and then civil law the true order of becoming. Civil law is only possible once the criminal

law is in place and has cleared a space for lawful transactions: the site of
the law courts for homicide was arranged prior to the laying down of a
single law (778c6–d3). What was presented to us as the experiential deviation from the law proves to be the precondition for the law. The ordinary
citizen, however, takes in, and is expected to take in, with his law-
abidingness a self-congratulatory vanity that assures him that the puni-
tiveness of this part of the law had not in any way contributed to his behavior (see, for example, 927c7–d3). The legislator can indulge the city in
this false belief as long as it does not spill over into extreme vindictive-
ness, and the Stranger will later devise a way to restrain the desire to punish without inducing the paralyzing belief in the universality of sin. The
Stranger proceeds in somewhat the same way as Socrates had when he
introduced complete communism as an institutional means to back up
the occasional failure in the education of the guardians. If everything is
out in the open and there is no place to hide, the guardians act justly
regardless of how poorly the laws of the regime have dyed their souls.
Likewise, the Stranger now is plugging the gaps in his educational scheme
and allowing even those who seemed initially to be in full compliance
with the preludes to draw the strength of their immunity, however uncon-
sciously, from the shameful part of the law. The openness of everything in
Socrates' project becomes in the Stranger's the concealment of motives. It
would be a terrible thing if the citizens were ever induced to lay them
bare. That the criminal law shores up the bulwarks against bestiality is
not to be known.

The Stranger offers two not entirely consistent reasons for criminal
legislation. The legislators are not gods or sons of gods (cf. 704d6), and
the citizens are not either, but human beings and born from human beings, and there are inevitably among them tough nuts (κερασβόλοι) to
crack, which no laws however severe can melt down.[3] The second reason
implies the rarity, the first the frequency of crimes: bad citizens had been
mentioned before, to whom at night the wide-awake magistrates were to
be as much a terror as they would be to enemies (808c2–4; cf. 880e1–3).
The first reason assigns the blame no less to the legislators than to the
citizens: the Stranger's laws are humanly defective and promote the

---

3. Consider the following sequence. The Stranger first established hunting in its
widest extension, both as to what it was and what of it deserved praise or blame, before he had the law confine it to its literal meaning; agricultural metaphor established
blameworthy aspects of *erōs*, but agriculture proper was treated apart from its meta-
phorical extension; and now again agricultural metaphor is the entering wedge into
criminal law. Running through all three species is the issue of desire.

crimes they cannot suppress. The second reason reassigns injustice to fate, for which neither any man nor any god was responsible, or at least the sacrilegious is to believe: his suicide, before he has committed any crime, goes tragedy one better and represents to the city self-punishment for fateful guilt. The Stranger himself tries to reconcile the human-all-too-human with the odd exception by asserting that the first applies to metics, strangers, and slaves, in whom the humanly weak would be in full force, whereas the second applies to the citizens, among whom the hopelessly flawed may from time to time be found. Whoever has not been raised by the law must be given a second chance to reform; whoever has had the opportunity but has not been transformed by the law must be executed. The jury is to believe that the education has not taken rather than that the threats in the criminal law have failed (854e1–6). No one is to infer from the scourging of slave or stranger, which cannot be inflicted for evil and must either prevent him from becoming worse or induce him to become better, that a milder form of the same penalty could straighten out the citizen (854d1–5). If the better does not work, one must deny that the worse could.

That every man must honor the beautiful things and the just things is the burden of what the would-be sacrilegious is to hear from good men and speak himself (854b8–c2). In his distress he is to hearken once more to the call of morality. The exact measure of the difference between the eidetic structure of the good and the genetic structure of law is the criminal law. It separates the just from the beautiful in its prohibitions and the good from the beautiful in its punishments. Morality, however, measures the difference between the two structures not by acknowledging the difference but by displacing the difference onto a pattern of right, in accordance with which poetic justice acquits the criminal and absolves the law. "Evil desire" does not mean, as it would were it opposed to the Socratic principle, desire for evil; but it means that some ancient wrongdoing has remained unpurified, and if some ceremony can clean it up, the law is to leave well enough alone. Suicide could also clear the books. This appeal to involuntary violations of right is morality's way of ordering the world without having recourse to the eidetic structure of the good. Morality translates its own departure from the good into the surd of evil, which in the long run gets canceled and squares the account. It tells a story in which unwittingly evil comes out as its own unrecognizable image.

The Stranger does not explain why he begins with so marginal a crime as temple robbery, and not rather with incest as the criminal counterpart to holy matrimony, with which, after all, his laws were to have begun. He has achieved, it is true, a kind of symmetry, for his laws actually began with the consecration of each tribe to a god or son of a god, but it is at the price of some triviality. The Stranger also does not explain why in particular the failure of education should show up first in that crime. It is clear, however, from the Stranger's surprise that atheism of any kind should occur to anyone, that habits do not by themselves induce belief, for if they did no one would ever come to doubt the truth of what he from earliest childhood saw and heard being practiced by everyone with complete sincerity (887c7–888a2). The prohibition against incest, which is merely part of the unwritten law, with every voice of poet and tradition raised in its support, proves to be far more effective among most men, despite their being lawbreakers, than the more elaborate ceremonies of prayers and sacrifices, which the city sponsors and every parent promotes (838a4–d2). The holy sinks deeper into the soul than the divine: the holy has the support of comedy and tragedy, the divine apparently does not. It is far less likely that a bad egg will turn to cannibalism than atheism. The tyrannical soul occurs less often than the unbeliever's. One might therefore infer that the awareness on the part of men that not everything is permitted, despite the arbitrariness of where each people sets the limit, is of a different order from and, as it were, more natural than the awareness that there are gods, despite the equally universal belief in their being. In speaking of an evil desire that summons a man by day and wakes him up at night to steal from a shrine, the Stranger seems to be describing a Cambyses, who sets out to expose for all to see the folly of religious belief, rather than anyone motivated by a perverse desire for gain. Indeed, the very story the Stranger proposes to tell him makes no attempt to check his greed but rather to convince him of his place in a cosmic scheme of retribution. One is forced to wonder, then, whether the Stranger has not anticipated the consequences of the teaching of the tenth book, which, through its silent denial of any connection between the holy and the divine, would lead necessarily to sacrilege among the impressionable young. Would they not want to make a dramatic state-ment of what they had learned? What the Stranger first called a desire and a frenzy (οἶστρος) he later ascribed to opinions (δόγματα) (854b6). In the end, he leaves it up to the highest authorities to discern the difference among impious acts and decide which are playful and which not (910c6–d4).[4] He seems to have in mind the mutilation of the Hermae and the

---

4. That the Stranger already has this distinction in mind is shown by the provi-sion that no penalty is to be attached to the sacrilegious's children: he must be over thirty (855a3–4).

profanation of the mysteries in Athens (cf. Thucydides 6.28.1). The former would fall under temple robbery, the latter under insolence (885a7–b4).

A slave or stranger who gets caught robbing a temple is cast out naked from the city and becomes a walking text which everyone can read and discover his crime. The tattoo on his face and arms declares what he has done, and the blows on his back are given in order to make him better, "for no lawful punishment (δίκη) occurs for evil, but pretty nearly produces one of two things: it makes him who has submitted to punishment (δίκη) either better or less bad" (854d5–e1). The Stranger wants to alter the sense of punishment. It is not directed toward the past and designed for revenge, but for moderation and directed toward the future. The law proclaims its concern for noncitizens and induces in them a version of the σωφροσύνη it could not guarantee for its own. It prudently dispenses with the test whether its sobering has worked. Its only effect within the city, apart from the loss a slave's owner might suffer, would be to support the paradigmatic function of capital punishment for the citizen. The law would surely want to convince the city that it is better to be killed than to live a life of disgrace, and the evident ugliness of punishment and its concomitant painfulness should reinforce the superiority of death to life: Achilles' choice in the *Iliad* is the model and not his regret in the *Odyssey*. The Stranger, however, cannot but admit that it is the least of evils; it is still an evil, and therefore not quite in agreement with the fundamental principle the Stranger laid down, that under no circumstances is the community of body and soul better than its dissolution (828d4–5). This principle makes all capital punishment doubtful, for it cannot be expected that the good it bestows on the city coincide with a good the city bestows on the criminal. The city cannot afford for everyone condemned to spout Socratic defiance, and throw in the teeth of the city the lesson it itself has inculcated: "I don't know whether the goods of the gods there are not the greatest of goods for me" (727d4–5). The city, one might say, is spared the spread of this defiance by its confident belief that those it condemns are not on the whole the witty.

The Stranger puts three cases under one law—temple robbery, subversion, and treachery (856e5–857a2). That the education has not been effective seems clearer in the last case than in either the first or the second, for it is an easy inference that its perpetrators are permanently disaffected and can be safely judged incurable. The city, in any case, cannot afford to let them have a second chance. Treachery, on the other hand, is not on a par with subversion, for treachery involves the fatherland, and it is at least as possible for the traitor to believe he is destroying as for the patriot to believe he is upholding something more sacred than the laws (cf. *Republic* 575d3–8). Betrayal of the fatherland fits more easily with temple robbery than it does with subversion of the laws, for the Stranger later treats patricide as a form of temple robbery (869b1–4; cf. 854e3). Criminal law, then, begins with the assimilation of two different cases to a third, which thereby must expand to accommodate them.[5] Fiction is at the heart of criminal law. What certainly must happen in civil law if it is to keep up with changes and make up for oversights, criminal law declares to be its basic principle. This principle, however, if strictly applied, threatens to comprehend every crime. If all three crimes fall under unholy deeds (854e1–6), the city and its regime must have been consecrated, and the defiant innovator in song—the Stranger's first example of impiety (799b4–8)—should also be subject to the same law. The criminal law would then have a Draconian simplicity to it, and no violation in the city would not fall under it (cf. *Statesman* 297e1–3). Criminal law and education are thus mirror images of one another. Just as the collapse of the two meanings of νόμος was going to egyptianize Magnesia, if the Stranger did not go on to restrict that collapse to six species of song, so the slide between temple robbery and subversion harbors a similar threat. We know that the Stranger's solution in the first case only put off the crisis which he alone experienced—the contemptibility of the human. Is the tenth book, in discarding the holy, the Stranger's final way out of that experience?

2   THE BEAUTIFUL, THE JUST, AND THE GOOD

In reverting now to his distinction between free and slave physicians, the Stranger indicates that the criminal law occupies the range that those before him had originally assigned to law itself (857c4–e2). Even the civil law, he implies, is punitive and not educative. The Stranger formulates the jeer of the physician with experience but without logos should he confront a free physician handling the case of a free patient. His speeches, which are near to philosophizing in touching on the illness from the beginning, and reviewing the entire nature of bodies, would soon provide a

5. Antiphon V.10 puts temple robbery, treachery, and murder under the rubric of great κακουργήματα, but he goes on to say there are separate laws for each of them; cf. Demosthenes 22.26. Gaius in his *Institutes*, 3.194, discusses how what is not by nature *furtum manifestum* can by law be treated as if it were by way of the penalty imposed (*at illud sane lex facere potest, ut proinde aliquis poena teneatur atque si furtum vel adulterium vel homicidium admisisset, quamvis nihil eorum admiserit*).

scornful laugh: "Fool!" he would say, "You are not curing the patient but pretty nearly educating him, as if he had to become a physician but not healthy" (857d6–e1). Clinias is inclined to believe the rebuke well deserved. He certainly would not take the view that Socrates cannot cure Charmides' headache before he has conversed with him. He does not realize that in general the difference between knowledge and health of soul, or σωφροσύνη as self-knowledge and σωφροσύνη as self-control, is of a different order from that between medicine and health, and that in particular a majority of the citizens over time will be judges or arbiters of large and small disputes, and without the kind of education the Stranger is to supply, they would be applying the law in the dark (cf. 856e5–6; 861c1–d1; 957c1–958a3). What fine is to be imposed, or what punishment is to be inflicted, must in many cases be left to the discretion of the judges (876c3–d6): once culpability must be weighed against crime, the Stranger has no choice but to turn to the nature of the soul. Philosophy enters the city through the breach the lawbreaker effects.

In the *Gorgias*, Socrates represented the relation between body and soul in an elaborate eightfold scheme. The body supplies the model through the arts (τέχναι) that treat it for the arts that Socrates discovered or invented for the soul; and through the experiences (ἐμπειρίαι) that flatter the body, Socrates detected those experiences that were the phantom images of his arts. Just as the art of legislation is to justice as gymnastic is to medicine, so sophistry is to rhetoric as cosmetics is to cookery. One term deviates from what the scheme required: Socrates speaks of δικαιοσύνη (justice) rather than of δικαστική (art of punishment).[6] The Stranger now offers a way to explain that deviation. Just as he has put together throughout the art of legislation (though he never asserted there was such an art) with legislation, so now he puts together the art of justice with the laws of justice. The art of justice consists more in the detection and understanding of the disease than in its treatment, for criminal law largely handles that incurable element in the city which the youthful tyrant, had he been the ally of the legislator, would have excluded from the city at the start. The brevity of the prelude the Stranger directed at the would-be sacrilegious suggests the degree of effectiveness the Stranger thought could be expected from the kind of punitive rhetoric Socrates had devised against Polus and Callicles (*Gorgias* 475d6–7; 506c3–4). Punitive rhetoric is most effective in the disguised form of the criminal law itself.

The Stranger's astonishing turn from treatment to education implies

---

6. δικαστική is a variant reading at 464b8 and 465c3 and clearly represents a simplification; cf. *Clitophon* 408b3–5; *Erastae* 137d10–15.

that the disease that either torments the future criminal or has already erupted in some criminal act lurks in almost everyone in the city (cf. 862e1–6). This disease must thus have a lawful aspect, and the judges, in imposing penalties or punishments, are subject to the same passions as the criminals they condemn. In this sense, Polus, with his indignation at the tyrant's injustice and admiration for his happiness, is typical of the judge, whose severity in carrying out the letter of the law effectively cancels his secret envy. Clinias admitted as much when he separated justice from happiness and pleasure from virtue. The Stranger, then, wants to continue the education of Clinias in order to check the indulgence in phantom virtue that is all but endemic in any but the true and healthy city. The beating the law as slave-master inflicts does not do the citizen-slaves as much good as it harms the citizen-master if he comes to believe that body is prior to soul and rules it. Punishment necessarily inculcates this false belief, not only because the punisher then believes he is getting at the soul through the body but because he finds his own good in pleasure and the criminal's pain. The theology of book 10 is therefore the educative corrective to the effects of the criminal law. It limits the damage the genetic structure of law, through its presumed union of body and soul, inflicts on the eidetic structure of the good, which kept soul and body disjoint and their union problematic. Book 10, in separating the holy and the divine, maintains the separation of body and soul. It is the closest the city can come to the truly philosophic speech of the eidetic structure of the good.

The Stranger combines his answer to the sneer of experience—they are not legislating but educating the citizens—with an appeal to the happy chance that they are now under no necessity to legislate but are instead "engaged in an attempt to descry both the best and the most necessary [most indispensable] in regard to every regime, in what manner they would come to be in becoming" (857e10–858a3). The Stranger sets for himself a threefold task. The lowest is paradigmatic legislation, from which Clinias is to choose what he can use; the middle is held by education; and the highest is concerned with the nature of the political itself and is not restricted to either the needs of Clinias or the athenianization of a Dorian city. This third consideration has its particular applicability at the moment: the Stranger leaves it up to Clinias whether in the case of laws they are to examine the best or the most necessary. The Stranger alludes to the issue he is about to face. Neither the opinion of the many nor his own is consonant with the law. The common opinion is that everything just is beautiful, and his own opinion is that no one is willingly bad. The Socratic principle the Stranger endorses cancels criminal law;

the common opinion, which is the basis for the genetic structure of law, shatters on the necessity for punishment. Reflection on the necessary, which characterized criminal law, thus leads to the unwelcome conclusion that it cannot consist with the best. Experientially, regardless of what the many may maintain in speech, punishment simply drives a wedge between the beautiful and the just, and however irrational it may be to deny Socrates' thesis, the city cannot afford to let everyone off who mistakenly commits a crime and send him back to Socrates' "reflectory" until he has learned his lesson. Insofar as the judges are slave physicians and cannot be dialecticians, they are between the writing on the wall, which merely threatens, and the writing of the *Laws*, which merely instructs. Their education consists in learning the necessity of their compromised and compromising position.

Clinias understands the Stranger's offer of either the best or the necessary differently. The necessary for him is the circumstantially urgent; unlike legislators who cannot put off till tomorrow what they must do today, the Stranger, Clinias, and Megillus are at their leisure and like stonemasons can heap up building blocks beside their project and put some into their structure now and set aside others for selection later (858a7–c1). Clinias confuses the first of the three tasks the Stranger set for them with the third. For the Stranger, they are on the way to becoming legislators and are still learning their trade (859b8–c4); for Clinias, they are already legislators who have the time to collect better laws than any they can possibly use. Clinias's image is apt if one takes it in a way Clinias himself did not have in mind. The building blocks that go into the making of the criminal law cannot fit with the overall construction of the law. It is not just that criminal law forms an outbuilding, or that in being nothing but threats it abandons the loving intelligence of the rest of the law, but rather that it embodies principles that are out of tune with the song of the law. The just is a block of the law that cannot be squared with the beautiful and the good. This disharmony is far worse than the inconsistency in the many voices the poet adopts, for the impersonality of the law has the law contradicting itself.[7] It cannot slough off onto another whatever it does not wish to contaminate in its message to those

---

7. In light of what follows, the mention of Homer (858e1) could allude to the way punishment plays itself out in the *Iliad* and *Odyssey*. There are two stories of anger, one of which brings about a double reconciliation, first with Agamemnon and then with Priam (in-between there is the vain punishing of Hector's corpse); the other story ends with the killing of the suitors and the tortured execution of the slave girls and Melanthius. One could not have a better illustration of the difference between the best and the necessary.

who, in absorbing its advice about the beautiful, the good, and the just, are going to be happy (858d6–9).

The Stranger seemingly wants to do the impossible. He wants to get rid of the tyrannical character of criminal law and bring it back into line with the kind and thoughtful parenting all the rest of their written laws display (859a1–b4). He admits that they may not succeed, but they should at least show their zeal even if they stumble along the way. "May it be good," he says, "and if a god is willing, it would become so." The Stranger seems to anticipate failure; but it might not be altogether bad if they come to understand that their failure lies not in any deficiency on their part but in an impossibility of the law itself. The necessary can come to light only if the truly impossible emerges from behind the veil of the apparently impossible. Only the best can reveal the necessary. Clinias's choice of the best was therefore, as the Stranger says, the more natural way to gain a survey of the laws (858c2–3). The massive contradiction Clinias detected in the Stranger's treatment of theft, so that one variety pronounced the thief incurable while theft itself was all of a piece and the thief paid double at most, merely heralded the cacophony at the heart of the criminal law.

Clinias agreed that they should not bar the legislator from giving instruction about the beautiful, the just, and the good, and that written law advises no less than do other writings in meter and in prose; but he did not then know that the absurdity of writings that contradicted the law could lie in the exposure of the contradictions in the law (858c6–859a1). Law looks ugly once it is opened up, and what seemed to be somewhat shameful—the need for criminal law—now looks like a permanent blot on the law. Its ugliness turns on the impossibility of either inducing in the patient what is in the agent of punishment, or checking the agent from becoming the patient of his own agency. The assumption that the just things are all beautiful founders first on the ugliness or shamefulness of what the criminal undergoes and then on the disgracefulness of the pleasures the agent experiences in the satisfaction he has in seeing justice done. The ugly but just man, who Clinias believes can be rightly called beautiful, reflects inversely the surface beauty of his justice and the depth of its ugliness (859d5–e2). The Stranger leaves the disparity between the just and the beautiful at the first level only and does not turn the problem back, as Socrates had in the *Gorgias,* to the agent of justice; but he lets us infer, from the equality of whatever the agent does to whatever the patient experiences (859e3–5), the utter ugliness of the agent of right if the patient experiences the most shameful of things. He hints at this when he claims that they stopped at the punishment for sacrilege and subversion when they saw the infinite number and magnitudes of just but ugly experiences (860b1–5). Since it was in fact Clinias who stopped him, in expressing his puzzlement how the Stranger, in laying down the law of theft, could ignore the complexity of circumstances, the Stranger's arrogation of Clinias's primacy seems unwarranted, particularly since the Stranger seems to antedate the point at which he stopped. What justifies the Stranger's claim to precedence is Clinias's remark—Clinias had not interrupted him before—once the Stranger finished with the law about sacrilege and subversion. Clinias had then said "Beautifully" (856e4). This form of approval expressed Clinias's experience of the law. It comprehended not only the law's mildness in freeing the sons of the sacrilegious from any taint but also its punishment of their fathers. Clinias's "Beautifully" triggered the check on the Stranger's plunge into criminal law and reminded him of the willful and tyrannical brutality he had attributed to slave physicians.[8]

When the Stranger first spoke of education he formulated it entirely in terms of pleasure, and only when he reviewed the problem did he connect pleasure with pain (653a6). The reason for this subsequent enlargement of the issue is clear as soon as punishment becomes central. Criminal law has to confront three different kinds of experience: the experience of the justly punished, which is stripped of justice and consists of nothing but pain; the imagined experience of the punished, in which by a miracle his pain appears as just and beautiful; and the secret experience of the punisher in which at best he experiences what Leontius did when he saw the corpses of the public executioner (*Republic* 439e6–440a3). It might not be going too far to say that Leontius's "Oh beautiful sight!" has its gentle echo in Clinias's "Beautifully."

Now that the just has been isolated from the beautiful, the Stranger tries to rejoin it to the good. It seems again an impossible task. The just is universally understood under the rubric of voluntary and involuntary, the Stranger understands the good in terms of knowledge and ignorance. There seems to be as much dissonance between will and knowledge as there was between the beauty of justice and the ugliness of punishment. The resistance the just puts up against the good and knowledge can be measured by Glaucon's comparison test, in which the unjust man had all the advantages and the just man had not even knowledge to defend him.

8. The last time Clinias said "Beautifully" was at 832d8, when the Stranger spoke of the correct completion in speech of martial education and play (παιδείαν τε ἅμα καὶ παιδιάν) in their laws; he had not shared in Megillus's πάντη καλῶς about the legislation for pederasty (837d9; cf. 922d9).

At the same time, Glaucon's statue of the unjust man showed the power of the Stranger's case, for the unjust want what they hold to be good and never have the will to be unjust. They certainly do not go after what Glaucon himself holds to be good—harmless pleasures, health, thought, and sights. It seems, then, that the Stranger can easily set the criminal law on a new basis by simply laying it down that any act of injustice has its source in the citizen's failure to absorb the education to which he has submitted throughout his life, and either his nature was recalcitrant from the start or some alien influence has got to him despite the Stranger's efforts to quarantine the city from such contamination. In either case, execution would be the remedy, and the executed criminal would be held up as a warning against the contagion of false opinions about the good. Whether he was willingly or unwillingly unjust would not be an issue; his crime would hint at the same denial on his part of the good the regime upholds as that which anyone who set out to subvert all its laws would declare explicitly. Two difficulties stand in the way of instituting the equation of injustice with false opinion about the good. First, not all presumed acts of injustice are self-evidently due to a misunderstanding of the good; second, the genetic structure of the law had itself been framed entirely in light of the beautiful and the just, and the legislator cannot at the tag end of the law suddenly renounce the genetic structure of law and declare that what he meant all along was the eidetic structure of the good. The law itself, in deviating in its opinion about the beautiful and the just from knowledge of the good, stands in the way of a fully rational criminal law. The dissonance between the beautiful and the just gave the illusion that the just could be reanchored in the good. As it is, the just is now all by itself, and, however reluctant the Stranger may be, he has to make some concession to the ordinary understanding of the will.

The Stranger seems to refuse to distinguish between being unjust and acting unjustly, so that it would appear plausible to assert that the involuntarily unjust are addicted to injustice and have lost sight of whatever good they originally wanted, while to act unjustly is voluntary, since one is then aiming at some good and believes one can get away with it (860d9–e3). The Stranger does not want to wiggle out of his thesis in this way; but he admits that if all injustice is involuntary, the penalty should apparently be uniform (861a1–2). The Stranger has now returned to that point where Clinias interrupted him. He had made the penalty for theft the same, regardless of whether it was in public or private, and Clinias had expressed his surprise at his disregard of all circumstances. Now theft would be a clear case where a good the city wanted to rank eighth the thief had moved near to the top of his list (cf. 870a8–b1), and the penalty the Stranger proposed was meant to reform the thief through what would hurt him the most. The penalty, moreover, is relatively mild because the penalty is drawn up on the basis of the rank wealth has in the eidetic structure of the good; it is not in accordance with the thief's own reevaluation. A crime against mind should, accordingly, have assigned to it the gravest penalty, and what the Stranger proposes in the case of certain forms of atheism might be thought to confirm his attempt to put the eidetic structure of the good back into play. However that may be, it is hard to figure out how the other six goods would lend themselves to penalties that were strictly weighted in accordance with the difference in rank of the good that the criminal had assailed. The penalty the Stranger already meted out to sacrilegious theft shows that the Stranger cannot bring off a perfect match between crime and punishment. Indeed, the Stranger had already given up in the case of pederasty, even though the second place that moderation holds would have warranted something more punitive than a call for discretion. One might, however, suppose that the link the Stranger later makes between hedonism and atheism restores to moderation the rank it seemingly lost in book 8.

If the criminal law for Magnesia wanted to be as tyrannical as all other law was and is, the Stranger could have declared the difference between his view and that prevailing everywhere else as based on divine revelation and thus be done with any explanation (861b1–c1; cf. 859a1–6). The Stranger would put himself in an intolerable position if he established by fiat a rational basis for criminal law. The divine injunction he needed to control *erōs* was not up to him to supply (835c1–8), but it would not have been at odds with the common belief in the irrationality of *erōs*, and as it was something more than human, so something more than human had to be invoked; but now that he wants to make ignorance the ground for all injustice, he cannot appeal to the willfulness of positive law. Everyone in the city must be able to follow the decisions of the court and judge their propriety. The Stranger implies that he will compromise the principle of involuntary criminality by diluting it with a version of the difference between voluntary and involuntary injustice. The version of the difference proves to be the image. Some murders will be likenesses of the involuntary, others of the voluntary (866e6–867b1). Δίκη (justice) will assume the guise of its accusative form (δίκην), when it serves as a preposition and means "just like."

The Stranger begins by separating harm (βλάβη) from injustice and benefit (ὠφελία) from justice (861e6–862b2).[9] Just as he will deny that an

---

9. At 862a3, the Stranger replaces the prose word βλάπτει with the poetic

involuntary harm is an injustice albeit involuntary, so he will assert that the agent of a benefit if it is not really a benefit acts unjustly. A good bestowed on the wrong person on the wrong occasion is clearly a harm, but since it must be due to ignorance, the Stranger regards it as an involuntary injustice, the cure for which would be to deprive the benefited of the benefit and instruct the benefactor about his mistake (862c6–8). The Stranger does not say how the legislator would soothe the benefited, who would surely believe the loss of the gain was unjust. The Stranger is more explicit about agent and patient in the case of harm. He proposes that the harm be made good, "bringing the lost to safety and straightening upright the fallen," and agent and patient be reconciled and turned from difference to friendship. The Stranger mentions two cases of harm, the infliction of death or of a wound (τὸ θανατωθὲν ἢ τρωθέν). He casually gives the legislator the impossible task of resurrection and does not say what kind of compensation (ἄποινα), within the capacity of the law to deliver short of that, would conciliate the killed and the killer. The killer would know that he was innocent and might balk at paying anything. The Stranger implies that the harmed looks upon his harm as an injustice and has to be cajoled into believing otherwise, for else there would be no need to restore a friendship which an act, if it was mutually recognized as unintentional, could never have damaged. The Stranger proposes to split injustice into harm and enmity and through compensation cancel the harm and restore friendship. He proposes in short the disappearance of justice and injustice as they are ordinarily understood. His proposal cannot but remind us of what he had originally offered Clinias, that the judge reconcile the good and the bad in a divided family through law and make those at odds with each other into friends (627e3–628a3).[10]

If there are unjust benefits there ought to be just benefits. In the

πημαίνει. In Homer, πῆμα is always said by someone other than Homer (forty-seven times)—i.e., it is experiential—with one exception (Iliad 11.413); Hector uses it five times, Achilles once (24.547); at Ion 508a3, Socrates replaces Homer's κῆρα with πῆμα (Iliad 24.82). In Homer, ἄποινα, which occurs at 862c2, is confined to the Iliad, primarily in its first and last books; in the first it is of compensation for the return of Chryseis, which Agamemnon refused at first to accept, and in the last it is of compensation for the return of Hector's corpse, which Achilles is compelled to accept. In the latter case, a kind of friendship is established between enemies, even though there never was any injustice (unless of course Achilles is held to be punishing the injustice of the Trojans); in the former, Chryseis is part of the spoils of war, and the Achaeans are punished for not being reconciled through ἄποινα. Calchas says that because they did not accept ἄποινα, they have to propitiate (ἱλασσάμενοι) Apollo, and not receive recompense (ἀπριάτην, ἀνάποινον) (Iliad 1.93–100).

10. E. Klingenberg, op. cit., 23–24, observes that the principle stated at 862b6–c2 finds no echo in any legal regulation in the Laws.

Gorgias, Socrates asks Gorgias whether he shares in his own nature (458a1–7): he takes pleasure no less in being refuted if he speaks falsely than in refuting if another does, but he holds it to be a greater good to be freed from the greatest evil than to free another. Socrates tells Gorgias that he never acts out of justice, but if Gorgias is like him, Socrates' refutation of him will both please and benefit him; and if Socrates had not informed him of his disposition, he might have wrongly inferred that Socrates was just. If, however, he finds his refutation distressing and treats it as a hurt, he will be liable to believe, as Polus does, that Socrates was unjust (cf. 461d2). How justice can show up as its experience without any basis in the intention of the agent is clear in this case. The Stranger can thus retain the just and the unjust as experiential modes of good and bad while denying to them any support in the real. Since, however, the Poluses of the world, to say nothing of the Callicleses, who take the slap in the face to be the height of injustice, are more common than the Socrateses, the law must accommodate them and adopt their perspective. Were Gorgias to get angry at Socrates, it would be easier to convince him that Socrates did not mean it than to argue that he had rejected a benefit out of hand.

The law is an instrument of instruction and compulsion (862d1–4). If someone has committed an unjust harm, he is to be so turned around that he hates injustice and loves or at least does not hate the nature of the just. If, however, the legislation perceives (αἴσθηται) that he is incurable, then it is better for him not to live but become a paradigm for everyone else. The legislation can "perceive" incurability in only two or three ways: either the magnitude of the crime by itself, the repeat offenses of the criminal, or a combination of both determines whether he is fit to live or not. If the determination of curability were left to the judge, some would get away with murder and others would be executed for the most trivial violations which they could not help themselves from committing again and again. The law cannot be expected to lay down in writing the perfect match between crime and criminal. Indeed, it seems that extra-legal considerations will compel it to be both too lenient and too severe.

3 SOCRATIC IGNORANCE

Once the Stranger denied that he would treat certain harms as involuntary injustice, he left us in the dark how the voluntary played any role in his legislation. Clinias wants greater clarity about the difference between injustice and harm, and how the voluntary and involuntary form a com-

plex web with them (862a3–6). The Stranger begins to comply with his
request by combining a version of the soul that we know best from the
Republic with an account of ignorance that we know from the *Philebus*
(48a8–50a10). This combination is as awkward as it is astonishing. Its
awkwardness is due to our refusal to speak of ignorance as we do of anger
and pleasure, as something to which we do or do not succumb; and it
astonishes because Socrates had used this account of ignorance to distinguish his own unarmed ignorance from the strength Aristophanes showed
in the comedy about him. Even apart from this, no sooner does the
Stranger list five faults of soul than he doubles them with a distinction
that wipes out a difference with which he started between anger and pleasure (864c4–6). We did not know that criminal law could be as funny as
it must be perplexing if Socratic ignorance is at its core.

The Stranger separates at first anger from pleasure and not, as he does
later, pain from pleasure, and anger from desire (863b2–6; 864b3–6). Anger
(θυμός) is quarrelsome, hard to fight against, and overturns many things
by its irrational violence. Nothing is said of the pleasure it gives and the
desire it has to retaliate for an experienced wrong. Pleasure holds sway
from a contrary strength and does whatever its will wants by means of
persuasion and the force of deceit.[11] Nothing is said about its irrationality
or how pleasure can have a will. A slight modification in both accounts
would make pleasure as ignorant as anger is about the good, and neither
cause could then be punishable for its errors. It seems, then, that the
Stranger lets anger and pleasure have the character they have in popular
speech; but when it comes to ignorance as the cause of faults, the legislator steps in and divides it between simple ignorance, which is the cause
of light mistakes, and double ignorance, "whenever someone is foolish
(ἀμαθαίνῃ), caught in the grip not only of ignorance but of an opinion of
wisdom as well (καὶ δόξῃ σοφίας), as if he perfectly knew what he does
not know at all" (863c4–6). The Stranger had spoken of the dishonor that
accrues to soul if one believes that life is good without qualification and
the things in Hades are evils, and does not instruct the soul that it does
not know whether exactly the opposite is the case (727c7–d5); and Socrates had distinguished himself from everyone else on the score of his ignorance about Hades and thus challenged the city to teach him first before
they killed him.

The Stranger goes on to separate illusory wisdom (δοξοσοφία) if

---

11. πειθοῖ μετὰ ἀπάτης βιαίου recalls Aeschylus's βιᾶται δ᾽ ἁ τάλαινα Πειθώ (*Agamemnon* 385). τοῦ λογισμοῦ καλοῦ μὲν ὄντος, πρᾴου δὲ καὶ οὐ βιαίου (645a5–6) shows
that the text should not be altered.

strength and force accompany it from what it is when it has no power. The first, he says, is the cause of great and nonmusic mistakes—he alludes perhaps to what he had said about Athens after the second Persian War (701a3–7)—, the second causes mistakes that are either childish or senile, for which the legislator will set down the gentlest and most forgiving of laws. The Stranger does not say a word about how the legislator is to handle the first variety of false conceits. Instead, he goes on to remark that pretty nearly everyone says, "One of us is a slave to pleasure or anger, another rises above it," but no one speaks that way of ignorance, as if one could not be, like Socrates, superior to one's own ignorance through knowledge of it, or under its sway like everyone else (863d6–e1). The immediate consequence the Stranger draws from this disparity between anger and pleasure, on the one hand, and ignorance, on the other, is that he can define the unjust, without the complication the voluntary and involuntary would introduce, as the tyranny of anger or pain, of pleasure or fear, and of resentment or desire, regardless of whether it does harm or not, and he can define the just entirely in terms of opinion, regardless of whether it is simple or double, and regardless of whether it fails or not (863e5–864a8). If an action is done, either by a city or some private group, on the basis of an opinion about the best, and this opinion holds the upper hand in the soul of every man and orders it, then it must be declared completely just. What in the opinion of many is an involuntary wrong now has the stamp of right. Justice is simply the absolute right of ignorance. The Stranger thus indemnifies the jurors if they condemn or acquit the wrong man. They are just, they are not involuntarily unjust. If a harm is due to simple ignorance, as in accidental homicide, and this is what is called in Greek just murder (δίκαιος φόνος), it is just; and if it is due to double ignorance and strength accompanies it, it is the law. The Indian tribes who eat their dead are as just as the Greeks who burn them, the magi who let the birds consume them, and the Egyptians who embalm them; yet they all severally rely on δοξοσοφία, and would surely punish anyone who contravenes their beliefs in deed. The Stranger shares the view of Socrates and the Eleatic Stranger that the city is the locus of powerful δοξοσοφία, while the sophists who go around from city to city are merely the scapegoats for the cities' several conceits (*Republic* 498a5–493c8; *Statesman* 303b8–c5). The big and nonmusic mistakes, for which the Stranger failed to provide any legislation, are nothing but the city's own permanent opinions about the good, in accordance with which it arranges the soul of everyone in the city. The city translates the good into the just by way of opinion and resists the Stranger's attempt to translate the just into the good by way of knowledge.

The Stranger divides the soul between opinion and passion. Opinion ranges over the individual and the city, passion informs the individual. The division makes it look as if no opinion about the goods affects either anger or pleasure, and passion does not affect any opinion of the good. The Stranger further makes it look as if he is distinguishing between the order and the disorder of soul, calling the latter injustice or tyranny when passion takes over and has the upper hand, and the former justice when it makes everyone subject to its principle; but the order of soul that opinion maintains deviates from the true order of soul, however much its stability may give the contrary impression. The invincibility of the city's sophistry conceals its claim to know what it does not know. The Stranger indicates how much he has misled us when, in his summary, he speaks of three species of errors (ἁμαρτανόμενα) and thus pulls anger and pleasure into the orbit of ignorance, and then goes on to reformulate ignorance as characteristic of one who, in his expectations and opinion, is truly aiming at the best, and thus pulls ignorance into the orbit of desire (864b1–7).[12] The immunity the Stranger bestows on ignorance seems not to survive the legislation he proposes, for the tenth book handles atheism as a form of δοξο-σοφία and does not let some of its proponents plead ignorance (868b7–8; 888e1–2). At the end of the ninth book, however, when he reverts to the embarrassment the need for criminal law induces, he distinguishes between laws of instruction and laws for the sake of punishment, and he appeals again to δοξοσοφία as explanatory of the actions of mother and father beaters (880d8–b2). The Stranger, however, is apparently not quite consistent, for the criminal law is directed in general against natures resistant to education and, in the case of maltreatment of elders (αἰκία),

12. This is to read ἐφέσεως with L. A. Post, "Notes on Plato's Laws," AJP 60 (1939): 101; Bury's ἐφέσθαι τούτου for ἔσεσθαι τούτων (864a2) is consistent with this, though the future ἔσεσθαι fits the argument better. Post translates the phrase thus: "expectations and belief that we are really launched in pursuit of the ideal." T. J. Saunders keeps ἔφεσις and reads ἐλπίδων δὲ καὶ δόξης, τοῦ ἀληθοῦς . . . ἔφεσις, τρίτον ἕτερον; "The Socratic Paradoxes in Plato's Laws," Hermes 96 (1968): 432–433; but cf. K. Schöpsdau, "Zum Strafrechtsexkurs in Platons Nomoi," RhM 127 (1984): 124–130. At 863e2–3, the Stranger suggests how ignorance could be harmonized with anger and pleasure: πάντα δέ γε προτρέπειν ταὐτά φαμεν εἰς τὴν αὐτοῦ βούλησιν ἐπισπώμενον ἕκαστον εἰς τἀναντία πολλάκις ἅμα. If ignorance often provokes each man, just as anger or pleasure does, in a direction contrary to that of his own will, he must have a will for true opinion about the good that is based on an awareness of his ignorance. Ignorance, then, includes knowledge of ignorance, and is as double as erōs. The Stranger thus slips in Socrates as the paradigm of ignorance and declares him to be wholly just. Socratic ignorance may seem to be a fourth species of ignorance, but it is also possible to treat it as the core of the class, and that the other kinds borrow their justice from it and vindicate their own ignorance through it.

against those who act as if they know what they do not know, and what they do not know and do not fear is the wrath (μῆνις) of the gods above and the stories of punishment below. The Stranger accuses them of knowing to be false what the city does not know to be true.[13] The city's justice in punishing the mother beater consists in its ignorance of whether there is divine punishment for his crime. The city cannot instruct him in what it itself does not know, but it gauges his incurability by his failing to make the city's ignorance his own. The city comes forward as Socrates and punishes those who are not content with knowing that they do not know. This punishment is permanent exile from the city and excludes them from everything sacred (881d3–5). The city rejects them with as much finality as Socrates' *daimonion* barred some of his followers on occasion from association with him (*Theaetetus* 150e8–151a4).

4   VIOLENCE

When the Stranger goes back to the three crimes with which he started—sacrilegious theft, treachery, and subversion—he does not make it clear whether he wants us to subsume them under the tyranny of desire in the soul, as his prelude would suggest, or whether they might not rest as well on a claim to superior wisdom (864c10–d5). If the latter were true, the arrest and execution of such criminals would prove their weakness and nothing whatever about the falseness of their opinion about the good. In all three cases the Stranger makes an exception of madmen and those whose bodily infirmities make them equivalent to the mad. Are we to assume that δοξοσοφία is not a form of madness, and those who say they know what they do not know are in their right minds (cf. *Sophist* 228c10–d2)? The madman, we say, represents a certain form of simple ignorance—he does not know what he is doing—but it is just as easy to say of Don Quixote that he believes he knows what he does not know and shift him into the species of double ignorance. However that may be, the Stranger makes an exception to his exception, and whereas the mad or infirm pay simple damages and are quit of all other charges, those among them who are guilty of homicide have to go abroad for a year, and if they return beforehand are put in prison for two years (864e1–9). The Stranger thus introduces the legislation for murder. He enters into a second species through an exception to an exception about another species. He thus

13. The phrase ἀληθέστατα λέγοντες (sc. Πόνοι, 881a6) takes back the Stranger's ignorance but not, to judge from book 10, the city's (903b1–2).

makes it appear how the Socratic principle could be extended over all of criminal law and let everyone off the hook (cf. 888a2–4). The importance of this slide can be measured if one recalls that Socrates used the example of the madman who wanted the weapons he had left with a friend restored to him in order to establish implicitly the principle that no one has the right to anything, including his own life, if he does not know how to use it (*Republic* 331c5–9).

As soon as the Stranger turns to homicide as a species, he speaks of the involuntary; but it is clear from the first three cases alone—in a public contest, in war, or on maneuvers—that unwilling (ἄκων) is a name for ignorant (865a2–b2). This change in nomenclature, however, dictates another: the killer is not called just but clean (καθαρός). Purification in accordance with the law brought from Delphi colors the just with the holy. These cases need such coloration because the situation in which bloodshed occurs conceals whether it is premeditated or not. The risk the victim knowingly assumed absolves the killer of any intent; and the same holds for the patient whom the physician kills (865b2–4). It is better not to inquire into guilt and arouse the wrath of the living and the dead. One does not want Euthyphro second-guessing the law.[14]

Before he turns to the second kind of homicide, the Stranger makes a special provision if a freeman kills a freeman (865d3–866a1). He is purified in the same way as the other involuntary slayers are, but he must go into exile for a year. He is to uphold an old story: "Whoever suffers a violent death, having lived in the pride of freedom, is angry at the doer while recently dead, and filled with fear and terror on account of the violence of the event, and seeing his slayer haunting the places familiar to him, is in terror, and in his own distress distresses as far as he can— he has memory as his ally—the doer himself and his actions." The law now distinguishes between slave and free, and though the slayer of a slave, whether his own or another's, has to go through the same rite of cleansing as the killer of a free man, there is no story that urges the appeasement of the slain slave. Homicide law, which seemed as if it would conform with the five or tenfold kinds of fault, undergoes an accommodation to the structure of the city. This accommodation both supports the pride in freedom every citizen has and soothes the irrational feelings any violent death provokes. The resentment that the Stranger's story attributes to the dead is the same as the resentment the closest relative in the victim's family might experience—and the law makes sure through

14. Cf. David Daube, *Roman Law* (Edinburgh 1969), 164–175.

its penalties that he does experience it (866b3–7)—if he saw the slayer of his own kin gadding about in town or country, as if his formal acquittal could compensate for his loss; but the Stranger's law removes, through the exile of the slayer for a year, any occasion for the relative to express his own anger. What looks like a pious concession to ancient beliefs is an up-to-date device to hinder the tyranny of anger in the soul, regardless of whether such injustice would result in harm or not. No theology can do as much in maintaining the eidetic structure of the good as the holy does in keeping the genetic structure of law intact. The hold that unwritten law must have on the written law could not be more plainly spelled out.

That the law must order the nearest relative to forgive the killer and be at peace with him, but cannot say what the penalty should be if there is no forgiveness and reconciliation (866a1–5), necessarily leads to the next topic, homicides committed in anger, of which the second kind— the premeditated—has to cover those cases where indignation has not faded in the course of a year, while the first kind—the unpremeditated— presumably is applicable when anger flares up again on the killer's return from exile. If the Stranger's law about such homicides had been in effect, Achilles, if Athena had not stopped him but he had gone through with his desire to kill Agamemnon, would have gone into exile for two years, and Ajax, whose plan was to kill at least Odysseus, Agamemnon, and Menelaus (if not more), had he succeeded and Athena not thwarted him, would have been exiled for three years (867c4–d3). The Stranger seems to be very easygoing when it comes to anger. The need for the citizens to be spirited (θυμοειδεῖς), and the rank of "great and perfect man in the city," which the Stranger had assigned to those who joined with the magistrates in punishing injustice (730d5–6), seem to have spilled over into an excessive indulgence of private vendettas. To kill in anger is by definition an injustice, but it is treated as if the relatives of the slain have to be given twice the time to chastise their anger, rather than that there can be any real attempt, with the slayer abroad, to temper his. The Stranger lets the insulted who retaliates determine whether he was in fact insulted, and he is wholly indifferent whether he deserved the insult or not, i.e., whether in fact it was a beneficial harm. Whether it was a cutting remark or a slap in the face, the dignity of the insulted is at his own evaluation. That Ajax perhaps did not deserve Achilles' armor, or that Achilles was wholly in the right to claim the highest honor, makes no difference in the Stranger's scheme. Instant retaliation is unthinking; brooding gives rise to premeditated revenge: "If I kill him, I shall prove that I am not contemptible, for he treated me as if I were his slave." The precarious hold that the free have on freedom warrants the Stranger's support of vengeance (cf. 777b4–c1).

The Stranger has replaced injustice, as he defined it without the complication of the difference between voluntary and involuntary, with injustice as the vindicator of his dignity defines it. The injustice the Stranger assigned to whoever retaliates in anger has become the injustice the insulted discerns in whoever disparaged him. With this turnaround left unexamined, the Stranger tries to restore his original position through an image. He says spontaneous retaliation is an image of the involuntary and postponed retaliation an image of the voluntary (867a2–b1): it is as if ἑκών (willing) had its origin in εἰκών (image). If voluntary and involuntary are retranslated back into their Socratic equivalents, instant retaliation images ignorance and premeditated images knowledge. The former resembles ignorance since remorse often accompanies it (866e2–3), and remorse implies something like, "Had I but known." The Stranger further allows the victim of deadly anger to forgive his assailant on the grounds that he acted unwillingly (869d7–e2). His pardon amounts to saying, "He did not know what he was doing." Premeditated anger is often without regrets (886e3–6)—there is no contrafactual involving knowledge—and it is not as easy to say why its perpetrator should get off with so light a sentence. The sentence takes into account two different considerations. For the family of the victim, since premeditation makes it look like a greater evil (867b7–c1), the greater length of the exile allows them the time to forgive and the slain to forget; and for the perpetrator, the magnitude of his anger is driven home to him and not that it was deliberate (867d3). What the Stranger seems to be pointing to is the innocence of private δοξοσοφία. Precisely what the Stranger seemed not to take into account—the veil of ignorance the Stranger threw over the "rights" of the case—so he seemed not to take into account whether one party was right to take offense or the other right to put him down—is precisely the justice he is willing to extend to the lack of knowledge and self-knowledge on the part of one party or the other. The Stranger does not wish the city to examine too closely the self-estimation of virtue in its citizens. His benevolent condescension first showed up when he allowed the judges to believe that the sacrilegious were incurable and not that they themselves had heeded the threats in the criminal law. The Stranger does, however, limit his indulgence of anger. He grants the guardians of the law, who are charged with testing those who have returned from exile after two or three years, the opportunity to scrutinize with still greater care the original circumstances of the murder (867d3–868a1). He expects that their indignation too would have died down in the meantime and allow them to conduct a more impartial inquiry.[15]

The Stranger makes no distinction between a master's inadvertent killing of his own slave and his killing him in anger (865d1–3; 868a4–5); and he makes no distinction between a slave who kills his master in a fit of anger on the spot and one who bides his time. One might suppose that the slave has already been insulted at the moment of his enslavement, and a clear distinction between premeditation and spontaneity cannot be drawn; his possible remorse clearly does not count. The Stranger, however, is silent about how one is to handle the slave who kills his master or any other free man accidentally. He cannot, as England says (on 868b6), be sent into exile; but it is hard to believe that he can be treated leniently and be given a term in prison (cf. 882b3–c2). It is true enough that master and slave are equally at risk, but it seems the slave's innocence must be sacrificed to the social order. After all, the relatives of the victim can kill the slave at any time with impunity, and it might be better for the city not to rely on time or calculation but rather to forestall the buildup of their anger.

The structure of the city alters the consistency with which the structure of the soul would by itself be applicable to crime. The inalienability of a lot limits the amount of a fine (855a7–b2); slaves are punished less for sacrilege and more for homicide than a citizen; and the family dictates that self-defense does not excuse patricide (869b7–c6). Even though the Stranger's language—"whoever has lost control of his anger" (ἀκρατὴς θυμοῦ) and "dares in the madness of rage (μανίαις ὀργῆς) to murder one of his parents" (869a2–4)—would send the patricide into exile for one or two years, he must be executed. That the parent's dying forgiveness can reclassify him shows the strain the law is under to reconcile principles that are at variance with one another. Without the parent's forgiveness, the killer is guilty of three crimes—insolent assault (αἰκία), impiety, and temple robbery[16]—and deserves to be killed many times over (869b1–7). Since the law runs out of punishments so quickly, the holy must supple-

15. The trial of Lord Byron for the murder of William Chaworth (April 16, 1795) nicely illustrates the difficulty of distinguishing between instantaneous and premediated retaliation; see *State Trials Political and Social,* ed. H. L. Stephen (London: Duckworth, 1902), vol. 4, 229–272.

16. The alteration in meaning that temple robbery undergoes in being extended to cover patricide has the consequence that either the statues of gods are alive or the Stranger is laying the ground for the theology of book 10 (cf. 930e7–931a8; 931d5–9). The stark alternative is either superstition or no religion. At 864d1, the Stranger says the legislation about temple robbery was περὶ τῶν συλώντων τοὺς θεούς (cf. 909e3–4; Sophocles *Antigone* 198–201).

ment it rhetorically. Hades and all it stands for ekes out the poverty of earthly punishment and draws off the excess in the unsatisfiable demands of anger. Tortures could no doubt be devised to degrade the criminal and satisfy indignation, but they would violate the Stranger's demand that punishments be either corrective or exemplary, to say nothing of the need to distinguish slave from free (872b4–c2). There would be the danger as well that a regime whose aim was friendship would in that case place fear at the heart of the family. If, on the other hand, the scale of punishments were revised, so that death be reserved for the triply heinous crime, the fear of death would cease to be a deterrent, inasmuch as these kinds of crime happily do not occur often enough, and the threats of the law would soon fade and become a distant memory.[17] The late Roman Republic had virtually lost the legal right to execute a citizen for any crime. The Stranger is going to make imprisonment for the first time a form of punishment and not simply a means to detain someone before he either discharges a debt or is executed. That he proposes this reform particularly in the matter of atheism shows that in anticipating a new kind of crime he has to invent a new kind of punishment.[18]

When it comes to murders that can be laid to desire, the Stranger varies the law in two respects. First, nonburial becomes a form of punishment, and stories about future punishments accompany the punishment the magistrates can prescribe. Soul was mentioned once in the account of murderous anger (869b3), soul occurs seven times in the account of murderous desire. In the story the Stranger told in the former account, the slain (ὁ θανατωθείς) himself is the patient and agent of experiences (865d6–e6); in the second of two stories he tells in the latter account the killer's soul is the agent that must pay for his crime (873a1–2). "God" was mentioned once in the former account (865d1), "god(s)" and "divine" seven times in the second. The Stranger had originally treated the tyranny of either anger or pleasure as unqualifiedly unjust (864a1), but now premeditated murder, if one succumbs to pleasure, desire, or jealousies, is labeled total injustice (869e5–8). When the citizen kills in anger and thus puts an absolute value on himself, stripped entirely of any acknowledged virtue except the freedom the city has granted him, he is never called unjust, not even when he kills his parent; but when the citizen

---

17. In Aulus Gellius, Caecilius Africanus defends a provision of the twelve tables which allowed a debtor to be cut up in pieces among his creditors on the grounds that it fostered *fides* and acted as a deterrent even though the punishment was never inflicted (20.1.39–54).

18. Cf. Louis Gernet, *Les Lois de Platon*, vol. 11, 1re partie, ed. É. des Places (Paris 1951), cxc–cxci.

inverts the rank of the goods, in which the city's education has exercised him, he is unjust (871a2; 872d2). The Stranger, however, has to admit that the city's education cannot be completely effective unless it were worldwide, and that if it were, bloodshed would not be needed to purify bloodshed in cities (870b6–c3). A false belief infiltrates even Magnesia, and those who fall for it are to be punished and not the magistrates who failed to keep it out. Universal δοξοσοφία is no excuse.

The grounds for the difference in treatment of anger and desire seems at first to be this: Those who were murderously angry absorbed the teaching of the city and ranked the soul higher than the body and external goods, for they must have believed themselves worthy of something, regardless of whether it was true or not; but murderous appetite defies the city and subverts the laws as much as any direct assault on them would. The Stranger, however, undermines this suggestion by attaching to murders of desire murders of ambition: "A second species is the condition of soul in love with honor; it breeds resentment, a harsh cohabitant, in the first place, with the possessor of envy, and secondly for the best of those in the city" (870c5–7). Everything leads us to expect that anger and envy go together, for the most extensive and strongest desire among the many is the insatiable desire for money (870a2–6), and to make ambition a second species of murderous desire is to lump together Achilles and Thersites. To see someone in the city with the honors you believe you deserve generates anger and, if the retaliation is as planned as Ajax's was, it looks like premeditated revenge. What makes the Stranger shift the category of murderous envy is the phrase he uses to describe the victims of the envious: they were "the best of those in the city." Their murders are always unjust because the city never makes a mistake about those who are best. In this case, the structure of the city interferes decisively with the structure of the soul, and the Stranger seemingly condemns false opinion: they should have known they were undeserving of the highest honors. Agamemnon, then, could never have been Achilles' inferior, and Achilles' rebuke—"With the eyes of a dog and the heart of a deer"—for all its concentrated beauty would have just been idle talk (cf. *Republic* 389e12–390a2).

The soul is at the heart of the preludes that are to frighten the obedient; the body is at the heart of the law that is to deter the criminally minded and confirm everyone else in their obedience. The first prelude says that there is requital (τίσις) in Hades, and the doer must undergo the natural punishment—on his return to life he is fated to become the victim of the same kind of crime he himself committed (870d4–e3). The story combines an injustice that belongs to the structure of the soul with a pattern of right. Poetic justice—the view from the outside—is to coincide with the experience of justice from within. The law, on the other hand, forbids burial in order to point up the shamelessness and impiety of the criminal (871d4–5). The second prelude is directed against family murders. Its story is much the same as the first: the agent is fated to become the patient, but now under exactly the same conditions: his own children kill the father killer, the mother killer first becomes a mother and then her children kill her.[19] The law, on the other hand, prescribes that for those who dared to deprive a soul of a body, the magistrates take the killer's corpse to a certain crossroad outside the city, each of them hit the head of the naked corpse with a single stone, and then throw him outside the borders of the country without burial (873a4–c1). The magistrates perform a vain action if soul can be without body, but it still can be extremely effective if the living look on. The separation of body and soul, in which the stories and the law equally share, show in general the necessary apartness and impossible togetherness of the eidetic structure of the good and the genetic structure of law, and in particular how the criminal law forces the logos of the eidetic structure of the good to become mythical in the city (cf. 872d7–e1). The things that are have to become artifacts before an unnatural light can cast their shadows onto the wall of the Cave.

Suicide, if the city does not order it (we may think of Socrates), if an inescapable and overwhelming pain does not compel it (we may think of Philoctetes), or if an unlivable shame makes it the only way out (we may think of Adrastus), requires that the relatives conduct the burial in one of twelve uncultivated and nameless districts, and that they set no marker on the grave (873c2–d8). This is the punishment for the suicide's injustice, which consists in the idleness and cowardice of unmanliness. He jumped the gun on his fate and decided he knew that life was not worth living. What looks like δοξοσοφία is labeled cowardice. His wish not to be born gets fulfilled in the ingloriousness and anonymity of potter's field. The idle (ἀργά) soil in which the suicide is buried echoes the

---

19. The stories the Stranger tells have a strange implication that he does not spell out. If it is fated that Orestes become a mother and then be killed by his (her) children, it was fated that Orestes kill Clytaemestra, for Clytaemestra was once a man who killed his (her) mother. The prelude to which the story belongs transforms the injustice of the criminal code into the inevitable and clears the guilty of wrongdoing. What is sacrilegious in the law becomes opacity of motive in the story—he did not know what good he was after. This might explain why the Stranger is wholly silent about pleasure and desire when he comes to cases, and has them only as the category under which he puts them.

idleness (ἀεργία) of his soul (873c7, d7). He ceases ever to have been. What seems to be a favor to him is also a favor to the city. The city is not to know that someone took the Stranger at his word and concluded that no communion of body and soul was ever better than its dissolution. No one is to take nondialectically the disjunction of body and soul in the eidetic structure of the good (cf. 828d5–6). The uncultivated shirks from perplexity and holds it to be a solution (cf. *Meno* 81d5–e1). The Stranger is forced to hide from the city a parody of what he wanted to be a principle of the city. He did not want his most beautiful tragedy to end with a whimper.

In the case of murderous anger, the Stranger arranged for its chastisement through exile; in the case of deaths caused by anything alive or lifeless, the Stranger proposes a solemn condemnation, execution, and banishment in order to discharge the anger one might harbor against a mere instrument (873e1–874a3). The Stranger gives no reasons for his proposals, but it is clear that the anger which exile appeased in accidental homicide behaves just as irrationally in the face of any random event. Nothing ever happens unintentionally. The locus of the category "voluntary-involuntary" is θυμός; it is that which forces "knowledge-ignorance" to yield to its understanding of intention. Θυμός, however, is in its own eyes not willful but insightful. It knows what is behind the slap in the face, the fatal goring by a bull, or the deadly fall of an iron block off the wall.[20] The Stranger thus seems to have misplaced this item of the criminal law; he should have appended it to the section on anger and not put it after murderous desire and suicide. The displacement, however, coupled as it is with silence about θυμός, suggests how the city's need to maintain the thumoeidetic led the Stranger to absolve the tyranny of anger and heap injustice pure and simple onto desire. The criminal law gives into anger and lets it dictate its own classification. The Stranger never admits that anger drips a pleasure sweeter than honey into the heart.

The Stranger distinguishes between, on the one hand, the sequence, homicide first and wounding and maiming second, which even the worst legislator would know, and, on the other, his own sequence, which makes

---

20. Cf. Oliver Wendell Holmes, *The Common Law* (Boston 1881), 3: "Vengeance imports a feeling of blame, and an opinion, however distorted by passion, that a wrong has been done. It can hardly go very far beyond the case of a harm intentionally inflicted: even a dog distinguishes between being stumbled over and being kicked." Not much later, Holmes corrects this view, 6–15, 25–27; he implies by his correction that he meant it to apply only to men who are as rational as dogs, for, he admits, hatred "leads even a civilized man to kick a door when it pinches his finger" (11); also Herodotus 7.88.

a link between homicide and the issue of nurture and education of soul (and whether life is worth living for the soul that falls short), and attaches violent but nonfatal actions to the nurture and education of bodies (874d2–e5). The latter connection seems fanciful in the extreme. It looks as if the split between the virtues and vices of soul and of body, which the eidetic structure of the good set forth, has intruded into a split in the criminal law, whereby the degree of culpability in homicides, which plainly rests on a ranking in the evils of soul, has spilled over into the degree of culpability in woundings and maimings, as if it depended on a gradation of the vices of body. Now it turns out that the rank of an excellence of body gets its equivalent in the amount of the fine for damage to that excellence. The excellences of body were in order: health, beauty, and strength. If a wound occurs by chance, one pays for the damage; if a wound is inflicted in anger, and it is curable, one pays double; if incurable, quadruple; if one leaves a lasting disfigurement, which is the object of reproach, the fine is also fourfold; but if one takes away another's strength and makes him incapable of serving his country against its enemies, one has to serve in the army in his stead and discharge as well one's own obligation (878b8–d4; 879b1–2).

Whereas a matchup can be made between bodily injury and money fines, which not only inculcates through crime what rank the virtues of body are to have, but also links the common good of military service to the penalty for incapacitation, still no such matchups can be made between the vices of soul and homicide, so that it would be as evident that moderation takes precedence over justice and justice over courage, to say nothing about how good sense would be shown to top them all. It is not accidental therefore that the Stranger returns to the difference between the eidetic structure of the good and the genetic structure of law at exactly that point where he has finished with homicide and is about to begin a discussion of injustice to the body. Law and order can be alive to whatever holds for the most part, but they are incapable of overseeing everything (875d3–5). In light of the manifest success of the law's provisions in what follows, the Stranger puts in this proviso to justify the lack of equal success in the case of homicide. The severity with which criminal desire is treated no doubt shows that moderation surpasses in importance whatever virtue it was, whether it be justice or courage, that failed to control criminal anger (though one might have thought that self-knowledge would have been better taught if the murderously angry did not get off so lightly); but the supplemental need for stories, so that distinctions could be made among death sentences, and the fact that exiles of one, two, or three years are not conspicuously right,[21] all go to show that the political and true art, which knows that the public good binds together and the private pulls apart, cannot be put in charge of the city without the support of law and order (874e7–875d5).

The law serves to keep man from becoming the most savage of beasts; and it does this regardless of whether it has set mind and knowledge superior to itself or not, and thus graded the eightfold good in the proper order. Law has done its job when it has approximated very crudely and preposterously the order of soul. The interference of the political order with the individual good cannot be offset by putting the man with political knowledge in charge: "After all, even if one grasps by art in an adequate manner the knowledge that these things [the private and the public] are this way by nature, and he rules a city with full authority without being subject to review, he would never be able to abide by this opinion and live his life while cherishing the common good for its leading rank in the city, and letting the private attend upon the common, but his mortal nature will always impel him toward profiteering and minding his own business (ἰδιοπραγία), and irrationally avoiding pain and pursuing pleasure, he will place both of these in front of the more just and the better" (875b1–c2). The Stranger then takes exception to what Cronus knew (713c5–8): if mind were in charge of a private person, who had the political art, he would have no need of laws, for it would not be right (θέμις) for mind to be subject and a slave to anything (875c6–d2).[22] Socrates can live without law; but were the city turned over to him, he would soon fill the city and himself with evils. These evils would arise not necessarily from his sudden acceptance of conventional goods as the good, as the Gyges-story of Glaucon suggests, but equally from indifference and a refusal to drop his own good while he attended to the problem of runaway slaves. Socrates did not lift a finger to help out Leon of Salamis; he was content to go home and let the Thirty smear everyone else with their own guilt. There

21. A metic who strikes an elder is imprisoned for three years (880c3–d2); a premeditated murder, conceived in anger, merits a three-year exile. It is not clear why the killer could not be imprisoned in the *sōphronistērion*. There he would be out of sight of the relatives. Would the unreformed atheists then be at risk?

22. That mind is not to be a slave to anything, "if one is really and truly (ὄντως) genuine (ἀληθινός) and free by nature" (875d1–2), was first hinted at when the Stranger, in a discussion of our contradictory attitudes toward slaves, misquoted Homer and replaced Eumaeus's "virtue" with his own "mind" (777a1). Cronus knew only of the virtue that prevailed at the beginning of political life (679b8–c4). The implication that the age of Cronus could not consist with philosophy is the same as that of the myth in the *Statesman*.

are many risky, painful, and unpleasant things the ruler must do, and it takes something more than knowledge not to mind one's own business.

The Stranger now comes around to acknowledging the force of the slave physicians' derision. By way of analogy the Stranger had him anticipate his own line of discussion, which would teach the political art and not cure injustice; and the Stranger admits one could have the political art and be incapable of ruling justly. Law and order, then, must be part of the ruler's makeup. The real force, however, of the Stranger's concession is not directed at the ruler, but at the limitations the law itself imposes on the courts. The penalties of the law for bodily harm, if it is inflicted in anger, ignore entirely the false opinion on the basis of which the angry man struck out at his denigrator. He believed he could get back at an injury to his pride or vanity by harming the other's body; and the law figured out how to assess the fine on a scale neatly adjusted to the harm itself and the needs of the city; but it did not even try to chastise his anger through a reformation; rather it decided that the penalty could be severe enough to make one think twice before doing it again and, at the same time, though it could handsomely compensate the other, it could not know whether he wanted anything more than a physician to set his arm. Perhaps he despised his injurer even more for believing in the magical translation of a bodily hurt into a psychic grief. The law thus made a double concession to the lack of education (ἀπαιδευσία). It let the agent nurse his anger while brooding over what it cost him, for it had no means to teach him his mistake; and simultaneously it elevated the good of money in its capacity to equalize the nonequatable. The law was not set up to fit the punishment to either crime or criminal when it came to murder, but at least it tried to bring them into line with the education; but the law simply gives up in the face of injury and discovers another way that, to the legislator's own chagrin, may prove to be more effective than that which is closer to his own intention. Despite the great leeway the Stranger proposes to grant the courts of Magnesia (876c8–d6), the prescriptions of the law stand in the way of their imparting a teaching along with the cure. The tyrannies in soul are left untreated in favor of law and order.

It has been the several claims to rule that mostly forced the criminal law to diverge from a strict compliance with the structure of the soul. The relation between master and slave and family structure dictated these divergences; but in the case of injurious insult (αἰκία), the claim of age determines almost entirely by itself the crime and the penalties (879b6–880–d7). The prelude to this part of the law recalls Socrates' solution to the problem posed by incest in his fully communized city (*Repub-*

lic 461c8–e2). Here, anyone twenty years older than another, who is to believe that he or she could possibly be his father or mother, has a certain right to beat the younger with impunity, in the expectation that he will quietly submit, while the other calculates that the same privilege is in store for him when he too gets to be that old (879c2–5; cf. Aristophanes *Clouds* 1331–1438).[23] The right of wrong could not be more sharply expressed. That a pattern of right has to be invoked to justify it, as if the city could duplicate cosmic retribution on its own, illustrates how the law relieves the courts of having any need for exact knowledge of the soul, and what a strain a judge with such knowledge would be under as he tried to make his sentence fit the circumstances. It would be better in a way for no one to know and to let the law keep the injustices it cannot extirpate within certain limits.

23. The obdurate bachelor loses this privilege (774b4–c2); his punishment of the young is automatically an injustice, regardless of whether he was in the right or not. He can never get even.

THEOLOGY

I ATHEISM

The Stranger proceeds from violence to insolence by way of a summary.
Its five kinds are listed in order of seriousness: desecration of shrines,
public or private, denigration of parents, disrespect to magistrates or fellow citizens. The Stranger then goes back to the beginning of the ninth
book: "It has been stated in general what one must suffer if there is violent and secret temple robbery; but in the case of everything that expresses insolence about gods, whether in speech or deed, one must state,
after the usual piece of advice, what one must suffer" (885a7–b4). The
separation of the holy from the divine is now explicit.[1] It can be expressed
in general either by the meaning to be assigned to the assertion of the
superiority of the separation of body and soul to any union or by the
difference between human self-contempt, which is at the core of what we
may call "Egyptian," and the contempt for the human race that Megillus
ascribed to the Stranger—φαῦλον carries this double sense throughout the
Laws—and it now shows up in particular in the legislation at the end of
book 10. The death penalty is exacted for a first offense in only two cases:
either the atheist sets himself up as a soothsayer and offers private initiations, or one of the unholy performs unauthorized sacrifices in private or
public shrines (908c6–d7; 910c6–e1). Anyone, in short, whose contraven-

---

1. This distinction first shows up in the section on hunting. The courage that is
"divine" in the praise of hunting confers in the law an inviolability on the hunters
themselves, in crossing property lines, which makes them "sacred" (824a9–12). The
difficulty in maintaining the distinction emerges plainly if one considers provisions
of the ninth book. That the belief in lawfully established gods, as the Stranger says,
would absolutely prevent any impious deed (885b4–6), does not square with the prose-
cution for impiety if, for example, a couple do not separate after one of them has
killed a son or daughter in anger (868c5–d6; cf. 868e6–869a2). Whether the songwriter
who is guilty of impiety confirms even marginally the Stranger's assertion is equally
doubtful (799b4–8). In the tenth book only Clinias uses the word ὅσιος (891a6, 898c6,
903a5); the Stranger uses ἅγιος, ἀνόσιος, ἀνοσίως, and ἀνοσιουργέω each once (904e1
[cf. 909e1]; 905b4; 907a8; 910c2).

tion of the theology intrudes into the realm of religion is punished; otherwise, there are various forms of correction or admonition. The theology indeed has so little bearing on impiety that its basic teachings are the preserve of the highest magistrates and are not expected of everyone else who practices the popular virtues (967d4–968a4).[2] They are to be forgiven if they go along with the solemn utterance (φήμη) of the laws (966c4–6; cf. 624b2).

The tenth book might thus seem both out of place and much too long. The Stranger's cosmology surely should be put before the nocturnal council as a problem they are to solve along with the unity of virtue, to which it seems not unrelated, and not made the prelude to the criminal law on sacrilege. The puzzle deepens if one takes the Stranger's word for it that Homeric and Hesiodic poetry, let alone explicitly atheistic writings, have not yet infected Sparta and Crete (886a8–e5). Clinias had no idea there were any nonbelievers anywhere, and thinks the cosmic order and the universal belief that there are gods dispenses with the need for any argument (885c7–886a5). The Stranger, then, goes out of his way to import an alien way of thinking into a Dorian city. He repeats within the context of legislation what he had done as a prelude to legislation when he induced Clinias and Megillus to discuss Dionysia and the symposium in speech. His argument had been that a training in resistance to pain did not prepare one for holding out against the blandishments of pleasure. One had to get inured to pleasure through pleasure. Now he argues that the inoculation against atheism has to incorporate the virus of atheism. It is the closest the Stranger can come, it seems, within the law to making the drink of fear potable. Atheism is as insidious as pleasure; indeed, according to Clinias and Megillus, and initially the Stranger confirms it, atheism is rooted solely in pleasure and desire, which take control of souls and set them on the path to the impious life (886a9–b2; 888a2–4).

Clinias himself calls our attention to the discussion about drunkenness and music (890c4–6). He sees the connection only in terms of the length of the two discussions; but the link goes much deeper. The atheists maintain that everything comes into being by nature, art, or chance; and it is clear from the Stranger's examples that art primarily means the arts of imitation (887c6–d4). These arts, they say, produce playthings (παιδιαί), which partake in truth to a very slight degree. The Stranger, then, in attempting to refute them, must show not only that soul has primacy over

---

2. Cf. V. Martin, "Sur la condemnation des athées par Platon au Xe livre des *Lois," Studia Philosophica* 11 (Basel 1951): 139 (on 966–967): "Il est à remarquer que dans la page à laquelle ce résumé est emprunté [966–8], le mot dieu ne figure pas."

body but music also has it over gymnastic, which the atheists say is
something serious because it shares its power with nature (889d4–6). The
argument of book 10 pulls into the law the argument of the first three
books of the *Laws*. It grounds the priority of music to gymnastic, which
was the dialogic relation of books 1 and 2 to book 3, through the real priority of soul to body. What gradually happened in the course of the second book, the separation of song from dance, and the emergence of the
gymnastic of the third book, which put the city in time, now has a basis
in the antecedent coming into being of soul. The Stranger thus pulls off
what seemed to be impossible when he suggested it at the end of book 4.
The paradigmatic legislation for a city in speech would at the same time
be a test of the argument he had already developed. The symposium in
speech of book 1, which served the political art, had its legislative counterpart in the analysis of choral music in book 2. It established the relation between θεωρία and παιδεία. This relation has its simulacrum in
book 10. It lies between the political art and legal punishment (δίκη). The
primacy of soul makes it possible to argue for a rational political art,
and the priority of soul makes it possible to go beyond the arbitrary in
legislation. What book 10 cannot do, and this is decisive for the limited
translatability of the prelude of the *Laws* into a prelude of law, is to preserve the disorderly order of the symposium in speech in a cosmic setting. Dionysus has to be sacrificed to the gods of law and order. The lawful
equivalent to the sobering of Clinias through intoxication is the establishment of a detox center (σωφρονιστήριον) for the curable.

One of the more peculiar theses of book 10 is not that the soul is
something nonderivative and has primacy over body—its rule of body
warrants the political art—but that it has a priority in becoming as well.
This latter thesis seems to be a requirement of the genetic structure of
law, while the former suffices for the eidetic structure of the good. Much
of the difficulty of book 10 has to do with its collapse of these two structures. The collapse is all in favor of the temporality of the genetic structure and against the atemporality of the eidetic. Being, with no admixture
of becoming, characterized the eightfold good; becoming, with a single
mention of being, characterized the beautiful and the just in the genetic
structure of law. In his theology, the Stranger speaks of the indestructible
but not eternal being of body and soul once it has become (ἀνώλεθρον ὂν
γενόμενον, ἀλλ᾽ οὐκ αἰώνιον, ψυχὴν καὶ σῶμα), just as are the gods according
to law (904a8–b1). The Stranger's first attempt at this kind of fusion had
occurred when he had replaced the divine of the eidetic structure of the
good with the gods of his first prelude within the law. In the first part of
that prelude, gods had been by themselves, and soul was placed second

as the most divine of possessions after gods (726a2–3). God himself had been characterized in a double way. Insofar as he held the beginning, middle, and end of all beings, man was to be just and obey god; insofar as he was the measure of all things, man was to be moderate and imitate god (715e7–d4). In the prelude, sacrifice and burial seemed to be the practices most in accordance with those virtues; in the theology, it is finally admitted that neither justice nor moderation depends on belief (980b4–c6), and the holy has lost all connection with the divine.

In one respect, however, the sequence of books 9 and 10 does echo the first prelude to the law. There, in a sentence that syntactically put things backward, the chthonic gods were in first place while they were said to be second in honor, and the Olympian gods were never assigned their primary position while they were spoken of as first (717a6–b2). Hades was essential in the form of stories and practices for the criminal law. Whether burial was to be granted and in what form, and how future punishments awaited some in Hades, were parts of the prelude and the law in book 9. The gods above were invoked once (881a1). Now the primacy of soul brings the gods of heaven along with it, and the sun is cited as a paradigm for all the rest of the stars and planets (898d6–9). Hades now belongs to "the so-called below of places" (904d1–2), for in a spherical universe there is no up or down. The cosmology of book 10 turns the topsy-turviness of the law right side up.

The theme of the ninth book had been the relation between anger and desire; the theme of the tenth is mind. It thus seems as if the structure of the soul in its three parts has its counterpart in the relation between the two books, with the tyranny of anger and pleasure dividing the two kinds of homicide between them, and the conceit of wisdom, in its most extreme form of materialistic atheism, getting its refutation now (886b7–8). This straightforward plan gets complicated through the anger that has to be put under control if there is to be any discussion of atheism—it recalls the indignation the sight of authorized drunkenness aroused in Megillus—and through the initial assumption that hedonism is at the heart of atheism (887c7–d2; 888a2–6). The craziness that pleasure and anger equally induce is the obstacle to a gentle conversation about gods. It thus looks as if the criminal law, in being so easy on anger and harsh on desire, had been blind to the alliance it surreptitiously formed with anger; but now mind is going to be fully in charge and not let indignation spoil its chances of making the young see reason. Clinias is shocked—shocked—to hear that impiety leads the young to believe that the right life according to nature is in truth a life in which one holds the upper hand over everyone else and is not a slave to others according to law (890a5–b2); but this had been Clinias's own viewpoint in its political form—freedom and empire—that he had deduced from his experience of the law itself (626b2–4), and he had stated later that the most pleasant life was the best life and wholly separate from justice. There seems to be a perfect fit between the nature of the city and atheism. Just as body is first for the city, and the Stranger himself had argued that mind and thought were never at the beginning of either animal or city, so it is for the materialists; and just as the city believes there are no limits to its expansion, so the atheists believe the constraints of the law are against the natural un-boundedness of man's desires. On this level, book 10 matches themati-cally the beginning of the *Laws:* Clinias comes face-to-face with himself and fails to know himself. Rather than the Stranger's argument being directed against an alien importation, it is needed to counteract the na-tive growths of the city and its divine law.

There are three stages in the argument of book 10. The first argues for the priority of soul, the second for the natural order of the cosmos, and the third for particular providence. The link between any two of the arguments seems extraordinarily weak. They would be strengthened per-haps if the first became the primacy of soul, the second the disorderly order of thinking, and the third the indifference of the gods to vulgar justice. These corrections, which are hinted at as the arguments develop, would have the effect of reproducing entirely within the law the prelude to the law, or of separating entirely the eidetic structure of the good from the genetic structure of law, and thus simultaneously casting legislation adrift from the political art and ruining the primary purpose the theology is meant to serve: to minimize the effect that punishment must have in turning the relation of soul and body inside out.

2 SOUL AND BODY

The prelude of which book 10 mostly consists is in one sense a part of the education of the young and belongs to the outline of the mathematical cosmology put towards the end of book 7; but in another sense it is like most other preludes a postlude, for it only has to be spoken after the beliefs have in fact not taken, though the young are supposed to have taken them in with their mothers' milk and had them confirmed in the ceremonies of a public and private kind throughout their life.[3] This pre-

---

3. The Stranger inserts a kind of logos (λόγος οἷος) between the prelude and the law (907d4–6); this is the real prelude to the law.

lude begins as an exhortation to philosophy, in which the Stranger asks a young man, with whom he imagines he is conversing, to postpone his atheism and examine whether the dogma about the gods is or is not the case, and in the meantime not dare to commit any impiety about the gods (888c1–3). He is to refrain from impiety about the gods while he does not know not only whether there are gods but also what the gods are. He is to obey the law and question it: the Stranger extends to the young the privilege Dorian law accorded the old. The young have the assurance of the Stranger that no one who while young was a strict atheist ever stayed that way (888c1–3). The Stranger's addressee reminds one of Theaetetus, who confesses that he has often been in doubt, perhaps on account of his age, whether there is only the randomness of nature or nature generates everything with the help of logos and divine science direct from god, and the Eleatic Stranger assures him that his nature will advance him, without any speeches from him, towards that position which Theaetetus discerned in the Stranger's face (*Sophist* 265c7–e2). The Eleatic Stranger further remarks that had he believed Theaetetus would come to hold other opinions later, he would now be trying to gain his agreement "by means of an argument coupled with compulsory persuasion." The Athenian Stranger seems to be composing a speech for a Theaetetus who would turn out otherwise. He certainly allows for the possibility that someone without Theaetetus's nature would find the Eleatic Stranger's arguments unconvincing. One cannot be more generous than that (cf. 899c2–d1).

There are three kinds of irreligion: disbelief that gods are, belief that they are but do not concern themselves with human beings, or that they do care but it is easy to dissuade them from strict justice (885b4–9). The Stranger is to prove that the gods are perfect and just, or they are beautiful and just (cf. 900e4–8). His theology is to put back together what the criminal law had burst asunder, and restore to the genetic structure of law the causal unity of its two principles. Socrates' theology was different; he wanted Adimantus to accept the premise that the gods were good and beautiful, but neither his argument nor his city allowed the gods to be just. Socrates did not have to prove to Adimantus the existence of the gods, for they were founding a city which needed Socrates' two postulates about the gods, so that he could have a free hand to design the city he wants without any interference from gods and could censor whatever lines of the poets did not suit his purpose. The Stranger, however, is forced to resolve a dilemma he brought upon himself. His opponents quiz him with banter and make fun of him (προσπαίζοντες), for they pick up on his own experience of the insignificance of human things and challenge him to be serious and follow his own model of persuasive prelude and threatening law. The Stranger is being forced to step beyond the law in order to defend the law (cf. 891d9–e3). He has never before had to give anything remotely resembling a proof of existence, and the gods more than anything else in the city exemplify what it means to be by law.

The irreligious want the Stranger to live up to his purported gentleness and not be savage (885e1–2). They thus bring out into the open what had been lurking in the criminal law, that the laws are savage in their domination of the savagery of lawless man. Those who bring this charge are not the atheists but the unjust—"We do not turn to not doing the not-just things" (885d7)[4]—who hide behind the atheists and pretend they would stop being unjust if the Stranger convinced them that they could not bribe the gods. They appeal to the assurances of the best poets, rhetoricians, soothsayers, and priests that the gods are not as savage as the laws but can be appeased. The insincerity of their appeal, however, does not make the Stranger's task any easier. The gods of the poets bring some relief to the unforgiving law (cf. 921a1–4). Are you going to deprive the city of this consolation, they ask the Stranger, and rigorously prove that the exaction of right is truly as harsh as the law wants it to be, even though you have neither proved the existence of natural right nor shown the conformity of law with it? Indeed, they could argue, law is incompatible with natural right, since the one needs enforcement and the other carries automatic penalties. Did not a sacred law once suspend a city's law and keep Socrates alive for some time after the city had consigned him to immediate execution? Did he not then write a hymn to Apollo in thanksgiving and question whether nonphilosophic music should have been his life's calling? The poets, they say, have the power of rhetoric on their side, even if the Stranger might be superior in point of truth. They doubt whether he can usurp entirely the poets' role and persuade them to face the music.

One can gauge the difficulty of the task the Stranger has set for himself if one considers that Clinias, who believes the true speech about the gods to be easy, still cannot hold together the beautiful order of the visible cosmos with the gods who support justice and are behind his appeal to the belief in gods among all Greeks and barbarians (cf.902b4–6).[5] The

4. The triple negative seems to imply that, though not devoted to justice, they do not automatically turn to injustice, but when the possibility of acting unjustly comes up they do not turn away.

5. The sacred precinct in which the city assembles to elect the three commissioners of review belongs jointly to the Sun and Apollo, but it is to the god [singular] that they are to show the elected (945e4–946a1; cf. b7–c1). Ancient laws about the

Stranger will later bridge this gap by making public injustice into a metaphor for visible disorder (906c2–6); but now he alludes to this tension in his account of old writings, in which "the first nature of the sky and everything else" comes to be first and shortly afterwards a theogony is described (886c2–4). In narration at least, the providential order of right follows on the cosmological order, and the cosmological order itself shows not a trace of right, but, as Pindar says, it justifies the most violent.[6] The Stranger limits his criticism of the ancients to their not promoting the honor and care of parents: Euthyphro's abuse of the poets, so that he can prosecute his father, does not pose a serious threat to the law. The reason for the Stranger's mild strictures on the ancients is not just that he reveres the ancestral more than antiquity did, but he has to admit that not only do the young experience a difference between sun and moon, on whose risings and settings they hear the prayers and see the obeisances of their parents, and the gods in whose sights they take the greatest pleasure (887d2–e4), but his own presentation carries the same trace of this duality as do Clinias's proof and the ancients' stories. This duality in his own case is soul and mind. Soul gives him a certain kind of motion and mind an order, but in making soul first he must in his narration at least make mind subsequent, and soul without mind seems more disorderly than any motion of body.

The moderns, on the other hand, are responsible for evils, for the young whom they have won over assert that the sun is not a god or divine, but merely stone and earth, incapable of showing concern for human things, but this truth has been crusted all over with speeches designed for persuasion (886c4–e2). The Stranger leads us to expect that he will prove that the sun is a god after he has shown what a god is. He does neither. The Stranger gives an account of the being of soul, but he gives no account of either the being of god or the causality of soul. The causality of soul belongs to the being of soul, but the Stranger does not know how a being that moves itself can move bodies (898d9–899a4). For all he knows, the moderns may be right, and the sun is nothing but a lifeless body,

---

gods, the Stranger says, have been laid down by all in a double way (930e7–931a4; cf. *Timaeus* 40d6–41a5). Timaeus's first account of the cosmos does not allow for particular providence, his second allows for it once (*Timaeus* 90e7–91a4); Critias, however, can build in periodic cleansing of the earth precisely because he deals with Olympian gods, but the price he pays for it is the destabilization of the cosmic order (*Timaeus* 22d1–23b3).

6. One may compare Timaeus's narrative order, where the making of body precedes and that of soul follows, for which he apologizes and claims it is due to his participation in the random (*Timaeus* 34b10–35a1).

which soul, stripped of body, moves in an extraordinarily marvelous way, or else it moves it from within or from without through another body or bodies (cf. *Phaedrus* 246c6–d2). The mysteriousness of the agency of soul cannot but remind us of Socrates' failure on the last day of his life to explain the causality of the "ideas" (*Phaedo* 100d3–7). This parallelism is all the more striking because the Stranger's soul that moves itself operates without the "ideas." It is constantly becoming by itself, for there are no beings that inform it. Socrates turned to the ideas as a second sailing because he could not figure out a teleological physics; the Stranger seems to promise us a first sailing and then abandons ship.

In order to justify speaking at length about gods, and not simply dismiss the atheists—after all, as legislator, he can lay down whatever he wants (890b5–c5)—the Stranger imagines a situation, no less strange than funny, in which he is in the dock and has to defend himself before a jury of the impious, who have listened to a prosecutor charging him with the dreadful crime of legislating "as if there are gods" or "that there are gods" (886e6–887a1). Socrates' trial is inverted. The young are already corrupt and the Stranger is accused of bringing old gods into the city. The Stranger's figure points two ways. Clinias sees only one of them. What he does not foresee is that the Stranger's argument will establish gods at the expense of the sacred and undermine what the law should be, the common opinion of the city. These old gods, moreover, have more in common with the barbarian gods than with the Olympian gods of Greece. They are the culmination of the Stranger's rebarbarization of the city for the sake of setting it on sound foundations. Clinias is all for their helping out the ancient law (890c4), and since no one is on their tail they can mount a lengthy defense (887b1–c4). This defense, he believes, would be the best and most beautiful prelude on behalf of all the laws. It would replace, he implies, both the prelude on music and gymnastic and the prelude the Stranger had delivered in two parts to all the assembled citizens in book 4 and at the beginning of book 5, and whose first part in particular was a prelude only in retrospect (733d6–8). Clinias's proposal carries the same implication with it as Socrates' introduction of philosophy had in the fifth book of the *Republic*. The discovery of what justice is through the construction of the best city would give way, once philosophy knew what the just, the good, and the beautiful are, to a straight deduction from the "ideas" to a code of laws (*Republic* 484c6–d3). The way to the principles would have led to a way from the principles, and the philosopher-king could descend into the Cave and bypass the way of the *Republic* itself.[7]

7. A conspicuous difference between the *Republic* and *Laws* consists in Socra-

Likewise, Clinias wants to get rid of the way that led to the point that he could conceive of getting rid of the way. That way can be characterized, in light of book 10, as the ascent from the gods of Crete and Sparta through the god of drunkenness to cosmic gods.[8] The symposium in speech led the way; it had the same function as the best city in speech in the *Republic*. The heady draft of understanding that Clinias drank has made him forget himself. He wants to do it all over again from the top down. His proposed revision of the *Laws* is never carried out. The primacy of soul the Stranger establishes puts the second part of his own prelude first and certainly gives the impression that the gods are nothing but souls, but just as Socrates failed to deduce one single law from the "ideas," so nothing evidently comes of the gods by way of laws. The Stranger had inserted the marriage law between the first and second parts of his prelude; and one could certainly expect that the definition of soul as the first genesis could stand at the top of a reformulated prelude about procreation (cf. 720e11–721a4). Nothing of the sort happens or can happen. Sexual generation and soul as becoming have nothing in common; and this is all the more surprising if one considers that Socrates had once connected self-moving soul with *erōs*. Socratic *erōs* seems to haunt the Stranger. It hovered in the background of his gingerly treatment of *erōs* in the eighth book, where he confessed that his educational reform could not meet the sudden intrusion of *erōs* into the life of adolescents; and this failure led in turn to the criminal law, which meted out much harsher penalties to desire than to anger; and now, though the Stranger abbreviates the argument of the *Phaedrus*, in every one of his lists of the soul's attributes, *erōs* and *epithumia* are conspicuous by their absence (897a1–3; cf. 688b1–4).[9]

Murderous anger, if it were not premeditated, imaged the involuntary. We would now like to know whether the sentence of two years in exile

---

tes' failure to attach a cosmology to his ontology, so that one could determine what relation obtains between the sun, on the one hand, as the cause of becoming and becoming visible, and the good, on the other, as the cause of what is and is knowable, whereas the Stranger supplies a cosmology without the cosmos of the "ideas." In light of the Stranger's cosmological psychology, one can say that Socrates' failure is due to the constraint he is under not to give a precise account of soul (*Republic* 435c9–d5; cf. *Timaeus* 89d7–e3).

8. Book 10 could make one wonder whether the god to whom the Stranger refers at 637a7 as the god to whom their logos is to arrive is neither Dionysus nor Zeus, especially if one takes into account the Stranger's failure to handle the being of the gods.

9. In this list, all the motions of soul are verbs, all the motions of body are substantives: the transition between them is made by participles.

still holds if one gets angry enough to kill someone who is spouting atheistic talk. Murderous desire, in any case, was deliberate and could not be
reckoned as involuntary in any form. Now, however, atheism is not only
the extreme form of δοξοσοφία but its proponents adopt it in order to
pursue pleasure. One might suppose that in the young atheism and sexual awakening go together. If the disproof of atheism were as easy as Clinias believes it is, the chastisement of pleasure could be safely left to the
alliance of indignation with law; but if the thesis of the atheists cannot
be so overturned, and one cannot administer a beating to them while
saying, "You ought to know better," then the Stranger, in admitting that
hedonism can make a strong alliance with atheism—Clinias showed that
the traditional gods equally supported hedonism—has pushed the Socratic thesis into a domain where the identification of unbridled pleasure
with injustice seemed secure. Insolence (ὕβρις), which is by definition the
opposite of moderation, and thus a natural successor to outrage (αἰκία)
within the confines of the criminal law, gets elevated to being the antago-
nist to the Stranger's own enterprise. His σωφροσύνη, which allowed him
to descend and pull Clinias and Megillus up towards him, is being challenged by a doctrine that has no patience with the sober views the city
needs and the law fosters. That there is nothing but body and motion is
a thesis that, if true, would cancel the first two books of the Laws, leave
the third book as the true beginning of political science, and validate
Clinias's belief that freedom and empire suffice to explain political life
and law. The Stranger is now not just incorporating the prelude of the
first three books into the law, he is also giving an account of that prelude.
He is defending himself.

The Stranger divides the atheistic thesis into two parts (888e4–889e1;
889e4–890a9). The first part gives the general principles, the second the
political consequences. Nature, chance, and art are causes and principles
of all the things (πράγματα) that are becoming, became, and will become.
Nature and chance produce the biggest and most beautiful pieces, art the
smaller. Art contrives to take over the genesis of the big and first deeds
and remold them. Fire, water, earth, and air are by nature and chance.
They are the beings which are always, but there is no reason why there
should be just these four. As remnants of the originally unformed state,
they alone show themselves to perception; when they are in combination
and disguise they are bodies. These bodies come to be at random through
haphazard coincidences of the elements that fit in some appropriate way.
As the Stranger presents it, elements and motion are not necessarily together. Motion, space, and time are assumed but not explained. Motion
is perpetual, and though it is a random universe there is no entropy. The

present state of the universe came to be in a finite time, but there is infinite time both before and after when possibly no bodies ever came together or ever will come to be. All of life, whether of plants or animals, came to be in this time by chance. Their cause was neither mind nor any god. Art came to be afterwards; it is mortal and came out of mortal things. The unchanging understanding of everything is not grounded in the eternal intelligibility of anything. Their understanding too should have the characteristic of art: a plaything (παιδιά) with very little participation in truth, but rather a phantom image (εἴδωλον) of its maker. Its proponents do not draw this conclusion and leave themselves entirely outside of their account (cf. 967b6–c2). How the elements disclosed that they were the elements is not a problem for them; rather, they distinguish between the arts of painting and music, which stand apart from nature, and the arts of medicine, farming, and gymnastic, which share their power with nature. This distinction between the primacy of body and the posteriority of soul allows them to separate the political art from legislation: the former has a small share in nature but a lot in art (cf.714c4–6), while the latter is wholly unnatural, or totally artificial, "and its premises are not true."[10]

Gods, they say, are by art and peculiar laws, and they are different in whatever different way, in accordance with a mutual agreement, they get established by law. The beautiful things are by nature, but they are not the same as those that are beautiful by law; the just things, on the other hand, are not by nature, but they are subject to continuous dispute and alteration. The just things retain their authority for as long as they are posited; and that which establishes the just is the victory of violence. The young, who imbibe this teaching, conclude that to have the upper hand over everyone else is to live the life according to nature. We are now back at the beginning of the Laws. The Stranger outlines a teaching that gives theoretical support to the insight into the nature of things that Clinias gained experientially through the law. Clinias, however, is now superior to his experience, and wants the Stranger to support the ancient law by reason (λόγος)—there are gods (cf. 891e1–2)—and come to the rescue of law itself and art, "that they are by nature or not inferior to nature,

10. If one considers the context in which the Stranger says that men θαύματα ὄντες τὸ πολύ, σμικρὰ δὲ ἀληθείας ἄττα μετέχοντες (804b3–4), and that in which his opponents say that men have generated παιδιάς τινας, ἀληθείας οὐ σφόδρα μετεχούσας (889d1–2), the two sides are not far apart. The difference seems to be this: for the one εἴδωλα are solely of man's own making, for the other εἴδωλα are by nature and, in showing up to the highest degree in human speech and opinion, give one an access to the truth.

provided they are the offspring of mind in accordance with right reason" (890d4–7). Clinias separates the proof of the being of the gods from the proof of the naturalness of law and art. The latter, he suspects, can be shown to come to be by mind, but the gods simply are and do not come to be. Inasmuch as the Stranger assumes that there is nothing that does not come to be, and argues that soul was the first to become, he disappoints Clinias.

Neither the difficulty nor the length of the proof dismays Clinias. He and Megillus believe that "the injunctions of laws [about laws], laid down in writings, will offer a test [proof] for all time, since they are absolutely stationary, and one must not be afraid, regardless of whether they are hard or long: if they are hard at first hearing, whoever has trouble understanding them will be able to go back to them again and again and study them; and if they are long, it makes no difference provided they are beneficial" (890e4–891a7). Everything for which Socrates in the *Phaedrus* criticized writing Clinias counts in its favor. The authority of the law, he believes, will force the slow learner to study it until he understands it, and he will not dismiss it out of hand as gibberish. Its immobility, in imitation of that which is always, will guarantee that it will always be there to be consulted, despite its incapacity to answer any question the perplexed put to it. Clinias pictures a situation in which of necessity divergent interpretations will develop around an authoritative but enigmatic text. There is as yet no nocturnal council to cut off debate and restrict its study. It seems not to bother Clinias that he first heard of the atheistic account just a moment ago, any more than that everyone in the city will first hear of it from the law, and it is far easier to understand—he had no trouble with it—than its refutation. The Stranger, on the other hand, justifies the attempt to refute atheism by the virtually universal spread of the speeches he has summarized. The greatest laws are being corrupted by bad men, and no one can more fittingly restore them than the legislator (891b1–6). In retrospect, this absurd exaggeration seems to contain a prediction: there will be a successor to the religion of Greece whose theology will borrow its principles from him (cf. 948d1–3). If we do not look backward, the Stranger must at least have foreseen that (οὐ) νομίζομεν εἶναι will loom larger than (οὐ) νομίζομεν, or that the issue of belief and disbelief will take precedence over whether or not certain lawful practices are performed.[11] Socrates' trial would be the watershed, for on the question

11. The Stranger calls attention to this difference when he formulates the principle of piety with εἶναι (θεοὺς ἡγούμενος εἶναι . . . 885 b4), and the spokesmen for impiety without (ἡμῶν οἱ μὲν τὸ παράπαν θεοὺς οὐδαμῶς νομίζομεν, 885c7); cf. *Apology of*

of τὰ νόμιμα, Socrates could not be faulted (cf. Xenophon *Memorabilia* 1.1.2). This shift seems to be due to philosophy. Philosophy forces the city to confront being as a question; but one wonders whether the city does not resist such a confrontation. Otherwise, *Antigone* would have long ago been laughed off the stage. The Stranger seems also to point to its unlikelihood. His theology makes becoming primary, and though each thing can be conceived of in three ways—its being (οὐσία), the logos of the being, and its name—the Stranger says there are only two questions connected with them, the logos and the name. The philosophic question, What is being? is missing. The Stranger's theology is philosophy cut down to size.

Of the three terms that characterize the doctrine the Stranger opposes, art is that in light of which the other two are to be understood. They are concealed negatives: what happens by nature or by chance happens by whatever art is not. Causality looks to art as its model (cf. Aristotle *Metaphysics* 981a5–28). Now the perfection of art depends on the divisibility of art, and its divisibility in turn depends on the city. Socrates' true city is the city of arts. The city as the locus of art caters at first to the satisfaction of the needs of the body; but as the city expands or the arts develop, the imaginary desires find their satisfaction in the secondary arts of adornment and entertainment. Pleasure becomes the internal aim of the city as imperialism becomes its external motive. The freedom and greatness of the city are never out of step for long with the hedonism of the city. There is, then, a curious agreement between the imperialistic city of art and materialism. It is therefore conceivable that such a teaching would sponsor simultaneously the cancellation of religion and the total technologizing of the city; and the culmination of these twin drives would be the artful making of man himself. That πανουργία, armed with a crude arithmetic, has so far resulted only in the love of money (747c2–6), does not mean that it cannot become "theoretical," supply Empedoclean physics with what it needs to ally itself with the city, and prove literally true—"the making of everything."[12] The loss of freedom that follows in the wake of unchecked imperialism is the penultimate loss;

Socrates 26b4–d5, where Socrates first brings in νομίζειν εἶναι, and Meletus at first, in accordance with the charge, uses νομίζειν by itself; likewise, in the *Laws*, the atheists use νομίζομεν without εἶναι (886c7), Clinias with (886a5). Μὴ νομίζοντι θεοὺς εἶναι occurs at 908b4 (cf. 909b1). See further W. Fahr, θεοὺς νομίζειν: *Zum Problem der Anfänge des Atheismus bei den Griechen, Spudasamata* 26 (Hildesheim 1969): 158–168.

12. In Sophocles' *Antigone* 295–301, Creon brings up the πανουργία that the love of money breeds just before the Chorus sing of the unlimited uncanniness of man, who is a neuter "this" (τοῦτο), and over against which there stands Antigone alone.

the final loss occurs if it combines with unchecked technology (cf. 687a2–b2). Socrates had hinted at this as the only possible "real" solution to the self-contradictions in the structure of his own best city in speech. The self-contradiction would then dissolve politically at the expense of the elimination of man, for whom the solution was initially sought. It therefore looks as if the potential damage this solution poses to man would make it urgent to retard or divert it. Writing is the only means available for such an effort. The representation of philosophy thus becomes a necessity. The wisdom of the poets, which they conceal behind their representations, does not suffice to meet this emergency. Philosophy must come forward. One no longer has any other choice than to write up the speeches of Socrates. The *Laws* complements the *Phaedrus*.

The Stranger refocuses the issue when he first regards it as likely (ἔοικεν) and then as being really and truly (ὄντως) the case that those who say the four elements are the first of all things mean that soul is later and comes out of them (891c1–5). Soul is his substitution for their art (cf. 889c6–7). This substitution recalls Socrates' shift from art to soul when he moves from the city of arts to the education in opinion of the guardians. Here, the Stranger inserts a missing step in the argument. The lifeless products of art cannot be before there is life. As the cause of generation and corruption, soul is prior to mortal art; it is certainly prior to the speeches that produced the soul of the impious (891e5–7).[13] In order to be somewhat consistent, the Stranger implies, they would have to say that nature showed the way to this knowledge at least as much as body contributed to gymnastic and medicine. Self-forgetfulness is at the center of δοξοσοφία. It is prior to the insolence of the young. The crucial error, according to the Stranger, concerns in particular the genesis of soul, that it is first, came into being prior to all bodies, and rules over their exchanges and transformations (892c2–7).[14] As the Stranger works out the argument, one might be inclined to identify the Stranger's soul or some version of it with Timaeus's place (χώρα), particularly since the Stranger's kinematics requires place (893c1–2). Timaeus, to be sure, makes place prior to the elements, but the Stranger has no demiurge to help him out, and Ti-

---

13. F. Solmsen, "Textprobleme im zehnten Buch der Platonischen Nomoi," in *Studien zur Textgeschichte und Textkritik* (Köln und Opladen 1959), 266, thought ψυχήν (891e7) an intrusion that ousted δόξαν or the like; but the Stranger's entire argument turns precisely on this point, that the atheists, in order to be consistent, would have to give a materialistic account of logos as a causal agent for soul.

14. If one takes the Stranger strictly, soul is posterior to the elements, which are always and prior to bodies; but in his reformulation, soul is once again prior to the elements as well (892c2–5).

maeus, when he speaks of the demiurge, does not speak of place, and when he speaks of place, does not speak of the demiurge. Timaeus admits that his account is a myth, however likely, and it is the impossibility of making demiurge and place consistent that condemns it to be a story. The Stranger is not as forthright, though he too speaks of persuasiveness rather than of demonstration. The barrier to the technologizing of political man is necessarily weak in the face of the inevitability of the self-ignorance of art.

There are three peculiarities in the Stranger's argument. The first is that, though the Stranger insists that the primacy of soul entails the priority of soul, he never speaks of time (χρόνος) throughout his argument. There is older and younger, before and after, and first and second, but there is no time. Inasmuch as there is no measurable interval between one event and another, the Stranger's psychology can never become a physics.[15] The second peculiarity is that the Stranger, when he converses with himself, does not begin with the distinction between that which moves itself and others and that which can move others but never itself, but rather with a noncausal list of motions, the last two of which are genesis and corruption. A kinematics precedes a dynamics and leads apparently to the Stranger's miscounting the number of motions. He says there are ten when they are by any unforced count eleven. The Stranger talks to himself and speaks enigmatically. He puts a riddle at the heart of the proof which Clinias imagines will stay at rest forever. The third peculiarity is that the mistake about soul, the Stranger says, was the source of the mistake "about the real and true being of gods" (περὶ θεῶν τῆς ὄντως οὐσίας), but he never fully makes up for that mistake with his own account of the being of the gods (891e8–9). He asserts that souls with complete virtue are gods, but he never shows that such souls are, any more than that souls with complete vice can be, and he admits he does not know how they are and are causes (899b4–8).

The Stranger does not make it clear when he first lists five congeners of soul—opinion, care, mind, art, and law—whether they belong to it as soft and hard and heavy and light belong to bodies (892b3–8); but his second list implies that false opinion, neglect, mindlessness, artlessness,

---

15. Time without measure is typical of myths, whose introductory phrases— "Once upon a time" or "Long, long ago"—are meant to thwart the possibility of counting backwards to their place on a single time line (cf. *Timaeus* 22a4–b3). Myth is the image of chaos, when no temporal arrangement of events is possible: all time is local. In rationalizing Greek myths, the Persian λόγιοι, who start off Herodotus's *Inquiries*, put Io, Europa, Medea, and Helen in an ordered sequence that is dictated by the issue of right (1.1–4).

and lawlessness are equally characteristic of soul and are not attributes of body (896c8–897d2). Soul is neutral to the virtue and vice of soul. It is as much without structure as it is without parts, for either would deprive it of self-motion. At exactly this point, the Stranger ceases to be dialogic and divides himself in two. He represents himself as himself and another. The other calls him "Stranger"—someone he does not know—but he never addresses the other. The Stranger indulges in a version of that art which his opponents said scarcely partook of truth, but generated phantom images of itself. He himself warns Clinias and Megillus that his self-dialogue is deliberately deceptive (892d2). We are being asked to consider whether thinking can in fact be a conversation of the soul with itself, which the poetic art could imitate, or it is doomed to be as self-contradictory as the paradox with which the *Laws* began—Clinias's claim that one could be superior or inferior to oneself. The mechanical view, that the agent of thinking programs the patient, and nothing comes out that did not go in, however much altered it may appear to be, would settle at once the question of the priority of soul. The Stranger represents this question, he does not answer it.

The Stranger introduces the argument about motion with an image of motion (892d6–893a7). The image implies that he is younger than either Clinias or Megillus but with greater experience and strength. His qualifications are apparently indebted to body and are not prior to it; if there is a strength of soul that antedates body it does not appear in any of the Stranger's lists (cf. 894d10). According to the conclusion the Stranger himself draws from the image, he is prepared to go through the entire argument by himself, until it is complete and he has shown that soul is prior to body. The Stranger does not live up to his engagement. His self-dialogue is over before he ever gets to self-motion. He likens that dialogue to a turbulent stream, which he has to cross over to get to the other side, where there will be a demonstration that the gods are. The logos may cause Clinias and Megillus so much dizziness that they will whirl around in darkness. The logos in itself combines rolling and sliding, the second and third of the Stranger's list of motions, and as it swirls along (παραφερό-μενος) effects an unstable rotation. One would not even dream of pressing the Stranger's image so hard were it not that he finds in rotation around a point a perfect image of mind, whereas his very divisions suggest that thinking more closely resembles disjunction (διάκρισις) and conjunction (σύγκρισις), the fourth and fifth motions in his own list (893e1–5). The Stranger's juxtaposition of image and self-dialogue looks like a true representation of the relation between soul and mind. How Clinias and Megillus may possibly experience the argument and how the Stranger and another readily part and pair represent a difference of the same order as that between the symposiasts and the symposiarch at the symposium in speech.

It is not at all clear why the Stranger needs his kinematics. If we took him at his word, kinematics alone, or rather his dialogue with himself about kinematics, would suffice to establish the priority of soul. As it is, the only use he makes of it is to find an image of mind in rotation around a point, and when he does so he gives another description of it (898a8–b2). He could surely have imported it later. As it is, rotation around a point is a mathematical construction and cannot characterize any body: the Stranger himself says it is an imitation of circles turned on a lathe or by a compass (898a3–5). The Stranger labels all possible bodily motions the ninth kind (894b8–c8). Kinematically, then, it does not count, for it is nothing but the set of all other motions (with the possible exception of the first) both apart and together under the aspect of causality. Accordingly, once the ninth motion becomes the second in the Stranger's reenumeration, the eleven motions become ten (894d8–e2). The cause of all motions now heads the list, the motions it causes are second (cf. 896b5–8), and rotation around a point, which headed the list, either comes in as the first of corporeal motions, or stands off by itself.

Apart from this difficulty, there is another. Granted that the kinematical list comprehends all corporeal motions, what is the kinematics of self-motion? Such a motion must be both ahead of itself and behind itself and thus reproduce within itself priority and posteriority. It must involve both a being apart and a being together simultaneously,

> Di sè facea a sè stesso lucerna,
> et eran due in uno et uno in due:
> com' esser può, quei sa chi sì governa,

and go far to explain why there is no mention of time. The definition of soul thus seems to image the truth of dialectical division and collection. The Stranger, in any case, has failed to combine his kinematics and dynamics smoothly.[16] Had he started with causality, his divisions would

---

16. The difference between kinematics and dynamics is crucial for understanding Timaeus's two accounts of elementary body, the first of which involves the transition from visibility to tangibility through geometric proportions, and the second of which concerns the relation of a fundamental structure to its phenomenal states of gas, vapor, and solid (Timaeus 31b4–c4; 49a7–c7). The first is kinematical, is phrased in terms of knowledge, and considers fire as the source of light; the second is dynamical, deals with causality, and considers fire as the cause of heat. The second account is

have been as follows: (1) that which does not move and does not move another (893b8); (2) that which moves another and does not move itself—this is Clinias's hope for the written law on gods; (3) that which moves itself and not another; (4) that which moves itself and moves another; (5) that which another moves and cannot move itself; (6) that which moves itself and others move. The Stranger might well have been able to prove that some of these cannot be and that others must be the same. The fourth and sixth, for example, might coincide in soul, regardless of whether what moves that which moves itself is another soul or body, for the effect in either case is experience.

The Stranger adds another argument when he is approaching the identification of self-motion with soul. He cites the problem of entropy, or the necessary difference between matter and energy over time, and calls it insoluble if all things were once together, or, one might add, if all things were once completely apart (895a6–b3); but he does not show that the antientropic principle must move itself. The antientropic principle is decisive for the Stranger's account because without it self-motion is just a possible kind of motion and does not get tied into existence otherwise. Antientropy allows the Stranger to bypass the issue of being (οὐσία), when he establishes the equivalence of the name soul with the logos self-motion; but he cannot thereby establish the priority of soul. The antientropic principle requires that it always be in some causal relation to body; it cannot withdraw and be by itself. Soul as self-moving motion would simply then be equivalent to any animal, which, we say, moves itself (895c1–13). The Stranger, however, requires that soul be first and capable of both withdrawal into itself and contact with another. It must be the sole cause of all the things that are, have been, and will be as well as of all their contraries (896a5–8). The soul is the cause of nonbeing. It is the ultimate ground for the ultimate terror: everything that is will vanish into nothing and all that will remain will be soul itself. Soul by itself is the drink of fear: it is without any ground for its own becoming (cf. Timaeus 28a4–6). Cut off from either antientropy or the providence of the gods, whether general or particular, soul imports the symposium in speech, either in its Dionysiac or Plutonian mode, into the law. It is no wonder that the Stranger did not want to take Clinias and Megillus across the river of argument before he had tried it by himself.

The Stranger forestalls the crisis of his own argument by taking it over again and answering his own question. This resumption of self-

_____

put as a problem, in which what "we see" is "as we imagine" (ὡς δοκοῦμεν) and "as it appears" (ὡς φαίνεται).

dialogue carries him over one crisis in counting and into another (896c5–897b5). Clinias agrees that soul is the cause of all good and bad, beautiful and ugly, just and unjust things (896d5–9).[17] The Stranger then asks whether it is one soul or more, and answers before either Clinias or Megillus can, that it is not less than two. It seems, however, that there must be at least three kinds of soul. Soul as self-motion and universal cause resembles the will; but there is also soul with the addition of mind—this looks like the alliance of θυμός (anger) with reason; and there is soul in association with folly (ἄνοια) that moves crazily and in disorder—this looks like desire (897d1)—and in its limitation on soul with mind the equivalent of Timaeus's space. If these three kinds are only two, then the soul the Stranger has defined does not exist and is soul only in speech. Soul in speech is soul that the good, however it is understood, has not informed. It would correspond to a definition of number—a multitude of ones—but there would be no number which was not either even or odd (895e1–3). Soul, then, despite itself, would belong to kinematics alone. If, on the other hand, it does exist, soul with mind and soul without mind must have come into being after the coming into being of soul in itself. When would that be? Were perfectly ordered soul always, the cosmos was always ordered, and body was never second; and if perfectly ordered soul came into being first, when did the completely disordered soul come into being?[18] If they came into being simultaneously, order and disorder were always together, and no appeal can be made to the appearance of order in the cosmos. Indeed, one wonders whether the two kinds of soul are also just in speech. There is a deathless battle, the Stranger later suggests, between the two kinds of soul, and the disordered soul has the upper hand (906a2–5; cf. Republic 379c2–7). The appearance of order, he implies, can coincide with the prevalence of evil, and good and disorder be together.

There is another consequence of the Stranger's argument that he does not work out. His kinematics, once it was tied in with being, implied that there was no motion of body, no matter how complex, that could not be analyzed into simple motions, and in this sense corporeal motion would never be in disarray. Truly random motion, which resists any anal-

---

17. Note how postpositive τε jams the ugly and the just things together, in accordance with the criminal law, over against the connective καί as the link between the first two pairs: τῶν τε ἀγαθῶν αἰτίαν εἶναι ψυχὴν καὶ τῶν κακῶν καὶ καλῶν καὶ αἰσχρῶν δικαίων τε καὶ ἀδίκων; cf. Timaeus 87d1–3. In the Sophist, Theaetetus comprehends under "the not beautiful" the ugly and the just (257d7–11).

18. If the soul is the first genesis, it must conform with the riddling definition of genesis, but whatever else it means it implies that there is no genesis without perceptible body (894a1–5; cf. 966d9–e2).

ysis, belongs to mindless soul (890b5–8). Chance can be understood only in terms of soul and belongs to nature as much as art does insofar as nature means the genesis of the first things (892c2–5). If, moreover, rotation around a single point is to be associated with mind, then all the other congeners of soul must have their own motions—vertigo was just one of them—the structure of which must be soul. Whatever the others are, they must in the case of perfectly ordered soul be different from and yet in consonance with the rotation of mind.[19] The mind boggles at the possibility that these motions may be unimaginable. The Stranger, in any case, when he asks which kind of soul is in control of heaven, adds virtue to the soul with mind, and he counts virtue and good sense (τὸ φρόνιμον) as two (847b7–c1).[20] If they are two (and it seems they would have to be if justice as it is ordinarily understood is going to be an attribute of the gods), the Stranger would have already settled the issue he is to hand over to the nocturnal council; and if, of these two excellences of soul, at least one could be without the other (in accordance with the genetic structure of law), soul would cease to be without parts, and the Stranger would have to give up his definition of soul as self-motion.

The Stranger's third intervention, when he jumps in to answer his own question, deals with the motion of mind (887d3–6). He despairs of giving a straight answer, looking directly at mind, as it were, but though he believes he can give an image of it—circular motion around a fixed point—he does not go on to prove that the movements of all the elements of heaven are also of the same kind. He himself had left it as a problem to be solved if a rational cosmology were to be taught in the city (822c7–9). He leaves the question open as to which soul guides the cosmos, and lets Clinias complete it in favor of mind:

> Now, then, it is no longer difficult to say expressly that, since soul, on the one hand, makes everything for us revolve, and, we have to state, on the other hand, that soul, whether it be the best or its con-

---

19. The description the Stranger's other gives of circular motion, in implying that it jumps from zero to a speed, which is always less (but not zero) than any speed one chooses, makes it absurd that it images the motion of mind (893c7–d5). It further checks the possibility of understanding the priority of soul without time as asserting that whatever point one chooses for the beginning of motion of body there is always a prior motion of soul, for the same holds for the motion of body.

20. A distinction between good sense and virtue first occurs as that between understanding and doing the serious and laughable things (816d5–e5; cf. 890b6–c3). The Stranger cannot make use of, however much he could use, Socrates' account in the *Philebus* of the relation between feelings and motions, for it was grounded in a proof that mind and the unlimited were together, and without mind there would be no disorder.

trary, makes the circuit of heaven revolve in caring for it and ordering
it—. (898c1–5)

In this surprising half-sentence, the Stranger admits that caring and ordering are not a preserve of mind, for otherwise the bad soul could not
be as likely a candidate as the good. Opinion, which the Stranger had
listed as the first congener of soul, must be either true or false (892b3;
897a2). The Stranger, moreover, fails to supply a crucial step: he does not
and cannot show that his image of the motion of mind is mind's own
imaging of its motion. The Stranger could not answer the question
whether the true motion of heaven is like the true motion of mind; he
asked instead whether the true motion of heaven is like the image of the
true motion of mind. If the point of resemblance between mind and circular motion lies in sameness (κατὰ ταὐτά, ὡσαύτως, ἐν τῷ αὐτῷ, περὶ τὰ αὐτά,
πρὸς τὰ αὐτά, 898a8–9), it is impossible to establish this missing step without a proof that mind makes representations of itself, or that the mind is
involved in the production of the image as "the other of the same sort"
(ἕτερον τοιοῦτον) (cf. Sophist 240a7–b1). Soul, he had said, was also the
cause of nonbeing, but he had not attributed that power to mind. The
Stranger, one can say, wants and does not want soul to vanish into mind.[21]
His theology cries out in vain for Socrates' second speech in the Phaedrus.

The Stranger does not explain why there must be more than one soul
endowed with complete virtue (cf. 898c6–8). If of course each heavenly
body had such a soul within, their multitiplicity would follow; but the
Stranger does not know this. If there are many, there would have to be
one soul in addition, which would be necessarily without a body, to order
all the rest into a coherent whole (cf. 904a6); but then all the other souls
could not be its equal in either mind or virtue without there being on
their part either an interference with its guidance or a voluntary abstention from exercising their full power. If the former were true, the order of
the whole would not be known to such souls; if the latter held, the invisible order of causes, with its resources underused, would be ugly and vain.
If all the souls were perfect and in harmony, the bad kind of souls would
not stand a chance against the excess of power they would then display.
If, on the other hand, some souls were imperfect in either virtue or power,
the disorder in the cosmos could be explained without any appeal to the

---

21. At 897b1–2, if νοῦν μὲν προσλαβοῦσα ἀεὶ θεὸν ὀρθῶς θεοῖς is the correct reading, mind is a god in the eyes of gods, and is so rightly [just as it is in those of men];
cf. E. Dönt, "Bemerkungen zu Phaidros 249 und Nomoi 897," Hermes 88 (1960): 369–
371. For the phrase θεὸν ὀρθῶς θεοῖς, compare ἀνθρώποις θεός (818c1).

soul of perfect vice and ignorance, but such an hypothesis would entail that the soul of perfect virtue and knowledge was not omnipotent, or that its ordering power either does not extend beyond the soul to which it belongs or falls off rapidly beyond its proper domain. The Stranger's psychology, once it becomes a cosmology, lands him in a paradox: omnipotence belongs to soul in itself, but soul in itself does not exist.[22] Once the Stranger admits that the motion of mind cannot be perceived, the way in which its order would show itself among bodies must be equally imperceptible. That a regular kinematics of circular motion can be constructed to yield the appearance of irregularity does not have anything to do with the true dynamics of self-motion. It was this inconcinnity that led the Stranger to tack his dynamics onto his kinematics and fail to integrate them. This perplexity haunts his theology. The Stranger invites the young to examine whether there is any way to resolve it or he has handed them an eternal problem. It should certainly keep them out of trouble.[23]

3   PROVIDENCE

The Stranger distinguishes between the logos he has given against the atheists and the assuagement (παραμυθητέον) he proposes against the irreligious (889d4–6). The irreligious are those who believe there are gods, but not necessarily those gods Clinias believed were adequately proved to exist (899d3). Either the gods do not concern themselves with human affairs, they believe, or they can be bribed. Of the irreligious in the former sense, there are several groups, which the Stranger does not distinguish as precisely as one might wish. The public or private fortunes of some bad and unjust men, extravagantly pronounced happy in opinion but not in truth, and celebrated in poetry and all sorts of speeches, can draw one to impiety. Or else one has been an eyewitness to or knows by hearsay of many dreadful impieties, by means of which men have become great from small, and at an advanced age left grandsons in the greatest honors

---

22. Plutarch's way out of this difficulty was to identify soul in itself with disorderly soul; On the Generation of Soul in the Timaeus 6 (1014DE).

23. Timaeus encapsulates the problem in speaking of mind's persuasion of necessity, which is nothing but the presumed fit between mathematics and physics, or, in his account, the coincidence of noncausal structures with causal processes. It is certainly striking that Ibn Bājja, using different principles, recovered in the eleventh century a version of this problem, which Maimonides called "the true perplexity" (Guide of the Perplexed, tr. S. Pines [Chicago 1963], II.24, p. 326).

(899d6–900a5). Injustice marks the blessed of fiction, impiety the tyrants of hearsay or experience.[24] The former are thought happy but are not, the latter are honored in deed. It is not clear at this point whether the gods ignore human opinion and show their justice without depriving men of their false goods, yet still get them and everyone else to understand that they are miserable (cf. 661c8–d3; 716a4–b5), or they punish men for their injustice but not for their impiety, and they do it in such a way that everyone else knows they are punished regardless of whether the unjust are aware of it or not. To devise a punishment that fits the crime but does not affect the specious benefits of the crime is not readily conceivable, for any punishment that satisfies resentment fosters the false opinion about the good that the education was designed to deny, even if such a punishment also happens to bring about a true misery, though the truth of the misery may be experientially inseparable from the loss of false goods. The coincidence of the two shows up perhaps in the unhappy endings of tragedy; but the Stranger cannot want to contaminate his truest tragedy with the union of peripety and recognition that the tawdry grandeur of poetic fables displays. As for the dreadful impieties that lead to high honors, it is again unclear what the Stranger wishes to include among them. Does the contravention of the holy or that of the divine constitute the impious? If it is the latter, the Stranger himself admits that no criminality attends by itself on atheistic belief; and if he means the former, his theology cannot apparently supply anything holy that can be violated. When the opportunity later offers itself for a simple and public test of impiety, the Stranger refuses to make it part of the law.

From the first argument, which the Stranger imagines the irreligious have overheard, the Stranger has them assign three of the four virtues to the gods (900d5–901a10); but he also lets them on their own, against his own ignorance of what is the case, attach some of the virtues of ensouled body to the gods, and thus bridge the divide between the divine and the human in the eidetic structure of the good. He does this in two steps. The first step involves the second group of the irreligious, the second step the third group. For the first group, neglect (ἀμέλεια) is strictly defined, so that one cannot say of anyone, whether a god or a nobody (φαῦλός τις), that he neglects, unless he also has the capacity to care (901b1–c7). The Epicureans, with their sublimely indifferent gods, are not included among those who deny special providence, for they are not indignant at

---

24. Is one to think of the Athenians' false association of tyranny and impiety at the time of the mutilation of the Hermae and the profanation of the mysteries (Thucydides 6.54.5)?

the injustices of the world. Neglect has to arise from either laziness or conviction that certain small things do not matter in the whole. The contrast between small and great obfuscates the issue whether human beings estimate the happiness of the unjust correctly or not, for the gods may care for the small things in their reality without concerning themselves with the petty resentments of men. The second step, in which the Stranger has the two groups answer the three of them, adds perceptions to knowledge as an attribute of the gods (901c8–d5; cf. 927a8–b2). The third group needs this postulate, for otherwise their propitiatory sacrifices would not be effective; but the second group does not need it unless they adopt the Stranger's first step as their own.

The model for divine providence is art. Just as a stonemason cannot lay properly the large stones of a wall without the small, so the gods cannot overlook the small if the whole is to come out right. The Stranger implies that just as the stonemason must employ small stones in order to accomodate his wall to irregularities in the terrain, so there are preexisting wrinkles in the cosmos that militate against the use of uniform building blocks throughout its expanse. His argument goes no further than to establish cosmic order; but it is conspicuously deficient in two respects. No scale is introduced, so that a common measure would determine where the small ceases to be a concern to the most precise of artisans; and, what is more of a surprise, there is not a word about divine justice.[25] Everything was leading us to suppose that the Stranger's argument was modelled on Socrates' discovery of justice in the *Republic*. There he had ticked off one by one three virtues of the best city in speech, and then declared that justice must be its fourth remaining excellence. Here, the Stranger easily endowed the gods with three virtues, but of justice, in the sense that the irreligious want it to be secured for the gods, the Stranger offers nothing. This is all the more remarkable since for Socrates the order of the best city in speech, where each part minded its own business, was in fact justice. So it would have been possible for the Stranger to say that the parts of the cosmos, in not overstepping their boundaries, manifest the justice of the whole. Justice for human beings would thus consist in not transgressing the human, either by sinking to bestiality or rising to divinity. Before no man is anyone to bow down as if he were a god, and no man who becomes a beast is to live among men. The structure of the free city with its laws would thus be the realization

---

25. This silence recalls the Stranger limiting human life to four kinds—the sensible or not, the moderate or not, the brave or not, the healthy or not—with no mention of the just or unjust life (733e3–6).

of divine providence, and the *Laws* itself, prior to book 10, would be its epitome.

Now both these limits on man are to be found in the laws regulating impiety; but the foundation for them, which would link the theology with the holy, is not where it ought to be. Its absence could be due either to the independence of the city from any theological demonstration or to the inadequacy of this kind of providence in the eyes of the irreligious, who want the gods to be more solicitous of man than the Stranger's implicit argument could supply: he had already admitted several times that the contingently small was beyond his capacity as legislator (cf. 723c6–d4). Irreligion of the kind the Stranger is examining could occur only if the city were so successful in bringing man up to the human that man forgot what he owed to the city. If self-forgetfulness is a necessary consequence of civilization, then the theology of book 10 is an indispensable means for keeping self-forgetfulness at bay. The Stranger himself realizes that his argument needs an enchanting supplement of stories (903a10–b2). In this supplement the Stranger supplies the scale: the individual human being is at the outer limit of minuteness, and whoever rails against the system is urged to consider his ignorance of the part he plays in the whole. Whereas the Stranger's argument would have stopped at the human species, organized into not natural parts, whether of cities or tribes, the irreligious demand a finer gauge, and the Stranger wishes to persuade them that they do count despite the immensity of their insignificance. This is the closest the Stranger can come to finding an equivalent for others to his own experience, which Megillus thought involved the total vilification of man (804b5–8). The vanity of man is inseparable from his religiosity (902b5–6; cf. 687c5–12), and without the establishment of his humanity apart from any theology, there would be no stopping to his bestialization.

The Stranger adds a curious inducement to belief in divine providence (903d2–905c7).[26] He starts off by implying that there is a stable and intelligible order of kinds that limits the apparent capacity of soul to affect and undergo every possible change. If living water (ὕδωρ ἔμψυχον), for example, were possible, the infinite number of variations that just three periods of becoming would produce, since there would be no set of ones out of which several kinds of many would come to be, would presumably have overwhelmed the capacity of the gods to manage the whole (903e4–

---

26. Cf. T. J. Saunders, "Penology and Eschatology in Plato's *Timaeus* and *Laws,*" *CQ* 23 (1973): 232–244. Saunders argues for a Heraclitean allusion in the possibility that the Stranger rejects, but it is his own account of soul that entails it.

904a3; cf. 965c1–3). Something on the order of a cosmos of "ideas" is suddenly postulated as a consolation. It seems to have a higher rank than the soul or souls of perfect virtue and, in restoring the hyperuranian beings to the Stranger's truncation of the *Phaedrus* myth, deny self-motion to the soul. The Stranger couples this limitation on becoming, which turns the gods into dialecticians, with a story about space. It is here where justice (δίκη), reward, and punishment (τιμωρία) are first introduced (904c10, e4; 905a1, 3, 7). Every soul, no matter how good or bad, makes a contribution to the order of the whole (905b2–c1). The irreligious are accused of seeing, as if in a mirror, the neglect of the gods in the seemingly successful actions of the impious. They are urged to give up their experience of right and attempt to detect the pattern of right. They are blamed for not knowing how to read images, which cannot be interpreted as if they conveyed an unscrambled message. The Stranger again brings in the image, but now, unlike the image of circular rotation, it is not to be discerned in any kinematical construction, for if there is to be a use of bad souls, disturbances in the regularity of motions are inevitable. If one may use the Eleatic Stranger's distinction, the Athenian Stranger grounds his astronomy in εἰκαστική, but his theodicy in φανταστική. The problem of nonbeing recurs. It is a challenge to the most manly of all to solve (905c1).[27]

The third form of irreligion would not need a separate refutation if the Stranger had not already argued that we are not too small to be a concern to the gods. Their care of everything ensouled, if it were on a sliding scale of importance, could easily have been limited in such a way that individuals did not matter enough for the gods to be susceptible to unjust pleadings; but as it is, the gods must be shown to be incorruptible precisely because they care. If, however, evil no less than good contributes to the order of the whole, the gods should not be able to be diverted from their proper tasks; but it seems not to settle the issue, since the orderly arrangement of souls, which makes up the invisible pattern of right, suggests that the gods are indifferent to everything of the body. The seven kinds of protection and guarding that the Stranger lists, in light of which the gods' actions may be understood, all have to do with the care of the body or bodies; and though six of them are arts, the seventh is not,

---

27. In the *Sophist,* divine making does not include φανταστική, either in body or in speech (266b2–c6). Note the similarity between *Laws* 903e4–5, εἰ μὲν γὰρ πρὸς τὸ ὅλον ἀεὶ βλέπων πλάττοι τις μετασχηματίζων τὰ πάντα, and *Timaeus* 50a5–7, εἰ γὰρ πάντα τις σχήματα πλάσας ἐκ χρυσοῦ μηδὲν μεταπλάττων παύοιτο ἕκαστα εἰς ἅπαντα. The Stranger's kinematics is to his dynamics as Timaeus's account of time is to that of space.

but likens the gods to dogs (906b5; 907a6). If the Stranger had not warned us against the illusoriness of images, we might now infer that the gods fawn upon us and love us whether we treat them well or not (*Republic* 376a5–7). The dogs of the shepherd resist the blandishments of the wolves not because they have knowledge, but because they are trained to harm enemies and benefit friends. On this model the gods cannot live up to the precept of the criminal law—never be other than corrective or exemplary—for they have enemies, and these enemies might be open to bribes. The deathless battle in which gods and *daimones* are engaged would seem to entail that there are other beings who struggle against them, and want either body or disordered soul to win: if it is up to us to be of whatever sort we desire, a concerted effort on our part might well upset the whole (904b8–c4). This Manichaeanism takes us back to Clinias's expression of his experience of the law. After the Stranger implied that the law and fate reconcile good and bad throughout the cosmos (904a8–9), it comes as something of a surprise:

> If then his providence
> Out of our evil seek to bring forth good,
> Our labor must be to pervert that end,
> And out of good still to find means of evil.

The Stranger divides the law of impiety into three parts, to each one of which the three kinds of disbelief correspond; he then divides each of the three in two, because there is no connection whatsoever between the virtues and vices of soul and belief and disbelief (908a7–b4). The duality he had introduced before, between the virtue of soul and mind (897c1), has its counterpart in this doubleness of the tripartite law. This scheme, however, proves to be more precise in the summary than in the exposition of the differences. The virtuous atheist seems to be one of the junior members of the nocturnal council, who in a spirit of levity mocks openly the sacrifices and oaths of the many and has to inform everyone of the difference between the holy and the divine (908c6–d1). Through his hatred of injustice, which includes lying, and his loathing of those who are just through their piety, he would denounce sacrifices as bribery and oaths as a crutch (cf. 913b3–8). That the nocturnal council could make a mistake about him, and declare him sober after they had kept him under close supervision in their σωφρονιστήριον for five years, so that he would have to be executed if he went back to his old ways (908e5–909a8), strongly suggests that any pronouncement on curability and incurability lies completely outside the competence of any magistracy however constituted. His ironical counterpart, on the other hand, who hides his atheism but is driven by uncontrollable gusts of pleasure and pain, becomes a soothsayer, inspired magician, tyrant, demagogue, general, sophist, or proponent of private initiations (908d1–7).[28] In his case, one declares him to be an atheist on the basis of his actions, and it would seem to make no difference whether he was a sincere believer in his subversive teaching or not; but the Stranger seems to suggest that the keenness of his understanding (μαθήσεις ὀξεῖαι) and the vehemence of his desires preclude his sincerity. Any claim to divine revelation would, it seems, condemn one to the charge of atheism. This formulation, however, cannot be right, since the Stranger proceeds to lump together the irreligious of all three types, and declare them bestial (θηριώδεις) if they prey on the gullibility of men, and promise for pay to resurrect the dead and persuade the gods by sacrifices, prayers, and magical incantations (909a8–b6). Whether these who act in this way believe in divine providence or not, and in the bribability of the gods or not, looks as if it makes no difference in their crime. What seems to be at issue is not the criminals, who in their contempt of mankind are the sophistical reflections of the Stranger himself, but their victims: they obviously believe that the gods can be bribed, and, if they believe in the resurrection of the dead, they deny the superiority of the dissolution of body and soul to any communion, and hence reject the theodicy the Stranger proposed in his consolatory myth. It is the victim, then, of fraudulent godmongering (θεοπολεῖν) who is to be treated with the greatest leniency, and even if he falls short of the virtue the frank atheist has, he will apparently not pay for his folly by any prison term (cf. 913b2). The justice of δοξοσοφία is reaffirmed.

The manipulators of false belief are not executed. Instead, they are locked up for life in a third prison, which England thought might be labelled Hades (908a6–7), located in a remote and wild region of the country (909c1–6). No citizen or stranger, if he is free, is to visit them, and when they die they are thrown out of the country unburied. It seems that they are judged incurable, and their punishment is meant solely as a sign of their bestiality. The citizens who fell for their cant are to be convinced that those who deceived them were not human beings. Their own sheeplike credulity is to be hidden from them, lest they come to believe they deserve the mockery of the just atheist. The Stranger seems to make a rare error in topography: he locates this prison for beasts in the middle of the country, where he had said the city was to be founded (745b3–4; 908a5; 909c1).

28. The Stranger seems to imply, by citing the general in this list, that his pleasure in killing warrants his inclusion among the atheists.

X I

PRIVATE LAW[1]

I MAKING GOOD

Theology interrupted the laws based on the eidetic structure of the good.
It introduced a distinction between virtue and good sense that that structure did not warrant. Its concession to the genetic structure of law consisted in the separation of soul from mind. Now, without any comment
by either Clinias or Megillus to mark the transition, the Stranger returns
to where he broke off in book 9, when he neatly assessed damages to the
body in accordance with the needs of the city and the rank of virtues of
the body, and considers property, the eighth of the goods. The sacred also
returns (914b5); but though everything is done to consecrate, nothing is
done to theologize. The theological implication, that anyone who swears
a false oath proves thereby his disbelief in divine providence, is not allowed to determine his punishment (916e6–917c7). Ὁ θεομισέστατος is
not a legal category (cf. 921a4–5). An oath is plainly a form of ψυχαγωγία
(909b2); it is uttered to convince others who do believe in divine providence to put their trust in the assertion that accompanies it (949a8–b6).
The Stranger had first sworn by Zeus and Apollo when he was arguing
Clinias out of his view that the tyrant with all the goods except justice
and moderation was not wretched (662e6). A perjurer, therefore, if his
action were treated under impiety, should be locked up for life and not
get off with a beating. In Egypt the penalty was death (Diodorus 1.77.2).
Oaths are not to be permitted in Magnesia by either plaintiff or defendant
in any court, even though there would be no easier way to reinforce the
second and third principles of the theology, and have the magistrates get
rid of any public trace of defiant irreligion (948d3–e4). Indeed, if all oaths

---

1. The difference between private and public law, which more or less separates
book 11 from book 12, is briefly indicated at 767b4–c1 (cf. 957a3–6) in the context of
law courts, which do not line up exactly with that difference. That book 12 begins
with a γραφή rather than a δίκη (941a6) also suggests such a difference, though again
this distinction is not maintained in what follows.

were true, for fear of what one would suffer if one swore falsely, the business of the courts would be vastly reduced (cf. 948b3–c2). The citizens
are not to believe that pretty nearly half of the population are liars and
thus treat with suspicion those with whom they are to be friends. The
charge of perjury would be a permanent obstacle to the reconciliation
that the Stranger wanted to follow on compensation for harm. To swear
truthfully by Zeus would of course not prove anything, and to swear
falsely by him would encourage the belief that the gods find perjury beneath their notice.[2] In regulating the relations we have with one another
without theology, the Stranger follows the laws on atheism and keeps
justice and piety apart (cf. *Euthyphro* 12c10–d4).

After a book about the soul as the first becoming, the eleventh book
deals with flaws in human genesis and time, everything in short where
there can be anomalies and irregularities, whether it be that contracts are
not kept, estates left intestate, or children orphaned (cf. 766c5–d2). The
necessary imperfections in human affairs and their regulation make the
eleventh book a proper foil to the tenth, for the ordinance of the sacred,
μὴ κινεῖν τἀκίνητα (913b9)—"Do not disturb the indisturbable"—, one of
whose applications is to property, meets with too many exceptions in the
course of human life. The Stranger's theological stories were designed to
counter the experience of the citizen and assure him that everything,
though subject to motion and change, was in place. His theology therefore is a fitting prelude to the civil law, for it urges everyone to temper
their irritation at the wrinkles in becoming and, in coming to acknowledge their subordination to the smooth working of the whole, put their
trust in an invisible pattern of right. Natural blemishes (κῆρες ἐπιπεφύ-
κασιν), as the Stranger says, grow on most of the beautiful things in the
life of human beings (937d–8), and in many cases the patient would not
survive their excision. There are seventeen topics in book 11, and though
they immediately fall into three large classes, each class is not evidently
well-articulated; but one does not want to jump to the conclusion that
their disorder mirrors the unavoidable disorder in human life:

2. As a confirmation of the Stranger's assertion that the laws alter with an alteration of opinions about the gods, consider Justinian's Constitution II.58.8 (A.D. 531),
which condemns those who accused of defamation refuse to swear: *sic enim non lites
solum, sed etiam calumniatores minuentur, sic pro iudiciis putabunt sese omnes in
sacrariis sisti. si enim et ipsae principales litigantium partes per iuramentum lites ex-
erceant et causarum patroni praebeant sacramentum et ipsi iudices propositis
sanctis scripturis tam causae totius faciant examinationem quam suum proferant ar-
bitrium, quid aliud, nisi pro hominibus deum in omnibus causis iudicem esse cre-
dendum est?* Contrast *Digest* 28.7.8 (Ulpian).

A WEALTH	B FAMILY	C DEFECTS
1 Treasure	6 Wills and	11 Poisons and
2 Buying and	intestacy	philters
selling	7 Orphans	12 Harm
3 Counterfeit and	8 Disowning	13 Comedy
deception	9 Divorce	14 Beggary
4 Retail	10 Parents	15 Slave damages
5 Contractual		16 Witnesses
obligations		17 Advocates

The book begins with things in place that appear out of place, like buried treasure and anything left unguarded, but it soon goes on to runaway slaves and freedmen whose wealth exceeds their former masters' (915a8–b1).[3] Freedmen can remain in Magnesia for no more than twenty years, with few exceptions, and if their wealth is ever more than the third property class, they must leave within thirty days (915b1–c4). If anyone disobeys, he is not forcibly evicted but executed. His presence is an affront to the system, which wants there to be no change unless there can be perfect exchange (cf. 953d8–e4). All exchanges must occur in a set location, and nothing is to be sold on credit (915d6–e9). The law does not back a transaction entered into on trust, and abstains from settling quarrels among friends. Every effort is made to keep partnership and fellowship apart, so that the former may conform with the compulsion of law and the latter display the persuasiveness of prelude.[4] Money is strictly a medium of exchange, by means of which "the being of things of any kind whatsoever (οὐσίαν χρημάτων ὡντινωνοῦν), being incommensurate and nonuniform," may become uniform and commensurate (918b3–4). Merchants and retailers are the discoverers of "uniformity for the beings" (ὁμαλότητα ταῖς οὐσίαις) (918c2–3). In light of the placement of this remark, the Stranger strongly hints at what a mathematical physics could

3. It might seem that the symmetry the Stranger gives to the law of treasure, so that if it is not reported, the citizen gets the reputation for vice, and the slave is executed (914a5–b1), is superfluous, for how would anyone else know about a nonreporting? The provision points, however, to how the law induces an internalization of shame or fear (cf. 957d4–6).

4. Cf. David Daube, "Money and Justiciability," *Zeitschrift der Savigny-Stiftung* 96 (1979): 1–16 (= *Collected Studies in Roman Law*, Frankfurt 1991, II, 1341–1356). W. G. Becker, *Platons Gesetze und das griechische Familienrecht*, 93–95, comments on the more extensive use of ἀτιμία in the *Laws*, but its milder provisions, than in Attic law. It is thus shifted closer to blame and further away from punishment. This is in accordance with the shift in meaning that honor had undergone in the second part of the prelude (727a2–7).

do in dissolving the differences among the beings and ordering them in accordance with uniformity and symmetry.[5] Still, regardless of whether the beings may ultimately resist their homogenization or not, the city at least is of two orders, and at a surprising point the Stranger remarks on their mutual interference.

The Stranger cites the innkeeper (918c9–919b3). He is in a position to comfort the traveler who, buffeted by the violence of savage storms or choked by summer heat, finds himself in a desolate spot and needs a friendly reception but instead is held for ransom as if he were an enemy. The use-value of the inn approaches infinity for the traveler, the costs to the innkeeper are finite and computable.[6] The disparity is so great as to defeat all but the strictest honesty; yet honesty is not so high a virtue that the city can afford to have its best young men and women serve in the lowest jobs in order to reveal how splendid it would be if the impossible were realized. The Stranger had already implied that even cosmologically the gods do not put the best souls in the lowest posts in order to burnish smooth the rough corners of the universe; but it would seem to make some difference to the goods to be found in Hades whether the best or the worst were in charge there. The rewards due to the best were implicitly in agreement with the order of the whole; but now the Stranger suggests that deserts and function, or the just and the good, which have their economic counterparts in exchange-value and use-value respectively, might not be harmonious in principle. Clinias had assumed that the gods led a life of ease, but the Stranger has them never idle as they scurry about in their strenuous effort to maintain the machinery of right. In the case of the city, the best cannot be denied their rightful place for the sake of establishing perfect exchange, not only on account of its injustice and the insurrection the Achilles of the city would lead, but because it would degrade the best and, in putting them at risk, tempt them with a corruption that few, according to the Stranger, could resist (cf. 919e5–9). The isolated inn appears to be the practicable equivalent to the symposium in speech, but unless the chief magistrates were out of town and

5. In the *Timaeus*, the demiurge first arranges for perfect exchange among the four elements; but once Timaeus belatedly introduces "space" and a geometry for the elements, he withdraws earth from the process of exchange and reassigns it the role of maintaining an order in motion through disorder, for without it the elements would separate into their kinds and not interact (31b4–32c4; 54b6–c5; 57c2–6).

6. In comparing the traveler to a prisoner held for ransom, the Stranger suggests the following proportion: just as the prisoner's price, if he were sold as a slave, is far less than the ransom, so a slave has infinite worth if one considers what he contributes to the freedom and leisure of the master.

presiding instead over the deskclerks and bellboys in a country inn, hardly anyone would pass the test (cf. 649e2–650a2).[7] Virtue is always cloistered virtue; one can no more put it to the test gratutitously than one ought to detect impiety at every turn. The best solution to the problem the innkeeper poses is something the Stranger wishes might never occur; his own solution is to minimize the use of exchangers, employ men whose corruption would harm the city least (cf. 904b3–6), and devise a way to keep those who engage in it from shamelessness and illiberality (919c2–920c8).[8] The Stranger, however, does not offer anything more than a solution on paper, for he does not address the issue whether anyone, who by definition has not been properly educated, would be willing to submit to limits on his gains. He is asked to earn less than he could elsewhere, and depart as soon as he has settled in. If the Stranger had not insisted that the artisans be good at their job (846d4–847a3), perhaps the worst of workmen might find Magnesia a refuge from competition. In order to prevent price-gouging, the Stranger forbids the seller to post two different prices during a single day (917b7–c3). He sacrifices the efficiency of the market, whereby the seller does not have to lug staples back and forth, and get nothing at all for the perishables he would otherwise have been willing to sell below cost, for the sake of a doubtful saving of his virtue.[9]

Socrates could not keep together the true city of arts and the good city of warriors. He could not afford to communize the entire city and extend to the artisans the education he devised for the guardians and auxiliaries; and he could not maintain the structure of the city without interposing opinion between the knowledge of the demos and the wisdom of the rulers. The Stranger apparently does not face these difficulties. After all, he does not have to decide whether Socrates' philosopher-king is the perfect innkeeper he himself wishes never to be. He turns the artisans into noncitizens, whether slaves, metics, or foreigners, and lets the

---

7. The sentence ταῦτά ἐστιν καὶ τὰ τοιαῦτα ἐν σύμπασιν τοῖς τοιούτοις ὀρθῶς ἁμαρτανόμενα τὰς διαβολὰς τῇ τῆς ἀπορίας ἐπικουρήσει παρεσκευακότα (919b1–3) looks at first as if it illustrates the tendency for polar opposites to gravitate toward one another, and one has to put ὀρθῶς with παρεσκευακότα, but since the Stranger argues that one cannot avoid missing the mark in cases of this kind, it seems to mean, at least secondarily, that the mistakes are made correctly.

8. If any citizen engages in trade he is to be imprisoned for a year; and for each time he goes back to it, another year is added to the prison time (919e5–920a3). Here is a clear case of incurability in which the death penalty is not exacted (cf. 937c3–5).

9. See A. Rameil, *Die Wirtschaftsstabilität und ihre Problematik in Platons Gesetzesstaat*, 26–27. Alexis (fr. 130 K–A) mentions a law of this kind about fresh fish. One is inevitably reminded of Lucius's friend, who, in his zeal to uphold the law, forced Lucius to go without his fish dinner (Apuleius *Metamorphoses* 1.24–5).

warrior citizens have their own families and land. The Stranger, however, now admits in a remark off to the side (ἐν παρέργῳ) that he is in the same difficulties as Socrates was, and, like him, he must sacrifice principle for the sake of structure (920d1–922a5). In generalizing for the sake of comprehensiveness, the Stranger takes the edge off the truth (ὡς . . . δίκαιον εἰπεῖν). The genus of craftsmen (δημιουργοί) is sacred to Hephaestus and Athena; and those who save the deeds of the craftsmen by other arts— those of defense (τέχναισιν ἑτέραις ἀμυντηρίοις), "being craftsmen as it were of another kind" (οἷον ἑτέροις οὖσιν δημιουργοῖς), are sacred to Ares and Athena.[10] They are the craftsmen of safety (δημιουργοὶ σωτηρίας) and are all endowed with art (τεχνικοί) (cf. 829d2–3; Republic 395b8–c3). Regardless of whether one takes the Stranger literally, and the entire citizen body has the art of war—they certainly have it to a greater degree than any other Greek city—or one restricts his expression to generals and senior officers, the Stranger now declares that either his citizens do not have that single art that distinguished them from other artisans and left them no time for anything else (846d4–7)—the warriors save the works of the craftsmen as if the craftsmen were citizens[11]—or the generals at least have two arts and therefore do not have the art that every other citizen has.[12] That Athena can be the patron of two kinds of art does not resolve the Stranger's dilemma, for "scarcely any human nature is capable of working at two practices or two arts with precision (ἀκριβῶς)" (846d7–8; cf. Timaeus 24d1). Socrates too had started out with giving his warriors a single art and a double education, and he did not get into trouble until he proposed that their double education was really a single art (Republic 402b9–c4; cf. 455e6–456a8). The true city of the Republic was riven by the untenable tension between a high-tech urban center and a citizenry who lived the simple life of real farmers in the country. The city

---

10. When the Stranger first mentioned the craftsmen and warriors together, he went out of his way not to make the two classes strictly parallel: Ἡφαίστου καὶ Ἀθηνᾶς ἱερὸν τὸ δημιουργῶν γένος, οἳ . . . , Ἄρεως δ' αὖ καὶ Ἀθηνᾶς οἱ . . . , and consequently had to add a clause—δικαίως δὲ καὶ τὸ τούτων γένος ἱερόν ἐστι τούτων τῶν θεῶν—to make them parallel (920d7–e4).

11. Cf. Timaeus 18b4. In some cases, the ignorance of the citizens is protected (916b2–c3); in others it seems that the citizen himself must be an expert (917c8–d5); and in others he must rely on experts (917e2–4). Citizen-travelers would be indispensable if the magistrates are going to set fair profit margins.

12. That art and virtue do not in principle coincide is shown by the pun on τέχνη—"a naturally straightforward and nonlying matter"—and τεχνάζειν (921b4–6). The craftsman knows the value of whatever he makes (921b3); if he also knows what it is worth to the purchaser, the arms maker, who can always leave if his price is not met, has the generals at his mercy, and they are no better off than travelers at an isolated inn.

of the *Laws* looks more coherent, but only if one discounts the spuriousness of the life they lead as farmers. It has an army, the true city did not.

The Stranger advises but does not force the citizens to assign second-
class honors to the good men who save the city by either acts of courage
or devices of war; and he suggests how that could be done by assimilating
their honors to the wages (μισθοί) of craftsmen, and treating their fulfillment of a public (δημόσιον) task as being no different from a "public-
worker" (δημιουργός) who fulfills a contract. Just as Socrates' guardians
became auxiliaries once the rulers were in place, so the Stranger, after he
had almost turned the city into a war machine in book 8, demotes the
generals to quasi-mercenaries—ὥσπερ ἐπίκουροι μισθωτοί in Adimantus's
phrase (*Republic* 419a10; cf. *Timaeus* 17b3)—and makes room for the
nocturnal council, or those who are capable of honoring the writings of
good legislators (922a3–5). The Stranger, however, pays a high price for
putting the generals in second place. He eliminates at a stroke the difference between honor and reward, upon which he had plausibly laid the
foundation for the difference between prelude and law (cf. 926d5–7). The
law now praises and blames (921e2–5; cf. 730b5–c1; 822e4–823a6). It is
not just the criminal law that infects the education, but the civil law does
it as well, for it must rely on money, or the lawful instrument for equating
the nonequatable: the word for price in Greek is the same as the word for
honor (τιμή). "Possession for possession" (κτῆμα ἀντὶ κτήματος), justice is
to be preferred (προτιμήσας) to wealth, and it is better to acquire the former in one's soul than the latter in one's substance (οὐσία) (913b3–8). The
Stranger comes close to suggesting that the best of legislators are the
worst of hucksters. For every drachma at which a counterfeit ware was
put up for sale, the seller is given one blow, but the intent to defraud does
not vary in degree with the price (cf. 941c5–d1), and no equivalence is dis-
cernible in the two kinds of assessment (917d6–e2). That the seller pays
for the counterfeit he wanted to palm off as genuine with an equally spurious equivalence would be an odd conceit for the law.[13]

2   ESTRANGEMENTS

Now pretty nearly all the most important parts of contracts—everything human beings do in contracting with one another—have been
arranged in order by us, except, of course, for what pertains to orphans

---

13. Herodotus labels a story as "sillier" (ματαιότερος) that said the Spartans accepted counterfeit money from Polycrates to lift their siege of Samos (3.56.2).

and the tutelage of orphans; but there is something of a necessity to arrange this after what has been stated. The desires of those about to die in regard to testamentary disposition have their start from this, as well as the fortunes of those who disposed of nothing at all by way of a will. I said it was a necessity, Clinias, when I looked at the peevishness and harshness about them. (922a6–b5)

One does not expect when one first reads of necessity (ἀναγκαῖον) that the Stranger means anything more than the formal arrangement of the civil law on contracts; but the Stranger means that this necessity has nothing to do with the proper order of items in the law, but with the necessity to stand in the way of the will. The necessity involves the impossibility of leaving this part of life unregulated: the cantankerousness of men is even more resistant to regulation than their love of lucre. This ambiguity in necessity recalls the two different versions of necessity that introduced the criminal law. The Stranger had offered Clinias a choice between the best and the most necessary, and Clinias believed that the absence of necessity consisted in their being under no compulsion to legislate, but the Stranger had meant that, despite their leisure, they had to acknowledge the disparity that could not be overcome between the necessary and the best. Now the civil law puts them once more in the same bind.

The Stranger treats everything from the beginning of book 11 up to halfway through book 12 under contracts (συμβόλαια), or mutual obligations (913a1, 956b4–6).[14] He singles out the handling of orphans because smooth succession has in their case suffered a break, and it is up to the legislator to devise for them a second coming to be (926d8). With this "fantastic description," as England puts it, the Stranger indicates that law wants to be the artisan of becoming (cf. 944d5–e2; 945e3–4). It turns out, however, that fathers too stand in the way of the law's need to make the past continuous with the future. The unqualified rule of contracts—"Let no one possibly tamper with my property" (913a1–4)—with which the Stranger began the eleventh book, cannot be allowed to support the whims of the dying. Ephemeral man protests against the sempiternal; he does not want to be nothing but a dot in the pattern of right. In wanting to put his mark on what he regards as his own, he appeals to the gods: "Oh gods! It's simply dreadful if I will not be allowed in any way to grant or withhold my things to whomever I will, to one more, to another less, of all those

14. On συμβόλαιον, see G. Beseler, *Zeitschrift der Savigny-Stiftung für Rechtsgeschichte*, Romanistische Abteilung, 50 (1930): 441–442.

who have plainly proved vile to me or good, [some] put to the test in illness, others in old age and every other sort of circumstance" (922d4–8). The exclamation ὦ θεοί does not occur anywhere else in Plato, and it is best known from comedy.[15] Indeed, many of the topics the Stranger discusses from now on belong to New Comedy, and it is not surprising if the Stranger, in reaffirming his acceptance of comedy, takes away its right to name names and thus deprives it of the harshness of Old Comedy (936a2–5). The Stranger, in any case, makes up a speech of the fathers which Clinias for one finds beautifully said. He calls attention to how the gods enter into speech whenever one wants to make oneself an exception to the law and gain a more forgiving form of right.

The will is an instrument of the will, and in testamentary dispositions the experience of right takes its legal form. How could I mistake who harmed and benefited me, one says to the legislator, and what is it to you how I distribute what is mine? The legislator is up against the malice of the old and dying, who are more likely to survive in memory if they withhold than if they grant a favor. The Stranger has to infer from the well-known curses mythical fathers uttered against their sons that blessings must also have been in their power, but he cannot cite any story to that effect (931b5–c8). The fathers certainly do not want to be as if they had never been, which would be the case were the law to allow them no discretion. They have no right to disinherit all their sons, but they retain the right to choose whichever one they want. Although the prelude declares that the Stranger will provide for what is best for the whole city and the whole family (923b4–5), there is a limit to the degree of his interference, and if one of a man's sons was an outrageous flatterer, the legislator has to yield, however reluctantly (923b2–c4). If the father in each family rejects the best son, or for whatever reason disinherits him, and no one adopts any of them, then the regime is finished in one generation, and one or more of Magnesia's colonies is the beneficiary. The Stranger never says anything about the regime of the colonies; but if in certain circumstances an heiress can choose her husband from the colonists (925b4–c3), she can import an alien education with the full blessing of the law, unless against all probability the colonies have the same laws as the mother country (cf. 637b3–5). An imperialistic necessity is built into a closed society against its will.

15. Demosthenes often has ὦ πάντες θεοί, ὦ γῆ καὶ θεοί, and ὦ Ζεῦ καὶ θεοί, but never ὦ θεοί. In one of the few occurrences in tragedy of this exclamation by itself, Euripides' Helen says, just before she is certain that she is seeing Menelaus before her, ὦ θεοί· θεὸς γὰρ καὶ τὸ γιγνώσκειν φίλους (*Helen* 560).

The whims of the fathers are matched by the wishes of the heirs. If a marriage would prove to be too great a burden, it is permitted to swear an oath (ἦ μήν) that the legislator, if he were alive and present, would never compel compliance (926c2–4). Apart from defects, whether of the body or soul, a cousin of a wealthy father might refuse to marry the daughter of his uncle, "directing his mind toward greater marriages" (926a9–b6). Even though there is a cap on the wealth of the richest class, the Stranger imagines a concentration of wealth and does not utter a word of reproach. The social climber who rejects the poor relative is on a par with him who will not marry the cripple or the mad. The Stranger admits that the commands of the law look as if they testify to the blindness of the legislator, who seems to be unaware of all the impediments that make it impossible to fulfill the law, and people would prefer to suffer anything rather than go through with a distasteful marriage (925d5–926a3). When the Stranger says this, he puts into indirect statement what would be, if he were quoting, just an expression like "I would rather die than go through with it," and no different in kind from the "Oh gods!" he put in the mouth of the fathers. It would be the sort of thing people say without necessarily meaning it or having any precise notion of what "suffer anything" could entail. They certainly do not expect the gods to take them up on it. The Stranger thus makes a much greater concession to human weakness than at first appears.[16] In this case, permission is granted to lie under oath with impunity. Does he also imply that God is not in the details, and though the gods cannot be bribed they can still forgive? It would be strange if the gods make the sort of concession to vices the Stranger does and do not establish everything in accordance with the eidetic structure of the good. Perhaps the cosmos runs perfectly, but some souls in the machine are as miserable with their reward as others are who are being punished.

The care orphans receive is unlikely to be equal to what their guardians bestow on their own (927e4–928b1); but the law orders that they be cherished more than one's own children, and their property receive better care than one's own. The law goes against nature, but it cannot enforce its threat except through a fine. The divergence of civil law from criminal law, no less than its closeness to it, emerges in the Stranger's appeal to a previous remark of his that now appears to be timely (926e9–927b4). In ordering exile for the accidental homicide, he had said that the murdered

16. W. G. Becker, *Platons Gesetze*, 21–22, begins by remarking on the dissonance between the programmatic equality of men and women and its absence in the legal code, and ends by asserting that in the case of divorce they are in unison (137–155).

man is angry at his killer and in his terror at the moment of his death is both the patient and the agent of distress (865d6–e6). Now this story is said to be true, and what was there attributed to the murdered man himself has become his soul. And just as there he had diverted the indignation of his relatives to the dead man, so here the dignified old show the same enmity or kindness as do the souls of the dead to the guardians of orphans (927b7–c2); but the penalty is not exile but a double fine for damages. This fine expresses the anger of the legislator, who translates the myth into money. The anger of the legislator seems to be of the same kind as that which the Stranger felt overtaking him in his need to refute the atheists, but again the maltreatment of orphans does not merit the accusation of impiety, even though it shows no fear of the gods above, "who have perceptions of the abandonment of orphans" (927b1–2). Perhaps the Stranger does not let his anger spill over into a charge of impiety because "though the speeches are true they are long," and it would not do to prosecute anyone on a missing proof. Not just the divine of the theology belongs to the prelude, but, to a large extent, the sacred does as well.

A son disowned and disinherited by the entire genus to which he belongs is still allowed to be a colonist; but it is not possible for him to remain a citizen unless someone adopts him (928e6–929d3). Despite the genus's confirmation of the father, whose anger may or may not have been justified, the city does not back its condemnation, "for it is natural for the character of the young to undergo many changes in the course of his life." Divorce is possible if husband and wife cannot abide one another, and a board finds that they are irreconcilable (929e9–930a7). It is then up to the board to find characters of a deeper and gentler sort with whom they could live. In all these cases the law is found to be sympathetic to what is intolerable experientially; but one wonders whether in practice it would be enough for the laws to provide for exceptions and still expect that no one will take them up on it. That one may get rid of a burden may be enough to ease it.

At first glance, the section on parents, how they ought to be honored, may look out of place, and that it would more properly belong before the discussion of divorce (930e3–932d8); but the issue it raises links it with the section that immediately follows it without any connective (932e1–933e5). The Stranger is now taking up a theme that structured the first part of the prelude he delivered to all the assembled citizens (715e7–718a6). There he had strung on a vertical line, reaching from heaven to below the earth, every class of beings to which some trace of divinity could be thought to adhere. The honoring of living parents followed the worship of the gods of the fathers (θεοὶ πατρῷοι) and preceded the appropriate way to bury them. We would expect that the intervening theology would alter in some ways how the Stranger treats them. He starts with the ancient laws about gods and distinguishes between "those we see plainly and honor, and those whose images (εἰκόνες) we ourselves set up as objects of worship (ἀγάλματα), and we believe that those ensouled gods are very grateful and kindly disposed to us who so worship them, although they are lifeless" (cf. Timaeus 41a3–5). Neither part of these laws conforms with the theology of book 10, for the sun, moon, and stars could not be shown to be ensouled without supplying the causal relation between soul and body, and the Olympian gods were not shown to exist. The Stranger seems prepared to elevate the parents at the expense of the Olympian gods. He consecrates them as living heirlooms (κειμήλιοι) and statues (ἀγάλματα), who have the power to curse or bless. The Stranger's theology clearly has an influence on this prelude to the law—the law is wholly free of any allusion to piety—through its doctrine of the primacy of soul to body. It thus holds out the possibility of its own vulgarization and the worship of bodiless souls as gods.

The next section raises grave doubts whether this kind of enlightenment is desirable. The Stranger here discusses imaginary causality, where either party to a supposed injury believes he has inflicted or has suffered harm by some form of voodoo. It is the vulgar equivalent of the unavailable drink of fear, with the double disadvantage that as some are not susceptible to it, others do not recover from it unscathed (cf. 649a4). "It is neither easy to know how everything of this kind is by nature, nor, if one should know, persuade others; and it is not worthwhile to attempt to persuade in the face of the suspicion men feel in their souls before one another in this regard, if ever they see molded wax imitations somewhere, whether at their doors, crossroads, or tombs of their parents, and urge them to disregard everything of the kind because they have no plain opinion about them." The Stranger himself had laid the groundwork for these beliefs, first when he had to restrict the power of soul to be in any body, in order to make it plausible that there was divine providence, even though he could not offer a proof for such a restriction (cf. 959b1–3), and just before when he affirmed the truth of stories about the power of dead souls and himself proposed that parents be treated as living gods. The Stranger has no better remedy for the spread of these beliefs that are naturally conducive to the childish terrors of most men than to beg, advise, and counsel against it, for he says no compulsion is to be put on the legislator and the judge to try to heal fears of this kind (933b7–c4). The attempt to bewitch is done by him who does not know what he is doing, and if he is not an acknowledged expert, his δοξοσοφία makes him innocent of every charge except the damage the court believes he caused, or, more precisely, it believes he is like the injurer (ὅμοιος τῷ βλάπτοντι) (cf. 845e5–9). The judges too are not exempt from such beliefs.

Immediately after the discussion of imaginary injuries follows a paragraph on real injuries that are due to theft or violence (933e6–934c6). This section lays down two principles: the damage must be made good, and, more importantly, one is to pay the penalty that accompanies the crime for the sake of σωφρονιστύς and not for the sake of the criminal action, for what's done cannot be undone. The Stranger revives an obsolete suffix in order to make up a new word. Σωφρονιστύς should mean a subjective disposition to or capacity for moderation.[17] It is what he could not even suggest should be the aim of the courts when it came to witchcraft. That he couples σωφρονιστύς with the impossibility of reversing time strongly suggests that the Stranger is thinking no less of the victim than of the perpetrator. How one is to reconcile the victim to the court's incapacity to put him back where he was before the injury is no less a problem than to distinguish among the possible motives of the perpetrator (cf. 924d1–e2), and decide how one is to go about curing that particular passion. The Stranger mentions one case. Whoever acted by the folly of another and was won over on account of his youth is to be handled more leniently than the agent of his own folly, or than one who succumbed to pleasures or pains, the terrors of cowardice, desires, resentments, or bursts of anger. The lighter sentence the Stranger proposes in the first case seems to be not unrelated to the insoluble problem of witchcraft, for he is dealing with the enchantment of one soul by another, and therefore of one who is as much patient as agent. Are we to think of Socrates and Alcibiades? What the Stranger now seems to be demanding is that the courts insert into their decisions a punitive version of the preludes that failed to check the crime. Given the extraordinary difficulty of combining in a single sentence the magnitude of the chastisement with perfect (παντελῶς) compensation, it is not surprising that the Stranger puts off giving the model cases which would stand in between the written law as outline and the decisions of the courts (934b6–c6). Indeed, one wonders whether

---

17. Cf. E. Benveniste, *Noms d'agent et noms d'action en indo-européen* (Paris 1948), 65–74; the Platonic example is discussed on page 73. Σωφρονιστύς is commonly taken to be a word Plato borrowed from the Cretan dialect, but his σωφρονιστήριον suggests otherwise.

there can be model cases, or could Socrates' enchantment of Thrasymachus, who gave up cash payment for the right to found the best city, be
what the Stranger has in mind?

3   COMEDY

The theme that gradually emerged in the development of civil law was
the relation that obtained between subjective claims of right and the express commands of the law, and how much the courts might concede to
the former, and how severe they ought to be in resisting these encroach-
ments on the law. A natural corollary to this theme was to what extent
the courts could correct faults of the soul, or whether it was enough to
compensate the victim of those faults. The Stranger did not know how
either the legislator or the magistrates were to disassociate his own theology from voodoo, and he did not offer examples the courts could use to
accomplish the second time around what the education had not done in
the first place. The relation between soul and body thus came to light as
a problem in two successive paragraphs, each of which began with almost
the same phrase, and neither of which had a sentence connective.[18] It was
as if the split between the divine and human goods in the eidetic structure of the good were now fully lodged in but still not incorporated into
the law. The Stranger now goes on to madness, which he divides between
madness as a disease and madness caused by the evil nature of anger and
a bad upbringing (934c7–936b2). At long last, the Stranger restricts the
license he formerly gave to anger in the criminal law, for the insulting
words that would initiate homicidal anger are now banned from all public
and sacred places of assembly, and if the magistrate in charge does not
check or chastise (κολαζέτω) the speaker, he cannot compete for the highest honors. If an angry exchange of words occurs outside a magistrate's
immediate jurisdiction, whoever of the citizens has seniority at the time
has the right to beat up those who are indulging their anger. The law anticipates the blows that would follow angry words and heads them off by
blows. It is hard to believe that any but those the Stranger called "great and
perfect" politically would be capable of such an intervention (730d6–7).
    A burst of anger is equivalent to the rebestialization of man, and all
of the soul that education once tamed is savage once again (934e6–935a7).

---

18. 932e1: ὅσα τις ἄλλος ἄλλον πημαίνῃ; 933e6: ὅσα τις ἂν ἕτερος ἄλλον πημήνῃ.
Note the use of the poetic πημαίνειν, which first occurred at 862a3: εἴ τις τινά τι
πημαίνει.

The law can do no more than prohibit the public expression of this savagery, for it is constrained to foster the thumoeidetic nature while it has to hope for the knowledge of how to gentle it (731b3–d5). Self-knowledge had been the burden of the second half of the Stranger's prelude at the beginning of the fifth book, and it reappeared when the Stranger rebuked the fathers for not knowing either what was their own or themselves (923a2–5). The ridicule to which the self-ignorant are subject is now connected with the taunts that anger brings in its wake, and the Stranger wishes to distinguish between playful joking and angry mockery. The Stranger's denunciation of the Dorians as pederasts with loose wives and Megillus's counterblast against Athenians as drunkards are perhaps over the borderline of the permissible. They seem, however, to fall under the Stranger's exception to no funny business, "if there is no need" (816e5), for they did much to clear the air and make it possible to get down to the serious business of symposia: the Stranger then for the first time addressed Clinias and Megillus as friends (637d1). The Stranger certainly does not want just anyone to slip from reviling to ridicule. He reviles any occasion where the two coincide, and presumably he is not joking. Aristophanes' *Clouds*, however, is prohibited absolutely, regardless of whether the poet was angry at Socrates or not. The Stranger assumes that the citizens are thin-skinned, and it cannot be left up to the butt of a joke whether he takes it in good part or not, and does not mind, as Socrates would not and Euthyphro does, whether everyone laughs at him (*Euthyphro* 3c1–d2). A loss of dignity or pomposity goes along with the telling of jokes if it becomes a habit (935b2–4), and the law cannot sponsor the nonseriousness of man, which Megillus thought was the same as his utter insignificance. We are a far cry from παιδεία as παιδιά. In one case alone does the Stranger allow for men and women to be funny, if they are at least fifty years old, with some beautiful and conspicuous deed behind them, and are themselves good and honored in the city (829c2–e5). The Stranger expresses indifference whether their lampoons, directed at one another, are rather boorish and are more like horseplay among soldiers than anything the Graces inspire.

Throughout book 11 there is a tension, which perhaps increases as the civil law unfolds, between justice and moderation (cf. 936b4, d2). It thus confirms what the Stranger acknowledged in book 8, the failure of his education to instill moderation; but we did not know then that not only *erōs* but justice too is an obstacle to moderation. The Stranger is concerned with how to control the unlimited demands of right, which culminate in the cancellation of time, but show up no less in the traveler's wish, which the Stranger does not share, for the honest innkeeper than in the wishes of the fathers to benefit friends and harm enemies. Book 11 ends with two items involving the courts. One can easily get away with not being summoned as a witness if one is willing to swear by three gods that one knows nothing of the matter (936e6–937a1): perjury is allowed no less if one cannot be bothered by one's neighbor's suit than if one wants him to lose the case without one's testimony. The Stranger ends with a blemish on right (937d6–938c5). It is of the same kind as that which haunted all commercial transactions. "How," he now exclaims, "is right or the vindication of right (δίκη) not beautiful? It has tamed all human things." Right civilizes the human, but education, he has just said, man's soul (935a5; cf. *Gorgias* 470e6–7). If, the Stranger goes on, right is beautiful, how would we not find advocacy (συνδικεῖν) beautiful as well? Advocacy has been so tarnished by the claims of a morally neutral art that no genuine art can be mounted in its stead, since even the most honest advocate, if he is successful, cannot avoid the suspicion that he supplanted the power of the just in the souls of the jurors with its contrary. He would be guilty of sorcery (ψυχαγωγία). No citizen can by definition acquire such an art, for otherwise he defeats the principle of the regime that the generals had already violated, and if he does it for free on the basis of experience, even if he does not abandon the practice of virtue, he incurs automatically the charge of ambition. No foreigner of course could help but be accused of a love of money. The city must simply resign itself to the unjust decisions of its courts if it does not want even its cover of moderation to be blown.

XII

PUBLIC LAW

I HEROIC VIRTUE

The three topics with which the last book of the *Laws* ends represent the three endings of the laws in the inverse order in which we were first introduced to the three structures of which each of these topics was the capstone or completion.[1] The first of the structures to be completed is that of the twelve magistracies, to which the courts did and did not belong (767a5–9; 768c3–d1). The Stranger had then told the courts to wait around for the end of the legislation when he would give them a precise arrangement and articulation. In some sense he now fulfills this promise (956b6–7).[2] The second structure to be completed is the genetic structure of law, which found its end or completion in burial, and whose penultimate theme was the just (632b1–c4). The temporality of this structure, from birth to death, differs from the spatial structure of the magistracies, whether they are in the city or country, and deal with either the soul or body. Both of these endings could have been anticipated. It is the eidetic structure of the good, which is the last of the topics, that was not forecast as exactly as the others were, though the Stranger dropped many hints along the way that a new or composite magistracy was in the offing. The Stranger thus brings the number of magistracies that support the regime full time up to the modular number of the regime and subordinates the courts to the temporal life of the citizens (958d1–2). What was not expected is that the Stranger would institutionalize the symposium in

---

1. μετὰ τὰ εἰρημένα (922b1)—it marks the shift from the contractual obligations of generals, in itself being an aside, to the wills of fathers—is the last such marker in the following items of the law until 956b6, where τὸ λοιπὸν δή, picking up but correcting the λοιπός at 765d4, introduces the courts; τὸ μετὰ τοῦτο at 958c7 introduces burial; and the announcement for the completion of the legislation is given at 960b4–c1. The last use of (ἐφ)εξῆς to mark a new item was at 914b1.

2. Susemihl rightly observes that the promise made in book 6, to complete the court system later, does not just refer to this passage in the twelfth book but points to everything handled from books 9 through 12; see his note 316 of the sixth book.

speech, or his own discussion with Clinias and Megillus, and start all over again with the relation of soul and body through setting before the nocturnal council the problem of the unity of virtue.

The orderliness with which the twelfth book ends stands in sharp contrast with the evidently haphazard or disturbed arrangement of the first half of the book. One could attribute this contrast to the intention, on the part of the Stranger, to underline the difference between laws and a book about laws. Laws cannot be ordered unless there are elements in the legislation that are not laws but explanations of the arrangement of the laws.[3] The issue with which the *Laws* ends, the unity and wholeness of virtue, was already at its start set over against the ordinary character of legislation. Just before he had introduced the eidetic structure of the good, the Stranger had opposed the search for laws in conformity with the species (κατ᾽ εἴδη) of virtue to the search present-day legislators undertake, who set before themselves species (εἴδη), whether of inheritance or outrage, or whatever else they happen to need (630d9–e7).[4] The end of the *Laws*, then, could not be further from legislation proper, which, even if it is articulated in accordance with the notion of whole and parts, can present only the parts but not the whole. Book 12 begins with public lying, public theft, military insubordination, and public malfeasance in that order (941a1–b1; 941b2–942a4; 942a5–945b2; 942b3–948b2). From the way in which the Stranger formulates the preludes to each, it is easy enough to see that impiety, shamelessness and illiberality, cowardice, and injustice are the vices he assigns respectively to each of these crimes, and that, accordingly, piety, moderation, courage, and justice are a version of the divine goods in the eidetic structure of the good. They are not in the same order as they were in book 1, but they are recognizable, provided one takes book 10 into account and, through its elevation of mind, grants some equivalence between piety and good sense. The law must meet various kinds of violations, whether they consist in misrepresenting an em-

---

3. The problem that now emerges recalls that which the Stranger briefly touched on when he discussed the need to survey the laws before he could finish any part of the laws (768c6–e1). He was prompted to mention this because he had completed the magistracies with the courts, which properly were not magistracies.

4. Just before the Stranger declares that the parts (μέρη) of the entire city have been explicated, and he proceeds to the court structure (956b4–7), he lists nine or ten items in a row with only two sentence-connectives among them to mark them as separate items (953e5–956b3). Cicero translates the last item and transfers it to his section on divine laws (*De legibus* 2.45). To single out birds as a suitable dedication to the gods, along with all imitations of the same order as whatever a single painter can complete in a single day, recalls Socrates' last words, as it offers a link between this item and the antepenultimate and penultimate parts of the legislation.

bassy, stealing from public funds, or running away on the battlefield; it cannot be concerned with the question whether virtue as a whole has been fragmented through a single crime, or one could retain every other virtue and still fail in one.

Insofar as the crime pronounces "incurable" on the criminal, the law seems in a sense to have decided that virtue is one; but insofar as it declares the criminal curable, it seems to grant that a number of vices do not automatically spread their contagion everywhere. This inference, however, from the penalty imposed to the character of the criminal cannot be drawn, since the crime itself carries its own weight that has nothing to do with whether reform is feasible or not. "Curable" and "incurable" are categories of the law that are independent of any evaluation of the soul and whether its virtue is one or many. There had been many occasions where the Stranger could have used a crime to prove impiety, but he refrained.[5] He begins the twelfth book with the first legal charge of impiety since the close of the tenth book; but whatever penalty the courts mete out—as a form of subversion or betrayal, it looks as if it requires the death penalty—their decision has no bearing on whether piety holds together the divine part of the eidetic structure of the good. The Stranger's way of bringing the divine goods into the law is to appeal to stories about gods and heroes in the first three vices he discusses in book 12, and, in the case of the review of public officers, to speak of the need for divine men (945c2), who might put an end at least practically to the insoluble problem, *quis custodiet custodes?* That need forces him to anticipate the ending of the genetic structure of law by describing the distinctive form of burial to be accorded the examiners (947b3–e5). The Stranger thus returns us to the beginning of the ninth book, where it was admitted that the citizens were no more divine than the legislators. He then concludes his "heroic" legislation with a remark about the age of Rhadamanthys—it takes us back to the very beginning of the *Laws*— when human beings believed with all the vividness of daylight (ἐναργῶς) that there were gods, and legal disputes were quickly settled, for the gods were the judges through the oaths men took (948b3–c2). The Stranger then brings in the three forms of impiety he discussed in book 10, which he now admits his theology will not alter, and, as he goes on to say, he will not allow it to be used to turn back the clock by fiat (948c2–949b6).

---

5. The removal of property left unguarded does not carry the death penalty for either slave or free, for it does not fall under ἱεροσυλία, even though one is to believe (νομίζων) that the goddess of the crossroads guards it and everything of the kind has been consecrated by the law to her (914b3–c3); see also 917c7, d4.

It is more important for the good and the bad to be friends than for disbelief to be publicly exposed or judicially punished. Indeed, the need for magistrates of magistrates is an acknowledgment built into the structure of the regime that "with changes in opinions about gods laws must also change among human beings" (948d1–3).

The law resists being a whole. It is incapable of being modeled on a living animal even though or just because it is meant for men as they live in time. Its elements pull in different directions and do not cohere even when the Stranger reduces them, as he does now, to a semblance of four virtues. At the beginning of book 12, the Stranger seems to go out of his way to dip the law in poetic fables and then immunize the law against them. He first links the penalty for ambassadorial falsehood with the impiety the city's envoys and heralds would have committed against Hermes and Zeus (941a6–b1); but he then contradicts the stories of Hermes the thief and Heracles the cattle rustler in order to impose the death penalty on public theft and not allow anyone to believe or plead that they are doing what the gods or sons of gods do (941b3–c2). Lying abroad and stealing at home have no connection in themselves with one another, though envoys and heralds may be said to be public advocates and thus rightly placed after the last item in book 11. Whatever connection exists between παραπρεσβεία (ambassadorial falsehood) and public theft is due to the Stranger's explicit mention of Hermes in the first case and his silent allusion to him in the second. The god unifies two crimes, he does not unify two virtues. A similar use had been made of Athena in the eleventh book: she linked the noncitizen craftsmen and the citizen soldiery and ruined the principle of the regime.

The poet is both the servant and the opponent of the legislator. He supplies the god the legislator needs if he is to consecrate envoys and cannot use if he is to execute thieves. For the poet, however, Hermes the thief and the god who brings Priam across enemy lines to ransom the corpse of Hector are one and the same (Horace *Odes* I.10.8–16). The poet gains a whole at the expense of morality; the legislator has to be fragmentary if he is to maintain the moral. The fragmentariness of law leads to such exaggeration of its parts that it is forced to take back its proposals almost at the very moment it puts them forward:

> The most important precept is: No one must ever be without a ruler, either male or female. The soul of no one is to get accustomed, either when he is serious or engaged in play, to do anything alone by himself, but whether engaged in war or in peace, he must always live with his eye on the ruler, being steered even in the smallest things by him, to

> stand or to go, for example, whenever one issues the command, to
> exercise, bathe, eat, or be awake at night for guard duty and conveying
> messages, and in dangers themselves, no one is to go forward or to
> retreat without the clear signal of the rulers; in short, everyone must
> teach the soul by habituation neither to have any know-how (γιγνώ-
> σκειν) or expert knowledge (ἐπίστασθαι) to do anything at all apart
> from everyone else, but there is to be as far as possible always a collec-
> tive and common life for all in everything . . . and this must be prac-
> ticed from childhood on—to rule over others and be ruled by others.
> (942a6–c8)

The Stranger wants all behavior to be collectivized, including knowledge,
and he wants all behavior to lead from the start to knowledge of how to
rule. No one is to be out of step, everyone is to know how to lead the
way. The horizontal uniformity of law collides with the vertical principle
of rule. The citizens must be trained to submit and learn to be free. This
doubleness had informed the difference between law and prelude as well
as the difference between god as the beginning, middle, and end of all the
beings and god as the measure of all things; but never before had one
aspect been expressed in such extreme terms that no room was left for
the other. The young are meant to imagine they hear these precepts as
praise of the life of war (943a1–3); they cannot possibly carry them out
without the support of a communized city and its institutions. Military
discipline has its natural counterpart in the individual body:

> This is the most important: do not corrupt the power of the head and
> feet by wrapping around them coverings that are alien to them, and
> destroy the natural becoming of the hair and shoes that are one's own;
> for these extremities, if they are preserved, have the greatest power
> over the whole and are as deleterious if they are not preserved, and
> one of them is most ministerial to the entire body, and the other most
> in charge, equipped with all the authoritative perceptions of it.

The head must go hatless if it is not to set a bad example for the feet:
nothing is said about gloves. The eccentric Socrates is the model for the
collectivized soldier (*Symposium* 220a6–c1). Even if Socratic endurance
were not at least as much an irritant as an incentive for the average GI,
the head and feet belong to a single body, and an army corps with a single
commander at its head can only be its poetic image. The law is forced to
express in the body the rule of mind over the eidetic structure of the good
and thus contradict the intention of the Stranger's theology, for it cannot
take back whatever impossibility it itself has introduced.

In refusing to treat battlefield desertion under treachery and hence as a capital crime, the Stranger does what he can to keep courage at its proper rank. In order to ensure that charges of cowardice are not recklessly hurled about, the Stranger wants everyone to hold that Right is the virgin daughter of Shame (943d4–e7). He makes use of two stories, one to limit the applicability of the law, the other to determine its penalty. A moral is drawn from a story that was not, and a penalty is devised from a story that could not be. "Had Patroclus been brought back to his tent without his arms but still breathing—it has happened to thousands—and Hector was then wearing his former arms—the poet says the gods gave them to Peleus as dowry on Thetis's wedding-day—it would have been possible for anyone at the time who was base to reproach the son of Menoetius with the loss of his arms" (944a2–8). The Stranger tells a contrafactual story, in which he strips Patroclus of almost everything—he was certainly not the model of the obedient soldier (Iliad 16.684–7)—and turns his story into something impossible: who would strip a man of his arms and not kill him first? If, however, the charge of cowardice sticks: "It is not possible for a human being to do the contrary of what they say the gods did, when Kaineus the Thessalian changed from a woman into the nature of a man, for the genesis contrary to that genesis would be in a way the most appropriate of all punishments for a man who throws away his shield, changing into a woman from a man" (944d5–e2; cf. Timaeus 90e6–91a1). Nature frustrates the will of the law; the closest it can come to what it wants is to bar the coward for life from service in the army and penalize the general who enrolls him (944e5–945b2). No magistrate may decide that the disgraced soldier has changed for the better and thus support the principle "One must always punish the bad [coward] in order that he be better" (944d2–3). Deterrence seems to override correction—it is absurd to suppose that one improves the man who ran away from battle by giving him the life he wanted—and forces the prohibition against indignant ridicule to be violated. Would not the official charge against the coward be translated into such common talk as "He became a woman," and license everyone to invent variations on this taunt? One would certainly like to know whether if the coward struck back and killed his tormentor he would be exiled for two years.

The problem of the relation between law and virtue first comes to a head in a discussion of magisterial review (945b3–948b2). Despite the fact that right (δίκη) holds together and binds into one all the institutions of the city (τὰ πάντα πολιτεύματα), the submission to review that every magistracy must undergo does not suffice to preserve the regime. It straightens out the parts, it does not and cannot look to the whole, for which the nocturnal council has to be devised. The Stranger thus opposes right to education, just as he had before, when he assigned in succession first to education and then to right the function of civilizing man (935a5, 937e1). The difference between them was that right puts man in a state of tameness (ἡμέρωκεν), but education vanishes in an instant at the moment a man indulges his anger and rebestializes his soul (ἡμερώθη). The very way in which right is experienced stands in the way of the establishment of right. Perhaps the argument for divine providence is nothing but a means to temper man's anger. Right was the civilizer when the advocate of right (σύνδικος) was denied to the defendant. That denial was connected with the necessary blotch on right; but now the Stranger tries to remove that blotch by requiring that every magistracy be reviewed after the close of its term. An attempt is made to reinsert virtue into a system of offices that was so organized as to give a place to every claim of right except virtue and good sense; and even in this magistracy, where the city needs the cynosures of every virtue, age and chance are still privileged (946a8–b3).

2   REVIEWERS AND OBSERVERS

The *Laws* seems to come to two false endings before the Stranger recovers his balance and gives us the endings for which he has prepared us. The first false ending concerns magisterial review, the second sightseeing. In the first case, the issue is right, in the second education. The review board handles the internal structure of the city and forestalls its springing apart horizontally; the city's observers allow the city to look at itself from the outside, in the perspective no less of the appearance (δόξα) than of the being (οὐσία) of virtue. The Stranger thus seems to have covered everything that he reasonably could within the confines of the second-best regime. There is a sign that the review board completes the internal structure of the city: after the Stranger recalls that the city is not being founded in the heroic age, he puts in a paragraph that is meant to cover any infraction of the city's laws that does not involve nonmonetary penalties (949c6–e2). A comparable sign that the regulations on going abroad complete the external aspects of the city is that nine or ten items the Stranger had not been able to insert elsewhere are listed immediately after them (953e5–956b3). The members of the review board are all priests of Apollo and the Sun, and the high priest gives his name to the year. The political culmination of the regime thus coincides with the teaching of the theology and the consecration of the ancient law (946c1). Since it is from these priests that observers are chosen for the common Greek sacrifices, the Stranger ties them in with the observers whom he treats almost immediately afterwards. They are, moreover, honored in an exceptional way in death. They illustrate the Stranger's prohibition of dirges and lamentations in public (800b6–e7); and they are celebrated in song as if they had become gods (947b7; cf. 801e1–2): priests and priestesses, if the oracle at Delphi approves, are to follow their bier, "as if the burial were pure" (947d3). The fact that they are corpses does not prevent the representatives of the gods from being present.

Within the city, the Stranger thus balances innovation against strict compliance with tradition; and in his handling of strangers, whether they be visitors to the city or Magnesians abroad, he leaves room for a kindly reception for someone like himself. The Stranger reiterates his objection to a commercial society, whose open borders are an invitation to corruption, though they can do no great harm in a badly administered city without good laws. In their case, the mingling of strangers with strangers is bound to induce a jumble of customs, and their own citizens are likely to go on a tear (ἐπικωμάζειν) when abroad (cf. 637a7); but he now admits that it is virtually impossible to be so isolated that no one comes in or goes out—he conveniently forgets that every teacher is a stranger—and besides one needs to test the city's homegrown virtue against the opinion of outsiders, whose fall away from the substance of virtue does not equally corrupt their judgment of virtue and vice (949e7–950c2). It thus seems that the Stranger has finally hit upon the real equivalent to the symposium in speech: the best representatives of the city are to display themselves to strangers and dare them to corrupt them, and, on their return, prove whether they have withstood the intoxication of freedom from supervision and the lure of foreign ways (952c1–d2). What further confirms that we are at the end is that the Stranger links the observers to the nocturnal council before whom some of them report, just as he had linked the reviewer-priests with the observers. The latter are to teach the young, after they have gone to one of the four pan-Hellenic games, that the lawful ways of everyone else are second to their own; but the guardians of the laws are also to send abroad other observers (950e2–951a5). These observers are indispensable:

> A city that was inexperienced of good and bad human beings would be just as incapable, if it were isolated, of being adequately tame (ἥμ-ερος) and perfectly complete (τέλεος) as it would be, in turn, of maintaining its laws without grasping them by understanding (γνώμη) and not only by habituation. There are always among human beings some

who are divine [the Stranger alludes to Megillus's praise of himself (642b2–d1; cf. 626d3–5)]—not many—and they deserve our acquaintance, growing no more in cities with good laws than without, on the track of whom the man who lives in cities with good laws must search, departing on land and sea, looking for whoever is uncorrupt, in order to confirm all of his own lawful ways that have been beautifully laid down, and to correct others, if anything is amiss. Without this kind of observation and searching a city never remains in a perfect and complete state (τελέως), any more than it does if they go about their observations badly. (951a7–c4)

Not only, then, can the city carry out an experiment on itself safely, but it can use the whole wide world to put everyone else on trial and discover everything about them without running any risk. What more could the Stranger want? The Stranger now gives the composition of the nocturnal council, the time of their meeting—it is to be just before daybreak and about the time the three themselves have reached in their walk—and what they are to discuss—their speeches are not only about the laws of their own city and whatever they learn about from elsewhere but also all the teachings (μαθήματα) that can illuminate the laws and if they are not learnt throw them into greater darkness (951e5–952a6). What seems to be missing so far in these two institutions—of reviewers and observers—is any reflection on the relation between virtue and law. The Stranger has just admitted that the best possible laws are no more effective than the worst in producing the rare. He thus suggests that the remaining problem is precisely what prevents the law from producing true virtue, or why its manifold of species must not just fall short of but cannot even aim at the one of virtue. The Stranger had challenged Clinias and Megillus to consider every law he proposed in light of virtue as a whole, but they had not done so (705e1–706a3). They had not done so because they did not know that there was a knot in virtue itself that had to be resolved before they could even question whether the Stranger's legislation was in conformity with virtue or not. They had not asked what virtue is once they had granted that courage is not all of it and achieved a greater sobriety through intoxication. Their experience was an obstacle to their understanding. The Stranger too had left it obscure whether courage should be extended to include resistance to pleasure or moderation had to be so balanced over against courage that one could not say whether they were two or one. The gods had given men the drink of hope, but not the drink of fear, for it would seem that the gods themselves were the ultimate hope, and their nonbeing the ultimate fear. Virtue, then, had

been left undefined because both the eidetic structure of the good and
the genetic structure of law had omitted piety, and without the tenth
book the virtue, on the basis of which the laws were to be framed, was incomplete.

It is not just virtue that has not been examined, but the law too has
been left hanging between being, on the one hand, the distribution of
mind (νοῦ διανομή) and, on the other, the articulation of the good, the
beautiful, and the just (cf. 957b6–c7). The triplet of good, beautiful, and
just was woven into the fabric of the *Laws*, but it was never presented
thematically. Initially, the good was apart from the beautiful and the just
because the eidetic structure of the good and the genetic structure of
law were apart; but the Stranger neither maintained their separation nor
reinterpreted them as a single whole. The elements of this triad split and
recombined in various ways, but there was no eidetic analysis of them.
There was no eidetic analysis because there was no appeal to an intelligible order or manifold in light of which both the virtues and the principles of law could be understood. Rather, the highest principle was soul
as the first becoming, which lent itself more readily to the temporal being
of man than to any unchanging structure. Piety thus looks as if it can be
attached only to the genetic structure of law and not to the eidetic structure of the good, to which all the rest of virtue belongs. The laws about
burial partly confirm this impression (958c7–960b5). On the one hand,
the divine and lawful practices of the gods below and in the country determine how the dead are handled, and, on the other, while the laws
about burial are the end of the legislation and pretty nearly complete it,
the Stranger presents the natural death of the citizen as being the same
as his putting in place the last element in the structure of law: "There
would be becoming after this [i.e., the courts] an end (τελευτή) according
to nature for a man born and raised, who bore and raised children, and
mutually contracted obligations in a measured way, paying the penalty if
he had wronged anyone and receiving compensation from another, duly
grown old with the help of the laws" (958c7–d3). The Stranger thus collapses the program of the genetic structure of law into the life of an individual; but the experiences of this individual, though they are saturated
in the law, are wholly apart from virtue. The afterlife brings back the
issue of virtue, but it is restricted to justice and piety:

> One should obey the legislator in everything else as well as when he
> says soul is entirely superior to body: that which makes each of us in
> the course of life be this [i.e., an each] is nothing else than the soul,
> but the body is an accompanying semblance (ἰνδαλλόμενον) of each of

us, and when we are dead it is beautifully said that the bodies of corpses are phantom images (εἴδωλα), but that which each of us is really and truly (ὄντως) is deathless and named soul, and goes away to give an account to different gods, just as the ancestral law says—it is an account that gives confidence to the good and terribly frightens the bad—and he has no help amounting to anything when he has died, for his relatives should have helped him when he was alive, to ensure that he had lived, while alive, being most just and most holy, and that when dead he had gone unpunished for his evil faults in the life after the one here. (959a4–c2)

The Stranger leaves unexplained how the dead managed to escape all lawful punishments while alive or what the law-abiding citizen ought to have feared. Are we to imagine that the moderate moneymaker Cephalus lives on in Crete? The Stranger does, it is true, restore the eidetic structure of the good to the genetic structure of law but at a price: he has to drop the three goods of the body as well as three of the soul and solve the riddle of the disjunction between soul and body that that structure displayed by reidentifying the individual with his soul.[6] This reidentification, in making the body a shadow of the real, either drains any reality out of the law's inculcation of habits or asserts the direct transfer of habits and actions onto the soul. The causal nature of soul also becomes problematic: did the Stranger give primacy in becoming to soul in order to deny any being to becoming? Cebes' question returns: why is there becoming at all if soul is as good as always? The legislator's teaching, however, is not meant to be taken too seriously. Its purpose is solely to convince the family of the dead to keep funeral expenses low (959c2–d1). It is not meant to explain why corpses do not deserve to be thrown out more than dung, for the Stranger had reserved that punishment for certain crimes (960b1–3). The law thus trails off into a minor key and does not live up to the conclusion of its genetic structure that the end of the entire regime is to be found in the burial of the dead (632c1–4). Had the Stranger ended with the funeral of the reviewers he would have somehow fulfilled his extravagant claim.[7]

---

6. The identification of "each" with soul is the last of three phases of the *Laws*: at the beginning the Stranger posited "each of us" as one (644c4), and in the eighth book proposed that the artisans be compelled to be only one and not many (847b1–2).

7. If one considers that the reasoning of the legislator about body and soul does not support Antigone, that his law allows tears which Antigone does not shed but forbids dirges (*thrēnein*), and that the Stranger calls attention to the prior treatment of traitors at the end of the burial law, one wonders whether the law, which demands the death penalty for whoever sides with a friend who is not a friend of the city (955b8–

3 The Nocturnal Council

As the Stranger first presents the final task of legislation, it involves its own perpetuation and thus stands over against the final resting place of the dead, whose future is assured in another life (960b5–c1; compare 717a3–6 with 962d3–5). The coincidence of the end of the genetic structure of law with the end of human life is mere coincidence and a poetic flourish. A whole is not complete (ἄτελες) unless its future safety is perfectly (τελέως) secured. For a city and its regime, the safety and health of bodies is not enough: "It must also arrange for law-abidingness (εὐνομία) in souls, or rather for the safety of its laws" (960d1–3). The Stranger first suggests that health is to body as law-abidingness is to soul, and the nocturnal council is to ensure that law-abidingness is irreversible (ἀμετάστρο-φον) and does not unravel over time as men undergo experiential deviations from the law. But he corrects this plausible proposal with something much vaguer. "The safety of the laws" is no doubt a perfectly intelligible expression, but after all the safeguards the Stranger has already put in place, it is not clear what he has omitted and the nocturnal council is to supply. The appropriate model for security agents of any work is to be found in a living being, in which the two that form a natural pair are soul and head (961d1–10). There is a single virtue of this pair, when mind in addition to everything else comes to be in soul, and when sight and hearing in addition to everything else are present in the head: "In a word, mind, if it is in a blend with the most beautiful senses and becomes one, would justly be called the saving of each animal."

This model works perfectly for a ship, in which the mind blended with the senses is to be found in the captain and the crew, who blend the senses together with gubernatorial mind and save themselves and the ship (961e1–5). The safety of either animal or ship is presented as if it were the same as the goal (σκοπός); but in the next two examples, where "goal" is used for the first time, a difference emerges between them. Victory over the enemy is the general's goal, and the health of the body the goal of the physician's art (961e7–962a3). The general is not concerned

---

c5)—the formulation is in the language of Creon (*Antigone* 182–191)—does not require the execution of Antigone, and the Stranger has failed to make a truer tragedy than *Antigone*. He had allowed for that possibility (817d4–8). The statement about the friend who is not a friend of the city comes in the center of a nonordered grab bag of laws. Tacitus's account of Judaism points to a similar difficulty: God, as unique and inimitable, was meant to distinguish him from and prevent him from being confounded with the Egyptian gods, but the burial practices of the Jews did not differ from the Egyptians' (*Historiae* 5.5).

with saving either himself or his army, but he has a goal that might possibly call for the sacrifice of many or all of them; and the art of the physician secures the safety not of the animal but of the body's virtue and does not concern itself with the virtue of soul. The animal that the senses and mind save contains within itself the virtue that saves it; but while the captain and the crew save themselves when they save the ship, they are separable from it and could on occasion lose the ship and save themselves. The victory of the army secures the safety of the city, and the physician does not risk his art in restoring the patient to health. If the nocturnal council, with its mind, eyes, and ears, is comparable to the soul and head of an animal, its goal could be its own salvation along with the city's; and if the city is the trunk (κύτος), with the army its feet and the craftsmen its hands, and incapable of being more than healthy (964e1), then the virtue of the city belongs solely to the nocturnal council, while the health of the city, which is not to be taken as a virtue of soul, is its law-abidingness. The Stranger's correction, then, of his own proposal points up the ambiguity in εὐνομία, and regardless of whether it characterizes a city with good laws or a city whose laws are well administered, it seems to be limited at best to the popular virtues (δημόσιαι ἀρεταί) that necessarily are a manifold and cannot constitute either a whole of parts or a one (cf. 734e4–6).

This conclusion would fit the distinction the Stranger had drawn between the eidetic structure of the good and the genetic structure of law, in light of which one could now say that the beautiful and the just of the genetic structure of law reflect in the body the divine goods of the soul, and for this reason burial was the completion and end of the regime. The laws of cities vary in their goal. The determinant is either one or more of the claims to rule, but especially freedom and empire, or the right of masters over slaves with its complement, the right of the stronger, and the legislators who are wisest in their own eyes favor a hodgepodge of every claim (962d7–e9). The Stranger implies that legislators confuse the political art with the legislative, or the indispensable with the best, and the difference in ends that must be pursued on different occasions overwhelms the steady point to which every prudential purpose must be subordinate. It is something of a surprise, however, that Clinias supplies virtue with its leader mind as the political goal, and not what the Stranger himself had stated it was: "The city must be free, sensible (ἔμφρων), and friendly to itself, and the legislator must look at them when he legislates" (693b3–5; cf. 701d7–9). The Stranger then hastened to add that moderation (σωφρονεῖν), which he substituted for freedom, good sense (φρόνησις), and friendship were not different goals but the same. This political goal can now be understood as the friendship between the vulgar virtues and true virtue, which moderation, as both the equivalent of good sense and not, is to bring about (709e8–710b2; cf. 759b6–7).[8] The duality of moderation finds its image in the double meaning of man as divine puppet: there can be on its basis a consonance between feeling and logos throughout the city without everyone ascribing the same meaning to the logos (cf. 662b1–2). This goal is also consistent with Clinias's choice of the reconciler of family differences who establishes friendship through laws (627e3–628a5). He was there said to be third in point of virtue.

Clinias too goes back to the beginning of the *Laws,* but he is as unaware that the reconciliation of the genetic structure with the eidetic structure is the true political goal as that the perplexity of the relation between being and becoming no less than that between the good, on the one hand, and, on the other, the beautiful and the just lurks in that reconciliation. Clinias's failure to see what the Stranger is about to pose as a series of problems is equivalent to his failure to understand what he has experienced in the course of the *Laws.* The Stranger succeeded in reconciling the apparent opposites of Dorian and Ionian ways, and he inculcated a version of his own moderation in Clinias and Megillus so that they could all become friends. The Stranger now reveals to them the edge he took off his own understanding in order to make it possible that laws could be laid down that not in the experience of them but in the argument for proposing them would preserve an image of himself as a permanent watchdog of the laws. The edge the Stranger took off was not a falling away from his own complete understanding but a falling away from his understanding of what he did not know into the completeness of the law. The chief sign so far of the Stranger's conversion of philosophic perplexity into lawful certainty was the absence of being in his account of soul, or the elevation of soul to being the first in becoming from its being in truth that which is in-between being and becoming. With this elevation several problems arose that we could not even formulate properly without going behind soul to the so-called "ideas."

Clinias retains something of the true perplexity when he gives his version of the eidetic structure of the good, but he does not know it. In three steps, with the Stranger's agreement between the first and second, and his high praise of the conclusion, Clinias recalls what the Stranger had said: (1) "We were saying that all the elements of our laws must look

8. At the conclusion of the prelude and prior to the postponement of the outline of the law, in a sentence that exhibited a double break in its construction, the Stranger had alluded to this friendship (734e3–735a4).

to one thing, and we surely were in agreement that this was rightly spoken of as virtue"; and (2) "we surely laid it down that virtue was four things"; and (3) "mind was the leader of all of them, at which both the three of them and everything else must look" (963a2–10). Whereas the Stranger had separated mind from good sense and associated it only with moderation, Clinias runs them together, but he cannot face the consequence that a part within a whole would then be the one of the whole. The Stranger had implied that the good of mind was the sole aim of the four divine and four human goods (631d4–6); but Clinias's identification makes it impossible for him to catch the Stranger's piquing the vanity of political mind—"You who are of course superior to all sensible men (ἔμφρονες), as you would assert"—and say that political mind or good sense looks toward mind simply. He obviously shies away from having mind looking toward itself, and thus from partially equating the mind's goal with self-knowledge, or the comprehensive reflection on the conditions that make itself possible. Such a comprehensive reflection is none other than political philosophy, whose understanding the Stranger simultaneously represented in the symposium in speech and realized in his conversation with Clinias and Megillus.

Political mind is just one of many minds—the Stranger mentions three others (963a11–b1)—and once Clinias identifies it with mind simply, he would have to come up with something like the good or the idea of the good if he were to answer the Stranger's question, What is your goal? Such an answer would certainly appear to him quite empty when compared with the Stranger's well-defined set of goods for the other kinds of mind. The distribution of mind over the manifold of arts seems to leave nothing to political mind. Clinias senses somehow that he cannot say that its goal is either the human good or the divine good, for the former would make soul ministerial to body and the latter would imply that human institutions could partake in some way in the divine (cf. 962c7–8). What must baffle Clinias is that the separation the Stranger enforced between the divine and the holy, or theology and religion, blocked the possibility of any translation of the one into the other and in this sense the preservation of the divine. The Stranger had just recently emphasized that the laws of the present age, which had altered in accordance with a change in opinion about the gods, prevented him from bringing the three principles of the theology into the city and securing belief at the expense of friendship (948c2–d3). Consecration has been everywhere in the city, but piety is not one of the four species of virtue. Piety seems to stand outside virtue and thus pose the problem of the relation between the whole and the human whole. The Stranger, in taking Clinias up on his answer, the one and four of virtue, suggests that this contains a typical question to which the nocturnal council is to be devoted (964a5–b1).⁹ As a typical question, it is just one of many questions, and if the goal of political mind is not itself to fragment, all these questions must belong to a single structure of questions. This single structure of questions can only be that which the Stranger was looking at while he went through the *Laws* and its laws. It was completely invisible to Clinias and Megillus.

Clinias had inadvertently put forward a question about mind by his identification of political mind with mind. He had made mind a part of a one to which that one was to look. Mind contaminated with nonmind was looking to mind for guidance. If one lets mind take over all of virtue, one would still have mind looking at itself or mind becoming two. The two of mind seems to be the questioning and answering that mind must do if it is to think (διανοεῖσθαι), where διανοεῖσθαι, in meaning both to think through and think apart, thinks both the whole and its parts. The Stranger represents the doubleness in thinking just before he brings up the question of the one and four of virtue. He asks Megillus and Clinias to answer the question he first put to political mind: "Or else you [singular], Megillus and Clinias, can you [dual] divide it at its joints (διαρθροῦν-τες) and point out before me on its behalf what in the world you assert [plural] that [one] to be?" (963b7 8). The Stranger, in having Clinias and Megillus stand in for political mind, pairs and parts them and makes them one. After Clinias confesses that they cannot answer his question, he asks: "What is that whose comprehensive vision (συνιδεῖν) of both itself and those things in which [it is] we must be eager to gain?" Clinias and Megillus are asked to articulate a one, and when they cannot, he asks them to collect in a single view, or in the literal sense give a synopsis of, both that one and the many in which it is. He then proposes that the distribution (διανειμώμεθα) of question and answer between himself and Clinias should consist in his supplying the many and Clinias the one of virtue (963d9–964a4).

The Stranger prepares the ground for asking the question about virtue

---

9. In the *Timaeus* the four elements in their distinctness and unity under transformation imitate the four noetic kinds of animal and their unity in "animal itself"; but it is not made clear whether the noetic parts are a whole of indifferent parts, so that gods and lice are the same eidetically, or there is a hierarchy among them, comparable to the relation of mind to the four kinds of virtue. The unity and diversity in the genetic is in any case plainer than in the eidetic. This is to say nothing of the problem posed by the demiurge, as Atticus observed, and, at the other end of the scale, by the omission of plants in the original count (77b1–3; Proclus *In Platonis Timaeum commentaria*, ed. Diehl, vol.1, 431–432 [131CE]).

as one and many by representing himself as the multiplier of virtue and Clinias/Megillus as its unifier. He distributes between himself and them, who are in succession one, a pair, and a plural, the many and one of virtue. He juxtaposes the issue of dialectic, or of collection and division, with the issue of mind itself as both one and two. He lets us sense a connection between διαλέγεσθαι and διαλεκτική. The connection between them appears particularly tight because the one and many of virtue involves the relation of mind and soul. The self-motion the Stranger ascribed to soul seemed to be unconnected with mind, for the Stranger simply jumped from the self-motion of soul to the virtue and thoughtfulness of soul and failed to put together either virtue with thoughtfulness or the pair with self-motion; yet now that thinking as conversation seems to be hinted at, it seems all but inevitable to link the self-motion of soul with the doubleness of thinking as question and answer, particularly since the question put to thinking is the one of the many of soul. Thinking is to address the question of its own structure. If we import the *Phaedrus* into the *Laws*, as we have been invited to do on several occasions, so that the *Phaedrus* would represent exactly what the Stranger had fallen away from, then we can say that the Stranger, in reinserting the hyperuranian beings into his account of soul, suggests that he is now redirecting his team away from the whole of the laws to the whole of questions, and he gives them a glimpse of what lies beyond the laws and must feed them.[10] This beyond was the necessary ground for what they were doing together. The divergence from it and the motion toward it was the thinking of mind and the self-motion of soul. The *Laws* is the Zeus and Apollo of Cretan and Spartan law who have been turned toward the Sun that itself gains its power of illumination from the intelligible structure of the whole of questions.

The Stranger asks Clinias to account for how the four species of virtue can still be one. He does not remind him of his own account of soul, which, dictated by the needs of criminal law, had divided it into three vices—pleasure, anger, and ignorance—and implicitly united it into the two virtues of moderation and knowledge, whose union could be found in turn either in self-knowledge or the indeterminate dyad of moderation itself. In the eidetic structure of the good he had at first united the goods

10. The way of inquiry the Stranger recommends, τὸ πρὸς μίαν ἰδέαν ἐκ τῶν πολλῶν καὶ ἀνομοίων δυνατὸν εἶναι βλέπειν (965c2–3; cf. 965b8–10), recalls *Phaedrus* 265d3–4, εἰς μίαν ἰδέαν συνορῶντα ἄγειν τὰ πολλαχῇ διεσπαρμένα, but Socrates couples this syncritical way, which is fit for teaching and manifest in his first speech, with the diacritical way of his second speech, which is both the whole and part of a single speech. The Stranger only hints at this second way (964a3–5; cf. *Sophist* 253d5–e2).

of soul in justice and denied to either mind or thoughtfulness a unifying role (631c7–8); but he then had set mind over against all the human and divine goods and hinted that mind was either a fifth virtue or the one of the four of virtue. On the basis of the first book, where courage first came to light as resistance to pain but was in principle extended to cover resistance to pleasure as well, courage could have as easily been united with moderation as moderation with it, and the moderate way the Stranger took to bring Clinias and Megillus around to this could have easily elevated them into thoughtfulness as the one of virtue. If one adds that Clinias's choice of reconciliation under law, over against his rejection of either the extermination of the bad or their voluntary submission to rule by the better, diluted strict justice with moderation, it seems not to be too difficult to make moderation once more the one of virtue.

In posing the problem of the four of singular virtue, the Stranger illustrates the difficulty by challenging Clinias to link up the naturalness of courage, which even small children and wild beasts have, with the rationality of good sense (963e1–e8); and he had already made a similar remark about moderation, that in its vulgar sense it is the characteristic of both some children and wild beasts, and the young tyrant could dispense with its fancier version, good sense (710a5–8). Insofar as the Stranger sets irrational nature against rationality, he seems to connect his theology, which argued for either the primacy of soul over nature or their identification (892c2–5), with the problem of the unity of virtue. That courage or moderation, however, could be at the beginning but mind could not seems to distinguish the gymnastic of book 3 from the Stranger's cosmology; but he had in fact failed to put the priority of soul, with or without mind, into time, so that we could not tell whether the self-motion of soul and the complete virtue of soul were together from the start, or like man the cosmos evolved and acquired thoughtfulness in accordance with some pattern not laid up in heaven. When the Stranger requires that the members of the nocturnal council learn his theology, he divides it into two points and leaves it as obscure as it was before whether they are one or two. He asks Clinias whether there are two of a pair of teachings about gods (δύ᾽ ἐστὸν τὼ περὶ θεῶν) that lead to trust in his theology: "One (ἕν) is, as we were saying about soul, that it is older and more divine than all the things whose motion, on its reception of coming into being (γένεσις), supplies ever-flowing being (ἀέναον οὐσίαν), and one (ἕν) is that which concerns the locomotion, as it pertains to order, of the stars and everything else that mind has mastery over and the whole (τὸ πᾶν) of which mind has marshalled into a distinct order" (966d9–e4). The inherent dissonance between motion and order, which the Stranger underlines by separating so distinctly these two points, seems reflected in the naturalness of moderation and courage, on the one hand, and, on the other, the rationality of good sense. One could perhaps begin to resolve the human puzzle by demoting courage and moderation to corporeal virtues and discovering their true counterparts in soul, but one does not know whether this would entail a revision of the Stranger's theology and involve some ground beyond both mind and soul.

The Stranger picks out courage and good sense by name and calls moderation and justice "the two others." We speak of all of them, he says, as virtue, "on the grounds that they are really and truly (ὄντως ὄντα) not many but only this one, virtue" (963c8–d2). The truth of the four kinds of virtue lies in their common name, but the cause of their being numbered and addressed separately is far easier to give than the grounds of their oneness. The Stranger does not say whether moderation differs from justice in the same way as courage does from good sense. Justice seems far more "natural" than reason, and not as independent of anger as moderation may be of desire (cf. 731b3–8). In the *Republic*, Plato had known how to put together, as al-Farabi said, the way of Thrasymachus and the way of Socrates. Socrates there had to adjust his original position that justice was an art to the thumoeidetic basis of justice before he concluded that justice was neither one nor the other but philosophy. Before he reached that conclusion, he seemed somewhat reluctant to give an account of moderation before defining justice (430c8–e2), as if the harmony between rulers and ruled that moderation brought about could hardly be separated from the justice that kept each class minding its own business.

If we take the *Republic* as an example of what the Stranger has in mind when he asks Clinias to unite what he has pulled apart, we are driven to add the *Laches* and the *Charmides* as two additional paradigms of how Clinias should go about answering the Stranger's question about courage and moderation respectively. In the *Laches,* the extreme positions that Laches and Nicias adopt about courage, with Laches appealing to its natural basis in wild beasts and Nicias parodying Socrates and turning it into a kind of wisdom, recall the way in which the Stranger now formulates the problem; and in the *Charmides,* the blush of Charmides, which looks like the natural basis of moderation, and the knowledge of knowledge, which Critias boldly puts forward as its definition, again in parodying Socrates, represent the same duality that the Stranger implies would have to be overcome in the difference between moderation and good sense. We thus have three Platonic dialogues in each one of which a version of the Stranger's question is at work. They represent the manifold in which the one of virtue shows itself; but there is no dialogue devoted to good sense in which the one of that triad would not be another showing of virtue but the being of virtue as it really and truly is one. This missing dialogue seems to be the Platonic model of what Plato represents the Stranger as falling away from in order to lay down the law. What lies beyond the *Laws* and behind it is that law wants to be the discovery of what is.

The virtue of the guardian of the laws is itself at stake in the question about virtue. He can be a somebody (τόν γε ὄντα τι) only if he knows what makes him be a some one (964a5–c4). His knowledge of difference within sameness and sameness within difference differentiates him from everyone else. The Stranger expresses the difference by distinguishing between two needs—the need someone may have to know and understand (γνῶναί τε καὶ ἐπίστασθαι) and the need someone may have to be punished and rebuked (κολάζεσθαί τε καὶ ἐπιπλῆξαι)—that the guardian must know how to satisfy by teaching and making perfectly clear what power virtue and vice have, and he expresses the sameness by adding in the second case that the one in need misses the mark or is at fault (ἁμαρτάνοντι). The unity of vice is as much contained in the double meaning of ἁμαρτάνειν as the unity of virtue is contained in that of σωφρονεῖν. The Socratic principle of the criminal law, which crowns self-knowledge with knowledge of ignorance, and the principle of the cidetic structure of the good are one and the same.

The guardians who are likened to mind are assisted by younger members who are their eyes and ears (964e1–965a4). It is not immediately obvious why the Stranger splits the single virtue of head and soul into two groups, as if the older were so decrepit that they were not aware on their own of what was going on throughout the city. The observers who go abroad and report back on what they have seen and heard are more clearly the eyes and ears of the council. When he had first stated the need for the political goal to be known to some element within the city, the Stranger had made the second task of the council to figure out how the city must partake of this goal, and what or who advises it well or not; and these advisers were in the first place the laws themselves and in the second human beings (962b4–9). The laws themselves are the chief representative of what is known solely by hearing, and the younger members, for all their natural acuteness, would primarily express in council what their experience of the laws was (cf. 632c5–6). Clinias exemplifies within the *Laws* what kind of knowledge could be expected to come from the eyes and ears of the council. This knowledge would be essential for the senior members if they are to keep together the political goal as such with awareness of the degree to which and the manner in which the city as a whole shares in it. Despite their great age, Clinias and Megillus, whom the Stranger rejuvenated in the first book, are the models for the junior members. The senior members take after the Stranger. Megillus is the first to realize this and urge Clinias to recruit the Stranger into the city or else abandon its founding altogether (969c4–7). Megillus realizes that the city cannot by itself initiate the more precise education of the guardians. A stranger must be at the beginning with a knowledge greater than any that can come from either the laws or the reading of the *Laws*.

The more precise education consists in one, two, three, or four elements. They are four if one distinguishes between the one and four of virtue, the one and many of the beautiful, the one and many of the good, and the theology (965b4–966c2). They are three if the one and many of virtue fall under the one and many of the good; they are two if the theology, which the Stranger says is one of the most beautiful things (cf. 966d4–5), falls under the one and many of the beautiful; and finally they are one if the general procedure of comprehending a dissimilar many into one comprehends everything else. In the last case, law as the distribution of mind would prove to be the image of dialectic. The Stranger expands the knowledge the guardians need so as to include all the serious things (περὶ πάντων τῶν σπουδαίων). But we know from what he said about tragedy and comedy that knowledge of the serious is inseparable from that of the laughable (816d9–e10), and the laughable, at least in the Stranger's experience of it, was the religion of the city: he had, after all, forbidden the doing and saying of the laughable things only if there were no need. Even apart from this indispensable expansion of the guardians' knowledge, which leaves behind the hearsay of the laws everyone else is to be forgiven for following (966c4–6; cf. 624b2), the Stranger is also silent about the just. Had he added it, we would have been able to say that the knowledge the guardians have is nothing other than of the sameness and difference of the eidetic structure of the good and the genetic structure of law. The just, one could say, falls under both the beautiful and the good, in just the way that Glaucon wanted Socrates to show him that it was both good in itself and in its consequences, or that it combined the best and the most necessary (*Republic* 358a1–3). If one sets the just aside, the Stranger clearly proposes that the beautiful and the good be articulated separately, and, as he presents it, this amounts to the theological problem of becoming, on the one hand, and, on the other, the ontological problem of the good.

Within the theology there was an eidetic problem that the Stranger left unresolved. He gave both a kinematical and dynamical articulation of motion that split apart the mathematical and the causal, and within the causal he failed to show how soul and mind cohered. Mind, in turn, brought in the duality of virtue and good sense that was at one with the problem that Clinias raised in putting mind among the four of virtue. The four of virtue was the exemplar of the eidetic problem. The eidetic problem is inseparable from the ontological problem of the good because any whole of parts always seems to yield a number greater than the number of the parts, and the being of the parts seems to exhaust being and leave the whole no less uncountable than beyond being. Piety represents this difficulty in the *Laws,* and in the *Republic* it was the ultimate problem that Socrates explicated only in an image; he likened the good to the sun, but left it obscure whether his image entailed a cosmology, so that as being is to becoming so the good is to the sun, and the good is the being of being and becoming together, or, alternatively, the causality of being and being known would not include the causality of becoming and being seen. This unresolved perplexity shows up in a minor key in the composition of the nocturnal council, where mind and the senses are together yet apart, and it shows up in a major key in the Stranger letting the two points of his theology be two and not one.

The two points of his theology correspond historically to Anaxagorean mind, on the one hand, and, on the other, the Socratic discovery of soul (967a1–c5). The Socratic discovery carried with it the renunciation of a teleological physics and the recourse to the so-called "ideas." The Stranger does not present outright the import of Socrates' second sailing, but he does suggest how uneasily Anaxagorean mind and Socratic soul fit together by reaffirming that soul is the oldest of everything that partakes of becoming or birth (γονή), while assigning to mind the mind of the beings (νοῦν τῶν ὄντων) among the stars (967d4–e1). The Stranger lists what the god-fearing mortal must know, but not how the two points of his theology and the mathematics that are indispensable for it are to yield him a synoptic vision (συμθεασάμενος) of the participation in them of "the things in conformity with the Muse," which in a harmonious way (συναρμοττόντως) he may use for the lawful things and the practices of his ways (967d4–968a1; cf. *Timaeus* 24b7–c3). The Stranger certainly suggests that the theological prelude Clinias wanted for all the laws could be put in place by the nocturnal council (887b5–c2), for he insists that it have the capacity to give an account of everything that admits of an account; but he himself has not done so, any more than Socrates had when, having advanced the *Republic* from the true city in speech to the philosopher-king, he proposed a deduction from the ideas to the laws of the best city in speech. The way to the principles and the way from the principles are not one and the same.

The last law the Stranger proposes constitutes the nocturnal council (968a4–b1); but they are to lay down no laws that govern the nocturnal council (968c3–7). The nocturnal council, once it is organized, must determine what laws hold sway over itself; and as for what its members are to learn, "it is not easy either to discover it or when someone else has made the discovery learn from him; and besides it is pointless and vain to state in writings the time periods, what they are and in which they must take on each lesson, for it would not even be plain to the learners themselves what is being learnt opportunely, until the knowledge (ἐπιστήμη) of the teaching had come to be within the soul of each" (969d3–e2). It is here where prudence and philosophy diverge. That there can be no order in understanding prior to the understanding of the experience of understanding is equivalent to the Stranger's denial that the *Laws* could be turned on its head and that either he or Socrates could have descended before they had ascended, or that the royal road of geometry holds for philosophy. The Stranger makes a pretty jingle out of this principle. He denies that the teachings have any trace of mysticism in them and are some secret doctrine (ἀπόρρητα), but he affirms that they cannot be stated ahead of time (ἀπρόρρητα). It is not religion that veils but ignorance that prevails over the teachings. If this were not the case, time, as the Eleatic Stranger says, would be superfluous (*Sophist* 265e2). The disorderly order, which began in the element of experience, returns at the end in the element of knowledge.[11] The laws that govern the nocturnal council are the sympotic laws (671c4). They are designed to save the laws from themselves.

The Stranger's last words concern the risk Clinias is running in founding the city and the risk he himself is willing to run in helping Clinias. His risk is confined to exploring at greater length the settled opinions he has about upbringing and education, now that the issue has been stirred up a second time, and to lending his assistance in finding others besides himself to found the nocturnal council (968b6–9). He does not say he is willing to be a citizen of Magnesia, and Megillus rightly takes him as not making such an offer, for otherwise he would not advise Clinias to enlist him and Clinias would not then ask for Megillus's help. The Stranger's risk has to do with starting out at the top of the city or, as he says, throw-

---

11. Timaeus recommends disorderly order when he urges the imitation of the random motions of space, which would put into order in a measured way the affects that wander around the body (*Timaeus* 88d6–e3). He leaves it open whether his recommendation applies solely to body, or, since space is coextensive with the whole and disorder is built into the world-soul, it necessarily must apply to mind as well (cf. 34c2–4; 69a6–b2).

ing a triple six on the first cast; Clinias's risk is to be thought the most daring (ἀνδρειότατος) if he sets out to found the city without the luckiest of all throws. The Stranger all but tells Clinias that he cannot get started if he does not know how courage and good sense are one and the same.[12] Then, he tells him, he can put together the *Laws*.

12. φρόνησις and ἀνδρεία had first shown up together as the qualifications the judge of any theatrical performance needed (659a1–4).

EPILOGUE

We have been looking at the *Laws* more or less in itself, with digressions elsewhere, whether within the Platonic corpus or without, only when they seemed relevant; but we have ignored what effect the *Laws* as a whole might have had on other writers on law, and in particular what interpretation they gave it. Cicero's *De legibus*, though we have but less than three books of it, is the closest in time as well as in spirit to the *Laws*.[1] It is the best place from which to look back at the *Laws* and gauge its meaning once it had been translated to another setting. Cicero's *Laws* throws a special light on Plato's because it begins by crossing the beginning of Plato's *Phaedrus* with the beginning of Plato's *Laws*. Of all the relations that the *Laws* has to other dialogues, the most perplexing is that to the *Phaedrus:* the *Phaedrus* and the *Laws* are the only dialogues that have their setting outside the city, and as the *Phaedrus* is concerned with writing, so the *Laws* restricts "laws" in the strict sense to written laws. Socrates is conspicuously absent from the *Laws,* for after he has defined law in the *Minos* the elaboration of a written code would seem to be of no interest to him, and Socrates denounces writing in the *Phaedrus* in favor of speaking and his own erotic art. To write the *Laws,* however, seems to be a greater deviation from Socratic principles than to imitate Socratic speech in writing. Cicero's own devious way into law shows his awareness of this. Although the transitions of his *Laws* from one topic to another are managed adroitly, if one considers them dialogically, their

---

1. Cf. Leo Strauss, *Natural Right and History* (Chicago 1953), 137n: "Cicero has indicated the higher dignity of 'regime' as distinguished from 'laws' by the contrast between the settings of his *Republic* and his *Laws*. The *Laws* are meant as a sequel to the *Republic*. In the *Republic* the younger Scipio, a philosopher-king, has a three-day conversation with some of his contemporaries about the best regime; in the *Laws* Cicero has a one-day conversation with some of his contemporaries about the laws appropriate to the best regime. The discussion of the *Republic* takes place in winter: the participants seek the sun; in addition, the discussion takes place in the year of Scipio's death: political things are viewed in light of eternity. The discussion of the *Laws* takes place in summer: the participants seek shade."

thematic purpose is obscure.[2] It is easy to see how historiography yields to legal philosophy, and that the poorness of Roman historians matches the narrowness of Roman jurists (5–7, 14), but not how the opposition between poetry and history, and in particular that between Cicero the published poet and Cicero the historian yet to be, introduces properly the question of law. Cicero, however, in suggesting how we can go about trying to put together the argument with the form of the dialogue, goes some way to explain as well the connection, at which Plato hints, between his *Laws* and *Phaedrus*. As the *Phaedrus* is one remove from Socrates' erotic art, so the *Laws* is one remove from the *Phaedrus*. It is third in rank.

Perhaps Cicero's clearest suggestion lies in the contrast implied between the published *De re publica*, which Quintus and Atticus have read, and *De legibus*, which is happening now and turns out to be written behind the backs of Quintus and Atticus. *De legibus* is to *De re publica* as the *Phaedrus*, in its illusion as spoken dialogue, is to the *Phaedrus* as written. Its air of unrecorded speech is against its theme of written law. Quintus and Marcus have read a book that assigned the death of the Roman republic to the moment at which Scipio, through a natural death or assassination, could not assume the dictatorship (6.12). *De legibus* is meant to supply the legislation for a regime that no longer exists except in speech. It is accordingly even more imaginary than the idealized version of the Roman republic that Cicero gave. His had a chance; this has none (cf. 3.29). The Rome of *De re publica* is now like Marius's oak; it has taken the place of, or is indistinguishable from, the real Rome. Cicero's Marian oak can be pointed out at Arpinum, but no one can ever be certain that the deictic pronoun *haec* points any further than from one text to another. Atticus begins the dialogue: "I have often read of that grove (*lucus ille*) in [your] (Cicero's) *Marius*, and I recognize this oak (*haec quercus*) of the Arpinatines, for if that oak remains, then this is surely it; it is at any rate very old" (1.1).[3]

The translation does not capture the oddness of the grammar: the irregularity of *lectus*, in agreeing with the more remote *lucus* in Atticus's speech, leaves *haec . . . quercus* something he recognizes but has not read.[4] He can thus refer to the Marian oak as *illa*, as if it were not a

2. Cf. M. Pohlenz, "Der Eingang von Cicero's Gesetzen," *Philologus* (1938): 102–127.

3. *lucus quidem ille et haec Arpinatium quercus agnoscitur, saepe a me lectus in Mario: si enim manet illa quercus, haec est profecto; etenim est sane vetus.*

4. A. E. Housman cites this passage in his edition of Lucan for Lucan's far easier *hinc leges et plebis scita coactae* (1.176).

Ciceronian fiction but something once real, whose survival would allow for its possible identification with the *haec* he sees before him. Survival in speech, however, replaces survival in deed: "No stock cultivated by a farmer," Quintus says, "can be as long lasting as that propagated by a poet's verse [or furrow (*versus*)]." Quintus's apparent misunderstanding of Atticus's *manet*—"Of course it remains and shall always remain, for it was planted by a native intelligence (*ingenium*)"—seems to indicate that the problem of law is bound closely with referents that cannot be fixed.[5] Atticus's *haec* is the same as Quintus's, but Quintus's *illa* is not necessarily the same as Atticus's: Quintus's *illa* is that from which "once upon a time the tawny messenger of Jupiter flew up" (1.2), and Atticus's "Then this is surely it" must become Quintus's "Now let this be it." Indeed, if one takes Quintus's *commemoratio* as ambiguously as his *versus*, he anticipates inadvertently the theme of the dialogue, for he can be said to adduce the principle that nothing is as fixed by nature as that which has been stamped by a visible mark of the law: *multaque alia multis locis diutius commemoratione manent quam natura stare potuerunt.* In nature, things grow old, decay, and disappear; in written memorials, they simply become hoary with the patina of antiquity (*canescet*).

Atticus wants Cicero to imitate his master Plato and follow up the writing of *De re publica* with its counterpart *De legibus* (15). In Cicero's reply, Plato the writer becomes the *ille* who disputed with Clinias and Megillus. The Athenian Stranger thus ceases to be without a name and is no more a mask than Cicero himself is. Since Clinias and Megillus are the pair whose kinship, through the similarity of Spartan and Cretan laws, sets them apart from the Athenian Stranger, the kinship of Quintus and Marcus, we might suppose, as well as their political activity, would set Atticus apart and make him the spokesman for Cicero's views, especially since his cognomen recalls Clinias's refusal to address the Stranger as Ἀττικός (626d3). Atticus, however, cannot possibly be the spokesman, for Epicureanism has no political philosophy at all (at least in the required sense of what the best political order is), and everything Marcus says, from the divine principle of the universe to the separation of the noble from the pleasant, is wholly alien to it (31). Cicero has a friend stretch his friendship to its utmost and thus deny dialogically what Marcus asserts dogmatically, that the slightest difference nullifies friendship

---

5. Cf. M. Ruch, *Le prooemium philosophique chez Cicéron. Signification et portée pour la genèse et l'esthétique du dialogue:* Publ. Fac. des Lettres de Strasbourg CXXXVI (Paris 1958), 252, on book 1: "L'absence de toute indication chronologique—fait unique—donne à la fiction un caractère indeterminé."

(34). Not despite their differences but because of them, the association the three speakers have with one another seems to be a sounder and more realistic ground for political community than the friendship of the wise with the wise, which is so perfect as to be indiscernible from self-love (34). The deictic pronouns of Stoic doctrine are self-referential and no more point to another than do those assigned to the Marian oak. Atticus's goodwill lets Cicero win a case that Atticus cannot be a party to. He is in fact the representative of a view—it chiefly consists in maintaining the priority of body to soul—that the Athenian Stranger combats in the tenth book. So Cicero has law pit itself against the most refractory of opponents and appeal to principles for which it could not argue. At the beginning of the first book, Cicero reproduces the Athenian Stranger's intoxication of Clinias and Megillus by elevating the view of Atticus, and at the end he again reproduces the Stranger's condescension by taking something off from his starting point. What prepares the way for this movement within the argument about law is the tangential manner in which law itself gets broached.

As the first word of Plato's *Laws* is θεός, so the first principle that Atticus has to accept is that all of nature is ruled by some indeterminate character of the gods (21). Cicero thus alludes to his putting a weaker version of Plato's tenth book at the beginning. He adopts for his own purposes Clinias's proposal that the Stranger start all over again and make the tenth book the prelude to all laws (887b8–c2). Just as the discussion of the two suns at the beginning of *De re publica* alludes to Cicero's putting there a weaker version of the seventh book of Plato's *Republic*, where Socrates proposes to replace the mathematical astronomy of his own day with a purely mathematical science of motion, based on the not yet developed science of solids, so *De legibus* starts with a natural law teaching and only later introduces a doctrine that does not depend on any special premise but, with the exception of the Epicurean and the skeptical Academy, is acceptable to all the schools. Cicero thus goes back to Socrates after he has acknowledged the changes that Socrates through Plato effected. Socrates becomes a discovery of Cicero rather than part of the philosophic tradition.

Cicero first speaks in answer to a question of Atticus, who wants to know, "Did your verses plant this oak, or did you take over a tradition that what befell Marius happened in just the way you write of it?" (3). Cicero is not asked whether the story of Marius's oak is true; he is asked whether he made it up on his own or took over an older account. Cicero's counterquestion therefore puzzles Atticus, for he is asked whether Romulus announced to Proculus Iulius that he was a god and Aquilo raped Orithyia. Atticus's answer would of course have to be no to both questions; but Cicero implies that tradition does not differ from a poet's free invention, and *fabula* covers them both. Such a shift in the issue certainly allows the "laws of history" to be introduced, but at the price of confining history, as Atticus wants to do, to contemporary eyewitnesses (8). The question of identity, however, which the Marian oak raised, is not settled. Cicero assigns to Atticus two houses, one in Rome, not far from Romulus's epiphany, and one in Attica, not far from the rape of Orithyia. These two places are known to Atticus through his dwellings; they are known to everyone else through the stories attached to them. Atticus's local knowledge cannot help to dismantle or confirm the tradition. It can only do so elliptically, by recalling a passage in Plato's *Phaedrus* (229b4–c5):

> Phaedrus: Tell me, Socrates, is it from somewhere here abouts that
>   Boreas is said to have snatched Orithyia from the Ilissus?
> Socrates: Yes, so it is said.
> Phaedrus: Is it really then from here? Its waters, at any rate, appear
>   charming, pure, and transparent, and suitable for girls to play
>   along its banks.
> Socrates: No, it's one or two stades further down, where we cross
>   over to the precinct of [Artemis] Agra. Nearby there is an altar
>   of Boreas.
> Phaedrus: I scarcely have it in mind. But, by Zeus, Socrates, speak:
>   are you persuaded that this story (μυθολόγημα) is true?

Socrates' curt denial that the place that, Phaedrus reasons, might be where Boreas raped Orithyia prompts him to ask whether Socrates is convinced the mythology is true. Phaedrus's inference from the appearance of the waters of the Ilissus, that it could be the place, since it is such a suitable spot for girls to play near, recalls Atticus's own inference, "For indeed it is very old," that led him to ask whether *illa quercus* was *haec quercus*. Cicero, then, in alluding to the *Phaedrus* in the context of his imitation of Plato's *Laws*, has urged us to consider Socrates' refusal to rationalize mythical monsters (τερατολόγοι φύσεις) as long as he does not know himself as the proper way to approach his *Laws* (*Phaedrus* 229c6–230a6). Self-knowledge proves to be the last theme of the first book (59–62). It is there linked with the word *philosophia*, which Cicero has to transliterate; he cannot either "calque" it or find its native equivalent. *Philosophia* is thus separated from *prudentia* and *sapientia*, both of which belong to the context of the natural law teaching (19). The philosophers are at first *doctissimi viri* (18), but in the second half they are *philosophi* (36, 50, 53).[6]

People say, Atticus reports, that Cicero as a native of Arpinum and a near contemporary of Marius should tell the truth. Cicero evades the challenge these people pose and identifies them with those who believe that Numa talked with Egeria and an eagle placed the hat on Tarquin. They are not the skeptical but the credulous. They no less than Atticus want his *Marius* to be true. Poetry, it seems, makes them both uneasy. They do not recognize that, as Quintus says, it has its own laws. Quintus thus supplies the thematic word of the dialogue but with a deviant sense, even though the mention of Numa offered the occasion to slide over into the issue of divine law. Why, then, is law postponed until after history has been discussed? Does history strike up a more suitable prelude than poetry? This deviant sense of *leges* recalls the deviant sense of νόμοι in Plato's *Laws*.[7] The laws of history amount to one—to tell the truth; the laws of poetry are more than one, for only a greater part of it looks to pleasure. Law, then, in its ordinary sense, would seem to be closer to the truth telling of history than to the delightfulness of poetry. The identification of law with right reason would confirm this (23; cf. Plato *Laws* 645b4–8). Cicero admits, however, that not only the father of history but also Theopompus relate countless *fabulae* without either of them ceasing to be historians. It would seem that truth is the aim of history to which it does not necessarily measure up. Socrates also had defined law in terms of its intention to be the discovery of what is. Law is not the discovery of what is. The meaning (*vis*) of law is the assignment of things to their proper place; it therefore must also mean the selection of things to be so assigned; but it only means this if its Latin significance is put together with its Greek. Law is in intention both *delectus* and *aequalitas*, or, once more in Greek, dialectic (19). It fails, however, at both selection and assignment. It deviates from what is. Its deviancy first comes to light in the deviancy of *leges*. It is therefore the inadequacy of Roman historians rather than their fulfillment of the "laws" of historiography that serves as the proper introduction to law.

Atticus faults the Roman historians not for their failure to observe the sole law of history but for what Cicero had told him was especially

6. For the difference between *sapientia* and *philosophia*, see *Tusculan Disputations* 5.7–10.

7. Cf. 2.29: *negat (Plato) enim mutari posse musicas leges sine mutatione legum publicarum. ego autem nec tam valde id timemndum nec plane contemnendum puto.*

the task of the rhetorician (5).[8] This is perhaps the most surprising turn in *De legibus:* it anticipates the subsequent insertion of rhetoric into the usual tripartition of philosophy and confirms how well Cicero absorbed the lesson of the *Phaedrus.* If the annals of the *pontifices maximi* suffer only from dryness, and the rest of the historians from lack of various refinements, it is hard to see the relevance of stylistics to the discussion of law. Inasmuch as Cicero adopts for the formulation of the laws themselves an archaizing version of the language of the twelve tables and thus deviates from them (2.18),[9] it would seem that the old Roman annals are to the laws as the awaited Ciceronian history would be to his *De legibus.* *De legibus* must be stylistically advanced. It contains no *res gestae,* except as they emerge in the speeches of the speakers. *De legibus* is a poem about law: delight is an ingredient in it (14; cf. 2.14). It conforms with the laws of one kind as it argues about the laws of another kind. It thus subjects law in its original sense to a deviant mode. It is only possible long after the beginning because its theme is the true beginning, not the beginning of Rome or any other city (19).

The conversation that immediately precedes Cicero's exposition of law does not prepare for that exposition in a straightforward manner. The sequence that focuses on some aspect of law is this:

1. Marcus reserves for his old age along with philosophy the writing of history, while public duties would be confined not unwillingly to giving *responsa* "in the ways of the fathers" (10).
2. Atticus remarks that Cicero's more philosophic style of speaking will let him continue the pleading of cases up to extreme old age (11).
3. Quintus insists that the role of *iuris consultus* would meet with wide approval.
4. Marcus, in tacitly accepting Atticus's view that he never has to give up forensic speaking, remarks that he would be increasing his labor, since he always devotes long study to his briefs (12).
5. Atticus proposes that Cicero in this fractional time write (*conscribis*) about the *ius civile* more subtly than others (13).
6. Marcus accepts, on Quintus's approval; Quintus is delighted to spend the whole day on it (13).

8. Cf. Pohlenz, op. cit., 110–111, for *De oratore* 2.62 as Atticus's source for his presentation of Cicero's view.

9. For Ciceronian innovations in his archaizing, see D. Daube, *Roman Law* (Edinburgh 1969), 46–48.

7. Marcus proposes that they walk first and then rest (14).

8. Atticus suggests a walk to the Liris with a discussion of *ius civile* (14).

9. Marcus objects; others do it perfectly adequately for all practical purposes, though they do not treat *ius civile* as it deserves: *ius civile* is *ius civitatis*. Cicero knows of course that the possessive adjective is by usage not at all equivalent to the genitive of possession; but, just as Scipio began his account of *res publica* by decomposing it into *res populi* (*De re publica* 1.39), he has recourse to their equivalence in principle. Cicero imagines that he is being asked to compose legal treatises (*libellos conficiam*), even though he had just agreed to talk about *ius civile*. This is the second time that speaking has been confused with writing, but it is not the last.

10. Atticus now declares that he wants Cicero to imitate Plato and write a companion piece *De legibus* to his *res publica* (15).

This sequence contains two apparently unrelated perplexities. The first consists in the deliberate violation of dramatic illusion by the failure on the part of Cicero and Atticus to keep speaking and writing apart. This failure recalls the second half of the *Phaedrus*, where Socrates seems to speak indifferently of speaking or writing even though the topic is writing (258d1–5, 259e1–2). That it has some connection with the problem of law is suggested by Cicero's reminder that, since their whole *oratio* is popular in character (*in populari ratione*), they will necessarily speak popularly and call *lex* that which is written and sanctions what it wants by command and prohibition (19).[10] It seems that *lex* implies the written law to such an extent that the very mention of *ius civile* has Atticus speak of speaking as writing. Law is truly oral only when Cicero contemplates his adoption of the way of the fathers, and he is to sit in judgment in particular cases in which the decision does not have to be strictly applicable to any other case no matter how similar. Cicero thus opposes prudence operating within the confines of Roman law to both a juridical treatise on some point of Roman law and a treatise on law in general. Inasmuch as it is Cicero's decision to turn the present occasion into a discussion of law, he implies that it is through dialogue that he can combine the particularity of oral *responsa* with the generality of writing. Dialogue, even though written, preserves the circumstantiality of speaking. The

10. *quae sunt autem varie et ad tempus descriptae populis, favore magis quam re legum nomen tenent* (2.11).

context in which the *ratio* of Stoicism is presented compromises its presentation. Dialogue makes the community of reason deviate from reason.

That Cicero has been making the first principle of natural law—
reason and mind—more and more conform with the human condition
is clear enough; but it should occasion no surprise that Atticus is more
aware of the distant derivation of the principle of right than of the continual deformation to which Marcus has had it submit. The principle
Atticus has to understand—we are born for justice and right by nature
and not by opinion—is not as great and remote as he supposed (28). Cicero puts natural right not quite on a par with the very first of principles.
It would seem then that he should try to prove that there is natural right
independent of the concession Atticus made him. Cicero's proof has as
its centerpiece a contrafactual: if the original nature of man could be restored, the identity of every man with the highest in man would be self-
evident (29, 32); but as it is, the class-characteristic of man, rationality,
suffices to distinguish us only from beasts; it is not enough to make us
interchangeable with one another. Such interchangeability now occurs
only in the case of two strictly wise men, for each of whom the love of
another is the same as the love of himself (34). It is not clear whether
Marcus said that he knew of any friend of this perfect kind, for the gap
in our text between 33 and 34 cannot be filled with anything near certainty.[11] We can conjecture, however, from the change in the order of topics that Atticus makes in his summary of Marcus's argument that it was
not clear to him at any rate whether the society of right was derivable
from the natural goodwill of all men or natural goodwill was derivable
from the society of right (35). Atticus's inversion of the order makes reason far less potent as the basis of right than it presumably was in Marcus's
own presentation. Atticus's goodwill toward Marcus is independent of his
concession about the place of reason in the whole. Their friendship is not
a sign of their agreement but a compensation for their disagreement. It
makes up for all that divides them. Marcus's proof, then, has to be pronounced a failure, for it replaces the society of men with gods with the
society of the wise man with himself. The gods, to be sure, cease to be
members of human society, but human society is a society of one. Cicero
can bring men together if there are gods, but then there is no rule; or he
can put the gods aside, but then there is no plurality of men. The wise
man transcends the human as much as the divine mind was beyond the

---

11. Laelius discusses this radical form of friendship only to dismiss it, *fortasse
vere*, he says of the Stoic teaching, *sed ad communem utilitatem parum* (*de amici-
tia* 18).

society of gods and men. One has only to compare the place νοῦς has inside and outside the eidetic structure of the good, both at the beginning and the end of Plato's *Laws*, to see how Cicero has understood it. Structure, he implies, is not possible if principles are not diluted.

The second difficulty in the sequence is this. It would seem to have been enough, if Cicero had wanted to prepare the way for law, for Atticus to ask Cicero to speak or write on *ius civile* as soon as Cicero himself spoke of *respondere* (10). Why should Atticus have to deny that Cicero will ever be free of advocacy and Quintus remark that if he devotes himself *ad ius respondendum* it will meet with the people's approval? Why should Cicero's superior skill in *ius civile* be tied in with the present? Why should it be something that does not have to be postponed but can be done at any spare moment? Law thus loses its connection with history and philosophy and has assigned to it the partisanship of the lawcourt (21). Cicero the arbiter yields to Cicero the controversialist, who will have to build the best possible case for law. Cicero's initial adoption of a Stoic teaching on law seems to be a direct consequence of this reorientation. Just as he had argued that the critics of his *Marius* were demanding truth from a poet as if he were a witness (4), so he will later ask for the silence of the skeptical Academy (39), and go on to dissolve almost all the substantive issues of the schools into merely verbal disagreements (53–4). Although the greater subtlety Atticus wants Cicero to bring to *ius civile* seems to make a parallel with what he is to do with Roman historiography (13), it turns out that Cicero has no fault to find in Roman jurisprudence as such, nothing in any case that he could do better (14); rather, Cicero is to do something that no one else could do because no one has written his *De re publica*. He defends his own (cf. 2.17). His defense is to be "somewhat richer than forensic practice demands" (15), and for all that it requires that he be unoccupied (*vacuus*), it does not demand that he be free (*liber*) and without a "hobbled mind" (8, 13).

Cicero's outline proposes a strictly deductive disputation on law: (1) the nature of *ius* expounded from the nature of man; (2) *leges* by which states are to be ruled; (3) the *iura* and *iussa* of people that comprehend the *iura civilia* of the Roman people (17). The first two parts of this outline recall respectively the eidetic structure of the good and the genetic structure of law, and the third the Stranger's legislation for Magnesia. It fails, however, to indicate where the best city of *De re publica* fits in. If it were not for the ambiguity of *leges*, one might say that the second part refers to it, and the third to the relation between the kinds of inferior regimes and the variety of laws to be found in various cities; but it is also possible that the second part alludes to those features indispensable in any legislation if it is to guarantee the peace and well-being of the city. This purpose of law emerges only in the second book (11), where Quintus replaces Atticus as the main interlocutor, and Cicero makes another beginning (2.1). There are altogether three beginnings, of which the first two can be said to place law in the light of reason and the third in the light of piety and religion. The third beginning is the Ciceronian equivalent to the Stranger's experience of the divine in the seventh book. In the first book, the universe is the common city of gods and men (23); in the second, it is the temple and home of the Persian gods (cf. *De re publica* 3.14–6), but the Greeks and Roman do better, since, for the increase of piety, they "wanted the gods to inhabit the same cities as we do" (2.26).[12] Anonymous *deus* yields to *summus Iuppiter* (2.10).

The perspective of piety allies Marcus with Quintus and makes Atticus an outsider who cannot share the love they bear their ancestral land (2.50). The ground of their subrational attachment to Arpinum has nothing in common with Atticus's to Athens, which by his own account mainly consists in his recollection of the wise men who lived there (2.4). The land of brothers is their real homeland (*germana patria*, 2.3), and Rome is only theirs by law and obligation (2.5). So alien is all this to Atticus that he goes out of his way to regularize it. Arpinum becomes the father that actually generated Marcus, and the island in which they sit to have their conversation was due to the action of the river Fibrenus, which almost had it as its duty and function (*tamquam id habebat operis ac muneris*) to arrange for such a place for them (2.6). Whereas Cicero in his prose and verse went out of his way to deny any allure to Arpinum (2.2), Atticus through poetry now rationalizes the irrational and proposes a teleology of the local and contingent. The second book thus begins with Atticus adjusting the particular to the universal and the real to the fictional (2.6),[13] just as Cicero in the first book tries to accommodate the universal to the particular through a double account of law.

The first account is from sections 18–35, the second from 36 to the end. The first account involves a teleological cosmology, the second separates off from it the discussion of natural right. The first goes from the beginning, the second to the beginning. The first aims at being didactic, the second at being dialectical. It is Cicero's adoption for the law of the

---

12. Macrobius discusses this movement "from mind to Jupiter," as it were, in the context of a defense of the philosophers' use of *narratio fabulosa* (*Commentarii in somnum Scipionis* 1.2.7–21).

13. *nec enim ullum hoc frigidius flumen attigi, cum multa accesserim, ut vix pede temptare id possim, quod in Phaedro Platonis facit Socrates.*

distinction Socrates drew in the *Phaedrus* between his first and second speech on *erōs* (265c8–266b1): only the second of Cicero's two accounts speaks of self-knowledge (58, 62). The first begins with *lex* as the *ratio summa* of the whole cosmos (18), the second with the phenomenon of conscience (40). The first starts with the divine, the second from the human. The first establishes the community of reason of gods and men (23), the second assigns the foundation of right to the natural affection among men (43). The first speaks of the perfect friendship of the perfectly wise (34), the second speaks of the controversies among the very philosophical schools whose unanimity was the basis of its argument (52–3). The first says we are born for justice (28), the second that we are born for civil society (62). These differences could be multiplied, and they would all point to the second argument's undercutting of the dogmatic postulates of the first; but they do not by themselves explain why Cicero proceeds in this way. For this, we have to look at the first argument more carefully.

Marcus's first long speech is in two parts: the first presents man's rationality as his essence (22–3), the second gives him a generational history and distinguishes him from all other beings in terms of the teleological character of his body, arts, and senses (24–7). We are again reminded of the Stranger's distinction between the eidetic structure of the good and the genetic structure of law. Speech (*oratio*) is the gathering power of human society (27), reason (*ratio*) of man with god (23). There is, then, even a double account within the natural law teaching, which can be characterized, following Cicero, as tantamount to the difference between *agnatio* and *cognatio*. *Agnatio* is ascribed to the relationship between gods and men on the basis of its legal stand in cities (23); *cognatio* is ascribed to that same relation without any appeal outside of nature (25). Indeed, *natura* does not occur in the first account until its last sentence (*in rerum natura*) and accordingly follows the introduction of *deus* and *lex*; but the second begins with the nature of man, and *natura* becomes the single principle of things that in the case of the arts *ratio* imitates (26); and god is brought in as the equivalent of nature only at the end (27). The rational animal of the first account is one "we call man" (22): he does not have a nature.

In the first account the uniqueness of man consists in his reason, in the second a concept of god that includes the worship of vices and animals void of reason (cf. 2.28). The teleology of man seems to bring the Fall along with it (*quae fragilia essent et caduca*, 24); and Cicero will later argue that vices point to the similarity of men to one another, but not of course to god (31). It would seem, then, that sections 24–7 show a tendency to weaken the principles of 22–3; but even those sections suffer in themselves from an apparently unnecessary weakness. In man and god there is reason; the first society man has is with god (*cum deo*); right reason is common to those who have reason, and since it is *lex*, we men are to be counted as being associated with gods (*cum dis*) by *lex*. *Cum dis* picks up *cum deo*, for the singular, it now seems, merely stood for the class name of the gods. Marcus then goes on to say that those who have a community of *lex* have a community of *ius*. *Ius* is not defined, but it suffices to introduce the consequence that gods and men belong to the same city. And this holds all the more, Marcus adds, if they obey the same commands and powers; and they do so because they obey *huic caelesti descriptioni, mentique divinae et praepotenti deo*. *Lex* as right reason becomes an authoritative and commanding principle by becoming a principle to be obeyed and shared, or only shared to the extent that it is obeyed. The community of gods and men is established through the equality of reason; but the order of the city they share is established through a principle of reason that transcends the common city. *In omni caelo et terra* is Marcus's phrase when he speaks of the unsurpassable dignity of reason; but he uses *universus hic mundus* when he now speaks of the single common city of gods and men. *Hic* is no easier to identify than the deictic pronoun with which the dialogue began, for the unity now implied is not perceptible and might allow for a god no longer imma-nent in either heaven or earth (cf. 3.3). The celestial revolutions that de-termine the generation of soul in men certainly seem to imply an intel-ligence beyond the heavens (24). Cicero, in any case, implies that right reason does not suffice for rule if the very society of men with gods in the universe prevents the gods of that society from ruling men. He thus adumbrates the following paradox: right reason brings gods and men to-gether, but only false opinions about the gods allow gods to rule men.

Up to this point there has been no discussion of morality; indeed if Ziegler was right to bracket *honesta* at 16 there has been no mention of it.[14] The new beginning brings in morality, and at the same time happi-ness. The implication seems clear enough: the first argument was pitched too high to involve the issue of happiness; but the implication is not clear, for Cicero invokes Socrates for his denunciation of whoever separated usefulness from right (33): "And rightly Socrates was accustomed to curse the one who first disjoined utility from right (*ius*)." This first mention of Socrates is mysterious, for it seems that Socrates anticipated the form of Cicero's first argument and denounced its starting point. If, then, we could imagine that Socrates' purpose was just that, to serve as the con-

14. See Pohlenz, op. cit., 114–116, for the reading.

necting link between the two parts of book 1, Cicero would then be hinting that the comprehensive character of the first argument has to be com-
plemented by the less global range of the second. The second argument
does not simply replace the first, but in harmonizing the differences
among the schools it casts doubt on the possibility of wisdom and restores the primacy of philosophy in the literal sense. We could then say
that the first argument differs from, and joins with, the second in just the
way that in the second book, the best and the oldest are and are not the
same (40). In book 2, *quasi* is the word that signifies the indeterminate
degree of equatability between them: "To preserve the rituals of the family and the fathers, that is . . . to save the religion handed down as it were
from the gods" (27).[15] In book 1, it is signified by a complex pun that involves Socrates.

Marcus has been trying to reduce the difference between Stoicism
and the old Academy (including the Peripatetics) to a terminological dispute; but that difference stubbornly resists dissolution and has to be set
aside, since, as Quintus decides, it is not relevant to the issue of *ius civile*
(57). Quintus can intervene in this way and declare that whether *naturam
sequi et eius quasi lege vivere* or *ex natura vivere* is the chief good is
perhaps undecidable (50), because Marcus gives him the chance by saying:
"On the basis of this discord not of things but of words a controversy has
arisen about ends (*fines*), in which since the twelve tables did not wish
there to be ownership by way of possession (*usus capionem*) within five
feet, we shall not allow this intelligent man (Zeno) to graze on the old
possession of the Academy, and we shall not set the boundaries (*fines*)
straight as we individually could do by the Mamilian law, but on the basis
of the twelve tables we three shall be the arbiters" (55). Quintus then
asks Marcus for his judgment, and he replies, "The boundaries (*termini*)
are to be those that Socrates fixed, and they are to be obeyed."

Finis is either a "calque" on τέλος and belongs to philosophy or a word
of native meaning and definable by Roman law. Cicero seems to have
discerned how the end (τέλος) of the Stranger's genetic structure of law
comprehended, along with the completion of law and the finality of the
grave, the purpose of law itself and found a way to convey some of that
triplicity in Latin and, at the same time, in pulling back from its implication, deviated from it and pointed it in another direction. His deviation,
however, makes him guilty of linguistic transgression while he asserts
that it is only a question of "semantics," and yet charges Zeno with the

---

15. *ritus familiae patrumque servare, id est . . . a dis quasi traditam religionem
tueri.*

crime of transgressing the boundaries of the old Academy. This type of category mistake was known to the rhetoricians as κατάχρησις or *abusio*.[16] When it first occurred Marcus had called attention to it and rejected the strict applicability of *virtus* to a horse or a tree (45). Why, then, can the philosophical extension of "boundaries" into "ends" be declared unlawful and its primary meaning fixed by Socrates? *Termini* is the equivalent of *fines* and not of τέλη.

Socrates, in drawing the line between the old Academy and Stoicism, must be keeping for himself the five feet of no-man's-land between them, inasmuch as the law states that so much room must be left behind for the turning of the plow. If this is the correct inference to be drawn, Cicero would be proposing, by way of his abrogating the newer Mamilian law in favor of the procedure of the twelve tables, to go back to a time even before the establishment of the Academy. He would be saying, "Back to Socrates!" Such a return would be that outlined in 58–62, where, through the cutting back of the extension of *fines* to the literal sense of *termini*, Socrates' failure to establish a teleological cosmology would be admitted, wisdom and philosophy would accordingly for the first time be distinguished (58), and self-knowledge become the hallmark of the philosopher. The consequence of this self-knowledge is that Cicero adds rhetoric to the usual tripartition of philosophy into ethics, physics, and dialectics: "And when he realizes that he was born for civil society, he will believe that he must use not only that subtle form of disputation, but also a more widespread and continuous speech, by which he rules peoples, confirms laws, punishes the wicked, defends the good, praises outstanding men, publishes precepts of health and praise that are fit for persuading his fellow-citizens, can encourage decency, discourage crime, console the wretched, and show in sempiternal memorials the deeds and deliberations of brave and wise men" (62; cf. 3.14).

Self-knowledge is bound together with the knowledge that "political animal" and "rational animal" are not separable definitions of man, and that *oratio* makes *ratio* possible no less than *ratio* does *oratio*. The greater rhetorical effects of Cicero's second argument, in contrast with the plainness of the first, give the actual evidence for the link between dialectic and rhetoric that, in echoing the *Phaedrus*, he finally suggests here; and of rhetorical devices none is of greater importance for the understanding of law than *abusio*. It allows for *caste* to be understood as

---

16. For its use in law, see Papinian *Digest* 48.6.1: *lex stuprum et adulterium promniscue et* καταχρηστίκως *appellat*. In order to make adultery criminal, Augustus had to assimilate it to what was already criminal.

primarily applicable to the soul without canceling ablutions of the body
(2.24),[17] and for gods to be shut up within walls without denying that the
mind is the god within (2.28). All of book 1, one might say, is one long
catachresis by means of which Cicero can fit together elements that seem
to resists harmonization. It is the technique of incremental deviation
that Adimantus recognizes as the source of Socrates' persuasiveness
(Republic 487b1–c4), and Socrates himself describes and employs in the
Phaedrus (261e6–262a4).

17. caste iubet lex adire deos, animo scilicet in quo sunt omnia; nec tollit casti-
moniam corporis.

INDEX

Achilles: and Athena, 273; choice of, 257; and Thersites, 74, 277

Adam and Eve: eidetic and genetic analysis of, 85

Adimantus: on justice, 59n.3

Adrastus: story of, xiv, 236; suicide of, 278

Advocacy, 328, 335

Aeneid: ending of, 215

Aeschylus: allusion to, 268n.11; in Aristophanes, 68n.9; on violent grace, 108, 135n.7; *Persians* of, 103n.11

Afterlife: and issue of virtue, 338–9

Agamemnon: and Achilles, 277; in image, 81

Agriculture: ignorance of, in Magnesia, 211

Ajax: and Athena, 273

Alcibiades: satyr drama of, 219; in Thucydides, 128–9; understanding of Socrates, 220

Alexis: on law, 317n.9

Amazons: and Spartan women, 196

Ambidexterity: and equality, 198; of Scythians, 195. *See also* Handedness

Ambition: as desire, 277

Anaxagoras: discovery of mind, 350; on moon, 224; writings of, 92n.2

Anger: alliance of, with reason, 287; chastisement of, 282; and desire, treatment of, 277; and pleasure, 268; restriction on, 326. *See also* Indignation and Thumoeidetic

Anthropeios: and *anthropinos* in *Laws*, 136

Antigone: man in, 297n.12

Antigone: criminality of, 339n.7; in image, 81

Antiphon: on *kakourgēmata* (evildoing), 258n.5

Apelt, O.: on third-best regime, 166n.13; on preludes, 222n.35

Apology of Socrates, 2, 130; summarized, 155; exemplifies truest tragedy, 222n.34

Apuleius: on law, 317n.9

Archaism: in law, 227n.39, 326n.18, 359

Archilochus: in Sparta, 214n.26

Ares: and Aphrodite, 32; and Athena, 318

Arion, xviii

Aristophanes: on Eros, 241; comedies of, 268

Aristotle, 8n.5, 64; on bestiality, 189; on causality, 297; on difference between good and beautiful and just, 22n.24; on *eupsuchos*, 194n.4; on flute, 120n.24; on the funny, 62; on *Laws*, 5, 161n.8; on population, 163; on purpose of laws, 10n.8; on priests, xvii; role of, in *Nicomachean Ethics*, 151n.23; on sacrifice, 201–2

Artisans: in Magnesia, 318; treatment of, 248

Arts: not at beginning, 88; development of, 297; invention of, 94–5

Astronomy: eikastics of, 310; in *De re publica*, 356; placeholder for theology, 224

Asymmetry: in divisions, 219, 241

Atheism: and city, 288; crime of, 265; *doxosophia* of, 270, 294; inoculation

TEXT PROBLEMS IN *LAWS*